AGRIBUSINESS MANAGEMENT

McGRAW-HILL BOOK COMPANY

New York | St. Louis | San Francisco | Auckland |
Bogotá | Hamburg | Johannesburg | London |
Madrid | Mexico | Milan | Montreal |
New Delhi | Panama | Paris | São Paulo |
Singapore | Sydney | Tokyo | Toronto

Second

AGRIB
MANAG

W. DAVID DOWNEY

Professor of Agricultural Economics
Purdue University

STEVEN P. ERICKSON

Associate Professor of Agricultural Economics
Purdue University

dition

USINESS
GEMENT

AGRIBUSINESS MANAGEMENT

1 2 3 4 5 6 7 8 9 0 DOCDOC 8 9 4 3 2 1 0 9 8 7 6

ISBN 0-07-017667-1

This book was set in Melior by The Clarinda Company. The
editor was Phillip A. Butcher; the production supervisors
were Diane Renda and Fred Schulte; the cover was designed
by Laura Stover. Project supervision was done by Chernow
Editorial Services, Inc. R. R. Donnelley & Sons Company was
printer and binder.

Library of Congress Cataloging-in-Publication Data

Downey, W. David (Walter David).
  Agribusiness management.

  Includes bibliographical references and index.
  1. Agricultural industries--Management. I. Erickson,
Steven. II. Title.
HD9000.5.D63 1987   630'.68   86-20036
ISBN 0-07-017667-1

ABOUT THE AUTHORS

Dr. W. David Downey is Professor of Agricultural Economics at Purdue University where he teaches agribusiness and agrimarketing courses. He has received six major teaching awards from Purdue University and the American Agricultural Economics Association. Over the years, Dr. Downey has worked closely with a wide variety of agribusinesses, in the United States, Canada, and Australia, as a cooperative extension specialist and consultant. He conducts numerous educational programs and monitors the financial and operating results of several hundred retail agribusinesses in the course of his research. Raised on a farm near Wabash, Indiana, Dr. Downey received his B.S. in agronomy and his M.S. and Ph.D. degrees in Agricultural Economics at Purdue.

Dr. Steven P. Erickson is an Associate Professor of Agricultural Economics at Purdue University, where he has received four major teaching awards. His teaching experience includes courses in agribusiness management, financial management, macroeconomics, retail merchandising, and the futures and options markets. He has monitored agribusiness compensation data for several hundred farm supply firms throughout the midwest as part of his ongoing research. He has recently returned from a sabbatical leave at Texas A & M University. Raised on a grain and livestock farm near Brookston, Indiana, Dr. Erickson received his B.S. and M.S. degrees in agricultural economics from Purdue University and his Ph.D. degree from the University of Illinois.

To the many students of agribusiness
who have challenged and enriched
our lives,
and
To our wives, Deb and Ginger

CONTENTS

PART III

MARKETING IN AGRIBUSINESS

PART IV

OPERATING THE AGRIBUSINESS

PART V

HUMAN RESOURCE MANAGEMENT IN AGRIBUSINESS

PREFACE

This second edition of *Agribusiness Management* was written for those planning for or currently involved in a career in agribusiness. This edition has revised and updated the first edition and added material that should further one's preparation for a career in agribusiness. This revision, like the first edition, is totally oriented toward management of the nonfarm agricultural business. Specifically addressed in this text are topics of relevance to managers, owners, and employees of firms which provide supplies and services to farmers or who market, process, or add value to farm products. While many concepts and tools presented are certainly applicable to the farm business and to businesses in general, our focus is intended to be strictly upon agribusiness applications.

We have attempted to build, in this edition, upon the strengths of the first edition of *Agribusiness Management* and have supplemented liberally with new data of relevance to agribusinesses and topics which were not covered in the first edition. We have made substantial revisions in the introductory chapter and have included data regarding the three important sectors of agribusiness. Chapter 4, "Cooperatives in Agribusiness," has been substantially revised to reflect the current standing and importance of cooperatives in the agribusiness sector. Additional production principles of microeconomics are presented in Chapter 5, "Economics for Managers." Finally, Chapter 16, "Production Planning in the Agribusiness," now includes a section on dealing with risk and uncertainty in the agribusiness.

Although the initial responsibilities of those entering a career in agribusiness may not include management decisions, it is essential that all those involved with the operations of an agribusiness firm have an appreciation for the problems involved in making management decisions. Thus, concepts and tools are presented that deal with many agribusiness management decisions. Those who begin their career as agronomists, nutritionists, horticulturalists, herdspeople, engineers, veterinarians, or salespeople may soon be faced with a variety of management decisions as they are promoted within the firm. The same is true for those who begin their career paths as drivers, applicators, field technicians, crop surveyors, mill hands, and operators. *Agribusiness Management* should serve as a good reference on which to build a management foundation for a productive career in agribusiness.

This book has also been developed with the practicing agribusiness manager in mind. From our dual responsibilities as undergraduate teachers and agribusiness management and marketing specialists with the Cooperative Extension Service, it is our belief that the optimal level of materials and approach for the college classroom is not greatly different from what is optimal for local agribusiness managers or middle management in larger firms. We have therefore included management concepts and tools that have proved valuable to the literally thousands of agribusiness managers we have worked with in solving specific management problems. We have also drawn heavily on these experiences for the wide variety of examples, illustrations, and cases that are included in this book. Consequently, we believe that this book will prove useful to the practicing agribusiness manager as well as for those just beginning their careers in agribusiness.

The second edition was also written with the teacher in mind. We consider ourselves teachers first and foremost—in the college classroom and through adult extension education seminars which we conduct. Thus, we have attempted to consider our subject matter and its organization for its teachability and applicability in the classroom environment. We hope that learning aids included in this edition of the book and in the teacher's manual will help provide the educator with the necessary support to involve students in illustrative discussions, and to create a proper learning environment. By adjusting the subject matter to fit their own experience and educational circumstances, teachers can adapt *Agribusiness Management* to a one-, two-, or three-term course setting.

Part I of *Agribusiness Management* is concerned with the role and organization of agribusiness. In it, the breadth and scope of agribusiness is illustrated, followed by a discussion of the role of management in agribusiness. Finally, different forms of business organization are presented and discussed. Particular emphasis is given the agricultural cooperative since it is an important and unique part of agribusiness.

Part II provides the student with a basis for analyzing and making economic and financial decisions within the agribusiness. It begins with a presentation of the principles of the free enterprise system and those economic principles which should be important to managers. This discussion is followed by a summary of the basics of the financial statement for the firm. Interpretation and analysis of the financial statements is emphasized as a guide for decision making. Also covered in this section of the book are the various methods of financing an agribusiness and recommendations for working with various financial institutions. Finally, the ways a manager can use several highly practical financial management tools for making a variety of critical decisions within the firm are illustrated and discussed.

Part III concentrates on marketing within the agribusiness. First, the macrosystem for marketing agricultural products is discussed. Then, micromarketing within the individual agribusiness firm is discussed. The critical elements of the marketing mix are presented along with methods to develop and implement a strategic market plan. Finally, the importance of selling in the agribusiness is presented. Since so many people enter agribusiness through sales, considerable emphasis is given to professional selling in agribusinesses.

Part IV focuses on managing the physical operation. It covers methods of purchasing materials, organizing, monitoring, and controlling operations in retailing, wholesaling, or manufacturing agribusinesses. The concept of risk and uncertainty analysis within the agribusiness firm is presented and discussed.

Finally, management of human resources in the agribusiness is presented in Part V. Various methods for structuring responsibility, authority, and accountability are discussed. Then students are presented with a variety of theories and methods of supervising, leading, and motivating employees, including a practical section on transactional analysis as a management tool.

We wish to express our thanks for the many useful comments and suggestions provided by colleagues who reviewed this text during the course of its development, especially to Daniel Kauffman, Virginia Polytechnic Institute and State University; Patrick D. O'Rourke, Illinois State University; Frederick A. Perkins, Cook College, Rutgers University; James Russell, Oklahoma State University; and Kathleen Simmons, Santa Rosa Junior College.

To summarize, *Agribusiness Management*, second edition, is a basic approach to the study of management and management decisions within the agribusiness firm. It continues to maintain a high level of application to real-world problems, like the first edition. In each part, basic principles and concepts are covered, then specific tools to solve important real world problems are discussed. It is an approach that we hope is readable, interesting, and highly practical and useful to your career in agribusiness.

W. David Downey
Steven P. Erickson

AGRIBUSINESS MANAGEMENT

I

THE ROLE
AND ORGANIZATION
OF AGRIBUSINESS

OBJECTIVES

• Describe the size and scope of agribusiness

• Explain the importance and impact that agribusiness has upon the total economy

• Categorize agribusiness by sector and describe the function of each sector

• Calculate the relative dollar amounts contributed by farmers and agribusiness industries in the input and product sectors

• Describe the importance of agribusiness as a major employer in our economic system

Agribusiness serves farmers by providing farm supplies and services and marketing agricultural products.
A. Retail farm supply center
B. Midwestern grain farm
C. Grain terminal market

AMERICA IS THE BREADBASKET OF THE WORLD.

1

AGRIBUSINESS IN PERSPECTIVE

B

C

THE BUSINESS OF AGRIBUSINESS

Food and fiber are daily requirements for everyone. Walking through the local supermarket, one might consider the number and type of diverse activities involved in producing food and putting it on that retail shelf. The process by which an 1100-pound steer is transposed from a west Texas feedlot to the table of a consumer in New York City is very complex, but it is performed every day of the year—it is a process that many consumers take for granted in the United States. Certainly there is no magic involved! But there has been a great deal of hard work and coordination throughout the food marketing system to provide food at a reasonable cost to United States consumers.

This food production system begins with many varied activities from the farm supply sector, which provides a myriad of production inputs and services to the farm, then continues through the marketing, processing, and distribution activities necessary to satisfy consumer wants. As the agricultural production process becomes increasingly complex and specialized, the farm supply sector takes on important new dimensions. Also, as their incomes rise, consumers demand more services with respect to the bundle of food products they purchase. As these trends continue, the agribusiness sector becomes increasingly important because it has the responsibility of providing not only the right type and amount of purchased inputs to the farm sector, but also the correct mix of service to products as they move through the food system to the final consumer.

Today more than ever before, every sector of the American economy is affected by agriculture. Although the number of farms has been declining for most of this century, maintaining or increasing output from this sector is important because the sector has a major impact on the economic well-being of the nation. Without agricultural products to trade with other countries, trade deficits would be even higher. In total, the agricultural sector exhibits the highest level of productivity in our economy. The production sector continues to adopt new technology in the form of machinery and equipment as well as new varieties of seed, all of which contribute to the sector's increased productive capacity.

In today's economic environment, the agribusiness sector combines diverse commercial enterprises, using a heterogeneous combination of labor, materials, capital, and technology. The food and fiber system is an extremely large, complicated system that is constantly changing to meet consumer demands and provide food and fiber to both domestic and world markets.

The USDA (United States Department of Agriculture) reports annually on the productivity and makeup of the agricultural sector of the United States. One statistic often quoted is the fact that one farmer now feeds about 79 people: 57.6 at home and 21.5 abroad.[1] This rather amazing fact is made possible, at least in part, by the highly competitive in-

---

[1] USDA, "Indicators of the Farm Sector," ERS, ECIFS 3–5, March 1985.

dustry that serves America's 2.3 million farms. Obviously farmers cannot do this alone; they need the help of thousands of firms on the input side of agriculture and hundreds of thousands of firms on the marketing side of agriculture. No longer do most inputs for agricultural production originate on the farm, as they did in times of horse-drawn vehicles and labor-intensive production. The importance to the farm sector of the input and distribution sectors of agribusiness has grown to tremendous proportions in recent years.

Today only about 3 percent of the United States work force is involved directly in farming. One hundred years ago about 50 percent of the work force was directly involved in the food and fiber sector. Thus, tremendous strides have been made in this sector, and advances in production techniques, technological innovations, and improved management practices have freed labor to seek employment in other sectors of the economy and allowed our overall economic system to evolve into the most developed one in the world. In contrast to the United States, Japan and the USSR employ 12 and 14 percent of their work force, respectively, in production agriculture. India, at the other extreme, still employs about 70 percent of the work force in food and fiber production.

This chapter serves as an introduction to the industry that (1) supplies inputs to the farm sector; (2) transforms the raw farm products to consumer products; and (3) moves these products through the food and fiber marketing system to the final consumer.

WHAT IS AGRIBUSINESS?

Agribusiness can be broken down into three economically interdependent sectors. These sectors, the input supply, farm production, and output sectors, are illustrated in Figure 1-1.

The input sector provides farmers and ranchers with supplies for production of crops and livestock. These inputs include seed, feed, fertilizer, chemicals, machinery, fuel, and many others. The farm production sector produces crop and animal products that are processed and distributed by the output sector to the final consumers.

Before we continue with our discussion of the significance and makeup of the agribusiness sector, it may be beneficial to define exactly what the term *agribusiness* means. Two definitions of agribusiness have generally been accepted. The first includes only the input sector as outlined above. Thus, the narrow or traditional definition of agribusiness would refer to producers and manufacturers of inputs for agricultural production. Some of the enterprises included here would be chemical, fertilizer, and farm machinery dealers; feed and seed establishments; and agricultural credit and other financial institutions serving the production sector.

Today, a broader view of agribusiness is generally accepted as more appropriate. This more encompassing definition includes any firm whose activities relate to any part of Figure 1-1. Here agribusiness includes the entire input, farm, and output sectors. Thus, agribusiness in-

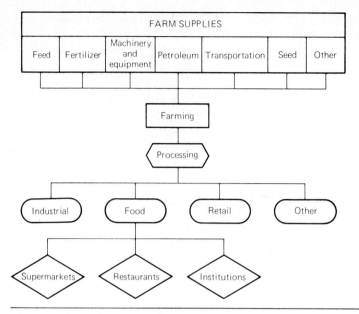

Figure 1-1 Breakdown of the input, farm, and product market sectors.

cludes all those business and management activities performed by firms that provide inputs to the farm sector, produce farm products, and/or process, transport, finance, handle, or market farm products.

In a survey of agribusiness-related occupations, the USDA defined very specifically what types of employment agribusiness encompasses.[2] The following is a breakdown of the types of skills and knowledge utilized by those employed in agribusiness:

1. Agricultural production and propagation of animals, animal products, plants, plant products, forests, and forest products

2. The provision of services associated with agricultural production and the manufacture and distribution of supplies used in agricultural production

3. The design, installation, repair, operation, and servicing of machinery, equipment, and power sources, and the construction of structures used in agricultural production

4. Any activities related to the inspection, processing, and marketing of agricultural products and primary by-products

5. Any aspects of greenhouse, nursery, landscaping, and other ornamental horticultural operations

[2]USDA, "Employment in Agricultural and Agribusiness Occupations," ERS 570, August 1974.

6. The conservation, propagation, improvement, and utilization of renewable natural resources

7. The multiple uses of forest lands and resources

Accompanying this definition of agribusiness is a list of over 950 occupations and 1900 selected industries that require or utilize agribusiness competencies. Thus our modern-day definition of agribusiness involves a broader view that encompasses the total food production and distribution system.

The Input Sector

Farm sector productivity has increased by more than 50 percent since 1967. A large proportion of this increased efficiency is directly attributable to the input supply sector. Improved varieties of seed and feed, farm machinery and equipment, and the facilitating services offered to farmers help improve the output-input ratio. In 1983 the input supply sector provided agricultural producers with a total of $135.3 billion of production inputs.

Production expenditures have increased dramatically on a per-farm basis since 1970. Production expenditures reached a high of $58,118 in 1982 and decreased slightly to $57,097 for 1983. In contrast, production expenses totaled $15,074 per farm in 1970. Table 1-1 illustrates some of the major input expense categories for 1983 and breaks these down in dollars and as a percent of the total outlay for all production input expenditure categories.

Today, farmers purchase roughly 70 percent of all the inputs they use for production. Thus, an efficient input sector that is capable of supplying the farm sector with the right inputs at the right time in the proper amounts is crucial to continuing the increases in production efficiency witnessed in the past few decades.

Some of the major input supply industries are discussed specifically below. Note that this is not a complete list of the industries that supply inputs to the farm sector. The brief look at some of the major input supply sectors should give the student an idea of the relative importance of each in terms of total farm outlays.

Feed The largest single out-of-pocket expense item for farmers in recent years has been purchased feed. Outlays for feed amounted to nearly $19.0 billion in 1983.

The structure of firms engaged in commercial feed production has changed significantly in the last 40 years. In the 1920s and 1930s elevator and flour businesses dominated the industry. Recently, larger feed industry firms that handle the manufacturing, processing, and distribution from start to finish have become predominant. Though these firms are becoming larger, their numbers have not declined significantly. To-

TABLE 1-1 Farm Production Expenditures, 1983*

INPUT	DOLLARS (BILLIONS)	PERCENT OF TOTAL
Feed	19.0	14.0
Livestock	8.8	6.5
Seed	3.5	2.6
Fertilizer and lime	7.4	5.5
Pesticides	3.5	2.6
Fuel and oil	7.7	5.7
Electricity	2.3	1.7
Repairs/operation	8.2	6.1
Custom/contract labor	3.3	2.4
Marketing charges	1.7	1.2
Other	6.9	5.1
Interest		
Real estate	10.9	8.1
Non-real estate	10.4	7.6
Wages	10.5	7.7
Rent	3.7	2.7
Depreciation	23.1	17.1
Taxes	4.6	3.4
Total	135.3	100.0

*USDA, ECIFS 3–4, January 1985.

day, the leading firms control a smaller proportion of the market. In 1930 the four largest firms accounted for one-quarter of total industry shipments. By 1972 this share had declined to about 22 percent of industry sales, and it was relatively constant at 21 percent by 1977.[3]

The majority of feed inputs, including grain and supplements, are sold through elevators. Some of these firms are affiliated with large corporations, while many are small family-owned businesses or farmer-controlled cooperatives. These firms often supply many other inputs, from nutrients to chemicals and pesticides as well as fuel and motor supplies.

Seed, Fertilizer, Lime, and Chemicals In 1983 farmers spent $14.4 billion on fertilizer, lime, seed, and chemicals. There are strongly competitive forces within the fertilizer-chemical industry, particularly among the approximately 5000 local outlets. Dealers must react quickly to market changes in their areas. Farmers are very price conscious but are also cognizant of the services provided by the individual firm.

Herbicide use on farms increased 22 percent between 1976 and 1982. This was due, in part, to expanded acreage, especially in soybeans,

---

[3]Conner, John M., R. T. Rogers, B. W. Marion, and W. F. Mueller, *The Food Manufacturing Industries*, D. C. Heath and Company, Lexington, Mass., 1985, p. 138.

and to increased use of tank mixes. Probably more than in any other input sector, changing technology affects how and what chemicals will be used on farms. In the future, government environmental restrictions may become a constraint on dramatic increases in pesticide and herbicide use. A trade-off clearly exists between use of pesticides, a plentiful food supply, and possible environmental problems. As farmers are forced to become more aware of the hazards of using chemicals on their land, continued increases in this input may be limited. Between 1967 and 1980 the use of chemicals on farms doubled. Over the next 15 years it appears that this trend is not likely to continue.

Petroleum Farmers spent a total of $10 billion for fuels and electricity in 1983. Farming consumes directly only about 3 percent of the petroleum fuels and electricity used in the United States. Input supply firms in this area are typically the larger oil companies that have integrated themselves into the farm supply area, and also agricultural cooperatives. Many of these firms also supply farm chemicals and pesticides.

Petroleum will continue to be a vital resource for agricultural production and for the input supply industries serving agriculture. The fertilizer industry is especially vulnerable to changes in the price and availability of petroleum. Roughly 12 percent of the United States' petroleum needs are used in the production, processing, and marketing of food.

Farm Machinery and Equipment Expenditures for agricultural machinery were $10.9 billion in 1980. By 1983 this figure had decreased to $7.9 billion as a result of higher machinery prices and dramatic decreases in farm income over the same period. Estimated machinery expenditures for 1984 are $8.1 billion, slightly above the previous year's level. The total value of machinery and equipment in 1983 was $110.9 billion, which represents about 10 percent of total farm assets.

An extremely efficient implement supply sector is needed to meet current demands of farmers. The structure of this industry approaches oligopoly, where a few large firms dominate the market. The purchase decision rests not only on the price of the particular piece of machinery but also on the service that the farmer expects from the dealer after purchase. Harvesting conditions change so rapidly in the Grain Belt that a delay of a day or two can mean hundreds of dollars in lost revenue to the farmer as a result of yield and quality deterioration. Today, farmers are concerned not only about paying over $100,000 for a new harvester but also about whether their local dealer can keep it running and supply spare parts as they are needed without delay.

The financial health of this sector of agribusiness, like many others, is directly related to the well-being of the production sector. As prices increase and farm income remains relatively stable, the machinery sector suffers. During the first half of 1984 farmers bought 65,740 tractors, down significantly from only a few years earlier. Combine purchases for 1984 are expected to be 26 percent lower than 1983.

Feeder Stock: Livestock Expenditures for livestock and poultry totaled $8.8 billion in 1983. The majority of animals move directly from producer to feeder. However, auction markets and country dealers play a significant role in feeder-stock movement. Terminal markets play a very minor role in providing livestock for breeding and feeding. Over the past 20 years there has been a dramatic shift in livestock volume handled, from large terminal markets to smaller country buying points. Many large producers today contract for feeder stock or go to the source and purchase feeder stock directly from producers as needed.

Financing In 1984 total farm debt was $201 billion: $103 billion for real estate and $87 billion in non-real estate debt. The remaining $11 billion represents CCC (Commodity Credit Corporation) debt. The largest sources of real estate loans are the Federal Land Banks, which are part of the Farm Credit System, and individuals. Many of the latter group are sellers of farms who provide loan funds to buyers. Banks and PCAs (Product Credit Associations) are the largest sources of non-real estate loans. Federal Land Banks held approximately $48 billion of the real estate debt in 1984, while PCAs accounted for about $14 billion of non-real estate debt.

In recent years, Land Banks, PCAs, and the Farmers Home Administration have become more important sources of loan funds, because they are now more competitive with commercial banks and insurance companies. Lending institutions in agriculture appear to be changing; they are becoming more competitive and are starting to adopt constructive innovations in lending policies that will ultimately benefit their farmer customers.

Cooperatives Farmer cooperatives are an important element in agribusiness today. They tend to be pacesetters and power balancers within the industry (see Chapter 4).

Farmer cooperatives today handle about 30 percent of all products from the farm gate to the consumer, and provide about 20 percent of all production inputs to the agricultural sector.

Cooperatives provide many innovative services to farmers and increase competition within the farm supply sector. In 1976 there were a total of 7535 agricultural cooperatives. By 1982 this number had decreased to 6125. Total annual business volume is about $70 billion, with a membership in excess of 5 million. The majority of these firms are marketing cooperatives, while about 35 percent are farm supply cooperatives. Farmer cooperatives today handle about 20 percent of the commercial formula feed business in the United States. Cooperatives continue to make competitive inroads in the fertilizer industry. They have progressed significantly in building and in acquiring manufacturing, storage, and distribution facilities.

The Farm Production Sector

At the hub of agribusiness is the farm production sector. As this sector grows in size, level of output, and efficiency, the other sectors of agribusiness are directly affected. The health of this sector has a vital and direct impact on the financial well-being of the input supply and output sectors of agribusiness.

Table 1-2 illustrates some important trends in the farm production sector which have dramatically affected the entire agribusiness complex. Farm income peaked in the mid-1970s, edged lower for a few years, and had a tremendous spurt in 1981 to $31.0 billion. Since then farm income has fallen dramatically to $16.1 billion in 1983. At the same time the cost-price squeeze continues to be a problem. While market participants in the supply and output sectors can set prices for their products, farmers are still price takers in the marketplace.

The government payment-in-kind program of 1983 set all-time records for financial assistance to the farm sector. In 1983 government payments to farmers represented almost 58 percent of net farm income for the year. Finally, Table 1-2 shows the sizable decrease in the number of farms—about a 50 percent reduction over the past 28 years.

Table 1-3 depicts one of the major problems in the farm production sector and the end result of this problem. As farm prices remain fairly stable and expenses increase, pressure is exerted on farmers and ranchers to improve efficiency. Today the cost-price squeeze is so serious that producers are unable to cut costs or improve production efficiency to the extent necessary to deal with the problem. Smaller farmers continue to exit the production process, and large farms become larger. The production expense per farm has increased almost fourfold in the

TABLE 1-2

The Agricultural Product Sector in Transition*

YEAR	NET FARM INCOME† (BILLIONS)	FARM PRODUCTION EXPENSES (BILLIONS)	GOVERNMENT PAYMENTS (BILLIONS)	NUMBER OF FARMS (MILLIONS)
1955	$11.3	$22.2	$0.2	4.65
1960	11.5	27.4	0.7	3.96
1965	12.9	33.7	2.5	3.36
1970	14.4	43.0	3.7	2.95
1975	25.6	73.7	0.8	2.52
1980	21.2	128.9	1.3	2.43
1981	31.0	136.9	1.9	2.43
1982	22.3	139.5	3.5	2.40
1983	16.1	135.3	9.3	2.37

*USDA, "Indicators of the Farm Sector," ERS, ECIFS 3–4, January 1985.
†After inventory adjustments.

TABLE Production Expenses per Farm*
1-3

	YEAR	PRODUCTION EXPENSE PER FARM	FARM POPULATION, % OF U.S.
	1970	$15,074	4.7
	1975	29,767	3.3
	1980	53,108	2.7
	1981	56,243	2.6
	1982	58,118	2.5
	1983	57,097	2.5

*USDA, "Indicators of the Farm Sector," ERS, ECIFS 3–4, January 1985.

past 13 years. At the same time interest rates have soared to levels which cause further financial hardship to many producers.

As the average farm size continues to increase, people tend to be displaced from the farm sector to the urban sector. Since 1970 the farm population as a percentage of the United States total has declined by about 50 percent. The implications of this displacement in terms of the socioeconomic impact on the persons involved are far-reaching. On average, farm production sector workers have less education and lower levels of work skills compared with their urban counterparts. Thus, government training and other, more direct financial assistance often is necessary if these workers are to relocate successfully.

Table 1-4 provides a specific breakdown, identical to that of Table 1-1, of the history of farm production expenditures. As noted in the input sector discussion, sizable increases in expenditures for fertilizer, pesticides, and fuel and oil have occurred over the past 13 years. A dramatic increase in farm interest payments is also shown in Table 1-4. Interest rate increases have been singled out as one of the major factors contributing to the farm sector's financial problems from 1982 to 1984. The ability of the producer to renew lines of credit in the spring before planting is crucial. As interest rates increase, many bankers begin to question the ability of some farms to generate the cash flow necessary to repay these production loans. It will be more important, in the future, for lenders and producers to work closely with one another to develop an efficient, appropriate financing strategy for the individual farm or ranch.

The Output Sector

The final sector in the food production and distribution system is the output sector. This sector is responsible for the transformation of the raw farm output into a final consumer product at the retail level. It is the largest of the three sectors in the food system. About 600,000 establishments are involved in food processing and distribution. These firms em-

TABLE
1-4

Farm Production Expenditures, Selected Years*

PRODUCTION EXPENSE ITEM	PRODUCTION EXPENDITURES† (MILLIONS)					
	1970	1975	1980	1981	1982	1983
Feed	$ 8.0	$12.6	$ 18.8	$ 18.8	$ 16.9	$ 19.0
Livestock	4.3	5.0	10.4	9.0	9.7	8.8
Seed	.9	2.3	3.4	3.9	4.0	3.5
Fertilizer and lime	2.4	6.4	9.9	10.1	8.8	7.4
Pesticides	.9	1.9	3.3	3.6	3.6	3.5
Fuel and oil	1.7	3.3	7.9	8.9	8.3	7.7
Electricity	.3	.6	1.8	2.0	2.1	2.3
Repairs and operation	2.6	4.2	8.1	8.1	8.2	8.2
Custom contract work	1.3	2.5	3.3	3.8	4.1	3.3
Marketing charges	NA	NA	1.7	2.0	2.0	1.7
Other	2.6	3.9	4.8	5.4	6.0	6.9
Interest:						
Real estate	1.6	3.1	7.5	9.1	10.5	10.9
Non-real estate	1.6	3.0	8.7	10.7	11.7	10.4
Wages	4.3	6.3	9.2	9.1	10.8	10.5
Net rent	2.1	4.6	4.8	4.9	4.8	3.7
Depreciation	5.9	10.9	21.4	23.4	23.6	23.1
Taxes	2.4	3.1	3.9	4.2	4.4	4.6
Total	43.0	73.7	128.9	136.9	139.5	135.3

*USDA "Indicators of the Farm Sector," ERS, se-
lected issues.
†Totals may not sum due to rounding.

ploy almost 9 million workers. According to the USDA, a relatively small number of large business organizations own and control these establishments.

Structure Large corporate organizations are common in the output sector. Many of these firms have successfully integrated by combining marketing functions at different levels in the farm-food chain, especially in merging under one management for processing and marketing activities. A few firms have even integrated back to the farm level to guarantee a supply of raw materials with uniform quality. This type of vertical coordination is most prevalent in broiler, fruit, and vegetable production. On the East Coast, for example, Perdue chickens sell extremely well, due, in part, to the integration within the production-marketing chain and the quality associated with this particular product.

    The level of concentration among food and fiber manufacturing and processing enterprises varies widely. In twenty-two of forty-five industries, the four largest firms accounted for over one-half of that industry's total value of shipments in 1977.[4] By contrast, in eight other industries less than 25 percent of total shipments was provided by the top four firms in the industry. The highest level of industry concentration was found in the breakfast cereals, chewing gum, and tobacco industries. Three industries, meat packing, poultry, and fresh or frozen fish, showed the least amount of concentration. From 1963 to 1977, four-firm concentration, the percentage of a given industry's business that is controlled by the four largest firms, increased in twenty-five of the forty-five industry categories, remained unchanged in five, and decreased in fifteen categories.

Wholesaling Wholesale operations involve sales to retailers, other wholesalers, industrial users, and, to a lesser extent, the ultimate consumer. A wholesaler may buy directly from the farmer and sell to another wholesaler or food processor, or the wholesaler may buy from processors and sell to retailers. The makeup of the whole trade involves a large group of varied organizations. Wholesalers take title to the products they handle and are responsible for geographic distribution of the particular product.

Recently in the grocery industry, many wholesalers have integrated forward in the food distribution channel and actually own and operate or franchise retail supermarkets. This is another technique for coordinating different steps in the marketing channel under one organization, and it has been an extremely timely, profitable move for some wholesalers.

Retailing Retail food stores represent one of the largest industries in the United States. In 1985 there were over 156,000 retail grocery stores with a total business volume of $279 billion.[5]

Recent trends in the retail food industry are toward larger stores with more square feet of display area offering proportionately more products. The "superstore" concept has been successful in some regions of the United States since its introduction in the 1970s. This prototype operation has led to many other innovative ways to sell food and related products. An almost opposite concept, compared with the large supermarket, is the convenience store. This concept involves the use of very limited store space to move only the high-volume items found in a more traditional food store. Convenience stores stock a limited assortment of these high-volume, high-margin items. The success of these stores lies in their location relative to traffic patterns in the area. For example, consider the location economics of placing a convenience store directly across from three college dormitories whose cafeterias are not open on Sunday evening! These firms will continue to be successful as long as

[4]Conner, op. cit., pp. 135-147.
[5]Progressive Grocer, 52nd Annual Report of the Grocery Industry, April 1985.

the consumer is willing to pay a premium for this type of limited-item, quick service facility.

Today, chain stores account for roughly one-half of all grocery sales. A chain is defined as a supermarket firm that has eleven or more stores under one central management. Current chain store efforts involve reducing costs and increasing awareness of consumer needs. Chain stores are adopting mass merchandising techniques to handle more items and are employing technological innovations, like computerized inventory control and electronic scanners at the checkout, to improve their operation. The front-end scanners offer two distinct benefits: (1) relatively error-free, speedy checkout, and (2) better inventory control techniques for the individual store. Many supermarkets have also adopted unit pricing programs that facilitate consumer price comparisons. Generic brands have gained a fair share of the market in some areas of the country, indicating that this very competitive industry is always looking for ways to satisfy the varied wants of the consumer.

SIZE OF AGRIBUSINESS

Agriculture is the single largest employer in the United States and accounts for more business activity than any other sector of the economy. Table 1-5 provides a breakdown of employment in eight selected job categories in agribusiness based upon estimates provided by ERS (Economic Research Service), a division of the USDA.[6] Farming employs about 3.1 million workers, as many as transportation, the steel industry, and the automobile industry combined. The input sector of agribusiness is included predominantly in the "other manufacturing" and "other" categories in Table 1-5. Employment in the food and fiber processing and distribution, or product, sector was estimated to be about 15.3 million workers. The USDA study further indicated that employment in agribusiness varied greatly by state.

This study estimated that farming and agribusiness combined employed about 23 million people, or 22 percent of the total work force. Regionally, agribusiness as a percentage of total employment varied from a high of 27 percent in the Midwest to a low of 20 percent in the Northeast. California had the most food and fiber jobs, with 2.5 million people employed. However, Nebraska and North Carolina had the largest percentage of their work force employed in the agribusiness sector: 32 percent each.

In 1984 United States consumers spent about $400 billion on food at home and away from home. Roughly $280 billion of this amount was for services added between the farm gate and the retail establishment serving the consumer. Thus, for every $1 that consumers spent at the retail level, roughly 30 cents went to the farmer and the remaining 70 cents was paid to some middleman for services or utility added in the

[6]Edmondson, William, and Gerald Schluter, "The Farm: Source of Many Jobs," *National Food Review*, NFR-27, 1984.

TABLE 1-5 Agribusiness Employment by Sector*

JOB CATEGORY	PERCENT	NUMBER EMPLOYED (MILLIONS)
Farming	13.6	3.1
Food processing	7.8	1.8
Textiles	11.1	2.5
Other manufacturing	7.0	1.6
Trade	30.5	6.9
Transportation	3.5	0.8
Eating places	14.5	3.3
Other	12.1	2.7
Total	100.0	22.7

*Edmondson, William, and Gerald Schluter. "The Farm: Source of Many Jobs," *National Food Review*, NFR-27, 1984.

agribusiness product sector. Figure 1-2 gives a more specific breakdown of the expenses for the services performed or value added to farm products so that they reach the consumer in a timely manner and in the form desired. Farm value has remained relatively constant during the past 5 or 6 years. Thus, the marketing bill has remained at about 70 percent of the consumer's food dollar, even though various components fluctuate on a year-to-year basis.

Because of the highly efficient, competitive agribusiness environment, United States consumers have more selection of food and related

Figure 1-2 Components of Farm-Food Expenditures (a) E.R.S., "What's Happening to Food Costs", March 1984.

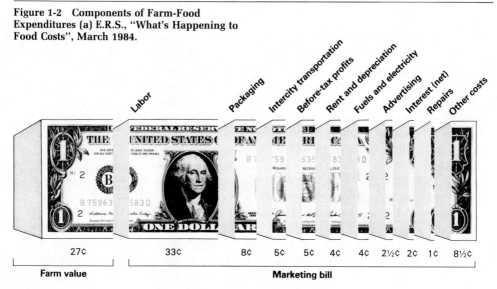

Labor	Packaging	Intercity transportation	Before-tax profits	Rent and depreciation	Fuels and electricity	Advertising	Interest (net)	Repairs	Other costs
33¢	8¢	5¢	5¢	4¢	4¢	2½¢	2¢	1¢	8½¢

Farm value: 27¢   Marketing bill

Includes food at home and away from home. Other costs include property taxes and insurance, accounting and professional services, promotion, bad debts, and many miscellaneous items.

products at the retail store than their counterparts in any other country in the world. Today, it is not uncommon for consumers shopping at a modern supermarket to have a choice of 12,000 to 15,000 items. Furthermore, food, measured as a percentage of disposable personal income, has remained a relatively constant cost component of the consumer's budget. During the second quarter of 1984 consumers spent 15.2 percent of their disposable personal income on all food—both at home and away from home.

WHY STUDY AGRIBUSINESS?

As later chapters in the text will argue, agribusiness is a dynamic, challenging area of employment. Students who seek careers in this sector should have a good foundation of agribusiness and economics courses and at least an appreciation and rudimentary understanding of the farm sector. Many large corporations have consolidated and will continue to consolidate with agribusiness-related companies. Opportunities for employment will increase, especially in the areas of sales and marketing. Students who seek jobs in agribusiness typically start in sales or first-level management. These jobs present unique challenges and will give you an opportunity to apply what you have learned in your four years of hard work in college.

The input and product sectors offer outstanding employment opportunities, but, like many other sectors of the economy, they are subject to cycles of unemployment. The relative health of the farm sector is closely related to employment in the input sector and less directly affects employment in the product sector as one moves up in the food distribution system and further away from the farm gate.

As an agribusiness manager, you may be required to deal with many externalities—factors that you must accept and over which you have very little, if any, control. Government programs seem to cycle from the arguments for "free trade" and all-out production to the other extreme, like the payment-in-kind program of 1983 that greatly restricted crop acreages. You must be ready to accept and deal with these problems if you are to be a successful agribusiness manager. Hopefully, agribusiness courses will give you some guidelines to go by which will be useful in evaluating decisions in the uncertain economic climate that lies ahead.

The chapters ahead are written to give the student a basic understanding of some of the critical areas of agribusiness management. Part I of the text is designed to present an overall view of agribusiness—what it is, what management concepts are important, and how agribusinesses might choose to organize. Part II reviews some important economic principles and presents the "numbers" part of agribusiness management. The principles of accounting as they relate to performance evaluation by agribusiness managers are developed and discussed. Finally, important management tools are developed which are used on a daily basis by successful agribusiness managers.

Part III discusses marketing—both at the farm level and at the consumer level. Tools for marketing decisions are presented. The selling aspects of agribusiness are carefully developed and discussed in the last part of this section. Part IV briefly discusses the importance in agribusiness of production planning and control. Principles of planning for production are developed in this section. The final section of the text presents an in-depth discussion of the human resource part of agribusiness. People management skills are presented and discussed. These interaction skills may be among the most important management skills to be learned by the prospective agribusiness manager of the future.

SUMMARY

Agribusiness is the sector of the American economy in which producing and distributing inputs to farmers, and marketing, processing, and distributing farm products to final users take place. The USDA lists over 950 occupations in 1900 agribusiness industries employing roughly one out of every five people in the United States work force.

The input sector has increased dramatically in the past 15 years because modern agriculture relies very heavily on new technology to improve operating efficiency. Farmers purchase over 70 percent of their inputs and are moving toward larger, more capital-intensive operations. The agricultural input industry is indeed large and growing to serve the needs of farmers. Agricultural producers had nearly $200 billion in outstanding debt in 1984.

The system for marketing, processing, and distributing farm products to consumers is also large and very complex. Although there are more than one-half million firms involved in processing farm products, much of the volume is concentrated in a few very large firms in some selected industries in this sector. Over the past 5 or 6 years, however, food expenditures as a percentage of disposable personal income have remained fairly constant.

The study of agribusiness includes understanding the economic and personal skills prospective employees need if they are to be successful in this sector. Many important agribusiness management tools are presented and discussed in detail in this text. It is up to you to study and be able to apply these management principles so that you can take appropriate action when a decision must be made.

DISCUSSION QUESTIONS

1. How can the food system justify the tremendous "middleman bill," which amounted to almost $280 billion in 1984? Are consumers paying too much for food? Are farmers receiving their fair share?

2. Pick two food products and follow them through the food processing and marketing system. How many different agribusiness firms do you estimate add value to each of these products?

3. Each farmer today is responsible for feeding seventy-nine people.

Explain the importance of the agribusiness input and output sectors in this statement.

4.   Do you see any "structural" problems in the output sector of agribusiness? What is being done to ensure that these problems will not worsen?

5.   List as many separate agribusiness industries as you can in the input sector; repeat the list for the output sector. How important are these firms to the total economy?

6.   What do you suspect are the major growth areas in terms of future employment opportunities in agribusiness? How might you best prepare for jobs in these areas, i.e., what specific skills do you think would enhance your chances of locating employment with firms in the areas you've listed?

- Define management and explain the role of a manager

- List the ways in which the agribusiness manager differs from other managers

- Summarize the various well-known approaches to study management

- Describe the functions of planning, organizing, directing, coordinating, and controlling in agribusiness management

- Explain the differences among policies, procedures, and practices

- Identify the importance of setting objectives for the agribusiness and describe the planning process

- List the four basic agribusiness areas that utilize the functions of management

Managing the agribusiness firm requires planning, organizing, controlling, and directing.
A. Record keeping for control
B. Planning and communicating
C. Directing human resources

MANAGEMENT IS A LOT LIKE JUGGLING. IF YOU DROP ANY BALLS, IT MESSES UP YOUR ACT.

2

MANAGING THE AGRIBUSINESS

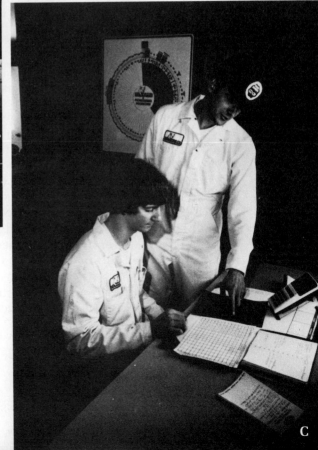

C

THE IMPORTANCE OF GOOD MANAGEMENT

Recently, Dun & Bradstreet conducted a survey to determine the single most prevalent cause of failure in business. After studying hundreds of cases, they concluded that 88 percent of all business failures could be traced directly to ineffective management.[1] The manager's concept of the management role, of what managers are and what they do, was the single most important factor in determining whether managers were effective or ineffective in their roles.

Thus success or failure of any agribusiness rests primarily on its managers' effective or ineffective utilization of the organization's resources. The ability to manage does not surface as an inborn gift; rather, it is a skill that can and must be learned. To some, management represents a land of mystery and games. To such people the messages transmitted by the present inhabitants of the management world often seem incoherent and vague. Only firsthand experience and exposure to the management perspective can correct this impression.

Because people and situations differ, an individual management pattern may be difficult to define. The myth that it is possible to formulate a list of perfect traits or styles of management has been dispelled once and for all by the realization that although certain management skills and principles can be learned, they must be adapted by each individual to fit the unique situation.

Management as a Profession

During the time when he served as president of the American Management Association, Lawrence A. Appley observed:

> Management is evolving as a profession with defendable principles and with a body of reference points strong enough to differentiate manager from nonmanager, and to correlate basic goals for its members, regardless of the nature of their business, their geographical location, or the activity with which they are affiliated.[2]

It is inescapable that during the past generation business education has come of age. It is now recognized that there are identifiable reasons why some organizations succeed while others fail. Today it is a widely accepted fact that managers of successful business are guided by principles and knowledge of management. An awareness that management skills can be learned is shown by the estimate that business spends $14 billion each year to train managers. That is a tremendous amount of money; however, this figure may be misleading. Many firms spend very little on internal or external training programs for their employees. In tight economic periods, when efforts are made to "trim the fat," the training budget is often a likely target. Businesses must learn, some the

[1] Dun & Bradstreet, "The Business Failure Record," 1978.

[2] Lawrence A. Appley, *Management in Action,* 3d ed., American Management Association, 1956.

hard way, that they must be as willing to invest time, money, and effort in their employees as in new plant additions or equipment.

What Is a Manager?

Successful managers feel like managers, see themselves as managers, and are both ready and willing to play the managerial role. When successful managers look in the mirror, they see a *leader*, a person who is willing to accept the responsibility for change and become the catalyst for action. The success-minded manager is comfortable with the managerial role, and accepts responsibility and power as a challenge rather than as a curse. The famous educator Nicholas Murray Butler once placed managers in three classes: "the few who make things happen, the many who watch things happen, and the majority who have no idea what has happened!"

Thus the *manager* can be defined as that person who provides the organization with leadership and who acts as a catalyst for change. Good managers are most effective in an environment that permits creative change. Such managers live to make things happen. Peter Drucker has remarked that "The ineffective manager concentrates on doing things right, rather than on doing the right things."[3] Success as a manager, then, necessitates the ability to understand and be comfortable with the managerial role, to accept responsibility, and to provide leadership for change.

What Are the Distinctive Features of Agribusiness Management?

In many ways, management principles and knowledge are the same for any business. Both the largest business in the country, General Motors, and the smallest one-person agribusiness are guided by the same general principles. The differences between large and small businesses, between agribusinesses and other kinds of businesses, rest in the art of applying basic management principles to the running of the business. All the functions of management discussed in this book are used in different ways by different business enterprises.

As a professional, the manager might be compared to a physician. The knowledge and principles of medicine are the same, but patients differ in such vital details as age, sex, build, and general health. The physician's skill is to apply general medical principles to the individual patient's unique circumstances.

In this chapter general management principles will be applied to the unique qualities of agribusiness and agribusiness management. Some of the reasons why agribusiness management differs from other kinds are the following:

1. The tremendous variety in the kinds of businesses in the agribusiness sector; that is, from basic producers to shippers, brokers,

[3]Peter F. Drucker, *Drucker on Management*, Management Publications, Ltd., 1970.

wholesalers, processors, packagers, manufacturers, storage firms, transporters, financing institutions, retailers, food chains, restaurants—the list is nearly endless. Following a loaf of bread from the time it is a seed to its positioning on the grocer's shelf would involve nearly every conceivable kind of business enterprise known to civilization.

2. The sheer number of agribusinesses. Literally millions of different businesses have evolved to handle the route from the producer through the retail marketer.

3. The way in which basic agribusiness is built around several million farm producers. These farmers produce hundreds of different food and fiber products. Most agribusinesses deal with farmers either directly or indirectly. No other industry is built principally around the basic producer of its raw product.

4. The infinite variety in size of agribusinesses, from giants like Dow Chemical to the one-person or one-family organization. Most agribusinesses tend to be small when compared with other business and industrial segments.

5. Agribusinesses are small and compete in a relatively free market in which there are many sellers and fewer buyers and in which the numbers and sizes of agribusinesses do not allow monopoly-like enterprises. Product differentiation is also difficult in most agribusinesses—a ton of 20-20-20 fertilizer or a bushel of corn will vary little from producer to producer.

6. The traditional philosophy of life exhibited by many agribusiness workers, which tends to make agribusinesses more conservative than some other businesses.

7. The fact that agribusiness firms tend to be family-oriented. Many agribusinesses are run by families or deal with businesses that are run by families. Husbands and wives are often involved heavily in both the operational and decision-making phases of the business on a full-partnership basis.

8. The fact that agribusinesses tend to be community-oriented. Many of them are located in small towns and rural areas where interpersonal relationships are important and associations are long term. People know each other and each other's families, perhaps for several generations.

9. The fact that agribusinesses, even those that are industrial giants, are likely to be highly seasonal in nature. Because of the intimate relationship and interdependence of agribusiness and farm producers, and because of the nature of planting and harvesting seasons, special problems often arise.

10. Agribusinesses deal with the vagaries of nature. Drought, flood, insects, and diseases are a constant threat for most agribusinesses. Everyone from the banker to the chemical manufacturer is concerned with the weather.

11.   The direct impact governmental programs and policies have on agribusinesses. The price of wheat, for example, may be heavily influenced by government regulation. Many agricultural products are directly influenced by government programs. The 1983 payment-in-kind program, along with severe drought in many areas of the country, had a great impact on the agribusiness sector.

Each of these special features of the agribusiness world requires the agribusiness manager to use the principles of management in a very special way. Agribusiness is unique, and requires unique abilities and skills of its managers.

THE ELEMENTS OF GOOD MANAGEMENT

Our definition of *management* is "The *art* of *successfully* pursuing desired results with the *resources available* to the organization." Several key words in this definition are italicized to stress the elements of successful management.

The first is the *man* in *management*. There are two dimensions to good management—the human dimension and the technical dimension—but the former is by far the more important one. A manager's ability to achieve results through others (both men and women) is the very essence of good management. Investment of time and energy in one's subordinates can pay handsome rewards.

Art is the second key word, for management is an art, not a science. Because management deals largely with people, we must regard management principles as imperfect equations at best. Everyone cannot become the Rembrandt of management art, but everyone can use management principles to foster continual growth and progress toward managerial potential.

The third key word is *successful*. Whatever else good management is, it must be successful in meeting desired and predetermined goals or *results*. Managers must know where they are headed in order to achieve success.

Finally, consider the *resources available*. Each organization possesses or has at its command a variety of resources. Successful managers stimulate the highest potential returns from the resources available. They recognize the difference between what should be and what is. They use what they have to get what they want, and deal in the realm of the possible.

Concepts of Management

Management has been dissected and described through as many concepts as there are writers in the field. Some describe management as a division of areas of responsibility, such as finance, marketing, production, and personnel. Others view it as coordinating a series of resource inputs, such as money, markets, material, machinery, methods, and manpower. Here once again management is conceptualized as obtaining desired results through the effective utilization of available resources. This approach is often called the *Six M concept*.

Another concept of management involves its division into approaches or processes. This is the realm of the industrial engineering, organizational, and behavioral concepts (see Chapter 18).

The *industrial engineering* approach assumes that whenever the process of work is scientifically analyzed and organized, maximum productivity will result. The most famous proponent of this management concept was Frederick W. Taylor. Job descriptions, time and motion studies, and production standards form the basis of this school of management. Industrial engineers believe that if the best and simplest way of doing things were discovered, productivity would result automatically.

Organizational theorists, on the other hand, have concentrated their focus on such areas as specialization; division of labor; the ways in which power and authority are distributed through the organization line; staff relationships; span of control (how many subordinates can be controlled by one manager); and span of attention (how many different operations can be controlled by one manager). This school of management asserts that if the aforementioned relationships and tasks were carefully designed, productivity would be the natural result; and that the informed use of power and organizational authority will result in maximum effectiveness.

The *behavioral* concept is the most recent development to appear on the management scene. This school of thought urges the manager to enlarge and enrich jobs; to give individual workers more responsibility and authority; and to provide a working environment in which employees can satisfy their own needs to be recognized, accepted, and fulfilled. Douglas McGregor, Abraham Maslow, Rensis Likert, and Frederick Herzberg were leaders in developing this new approach to management. The behaviorist believes that if the worker is happy, productivity will follow in the natural course of events.

Still another popular concept views management as a series of functions. This school of thought generally describes management as PODCC; that is, *planning, organizing, directing, coordinating, and controlling*. Two other functions should be added—communicating and motivating—since these functions underlie the success or failure of the first five functions.

* *Planning* describes the adoption of specific programs in order to achieve desired results.

* *Organizing* involves fitting the organizational pieces together.

* *Directing* indicates an attempt to point out the best way.

* *Coordinating* represents an effort to ensure that all the gears are meshing smoothly.

* *Controlling* means checking whether objectives are being met.

Under this approach, the best of all schools of management philosophy can be combined.

Figure 2-1 illustrates the concept of management as a wheel. The five functions of management are the spokes that connect the manager with the objectives and results that are sought. It is only through planning, organizing, directing, coordinating, and controlling that the manager's results and objectives are achieved. Overall management can be no stronger than the weakest spoke in this wheel.

One of the places where confusion often arises among students of management is in their attempt to separate each function of management from every other function. The wheel illustrates the need to view management as a whole, with each function tied to an interrelated function in unison and all overlapping one another; each one is as necessary as the spokes on a wheel.

Now add motivation as the torque, or speed, with which the functions are accomplished. Motivation provides the motion by which the wheel either moves forward or reverses. Good motivation results in speedy, efficient, successful, forward-moving management, while poor motivation can result in a discouraging reversal.

The axle on which the entire wheel of management turns is communication. Without good communication the wheel of management

Figure 2-1 Management as a wheel, with the manager as the hub. The five functions of management are the spokes leading directly outward to the manager's objectives.

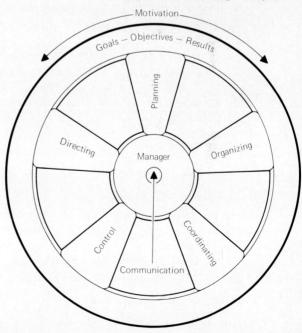

soon begins to wobble and squeak; if attention is not given soon enough, the entire wheel is likely to break down.

It is important to recognize that not all management is good or positive in its effect. Management that is poor can hold back the progress of the entire business enterprise. Because most management results in activity, the crucial question becomes whether that activity is positive or negative in each management situation. The running of the business or activity must not be mistaken for successful management simply because it is active. An agribusiness manager who charges from one crisis to the next is probably putting out the fires that good management would have prevented in the first place. It is not how hard a manager works, but how intelligently the work is handled that determines the manager's success.

All these approaches to management are of value, and each offers something to the student. The functional or traditional approach will be developed in detail because it encompasses the best of all the other philosophies, because it is simple and precise, and because it has withstood the challenges of time.

THE FUNCTION OF PLANNING

In the body of management knowledge, the function of planning provides the muscle and sinew, that is, the part of management that allows movement in the desired direction.

It is undeniable that aimlessness produces unpredictable results. A decade or two ago, planning was often extremely casual, even in large companies. But according to a survey reported recently by the American Management Association, four out of five contemporary companies prepare and use planning consciously as a part of their business life.[4] In today's dynamic business world, planning is a necessity for consistently achieving success.

It is no longer possible to excuse a lack of planning with such vague justifications as, "as long as we are getting somewhere, that's what counts." It is getting somewhere *that you want to go*, with specific routes and timetables for success, that counts.

That is why most success-minded managers are now committed to formal planning. They would never consider operating without a plan in such vital functional areas of business as production, marketing, work force, and finance. Planning has become a way of business life.

Definition of Planning

Planning can be defined as forward thinking about courses of action based on full understanding of all factors involved and directed at specific objectives.

When this definition is dissected, the first segment is seen to be *forward thinking*, which means just that, looking ahead. It is not a fore-

---

[4]Ernest Miller, "Marketing Planning," American Management Association, 1966.

THE ROLE AND ORGANIZATION OF AGRIBUSINESS

cast but an action-oriented statement, which leads to the second element of the definition.

The second element is *about courses of action*, which implies developing alternatives or methods of getting ahead.

Then comes *based upon full understanding of all factors involved*. Here is where the facts and consequences of the various factors impinging on the alternative courses of action are weighed.

Finally, there is the most important part of all, as well as the most neglected: *directed at specific objectives*, or, in other words, going exactly where the forward-thinking actions are intended to lead.

Types of Planning

Figure 2-2 illustrates in a graphic manner the levels at which different types of planning occur.

Please note that as the level of planning moves from the chief executive to the worker, several changes occur. At the top levels, plans have a tendency toward flexibility, are longer range, are usually written, are more complex, and are broader in nature.

At the lower levels, plans are detailed and specific in nature, are for immediate action, are usually unwritten, and tend toward simplicity.

Almost all plans would benefit from being written down because written plans tend to organize and consolidate thoughts, are easier to communicate, and provide a source for further reference.

Top executives make plans that generally add or subtract resources from the agribusiness, while those plans that are made at the lower levels generally relate to using the existing resources in the most efficient manner.

Figure 2-2 illustrates the need for all these plans to mesh in a correlated manner so that the long-range, complex objectives and plans of the organization can be achieved.

The challenge is to help those at all levels of the organization un-

Figure 2-2   The levels and nature of planning in the agribusiness.

POLICY LEVEL	MIDDLE MANAGEMENT	SUPERVISOR LEVEL	PRODUCTION EMPLOYEE
Very flexible	Somewhat flexible	Discretionary changes	Inflexible
Long range	Intermediate term	Short term	Immediate
Written, analyses	Written, reports	Outlined	Unwritten
Complex, detailed	Less detail, outlined	Highlighted	Simple
Broad	General	Somewhat specific	Very specific

derstand their common objectives. *Policies, procedures,* and *practices* are developed to help ensure cooperative action toward common objectives and goals.

Policies, Procedures, Practices

Policies are used to guide one's thinking process during the planning or decision-making stage. The formulation of policies allows everyone to consistently make decisions that are in line with organizational objectives. The policy sets the boundaries within which an agribusiness employee can exert individual creativity. Policies make it unnecessary for subordinates to constantly clear plans and decisions with top management. For example, one farm equipment supply store in the Midwest instituted a policy that the general manager must approve all purchases that totaled $500 or more. The purpose of this policy was to protect the business against unexpected large cash drains.

Policies are best adapted to recurring problems in areas that are vital to achieving the agribusiness objectives. Policies are not objectives, although they are closely tied to objectives. Because they are not objectives, policies should never be used to fence in managers as they make decisions about long-range, complex problem situations.

A *procedure* is a step-by-step guide to a specific activity or function. In many cases, there is a definite need to set out just such a precise course of action. A procedure should not, in most cases, be applied to complex tasks of a long-range nature.

When the aforementioned farm equipment supply store sought to implement its new purchasing policy, the procedure involved called for an employee to fill out a requisition form, submit it to the general manager for approval, then send it to the purchasing director. Procedures work best when they are applied to routine and recurring tasks of a relatively simple nature that require control.

Both policies and procedures are of tremendous value to the new or newly promoted employee who is learning on the job. They also ensure uniform performance by all employees and prevent unauthorized actions.

Practices represent what is actually done in the agribusiness, and they may conflict with policies and procedures. Managers have to be sure that policies make sense, are relevant, and are enforced, in order for them to become widespread practices. If employees of the farm equipment supply store ignore the policy and procedure regarding the limits on spending, the store may find itself in a serious cash bind.

A course of action that is established on a recurring basis becomes a practice, often by tradition or habit more than anything else. The status of practices can become as important as that of either policies or procedures, and even more difficult to change, so the agribusiness manager must see to it that practices coincide with policies and procedures.

For instance, some agribusinesses make it a company *practice* to give Christmas turkeys to their employees, while other agribusinesses follow a *policy* of sharing a portion of their profits with their employees.

Setting Objectives

The planning process starts with objectives (see Figure 2-3). *Objectives* are statements developed by top management, boards of directors, and chief executives to define what they believe to be the organization's mission. These are the shining stars that light the path of subsequent planning and thinking. They are the targets toward which goals are aimed. They are also the most neglected of all planning segments. This neglect occurs because managers either avoid the mental exercise needed to set objectives or fear the failure that might be evidenced by an inability to reach them.

Nothing is so important to the long-range success of an agribusiness as written, well-thought-out objectives. Quite simply, an organization that knows where it is going is *much more likely* to get there than one that depends on arriving by accident.

Well-stated objectives should:

1. Record the direction the agribusiness should take

2. Provide guides for the goals and results of each unit or person

3. Allow appraisal of the results contributed by each unit or person

4. Contribute to a successful overall organizational performance

5. Indicate the philosophy and desired image of the organization

Objectives should be broad, long-range, flexible, and not necessarily time-oriented. Most agribusinesses will have at least five objectives, and a few might have ten or more. An organization with more than ten overall objectives is almost certainly mixing goals with its objectives.

Objectives are usually found in the following business areas:

1. Market standing (Position compared with competitors?)

2. Growth and development (How much and how fast should growth be?)

Figure 2-3 Objectives are the targets toward which a web of interrelated goals and subgoals is directed.

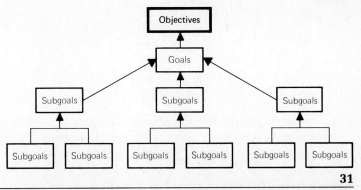

3. Profitability (What kinds and amounts of profit are feasible?)

4. Employee relations and performance (What rewards and share of income should go to employees, and what is expected of them?)

5. Investor relations and returns (What portion of earnings should go to investors?)

6. Public responsibility and relationships (What kind of business citizen does the company want to be?)

7. Physical resources (What plant equipment, tools, etc., are needed?)

8. Products and innovation (What emphasis will be placed on new products and research?)

The Planning Process
There are six steps in the planning process. These are:

1. *Gathering facts* and information that have a bearing on the situation

2. *Analyzing* what the situation is and what problems are involved

3. *Forecasting* future developments

4. *Setting goals,* the bench marks for achieving objectives

5. *Developing alternative* courses of action and selecting those that are most suitable

6. *Developing a means of evaluating progress,* and readjusting one's sights as the planning process moves along

Step 1: Gathering Facts Gathering of facts and information has been dubbed the first step of the planning process, even though information gathering is a constant, recurring part of the planning process. Its place as a first step is easily justified, since adequate information must be available to formulate or synthesize the fuzzy problem or opportunity present.

Fact gathering is subdivided into two parts: gathering sufficient information to identify the need for a plan in the first place, and systematic gathering of specific facts needed to make the plan work once it has been decided upon.

Because of the difficulty of gathering facts, some managers tend to slide by this step of the planning process and resort to the "seat of the pants" philosophy, which reduces the likelihood of success.

On the other hand, one should not become so engrossed in fact gathering that inaction results.

Step 2: Analyzing the Facts The groundwork for developing a sound plan is laid in the process of *analyzing facts.* This process answers such questions as "Where are we?" and "How did we get here?" It helps pin-

THE ROLE AND ORGANIZATION OF AGRIBUSINESS

point existing problems and opportunities, and provides the framework upon which to base successful decisions.

An analysis of facts will prevent the making of foolish mistakes and allow for the wisest use of the organization's resources.

Step 3: Forecasting Change   The forecasting of change is the ultimate test of good planning. It has been truly said that the ability to determine what the future holds is the highest form of management skill.

As managers ascend the organizational ladder, the demands on their abilities steadily increase. The broader, the more complex, the more long-range a plan is, the more difficult it is to foresee results accurately.

As with all of the steps of planning, forecasting is interrelated with all the other steps. Actually, it is simply the logical extension of analysis into a future time setting. Many say, "No one can predict the future in our business." While no one can be expected to predict accurately all future developments, this is hardly a good reason for not attempting to predict the future at all.

Many failures in prediction result from sloppy, ambiguous, generalized thinking. Forecasting change is not a guessing game; it is based on a hard, disciplined, tough approach to planning.

Step 4: Setting Goals and Results   Many management specialists consider goal setting to be the first step in the planning process. In a way they are correct, but in the present division of the planning steps, it seems that the formulation of information is part of goal setting.

All these processes are going on continuously in the funnel of planning. Goals cannot be set in a vacuum, but must be related to the attainable. Therefore, they must be formed as a consequence of the gathering of, and analysis of, information and facts. They should be aimed toward organizational objectives.

Step 5: Developing Alternatives   After the goals have been set, *alternative courses* of action must be developed; that is, agribusiness managers must explore the different ways of getting wherever they want to go.

Here again the relationship between *goals* and *results* can be seen. The *results* achieved depend upon the alternative activities selected to meet the *goals*. Alternatives must be weighed, evaluated, and tested in the light of the unique agribusiness' resources. Imagination is crucial, since new ways and/or new paths can blaze the route to success.

The individuality of this step must be stressed. For example, corn might be shipped to a distant city by truck when rail might have been the best and quickest way to get it there. But if one cannot afford to send it that way, or if there is no railroad available, a truck may well be the best alternative.

Step 6: Evaluating Progress   Surveillance and checking of progress have been found by management specialists to be one of the highest priorities.

Evaluation shows whether the plan is on course, and allows both the analysis of *new* information and the discovery of new opportunities.

Evaluation cannot be left to chance. It must be incorporated into the planning process as one of the most important steps, since a plan is only good so long as the situation remains unchanged. For this reason, the plan must be evaluated when it is formed into a program of specific activities, and once it is underway.

From evaluation one can tell whether goals have been achieved, whether results matched goals, and where the results fell short or overshot goals. It also points up weaknesses in plans and programs so that those portions that are ineffective can be changed. In a fast-changing world, planning is essential to management success.

THE FUNCTION OF ORGANIZING

The first function that will be discussed is *organization*. This is the beginning step, since the manager must recognize and implement the principles of organization before she or he can carry out the other functions of management.

Organizing involves:

★ Setting up the structure

★ Determining the jobs to be done

★ Selecting, allocating, and training personnel

★ Defining lines of activity

★ Establishing relationships within the organization and then staffing them

If management is seen as a body of knowledge, then organizing is the skeleton or framework on which management is built.

Some organizational structure exists in all businesses. It might be argued that even a one-person agribusiness contains a structure for accomplishment, with one person wearing many organizational hats. Organizing, then, involves formalizing a plan to show the interrelationships of each job and each individual within the organization.

But organizing is more than a formal plan; it is an action step in management. Until all employees understand their relationships to other employees and to the agribusiness as a whole, cooperation, teamwork, and coordinated action remain impossible to achieve, just as when the members of a band do not understand their relationship to the whole, discord, rather than harmony, will result.

Thus, as part of the organizing function, the agribusiness manager must see to it that each employee has a role that is clearly defined. The employees' work goals, the decision to place someone in charge, and the overall goals of the organization, coupled with the ways in which each person and department relate to each other, compose the organizational plan. Such a plan allows management to establish accountability for the results achieved; it prevents buck-passing and confusion as to who is responsible; and it details the nature and degree of authority that is given to each person as the activities of the firm are accomplished.

THE FUNCTION OF DIRECTING

It is important to reiterate that, in practice, one management function cannot be dissected or separated from another without incurring a breakdown of the whole management process. If, in the analogy of management as a body, organization is seen as a skeleton, then the heart of management would have to be the *directing of people*. Directing is:

★ Assigning duties and responsibilities

★ Establishing the results to be achieved

★ Delegating necessary authority

★ Creating the desire for success

★ Seeing that the job is done and done properly

Directing, then, involves leading, supervising, motivating, delegating, and evaluating those whom you manage. Managers are *directing* when they see to it that the efforts of each individual are focused on accomplishing the common objectives of the organization. Directing is at the very heart of the management process and is founded on a good organizational plan that provides for responsibility, authority, and evaluation.

The function of direction may also be described in broader terms as the task of making the organization take on life, of creating the conditions that make for interest in the job, vigor of action, imaginative thinking, and continuous teamwork. This goal is one that cannot be reached by magic formulas. Its achievement rests in large measure upon the qualities of leadership exhibited by the manager.

Leadership is helping individuals or groups to accomplish organizational goals. It is also, perhaps paradoxically, the process by which the manager attempts to unleash each person's individual potential, once again, as a contribution toward organizational success. Leaders recognize the *result* of a person's activities counts for more than the activities themselves.

Results represent the reason why a job exists. The results are what is produced by the activities undertaken by the employee. Only if these results lead to the accomplishment of the organization's goals and objectives are they successful.

In order to achieve maximum results, agribusiness managers must be aware of trends that affect the people they manage and, consequently, the need for a continual reevaluation of direction.

Patterns of Management Are Changing

One trend that agribusiness managers should be aware of as they provide leadership is the tendency for patterns of management to change rapidly with the dynamic changes in the socioeconomic structure of the United States. Many popular management "how-to" books have recently emphasized in many different fashions the importance of communication, involvement of subordinates in planning and profits, flexible organizational arrangements in the firm, etc., to ultimate business success. Figure 2-4 outlines in a simple manner how many management philosophies have changed in the last 5 to 10 years. Successful managers must have a leadership style and capability that allows them to modify their management patterns to fit these changing times.

A good manager today must help subordinates to find satisfaction and to identify themselves with their jobs and with the organization. A job is no longer a thing that is endured to exist; it is an outlet for individual human satisfaction.

At the same time, a sense of balance is required. Managers must recognize the usefulness of human behavioral principles; but they must also recognize that there are other objectives in running a business besides having happy, satisfied employees.

The Manager as Director

Successful agribusiness managers know that the measure of their output is but the sum total of the outputs of all those who work for them. Such managers recognize that no one is ever completely satisfied with any organization, and probably some will never be satisfied at all. What satisfies one person will not satisfy everyone. It is true that all of the people cannot be happy all of the time, but it is also true that most of the people should be happy most of the time with the satisfactions that they derive from their work. The good agribusiness manager will develop those qualities of direction and leadership that will help subordinates to succeed and to derive satisfaction from their work (see Chapter 18).

THE FUNCTION OF COORDINATING

Coordination deals with synchronizing and unifying the actions of a group of people. Coordination is the brain in the body of management skills. When a manager discovers continued difficulty in coordinating, he or she should suspect a poor program of planning, organizing, and directing.

Coordination is, in short, that area of management skills in which an ounce of prevention is worth a pound of cure. The less coordinating a manager has to do, the better. A good, sound command of the other management skills areas will keep the need for coordination to a minimum.

Even in well-managed organizations, however, there are areas that require coordination. It is the responsibility of the manager to see that

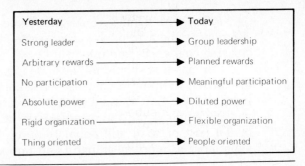

Yesterday		Today
Strong leader	⟶	Group leadership
Arbitrary rewards	⟶	Planned rewards
No participation	⟶	Meaningful participation
Absolute power	⟶	Diluted power
Rigid organization	⟶	Flexible organization
Thing oriented	⟶	People oriented

Figure 2-4   Changes in management patterns.

the operations, departments, divisions, and individuals under her or his direct control are properly integrated to produce results that contribute toward organizational objectives.

Coordinating is working together by:

1. Interpreting programs, plans, policies, procedures, and practices

2. Providing for growth and development of employees

3. Keeping in touch with employees and keeping a sense of perspective

4. Providing the climate for success

5. Providing for the free flow of information

The Manager as an Interpreter

The manager must interpret programs, plans, policies, procedures, and practices within the organization. Every department, division, or organization must have a court of last resort.

Human nature is such that even those with the best intentions may differ in their interpretations of facts or information. In such cases, it is the manager's task to deliver this interpretation; to become, in effect, the supreme court for those who are being supervised.

As the Individual Grows the Business Grows

Part of the manager's coordinating function involves the encouragement of employees' growth as individuals. An individual who is growing and developing is becoming more productive for the agribusiness as well as for himself or herself.

Special provisions for growth in responsibility should be built into the opportunities presented by any job, and job challenge must be maintained for the individual. Promotion policies should be formalized, and they should be understood by all concerned. Each employee should be appraised and evaluated for the unique contributions that the employee can make to the organization.

The good manager leads employees to discover hidden talents by stimulating them through varied assignments that offer continually increasing challenges and opportunities.

A manager should not hesitate to provide encouragement for more formalized training in courses, workshops, seminars, educational meetings, and the like. Formal education can benefit both the organization and the employee. If the organization participates by bearing all or part of the cost of such additional training, both parties tend to view the experience as more meaningful and important.

A Regular Schedule of Contacts with Individual Employees

A good manager maintains a regular schedule of interaction with subordinates. Application of this technique will acquaint the manager with the problems and personalities of employees. The manager will be able to consult and guide subordinates in the right direction, toward the objectives of the agribusiness.

A manager should develop an awareness of the subordinate's strengths and weaknesses. This, in turn, will help the employee to develop a confidence in "the boss." Both the manager and the subordinate will in this way be kept in touch and viewed in perspective.

Creating the Right Work Climate

It is mainly through the ability to create the climate for success that a manager can step up employee efforts to the point where employees approach their potential. Without a proper climate, none of the skills and principles of management can flower and bear fruit.

Six Principles of Creating the Climate

1. Set a good example.

2. Conscientiously seek participation.

3. Be goals- and results-centered.

4. Give credit and blame as needed: credit in public, blame in private.

5. Be fair, consistent, and honest.

6. Inspire confidence and lend encouragement.

Good managers know how to use these principles to create a productive working climate.

Provide for Free Flow of Communication

The key to the success of any of the management functions is the free flow of communication. The agribusiness manager is responsible for designing and implementing the communications process within a given area of responsibility. *Free flow of communication* means that communications must flow not only downward (from management to subordinates), but upward (from subordinates to managers) and laterally (at the same level) to be effective. Too often managers depend almost exclusively on downward communications and then wonder why policies, procedures, and goals are misunderstood. Successful communications require feedback. Feedback allows the manager to determine whether understanding has indeed occurred. It also allows the good ideas and potential contributions of each employee to be part of the success mix of collective wisdom and knowledge found in the organization. The manager must provide the opportunity for this feedback and involvement through a carefully designed communications process involving committees, meetings, memos, and individual contacts (more on this in Chapter 19).

THE FUNCTION OF CONTROL

The word *control* when used in a management sense does not mean restriction of or power over subordinates. The relationship of power over or restriction of subordinates comes under the function of directing. *Control* in management describes an information system that monitors plans and processes to be sure that they are meeting predetermined goals, and sounds a warning when necessary so that remedial action can be taken. In the body of managerial knowledge, control is the nervous system that reports the function of the parts of the body to the whole system.

If all people were perfect and their work were without flaw, there would be no need for "controls." Everything would come out according to plan. But all people make mistakes; they forget, they fail to take action, they lose their tempers, they behave, in short, like normal human beings.

Control is complementary to the other four functions of management. It compensates for the misjudgments, the unexpected, the impact of change. Proper controls offer the organization the necessary information and time to correct programs and plans that have gone astray. They should also indicate the means of correcting deficiencies. Managers can become aware of weak spots in the organizational, directional, and coordinating efforts of the business through proper use of control.

Control requires meaningful information and knowledge, and not that which is outmoded or not germane to meeting organizational goals. Much valuable time can be squandered or wasted by a control program unless a careful check of its *real* value is made periodically.

When the need for control information is not real, frustration, disrespect, and inaccuracy are likely to result. Employees cannot respect a program that is not used in a meaningful manner by management. Management can consume valuable time in reviewing useless control data, or it can fail to separate the relevant from the irrelevant, with poor performance as the consequence.

Comparing Results Achieved with Goals Set

All business activities produce results. These results should be matched carefully to well-conceived goals that aim toward organizational objectives. One of the most important purposes of control is to evaluate the progress being made toward organizational goals.

A good example of this type of control is found in the budget or forecast comparison. Is one over or under the budget? Are forecasts of sales and expenses in line with predictions? The information or control required in all areas must be based on predetermined, written goals and objectives. Only then can the agribusiness manager tell whether the reality matches the plans through which success is sought. A detailed discussion of control programs is presented in Chapter 9.

MAJOR AREAS OF MANAGEMENT RESPONSIBILITIES

Each of the functions of management—planning, organizing, directing, coordinating, and control—is used in managing the four major areas of an agribusiness. The management functions are implemented through the use of the various skills, principles, and tools that have become part of the professional agribusiness manager's knowledge and ability. To be successful, the agribusiness manager must apply this functional knowledge and ability to each of the four basic areas of the agribusiness; that is, financial management and planning, marketing and selling, production and operations, and personnel or the human dimension. The balance of this book is built around these four basic areas of the agribusiness, and is designed to help students acquire the know-how of the professional agribusiness manager.

SUMMARY

Management is the process of achieving desired results with the resources available. A key to successful management is accepting responsibility for leadership and making business decisions through the skillful application of management principles. Management of the agricultural business is unique because agricultural business is extremely seasonal, its products are perishable commodities, and it deals in local communities where long-term interpersonal relationships are critical.

The management process is often divided into five traditional functions: planning, organizing, directing, controlling, and coordinating. Planning is determining a course of action to accomplish stated objectives; organizing is fitting people and resources together in the most effective way; directing pertains to supervising and motivating people; the controlling function monitors performance and makes adjustments to stay on purpose; and coordinating synchronizes the total effort. Each of these is a necessary ingredient for accomplishing the established objectives.

DISCUSSION QUESTIONS

1. Define management, as separate from its functions.

2. Discuss some of the agribusinesses with which you are familiar in light of the distinctive features of agribusiness management.

3. Identify four different approaches or philosophies of management.

4. Define and discuss the management functions.

5. Describe some major changes in the socioeconomic system during the last decade or so, and explain the resulting modifications in management philosophy or attitudes.

6. Show how and why planning changes as one progresses up the organizational ladder.

7. Discuss some of the major objectives that an agribusiness should provide and the areas in which the objectives are usually found.

8. Examine and describe the steps in the planning process.

9. Discuss the components of the agribusiness manager's role as co-ordinator.

10. Discuss why there is the need to apply all the functions of management to the basic areas of an agribusiness.

THE CASE OF THE HART CHERRY COOPERATIVE

The Hart Cherry Freezers' Cooperative was organized 2 years ago to pit and freeze member-farmers' cherries. The cooperative is experiencing difficulty in keeping grower-members' cherries separate. Most of the cherries are harvested mechanically by shaking them from the trees. They are placed in pallet tanks by the farmer and brought into the plant for processing. The cooperative owns all the pallet tanks. When the farmer unloads the pallet tanks on the concrete pad, the cherries have to be cooled with running cold water until they are ready for processing. There is considerable variation in quality among the loads of cherries brought in by members. Some loads have large quantities of small twigs and leaves in them, some are rotten or soft, and some have some other undesirable quality. This is the first year that the cooperative has owned all the pallet tanks. The cooperative board decided that it was best for the cooperative to own them, since growers had been continually taking other growers' pallets whenever their own were unavailable. The *policy* of the cooperative board and management is that each farmer's cherries must be identified so that farmers can be paid separately, on the basis of the quantity and quality of their product.

The *practice* as it had developed this year was for the members to unload their pallets onto the pad. Each member was supposed to put a name card on each pallet.

The problem was that sometimes the farmers' new, inexperienced, or "Don't give a darn" truck drivers were failing to put cards on, cards were falling off, or sometimes two or more cards were on the same pallet.

QUESTION

1. Devise a *procedure* that will help to solve the problem by ensuring that each farmer's cherries are properly identified, and create a plan to ensure that the procedure will be carried out in practice.

OBJECTIVES

- Determine which factors are involved in selecting the best organizational form for an agribusiness

- Define the terms proprietorship, partnership, and corporation, and list the characteristics of each

- Summarize the advantages and disadvantages of each organizational form

Proprietorships, partnerships, and corporations are the primary forms of agribusiness organization.
A. Farm equipment proprietorship
B. Landscape partnership
C. An incorporated elevator

PRIVATE OWNERSHIP IS THE
BACKBONE OF AMERICA.

3
THE ORGANIZATION
OF AN AGRIBUSINESS

C

BASIC ORGANIZATIONAL FORMS

An agribusiness may boast billions of dollars of resources, or it may be as small as an individual who is a part-time seed-corn salesperson. Agribusinesses may engage in any kind of activity that is related to the production, processing, and marketing of food and fiber products. Though the one-person or one-family agribusiness is not uncommon, most of the true business volume in agriculture is carried on by enterprises that employ hundreds or even thousands of people.

All agribusinesses are owned by someone, and it is the circumstances of ownership that gives an organization its definite legal form. Four business forms are basic: the single proprietorship, the partnership, the corporation, and the cooperative (see Chapter 4 for discussion of cooperatives). The form of organization is not necessarily dictated by the size or kind of agribusiness; nearly every conceivable size and kind of agribusiness may occupy any of the four legal categories.

The many advantages and disadvantages of each of the four organizational forms must be weighed carefully because each form tends to fit some situations better than others. This chapter will clarify the important characteristics of each form and the factors that affect their selection for an agribusiness.

FACTORS INFLUENCING CHOICE OF FORM

Each form of business organization has its own individual characteristics. Owners and managers must choose the most appropriate one for each unique agribusiness. An agribusiness may want to change its legal form of organization as it grows or as conditions change. When deciding which form of organization is best, an owner or owners must analyze several factors.

1. How much will organizing cost and how easy is this form of agribusiness to organize?

2. How much capital is needed to carry on the agribusiness?

3. How much capital does the owner or owners have available?

4. How easy is it to secure additional capital for the agribusiness?

5. What tax liabilities and options are available?

6. How personally involved should the owner or owners be in the management and control of the agribusiness?

7. What factors of stability, continuity, and transfer of ownership are important to the agribusiness?

8. How desirable is it to keep the affairs of the agribusiness secret?

9. How much risk and liability should the owner or owners assume?

10. What type of business is it, where will it be conducted, and what are owners' objectives and philosophies for the agribusiness?

An evaluation of each of these factors will allow the selection of the most appropriate form of business organization in each case.

THE SINGLE PROPRIETORSHIP

The oldest and simplest form of business organization is the *single* or *individual proprietorship*, an organization owned and controlled by one person. In the United States it is the most popular form of organization. There are nearly 10 million single proprietorships, which together comprise over 80 percent of the country's business entities. It is estimated that these 80 percent of businesses transact only about 12 percent of the total business volume.

Proprietorships tend to be small businesses, although there are notable exceptions; the fortune amassed by Howard Hughes, for example, was largely accumulated from a single proprietorship. When a business reaches a certain size, other forms of business organization usually become more attractive.

Advantages of Proprietorships

The formalities that precede the organization of a single proprietorship are minimal. About all that is required is an individual's desire to start a business and the purchase of a license, if one is required for that particular kind of business. If the owner wishes to do business under an assumed name, that is, if the business is to be conducted under a name other than that of the owner, most states require that the assumed name be registered.

Ronda Green was an example of this. She decided to start a feed store, which she wanted to call Economy Feed because she preferred doing business under that name rather than using her own. Consequently, she registered the new name. Thereafter, those who did business with Economy Feed were aware that they were really doing business with Ronda Green.

The proprietorship gives the individual owner complete control over the business, subject only to government regulations that are applicable to all businesses of that particular type. The owner exerts complete control over plans, programs, capital, policies, and other management decisions. No one else shares in this control unless the owner specifically delegates a portion of the control to someone else. The owner need not seek permission from anyone to make decisions. All profits and losses, all liability to creditors and liability from other business activities are vested in the proprietor. The costs of organizing and dissolution are typically low. The business affairs are completely secret from all outsiders, except for select governmental units.

Whenever capital is needed it is supplied by the owner from personal funds or is borrowed against either business or personal assets. Personal and business assets are not strictly separated as they are in some other business forms; therefore, if the owner as an individual is financially sound, lenders will be more likely to extend funds. The proprietors can sell their businesses to whomever they wish, whenever they wish, and for whatever price they find satisfactory. They can assume as much risk or liability as they wish, and will often extend themselves far beyond the point at which they might retreat if others were involved as owners.

A single proprietorship pays no income tax as a business. All income that the business earns is taxed as personal income even though the IRS (Internal Revenue Service) requires the filing of a separate form to show business income and expenses. The proprietorship can conduct business in any of the fifty states without special permission other than whatever licenses are required for that particular kind of business. This is a right guaranteed to individuals by the United States Constitution, which provides that "citizens of each state shall be entitled to the privileges and immunities of citizens of the several states." The person who desires the cheapest, simplest, most self-directed, most secret, and most flexible form of agribusiness will choose the single proprietorship.

Disadvantages of Proprietorships

The most important disadvantage of the proprietorship relates to the generally limited amount of capital funds that one person can contribute. Lenders are also somewhat reluctant to lend to an individual owner unless the owner's personal net worth can guarantee the loan. Proprietorships often find that they are starved for capital, and this serious disadvantage may do more than stunt growth; thousands of bankruptcies each year can be traced to a serious shortage of capital at the onset.

Another distinct disadvantage is that the owner's personal liability for all debts and liabilities of the business extends even to the owner's personal estate. While freedom from business taxes is generally an advantage, it may be a disadvantage. Since business profit in a proprietorship is considered personal income to the owner, a high business profit may throw the owner into a higher tax bracket than the corporate form of business organization. This is especially disadvantageous if extensive funds are needed for the growth and expansion of the business. Corporate tax rates provide an advantage in such cases.

The concentration of control and profits in one individual may also be a disadvantage. Many highly trained and motivated employees want to participate financially in the business for which they work. They may also be uneasy about the fact that their futures depend on the health and viability of a single person. Thus, proprietorships may experience some difficulty in finding good people to hire. Without good, highly motivated employees, the owner may find as the business grows that he or she is wearing too many hats, with the end result that the business suffers.

Finally, the proprietorship lacks stability and continuity because it depends so heavily on one person. The death or disability of that one person, in effect, ends the business. Proprietorships may be difficult to sell or to pass on to heirs. This is particularly true if they become sizable businesses. Individual shares or parts of the business cannot be parceled out to several individual owners or to heirs in the same way that shares of a corporation can.

PARTNERSHIPS

A *partnership* is the association of two or more people as owners of a business. There is no limit to the number of people who may join a partnership. Apart from the fact that a partnership involves more than one person, it is similar to the proprietorship.

Partnerships can be based upon written or oral agreement, or on contracts between the parties involved. It is strongly urged, however, that partnership agreements be concluded in writing to avoid disagreement and misunderstanding at a later date. Partnerships can be formed by law whenever two or more people act in such a way that reasonable people would be led to believe they are associated for business purposes. There are slightly fewer than 1 million partnerships in the United States, and they account for about 5 percent of the total business volume. Partnerships are the simplest form of business organization by which a number of people can pool their resources and talents for mutual benefit.

There are basically two kinds of partnerships: general partnerships and limited partnerships.

General Partnerships

By far the most common form of partnership is what is called the general partnership. In a general partnership each individual partner, regardless of the percentage of capital contributed, has equal rights and liabilities. A general partner has the authority to act as an agent for the partnership, and normally participates in the management and operation of the business. Each general partner is liable for all partnership debts, and may share in profits, in equal proportion with all other partners. If misfortune befalls the partnership, all liabilities are shared equally among partners for as long as sufficient personal resources exist. However, when one partner's resources are exhausted, remaining parties continue to be liable for the remaining debt. General partners may contract among themselves to delegate certain responsibilities to each other, or to divide business revenues or costs in some special manner (e.g., according to funds invested or job responsibility). Each general partner may bind the partnership to fulfill any business deal made. While the partnership is usually treated as a separate business for the purposes of accounting, it is legally regarded not as an entity in itself, but as a group of individuals or entities.

Limited Partnerships

All partnerships are required by law to have at least one general partner who is responsible for the operation and activities of the business, but it is possible for other partners to partake in the business on a limited basis. This type of partnership permits individuals to contribute money or ownership capital without incurring the full legal liability of a general partner. A limited partner's liability is generally limited to the amount that the individual has personally invested in the business. The state laws regulating limited partnerships must be strictly adhered to. Most states have adopted the Uniform Partnership Acts, which generally require limited partnerships to be registered. These acts also spell out the limited status of any partners: first, that the limited partner can contribute capital but not services to the partnership, and second, that the limited partner's surname cannot appear in the business's name (unless the partnership had previously been carried on under that name, or unless a general partner has the same surname). Limited partnerships are relatively few in number; therefore, the balance of the discussion of partnerships will apply to regular or general partnerships.

Advantages of Partnerships

Partnerships are just about as easy to start as proprietorships. They require very little expense, although a good attorney should be engaged to draw up the partnership agreement. The partnership may operate under an assumed or fictitious name, providing it is registered in accordance with state laws. A partnership can generally bring together many more resources than a proprietorship because of the increase in the number of people involved. These added resources are not only financial in nature; the business likewise benefits from the variety of unique talents that many different individuals can bring to it. Partners are a team, and because each team member shares in the responsibility and profits, partners are more likely to be motivated than employees of a single proprietorship or corporation. Additional partners can be brought in if more money or talent is needed.

Partners as individuals pay taxes only on the income generated from their share of the profits. There is no business tax per se, and this can be a considerable advantage, depending on the income of the partners. Control or management of business decisions and policies is concentrated among the partners. Generally, partners split the responsibilities of the business; that is, one will head sales, another will head operations, etc. This can be done on either a formal or an informal basis. Partners may sell their interest in the business to others if the remaining partners agree. The business affairs of a partnership are confined to the partnership, and this element of secrecy is one of the prime reasons why many people choose to do business as partners. Partnerships share the same privileges of doing business in other states that proprietorships do.

Disadvantages of Partnerships

By far the biggest disadvantage of the partnership is the unlimited liability of each general partner. There are many known cases where one partner has run up bills against the partnership with those who sold in good faith, and then because that individual has been personally insolvent, the other partners have had to pay the bills. Even limited partners must be very careful that they do not give any appearance of being active in the management of the business. The law has frequently been enforced on the basis of a person's actions rather than on the basis of the written documents. If a person acts as a general partner *would* act, then the legal interpretation is that he or she is, in fact, a general partner, with all the liabilities that such status would incur.

The liability of general partners has created a second disadvantage: partnerships usually have only a limited number of members. Imagine a partnership with 100 members, each able to bind the partnership legally to contracts and to other obligations. Of course, the limited partnership was created to cure this problem, but it has not been very successful. A limited partnership suffers the lack of both ready funds and talented people as compared to a corporation.

Another disadvantage is the lack of continuity and stability of a partnership. When a partner leaves the partnership as a result of withdrawal, death, or incapacity, a new partnership must be formed. The old partner's share must be liquidated, and this can often place a severe burden on the partnership's capital position. Another problem is that which occurs if one of the partners becomes incapacitated by accident, ill health, old age, or insanity, or for some reason fails to pull a full share of the load. Often the only way to get rid of such a partner is to liquidate the entire business. When a partner leaves, it is often hard to determine what that individual's share is worth; for this reason, a formula and payoff method should be incorporated in the original partnership agreement. This will also help to solve the ultimate problem of partnerships, that of transferring the ownership of a partner's share. From a strictly legal point of view, whenever a partner leaves, the partnership is dissolved and a new one must be formed. However, if the means for establishing the value of the partner's share and the process for transfer and acceptance of new partners has been firmly established in the written partnership agreement, the transition can be reasonably smooth. Finally, while being taxed on income as separate individuals can be an advantage in some situations, it can be a disadvantage in others (just as with the single proprietorship).

One last and very important principle: the preparation of a carefully drafted partnership agreement in writing will do more to ensure the success of a partnership than any other factor. Find the most competent legal aid possible, a lawyer who is familiar with the problems of partnerships, and trust that lawyer to prepare the agreement for the agribusiness. When partnerships are formed, the members are all on good terms and cannot imagine feeling any other way about each other, but situations change and people change. Not only will a written contract of partnership provide many solutions, but it will serve as a ready reference to supplement all-too-fragile memories.

THE CORPORATION

A corporation is an artificial being, endowed by law with the powers, rights, liabilities, and duties of a natural person. Without the corporate form of organization it is impossible to imagine the creation of today's huge business entities, which employ hundreds of thousands of people and are worth billions of dollars. While there are only about 1.7 million corporations in the United States, they handle over 80 percent of the business volume. Many corporations are giants. The 500 largest corporations, as rated by *Fortune* magazine, generate two-thirds of all industrial sales in the United States. But most corporations are relatively small, and many are really one person businesses whose owners have chosen the corporate form of organization as the best for their unique businesses. As a matter of fact, 95 percent of all United States corporations have assets and annual sales of less than $1 million.

Nonprofit Corporations

Most corporations are formed for profit-making purposes; however, there are thousands of nonprofit corporations in existence. These nonprofit corporations embrace many areas of endeavor, including those of religious, governmental, farm, labor, and charitable organizations. Federal and state laws specify the numerous forms that these nonprofit corporations may take, along with very specific regulations as to their purpose and operation. A competent attorney can advise whether a nonprofit corporate form of organization is the most appropriate for a particular agribusiness. Again, the legal interpretation will be made on the basis of the ways in which the corporation acts, and not on the basis of how its organizational papers say it will act.

Examples of nonprofit corporations include some cooperatives, some agricultural trade and research groups, and some farm organizations, such as the Dairy Herd Improvement Association. Nonprofit corporations are exempt from certain forms of taxation, and generally they cannot directly enrich members financially. In many cases, the nonprofit corporation must secure a formal exemption from paying corporate income taxes.

The Nature of the Corporation

The corporation as we know it today is a rather recent innovation compared to proprietorships and partnerships. The early American colonists were very suspicious of this form of organization, and it was not until the 1860s that most states had provided laws allowing for the formulation of corporations. A corporation can own property, incur debts, and be sued for damages, among other things. The important distinction to remember is that the owners (stockholders) and managers do not own anything directly. *The assets of the corporation are owned by the corporation itself.*

Forming a corporation requires strict adherence to the laws of the state in which the business is being formed. Usually, one or more persons join together to create a corporation. A designated form is filled out and examined by the state's designated department for establishing corporations. If the legal formalities are in proper order, and if the proper fee for incorporation has been paid, a charter authorizing the applicants to do business as a corporation is issued. Additionally, a corporation maintains the following legal documents: articles of incorporation, which are filed with the state and which set forth the basic purpose of the corporation and the means of financing it; the bylaws, which set forth such rules of operation as election of directors, duties of officers and directors, voting procedures, and dissolution procedures; and stock certificates or shares detailing amounts of the owners' investments. The laws relating to the formation of proprietorships and partnerships are fairly well established and uniform throughout the nation, but considerable differences in the requirements for forming a corporation exist among the various states, so the individual state's laws and statutes must be carefully considered by those who wish to form a corporation. Selection of an attorney who is well versed in the corporate law of the individual state is essential to avoid potentially serious organizational problems in an agribusiness corporation.

Stock of the Corporation

When corporations are formed, shares of stock are sold to those who are interested in investing and risking their money in the enterprise. A *share of stock* is a paper, in prescribed legal form, that represents each person's amount of ownership in the corporation. *Common stock* normally carries the privilege of voting for the board of directors that oversees the activities of the corporation. *Preferred stock* differs from common stock in that it is usually nonvoting, and has a preferred position in receiving dividends and in redemption in the case of liquidation. Thus voting rights are exchanged for a lower-risk investment of capital. Each state has what are commonly called *blue-sky laws*, which regulate the way in which corporation stock may be sold and which protect the rights of investors. Individual states' laws must be consulted prior to the sale of stock in a corporation. The most common way of financing corporations is through the sale of stock, but financing through bonds, notes, debentures, and numerous means of borrowing against assets is also practiced (see Chapter 8).

How the Corporation Functions

The common stockholders in a corporation elect the directors. The number of directors may vary according to the bylaws of the organization. It is the responsibility of the board of directors to supervise the affairs of the corporation. In a large corporation the thousands of stockholders exercise very little actual control. Those they vote for to serve as directors are unknown to them and are often preselected by a small group of majority stockholders who are allied with top management of the corporation. The board represents the interests of the stockholders, and their major function is to elect officers, hire top management, and evaluate the progress of the business. In a small corporation there is usually a very intimate relationship; in fact, there could be only one stockholder who, in effect, is in complete control of the corporation.

Advantages of Corporations

The primary advantage of the corporate form of business organization is that the stockholders (owners) are not personally liable for the debts of the organization, and in most cases are not responsible for any liability that occurs through the corporation's business activities. The assets of the corporation are all that are at stake in settling most claims. With the corporate structure it is possible to delegate authority, responsibility, and accountability, and to secure outstanding, highly motivated personnel. Corporations can offer their personnel such benefits as profit-sharing and stock-purchasing plans, which encourage a high degree of dedication and loyalty to the corporation.

Transfer of ownership is also easier in a corporation than in other business forms. Usually, a stockholder can sell shares of stock to anyone for any price that the buyer is willing to pay. An owner can also transfer individual equity to heirs or to others much more easily. Sale of stock in a small, unknown corporation may not be easy. Finding someone who is willing to risk funds becomes much easier once the stock is *traded*; that is, as a corporation becomes larger and begins to develop a ready market for its stocks, the stocks may be traded by brokerage houses that specialize in the sale of stocks and are in constant touch with potential investors. New issues of stock may be purchased by a group of brokerage houses, which, in turn, sell the stock to the general public. Many companies have their stock traded in secondary markets which list daily price movements and facilitate buying and selling of these stocks. Examples of these markets include the New York Stock Exchange and the American Stock Exchange.

Because corporations' ownership rights are traded freely, it is relatively easy for them to raise large amounts of equity capital. The combined investments of hundreds and even thousands of investors made the huge corporate giants of American business possible.

Finally, the corporation is perpetual in nature. Death, withdrawal, or retirement of its shareholders has little effect on the life of the corporation. This is another advantage that makes investment in a corporation more attractive to those with funds to risk.

Disadvantages of Corporations

The greatest disadvantage of the corporate form of organization is taxation and regulation. The corporation is taxed on funds it earns as profit; then, after it has paid dividends to its stockholders, the stockholders must again pay income tax on the amount that is received as dividends. (This may not always be a disadvantage, as will be discussed later in the book.) In addition, there are many states that impose special levies and

THE ROLE AND ORGANIZATION OF AGRIBUSINESS

taxes on corporations, and there are many more laws and regulations controlling the activities of corporations than there are for other organizational forms. The corporation must withstand a lack of secrecy because reports must be made to stockholders and states and because the federal government may require disclosure whenever a stock offering is made to prospective purchasers. A corporation that is chartered to do business in one state may not do business in another state unless it complies with the second state's law of registration, taxation, etc. Finally, owners (stockholders) of larger corporations have little, if any, control over the management and policies of the corporation. Often their only recourse in the event of dissatisfaction is to sell others their stock, if possible.

The costs of taxes, records (which must be extremely comprehensive), and operation of the corporate form can be significantly higher than the costs for other forms of organization; for that reason, the corporate form should be evaluated carefully before it is adopted by an agribusiness.

Closely Held Corporations

A special form of corporation has been designed to offset some of the disadvantages of the regular corporation. This form is called the *subchapter S corporation,* or simply the *S corporation.* Subchapter S of the Internal Revenue Code makes it possible for the owners of a corporation to elect to be taxed as individuals, in the same manner as owners of a partnership or proprietorship. Several qualifications must be met: there cannot be more than thirty-five stockholders, the stockholders must be individual persons rather than corporations, and they cannot be nonresident aliens. The election to be taxed as individuals must occur prior to the start of the corporation's fiscal year. Owners, therefore, cannot simply wait to see which method of taxation would be better once the year is over and the returns are already in. There can be many pitfalls to this form of organization; agribusiness corporations should consult competent legal and accounting professionals before selecting it.

SUMMARY

Agribusinesses represent nearly every conceivable kind of business organization. A great many are owned and controlled by one person as a proprietorship, or by two or three people as partnerships. These forms of business are the simplest forms and allow their owners complete flexibility, minimize red tape, and incur no profits tax. But owners are personally liable for any debts or lawsuits against the businesses. Also, the longevity of the businesses is limited to the life of their owners.

Today, formal corporations are increasingly common, even for small firms that still operate mainly as a proprietorship or partnership. The corporation is an organization created for the purpose of carrying on business. Because it is a legal entity, it can own property in its own right, sue or be sued, and carry on business in its own behalf. Its owners are separate legal entities; thus their liability is limited to the amount of their investment. Also, the life of a corporation does not depend on how long its owners live. However, corporations generally must pay a special corporate-profits tax and must regularly report their activities to governmental authorities. The subchapter S corporation is a special type of corporation for small firms; they gain the benefits of a corporation, but are exempt from corporate-profits tax.

The best form of business organization for a particular agribusiness is an infrequent business decision for both management and owners, but an extremely important one. As businesses grow, they must consider moving toward becoming a regular corporation. The timing of that decision is highly important.

DISCUSSION QUESTIONS

1. List and discuss the factors involved in deciding which form of business organization is best suited to an agribusiness.

2. Define a single proprietorship and list its characteristics.

3. List the advantages and disadvantages of a proprietorship.

4. Define a partnership and list its characteristics.

5. List the advantages and disadvantages of a partnership.

6. Differentiate between a regular and a limited partner.

7. Describe how a corporation functions.

8. List the advantages and disadvantages of a corporation.

9. Design a chart to show how the three major forms of business organization rate for each of the factors that must be considered in selecting an organizational form.

10: How would you describe the importance to an agribusiness of choosing the best organizational form for conducting its business?

SHOULD I INCORPORATE?

You have started a new business with two other enterprising individuals on an equal share basis. You plan to produce Business Trivia games for adults. You estimate that the variable cost per game (i.e., the increase in total cost for each game produced) is $2.75 and that there are fixed costs (those that are the same regardless of output) of $70,000 per year. (Total cost = fixed cost + variable cost.) Your average selling price will be $8.95 per game. You expect to sell 25,000 games per year.

Business has been brisk, and the outlook was great until a hotshot agribusiness student visited your office and proceeded to tell you of the many advantages of incorporating. The student indicated that it would probably be profitable for you to incorporate. Each of the three partners would own one-third of the corporate stock and would work for the corporation.

Not desiring to hire an outside consultant, you plan to solve the incorporation question yourself. You have assembled the data and facts of the problem. The answer should be apparent if you work through the questions. Given the assumptions below, answer the following questions.

a. Tax rate for individuals: (1) 15 percent up to $10,000, plus (2) 30 percent for all profits above $10,000.

b. Tax rate for corporations: (1) 20 percent of first $25,000, (2) 22 percent of next $25,000, and (3) 46 percent of profits in excess of $50,000.

c. The corporation pays a salary of $20,000 to each shareholder for labor and management input.

d. Average per year "red tape" cost for the corporation is $700.

e. All corporate profits are paid out as dividends.

f. Assume that all other factors have no effect on the decision.

g. Personal income = income before individual taxes. Personal disposable income = income after tax.

QUESTIONS

1. What is the partnership's net income before withdrawals of salary, profit shares, etc.?

2. What is the corporation's taxable income?

3. The partnership would pay how much in federal income taxes?

4. The corporation would pay how much in federal income taxes?

5. In the partnership, what is the amount of each individual's profit share (before taxes)?

6. In the corporation, how much would each of the stockholders receive as annual personal income (salary plus dividends)?

7. In the partnership, each individual would have what amount in personal disposable income?

8. What is the personal disposable income for each of the stockholders in the corporation?

9. Based on these calculations, what should the current partnership do in terms of its organization?

10. If each individual suddenly decided that the value placed on acquiring limited liability should be $2000 annually (after all taxes), what should the firm do?

OBJECTIVES

- Determine the scope and sheer size of cooperatives in agribusiness

- Develop an appreciation for the heritage that has influenced today's farm cooperatives

- Describe how cooperatives have acted as pacesetters and power balancers in agribusiness

- Identify the basic principles that ensure that cooperatives serve the needs of member-patrons

- Explain how local and regional cooperatives are organized to serve members

- Examine some of the challenges and opportunities that face agricultural cooperatives

Agricultural cooperatives are a unique type of agribusiness organization
A. Cooperative board of directors
B. Local farm supply/marketing cooperative
C. Credit cooperatives

COOPERATIVES' HISTORIC ROLE HAS BEEN AS THE PACESETTERS AND POWER BALANCERS OF AGRIBUSINESSES. MAINTAINING THAT ROLE IS THE MOST SEVERE CHALLENGE OF THEIR FUTURE.

COOPERATIVES IN AGRIBUSINESS

LAFAYETTE CO-OP ELEVATOR CO.
CENTRAL OFFICE-GENERAL STORE
SERVING CUSTOMERS SINCE 1922

B

FARM CREDIT BANKS
OF LOUISVILLE
FEDERAL LAND BANK
FEDERAL INTERMEDIATE
CREDIT BANK
LOUISVILLE BANK
FOR COOPERATIVES

C

THE INFLUENCE OF COOPERATIVES

Agricultural cooperatives are a unique part of the American free enterprise system. Most are organized as business corporations (see Chapter 3), but their basic purpose—to serve the needs of their user-members rather than to make a profit on their own—distinguishes cooperatives from other forms of business organizations. The cooperative organization gives control to the member-users rather than to nonusers. Because cooperatives are owned by those who use them and are legally obligated to benefit their member-patrons, our political system has traditionally chosen to encourage their growth and development as a logical extension of the independent farm business. Special government policies and regulations have helped farm cooperatives to become a major factor in many supply, marketing, finance, and service industries of the agricultural sector.

Virtually every phase of agriculture is touched by cooperatives, either directly or indirectly. Cooperatives helped market over $20 billion worth of grain and soybeans and almost $17 billion worth of dairy products in 1984. Nearly 27 percent of all farm supplies are handled by cooperatives. More specifically, in 1984 cooperatives handled over $3.4 billion of fertilizer and almost $1.5 billion of chemicals. In total, marketing cooperatives helped their members sell over $54 billion worth of farm production in 1984, or nearly 30 percent of national production. Finance cooperatives, through the Farm Credit System (the Production Credit Association, the Federal Land Bank, and the Bank for Cooperatives), supply over $75 billion annually to help their members buy and operate their own farms and finance their businesses. And a wide variety of service cooperatives aid farmers by irrigating their land, insuring their assets, improving their livestock, and providing electric power and telephone service for rural areas. There is a total membership of nearly 5 million in 5781 separate cooperatives. Since there are only slightly over 2 million farmers in this country, many of them must hold membership in more than one cooperative simultaneously. Obviously, cooperatives are an important part of the American agribusiness community.[1]

Even consumers are directly affected by the wide scope of cooperative activities. Although they may not be recognized immediately as such, brand names such as Sunkist (citrus), Land O'Lakes (dairy and poultry), Welch (grape juice), and Ocean Spray (Cranberries) are all cooperatives that market their members' produce through these branch names.

Cooperatives have become big business. Today some cooperatives are numbered among the largest businesses in the country. In 1984 Farmland Industries, which is based in Kansas and operates throughout the central United States, had sales of $5.62 billion, making it among the top seventy-five United States corporations. Agway, Inc. (Syracuse, New

---

[1]"Farmer Cooperatives," USDA, Agricultural Cooperative Service, vol. 52, no. 7, October 1985.

York) had sales of $4.10 billion and was ranked as the 98th largest corporation in America by *Fortune* magazine in 1984. Land O'Lakes (Minnesota), Gold Kist (Atlanta), CENEX (Minnesota), Mid-America Dairyman (Missouri), and CF Industries (Illinois) were also ranked among the country's largest businesses by *Fortune* in 1984.[2] Table 4-1 shows the fifty largest farm cooperatives.

TABLE 4-1 1984 Top 50 Agricultural Cooperatives

1984 RANK	COOPERATIVE	TOTAL SALES (MILLIONS)	NET MARGINS (MILLIONS)
1	Farmland Industries, Inc.	5,620	11.2
2	Agway, Inc.	4,101	11.8
3	Harvest States Cooperatives	3,569	1.2
4	Associated Milk Producers, Inc.	2,532	5.6
5	AGRI Industries	2,284	(9.8)
6	Land O'Lakes, Inc.	2,277	10.5
7	GROWMARK, Inc.	1,954	1.3
8	Gold Kist, Inc.	1,600	50.0*
9	CENEX	1,488	15.7
10	Mid-America Dairymen, Inc.	1,300	5.0
11	Dairymen, Inc.	1,111	8.3
12	Indiana Farm Bureau Cooperative Assn.	983	(10.0)
13	CF Industries, Inc.	908	10.0
14	Ag Processing, Inc.	896	1.9
15	Calcot, Ltd.	876	32.0
16	Sunkist Growers, Inc.	784	545.0†
17	National Cooperative Refinery Assn.	730	13.3
18	Southern States Cooperative, Inc.	698	9.1
19	Tri/Valley Growers	663	25.5
20	Northwest Dairymen's Assn.	632	16.0
21	Landmark, Inc. (now known as Countrymark)	620	147.0
22	Union Equity Cooperative Exchange	606	4.5
23	Milk Marketing, Inc.	600	(1.3)
24	California and Hawaiian Sugar Company	589	N/A†
25	Riceland Foods, Inc.	576	(4.4)
26	Michigan Milk Producers Assn.	555	0.4
27	Sun-Diamond Growers of California	517	250.3†
28	MFA, Inc.	509	(4.9)
29	Ocean Spray Cranberries, Inc.	466	0.15†

Continued.

[2]"The Fortune Director of the 500 Largest U.S. Industrial Corporations." Fortune, April 29, 1984.

TABLE 1984 Top 50 Agricultural Cooperatives—Continued.
4-1

1984 RANK	COOPERATIVE	TOTAL SALES (MILLIONS)	NET MARGINS (MILLIONS)
30	Wisconsin Dairies Cooperative	447	5.7
31	Inter-State Milk Producers' Cooperative	455	(1.5)
32	Agri-Mark, Inc.	428	0.0
33	American Crystal Sugar Company	362	171.6
34	Dairylea Cooperative, Inc.	359	N/A†
35	Mississippi Chemical Corporation	349	37.1
36	Plains Cotton Cooperative Assn.	345	5.8
37	Universal Cooperatives, Inc.	340	4.2
38	Eastern Milk Producers Cooperative Association, Inc.	319	0.54
39	California Almond Growers Exch.	316	3.8
40	Ohio Farmers Grain and Supply Association	315	(0.25)
41	Northeast Dairy Cooperative Fed.	310	(2.1)
42	Dairymen's Cooperative Creamery Assn.	298	N/A†
43	FCX< Inc.	291	(7.0)
44	Citrus Central, Inc.	286	N/A†
45	Tennessee Farmers Cooperative	261	1.7
46	Welch's Food, Inc.	236	N/A†
47	American Rice, Inc.	233	N/A†
48	Upstate Milk Cooperative, Inc.	216	0.4
49	Rice Growers Association of California	194	102.0
50	Southern Farmers Association	192	0.5

*This is a pre-tax figure.
†Marketing cooperatives operating on a pool basis. Earnings figures comparable to those of the other cooperatives are not available. The figures provided for these marketing cooperatives are net proceeds distributed to members and include payments for crops as well as earnings.
N/A—not available or not provided.
Source: National Cooperative Business Association, Special Report, 1985.

Nonagricultural Cooperatives

Cooperatives are by no means limited to agriculture. Mutual insurance companies are cooperatives. Cooperative housing units and college campus bookstores are becoming increasingly popular. Cooperative apartment houses and supermarkets have also become prevalent in recent years. In fact, the federal government has established a special consumers' cooperative bank to lend money to newly established consumer cooperatives. Auto parts dealers, independent supermarket owners, and others are joining together cooperatively to gain the advantage of larger-volume purchases. United Press International (UPI) and the Associated Press (AP) are both cooperatively organized news agencies. Many savings and loan associations and mutual insurance companies are cooperatives. Although these organizations are not agricultural in nature, they are cooperatives and they play an important role in the economy of the United States. All these nonagricultural cooperatives operate very much like traditional agricultural cooperatives.

Cooperatives: A Brief History

It is difficult to determine the origin of cooperatives. There are traces of cooperativelike organizations in ancient Egypt as early as 3000 B.C. There are vestiges of cooperative ideas in Greek, Roman, and Chinese cultures. In the Middle Ages cooperative ideas developed in the form of "guilds," which united workers in an effort to meet common needs. The first farmers' cooperatives are reported to be those of Swiss dairy farmers, who made cheese cooperatively as early as the thirteenth century.

Early Americans also experimented with cooperatives. The colonists worked jointly on many self-survival projects. Benjamin Franklin organized a mutual insurance company (cooperative) in 1752. By the early 1800s dairy cooperatives had been organized in the Northeast. By the mid- and late 1800s there may have been as many as 1000 farm cooperatives—mostly dairy co-ops—in the United States.

Many people recognize the first formal cooperative of modern times to be the Rochdale Society of Equitable Pioneers in England in 1844. The original twenty-eight members of this early cooperative joined in an effort to purchase supplies for their businesses. Although theirs was not the first cooperative in history, their formal principles have served as a model for the development of a great many modern cooperatives.

Rochdale Principles[3]

1. That capital should be of their own providing and bear a fixed rate of interest.

2. That only the purest provisions procurable should be supplied to members.

3. That full weight and measure should be given.

4. That market prices should be charged and no credit given nor asked.

5. That "profits" should be divided pro rata upon the amount of purchases made by each member.

6. That the principle of one member, one vote should govern, and that there should be equality of the sexes in membership.

7. That the management should be in the hands of officers and committees elected periodically.

[3]Martin A. Abrahamsen, *Cooperative Business Enterprise*, McGraw-Hill, New York, 1976, p. 48.

8.　　That a definite percentage of profits should be alloted to education.

9.　　That frequent statements and balance sheets should be presented to members.

But it was not until the early 1900s that cooperatives really began to grow. The growing recognition that farmers could significantly improve their economic condition through cooperatives generated much state and federal legislation that encouraged the growth and development of farm cooperatives. Not only was there a sharp increase in the number of local cooperatives during this period, but many established cooperatives were reorganized and consolidated into larger units as well. Regional cooperatives were formed to support the activities of local cooperatives. The formation of national cooperative organizations, such as the American Institute of Cooperation, the National Council of Farmer Cooperatives, the Cooperative League, and the American Farm Bureau Federation, supported an increasingly favorable social and political climate for cooperatives.

In the early 1900s many important laws were passed to encourage the growth of cooperatives. The Capper-Volstead Act of 1922 is among the most significant cooperative legislation, since it ensures the right of farmers to organize and market their products collectively so long as:

1.　　The association conducts at least half its business with members of the association; *and*

2.　　No member of the association has more than one vote, *or* the association limits dividends to 8 percent.

Pacesetters and Power Balancers

The early 1900s provided many vivid examples of cooperatives that fulfilled two basic purposes: to set a competitive pace and to act as power balancers. Frequently, the United States' rural areas offered few alternative sources for essential farm supplies. In many cases, farmers were afforded woefully inadequate service, yet were forced to pay high prices. By organizing a cooperative, farmers gained both their own source of supplies and a place to market their products, one that they owned, controlled, and operated to serve their own interests. In the free enterprise system not only did this alternative serve to "balance the power" in the marketplace, but it also encouraged innovations in products and services for farmers. Since the primary objective of the cooperative organization is to benefit the needs of its farmer-members, cooperatives often "set the pace" for new products and market services.

Cooperatives were particularly effective as pacesetters and power balancers during the early years of cooperative development. They are often given the credit for developing open-formula livestock feeds with labels that spell out nutrient values, and for developing guaranteed-analysis fertilizer. Cooperatives were solely responsible for channeling electric power to much of rural America. Even a hint of the impending formation of a cooperatively owned livestock market or grain elevator has been known to cause local prices to move upward markedly. Cooperative lenders who specialize in farm loans have often been the only commercial source of funds available for farm expansion projects and annual operating capital.

The Role of Cooperatives Today

It is very difficult to determine how effective cooperatives are at playing the roles of pacesetter and power balancer today. Some opponents of cooperatives argue that whereas such roles were once the exclusive province of cooperatives, at the present time noncooperative competition has escalated to the point where it too plays this role. In fact, some argue that cooperatives themselves have become large, complex organizations that are top-heavy with many layers of management and bureaucracy, and that they respond slowly to farmer needs. According to these opponents, farmer control of cooperatives is only theoretical because individual farmers are far removed from executive and boardroom decisions. Larger regional cooperatives especially, they argue, operate very similarly to national corporations. As evidence, they point to small groups of farmers in some areas who have banded together into bargaining groups to negotiate with their own cooperatives.

Although such serious charges are difficult to prove, there may be enough truth in them to force cooperatives to take them seriously. Most of the problems are brought on by rapid maturity and burgeoning size. Cooperatives must work hard to avoid any problems that might undermine their very purpose.

Actually, the entire issue of whether cooperatives are needed to serve the roles of pacesetter and power balancer may be academic. The fact is that cooperatives do exist and do play an extremely important role in supplying, marketing, financing, and servicing American farmers. In many local areas and markets the cooperative is the only major factor in the market. Cooperatives are an established fact of life in the American agribusiness community and will continue to serve an extremely important function in the marketplace.

CHARACTERISTICS OF AGRICULTURAL COOPERATIVES

Basic Purpose

Agricultural cooperatives are organized to help member-patrons increase the profits from their own businesses. Cooperatives achieve this goal by providing member-patrons with the products and services they need to lower their costs and/or to operate more efficiently. The total emphasis is on the member-user of the cooperative. The purpose of the noncooperative business enterprise, on the other hand, is to generate a profit for the owners of the business.

Often cooperative and noncooperative businesses operate similarly in the marketplace, but there are many cases where their distinctively different purposes lead to distinctively different operating decisions. For example, in 1974 there was a severe worldwide shortage of fertilizer. At that time, the federal government had imposed price controls to control inflation. United States fertilizer manufacturers had the opportunity to sell their product on the world market at a price that was about three times greater than the controlled domestic price. Many noncooperative companies quickly moved to reap high profits by selling significant quantities of fertilizer to foreign markets. Cooperatives, however, were dedicated not to making huge profits but to providing their members with all-too-scarce fertilizer. So cooperatives sold all their fertilizer production to their members at the controlled domestic prices. In fact, some cooperatives even went so far as to purchase high-priced fertilizer from the world market for distribution to members at the lower domestic prices, in order to assure their members of an adequate supply. Thus the orientation of cooperatives toward meeting members' needs triggered a very different set of operating decisions from those of the noncooperatives.[4]

Operate at Cost

Cooperatives are obligated by the laws under which they are incorporated to return to their members income in excess of the expenses generated by member business. This income is distributed to individual members in proportion to the volume of business that they have brought to the cooperative. The aforementioned obligation is the primary factor that separates cooperatives from other forms of business. Noncooperatives are not so obligated and, after paying any profits tax that may be due, will return profits to the owners of the business in proportion to the owners' investment, or will keep the profits in the business as retained earnings for future growth (see Chapter 6).

From a technical point of view cooperatives do not make a profit, since they are obligated by law to return to their members all income that in noncooperative enterprises would be viewed as profit. This is why cooperatives are sometimes called *nonprofit organizations*. Actually, even noncooperatives are free to return their profits to their customers in proportion to the amount of business that the customers have transacted, just as cooperatives do. But since the basic purpose of noncooperatives is to return profit to their investors rather than to customers, few choose this alternative.

A cooperative may choose to retain profits rather than pay them out as patronage returns, but when it does, it must pay corporate profits tax just as any corporation must.

---

[4]An interesting consequence of this action was that cooperatives, in general, gained a significant market share nationally during this period as a result of the favorable reaction that farmers accorded their operating policies. Since the shortage, cooperatives have maintained much of their increased market share.

In the case of nonmember business in a cooperative, however, any excess of income over and above the expenses generated specifically by that kind of business does not have to be returned to the customer (although it may be in some cases). Instead, many cooperatives elect to treat this additional income as regular profit, to pay taxes on it just as any business would, and to use the profits for the growth of the cooperative. An agribusiness can maintain its cooperative status as long as not more than half its business is with nonmembers.

Usually, cooperatives do not make it a practice to sell at actual cost, but choose instead to operate at "normal" market prices, and then return any savings or profits annually to member-patrons. There are several reasons for this. One reason is that it is very difficult to know for sure what the actual cost of operation is until the season is over. And it would be extremely awkward if the cooperative were to underestimate actual costs, since members would then be required to contribute extra funds at the end of the season—a very unpopular remedy. A second reason is that operating at normal market prices allows many cooperatives to finance growth by special methods, such as retaining the cash savings and making patronage refunds in the form of stock. And a third reason is that publishing low at-cost prices would have a devastating impact on an industry, especially where commodity-type products are involved.

Revolving fund financing is a highly advantageous feature that is unique to cooperatives. Based on the theory that cooperative members should be willing to finance the growth of their own organization, this technique gives cooperatives the option of issuing patronage refunds in the form of stock rather than in the form of cash. The advantage to the cooperative is that since the ownership stock represents ownership of valuable assets, it satisfies the cooperative's obligation to return the excess of income over expenses, while at the same time the cooperative retains the actual cash earnings for use in the business.

Noncooperative businesses argue that this is an unfair advantage, since any excess of income over expenses (profits) that noncooperatives make is taxed first before it is retained for use by the business or distributed as dividends. Since 1962, legislation has required cooperatives to return a minimum of 20 percent of all patronage refunds in cash rather than in the form of ownership stock.

Refunds in the form of stock are considered to be income, so cooperative members are required to pay taxes on that stock. Farmers in tax brackets that are higher than 20 percent will find that this type of stock can cause a net outflow of cash, since they must pay out more in taxes on the stock than they actually receive in cash refunds. This can create a temporary financial hardship, although in the long run the cooperative stock may increase the farmer's overall net worth. This potential cash-flow problem has caused considerable concern in many cooperative relationships, particularly those where members fall into higher tax brackets. Consequently, many cooperatives elect to refund more than the minimum 20 percent in cash. In fact, cooperatives in general average over 40 percent of their refunds in cash. Despite this adjustment, some of the more successful farmers remain highly critical of cooperatives on this issue.

Some argue that is is not fair for cooperatives to issue patronage refunds as stock and then retain the cash for internal financing. However, an equally strong argument can be made that, since the cooperative is a logical extension of the farmer's own business, each farmer has an *obligation* to contribute directly to its financing in proportion to that farmer's use of the cooperative's services.

Theoretically, the cooperative "revolves" the stock periodically, thus allowing older stock to be cashed in. Sometimes a nominal cash dividend is paid on stock in force. (However, any dividends are limited to nominal rates by law to preserve the basic cooperative principle that savings must be paid to current rather than previous patrons.)

The decision to "call" or cash in older stock, and to fix the amount of dividend that will be paid on outstanding stock, is a board of directors' decision that depends on the cooperative's financial condition and on the availability of cash. In practice, many cooperatives find themselves in financial situations that preclude easily cashing in older stock or paying dividends. Many cooperatives are able to cash in stock only when a member leaves the community or dies. Although in these situations cooperative stock is a valuable asset and good life insurance, less loyal cooperative patrons and younger farmers are often disgruntled by their inability to convert their stock into cash easily. This generates considerable frustration in many cooperatives, and is a major point of contention among those who are critical of cooperatives. Cooperatives argue that members purchased products and services at competitive prices, and so the stock should be viewed as a "bonus" for doing business with their own organization.

Member Controlled, Member Owned

A fundamental and unique principle undergirding cooperatives is that they must be owned and controlled by the people who conduct business with them. It is imperative that cooperatives maintain their orientation toward servicing those who patronize them. And there is no better way to ensure this than to require that the cooperative be controlled by active member-patrons who are also owners of the business.

Originally, and even today in most cooperatives, this requirement means one vote for each active member-patron regardless of how much business that member transacts with the cooperative or how much stock the individual member may have accumulated. Democratic control has gained almost universal acceptance as a basic cooperative principle. Some cooperative leaders are extremely strong in their support of this concept.

But recently a small percentage of cooperatives serving a widely diverse membership find that limiting control to one person, one vote creates enough dissatisfaction to threaten the very existence of the cooperative. As a result, some co-ops, particularly in the West, determine

THE ROLE AND ORGANIZATION OF AGRIBUSINESS

the degree of individual control in the cooperative on the basis of patronage or investment in the cooperative. The important thing to keep in mind in either case is that cooperative control is always in the hands of the patrons.

Noncooperatives, however, place total control in the hands of owner-investors and base the degree of control accorded to each owner-investor exclusively on the amount that the owner has invested in the business. It makes no difference whether the owners patronize the business. In fact, in noncooperatives the owner may never see the business or take any role in decision making. This is particularly true in larger corporations.

Member control of cooperatives is executed through boards of directors, which are elected in open elections from the ranks of active members. The board shoulders the responsibilities of sensing and representing the best interests of all members, setting overall policy, making important management decisions, hiring and directing top management, and monitoring the cooperative's performance in achieving its objectives. However, some highly critical decisions involving such issues as mergers or large investments may be taken directly to the membership for a vote.

In a noncooperative business, on the other hand, the directors are elected by the owners, whose number of votes are determined individually by the amount of stock they own. Consequently, most board members are stockholders with relatively large ownership interests.

Those who are critical of cooperatives say that many of them—even the local ones—have gotten so large that the farmer is far removed from having any significant voice in the business. They say that professional management really determines operating policies, and that, for the most part, the elected boards of directors simply approve management suggestions. They also argue that the board of directors is sometimes elected on the basis of popularity rather than genuine ability to make policy decisions in a multimillion dollar business. Then they point to the longevity of some members' terms on the board as further evidence that the total membership is not well represented on a cooperative's board of directors.

While these charges are serious, and one could probably find evidence of some situations in which they are justified, it would be unfair and incorrect to assume that they are the general rule. Although there is variation from cooperative to cooperative in the manner in which member ownership–member control is interpreted and carried out, it is unmistakably clear that member-patrons maintain their control and ownership of most cooperatives.

Limited Returns on Capital

Since the basic purpose of cooperatives is to operate at cost in order to benefit member-patrons directly in their own businesses, it follows that returns on capital invested are limited. Limiting returns on member equity to a nominal amount, not greater than the going interest rate, simply ensures that members holding stock in the cooperative are not tempted to view the cooperative as an investment in and of itself, but rather as a service to their own businesses.

In fact, most cooperatives pay no dividends on their stock; therefore, limiting returns is merely an academic point. But it is important to recognize the limited-returns principle, since it ensures that the purpose of the cooperative—to help farmers help themselves rather than to become an investment company—is realized.

THE ORGANIZATION OF AGRICULTURAL COOPERATIVES

The cooperative system in the United States is highly complex and interwoven. It ranges from simple, local, independent cooperatives to the vast interregional cooperatives that link literally thousands of local and regional cooperatives into one complex organization.

The local cooperative is usually organized as a corporation; thus, it has the same general structure as any corporate organization. Stockholders elect a board of directors who, in turn, select a manager to carry out their policies and operate the cooperative on a day-in, day-out basis. Management then hires appropriate personnel to perform prescribed duties.

However, it is the local cooperative organization that creates many of the special problems that cooperatives often encounter. One of these problems has already been alluded to. Since the board of directors is generally elected on a one person, one vote basis, the election may be as much a popularity contest as anything. As a result, the directorate does not always consist of the members with the most insight and management savvy. Another problem is that farmer-directors are often reluctant to invest in the quality of management necessary to run the business. Sometimes they are unwilling to pay someone who works for them a considerably higher salary than they themselves earn, even though the cooperative business may be several times larger than their own individual operations.

Another problem is that farmer-directors are often personally affected by the decisions they must make on the board. It is often difficult for them to represent the best interest of the total membership when they are considering closing down an old, high-cost facility that happens to be conveniently located near their own farm.

These problems often hinder the ability of local cooperatives to reach their full potential. Many are criticized for operating inefficiently or for not adequately representing the interests of the membership. Yet despite all obstacles a great many local cooperatives are directed by aggressive, intelligent farmer-members who have shown great insight and leadership ability. They have hired and supported competent managers who have carried out their responsibilities well. There is great variability in effectiveness and efficiency among local cooperatives.

Regional cooperatives are conglomerations of local cooperatives, joined together in either a formal or an informal manner. Their primary purpose is to provide manufacturing, processing, and wholesaling services to local cooperatives. They are necessary because local cooperatives are often not large enough to compete effectively in a world of corporate giants. The regional cooperative offers local cooperatives all the advantages of the United States' largest organizations, which in turn lends the locals more muscle in the marketplace. There are even a few national and international cooperatives.

There are two basic types of regional cooperatives: federated cooperatives and centralized cooperatives (Figure 4-1). Each has a different type of organizational structure, which greatly affects the way it operates.

Federated cooperatives are really cooperatives whose members are other cooperatives, usually local cooperatives. Farmers own their local cooperatives. Then each local cooperative, in conjunction with other locals, owns and controls the regional. The control is from the bottom

Figure 4-1 Diagrammatic representation of the two basic types of regional cooperatives— federated and centralized.

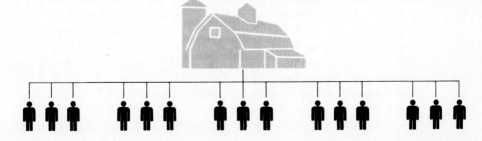

Federated

Centralized

up, with the regional responding to the voiced needs of the local cooperatives. Farmland Industries, Kansas City, Missouri; the Indiana Farm Bureau Cooperative Association, Indianapolis, Indiana; and CENEX (Farmers Union Central Exchange), St. Paul, Minnesota, are examples of federated cooperatives.

Centralized cooperatives differ in that the local cooperative outlet is controlled by the regional cooperative rather than by a local board of directors. In this case, local farmers elect regional directors, who control the regional cooperative, which in turn manages and controls the local cooperative outlet. There is no local board of directors per se. Instead, there is usually a local advisory committee that communicates regularly with local management, which reports directly to the regional cooperative management. Control is essentially from the top down. Good examples of regional cooperatives that are primarily centralized are Agway in the Northeast and the Welch Grape Juice Company on the West Coast.

Some regionals are actually mixtures of federated and centralized organizations. That is, a regional cooperative may simultaneously serve some local cooperative outlets that are federated and others that are centralized. This often comes about because some locally owned and controlled cooperatives have gotten into financial difficulty and have been taken over by the supporting regional to protect the financial interests of individual farmer members. Gold Kist in Atlanta, Georgia, and the Southern States Cooperative in Richmond, Virginia, are mixed regional cooperatives.

CHALLENGES AND OPPORTUNITIES

Coping with Success

Among the several issues that challenge agricultural cooperatives is the question of how to cope with success. Cooperative growth in many areas has brought renewed cries of concern from many corners. Pressures are increasingly being applied to cooperatives in an effort to slow their continued growth. Recently, serious questions have been raised about the legality of cooperatives' gaining large portions of market share. Pressures are mounting to remove some of the protections provided cooperatives by the Capper-Volstead Act. As the political power base in the United States shifts away from agriculture, cooperatives may experience fewer of the advantages that have significantly enhanced their growth in the past. Merger activity among cooperatives has been attracting increasingly closer attention from the Federal Trade Commission. A national association of farm suppliers has gone on record as favoring restraints on cooperatives in order to maintain a favorable balance of cooperative/noncooperative businesses. The same association has even funded a foundation to study "how cooperatives interfere with the free enterprise system."

Clearly, cooperatives are facing new and significant challenges to their methods of operation and to the favored treatment that they have come to expect and take for granted. There is a very real possibility that farm cooperatives may have to fight vigorously to protect their traditional organizational and financial operating methods.

Upgrading Leadership

Cooperatives face important challenges in upgrading professional and farmer leadership so that they can deal effectively with the complex organizational and business problems of large corporations. The past 10 years have brought some of the most significant changes ever in American agriculture. The impact of international economic and political issues has brought an entirely new dimension to farmers and their cooperatives. The agricultural prosperity of the 1970s, coupled with a very rapid growth in farm size, has caused agricultural cooperatives to grow at unprecedented rates. Many cooperatives have doubled and even tripled in size during the past decade. With this dynamic growth has come unprecedented responsibility to deal with highly complex multimillion dollar decisions.

Frankly, many cooperatives have not been ready to cope with this rapid growth. Management and directors have often just not had the experience or the training to deal with these problems. In many cases, large cooperatives are operated more like small businesses than the large agribusinesses they have become. These factors are growing pains that must be worked out.

Directors can no longer be elected as if the process were a popularity contest. The responsibilities and legal obligations of the directorate are far too great for people who do not understand the full scope of their responsibilities or are incapable of meeting the challenge. Directors of cooperatives must concentrate on upgrading their own business skills and competence.

Directors must also work to upgrade the quality of the professional management that they employ. Quality management capable of guiding a multimillion dollar business in an increasingly fast-paced, complex agribusiness environment must be developed or hired and supported. Although some cooperatives have obtained top-notch management, many have simply outgrown their management or have limited their growth by the level of management they have retained. Only when top managers' salaries are commensurate with their level of responsibility and competitive with salaries of their counterparts in noncooperatives will agricultural cooperatives attract the level of management that they so desperately need. Only then will the level of pay for rank-and-file cooperative employees be sufficient to attract top quality people. Some cooperatives continue to have a salary lag in many areas, and so attract only the "average" personnel or those who are willing to accept less pay because they just "believe in co-ops." Many progressive cooperatives have faced the issue and are competitive in their salaries, but there is still considerable variability among cooperatives.

Changing Membership

Another extremely important challenge for cooperatives lies in their rapidly changing membership. The relatively prosperous agriculture of the 1970s enticed many highly educated young people back into production agriculture. Most of these choose to become cooperative members because it is a sound business decision. Few are attracted to cooperatives for precisely the same reasons that their fathers and grandfathers were. And still fewer will loyally support their cooperative solely on the basis of past performance. There are few, if any, emotional ties between young farmers and their cooperatives; in fact, any attempt to suggest that members "should be loyal" regardless of the situation is likely to be met with defiant independence. Instead, cooperatives must be ready at all times to earn their members' continued support on the basis of their current performance records.

Stock patronage refunds that can be redeemed for cash only at retirement offer precious little incentive to a 25-year-old farmer. A young farmer who typically has to "beat off" five different fertilizer salespeople as they vie with each other to make a sale will probably remain unmoved by the argument that a cooperative will protect the farmer's market alternatives. And national cooperative meetings where long-time members discuss the "good old days" may alienate younger members even more.

Yesterday's and tomorrow's cooperative members are different people. Cooperatives face a formidable challenge in meeting the needs of all their members today. But, at the same time, cooperatives that can simultaneously offer young, aggressive farmers both an opportunity to be actively involved and some sound economic benefits will find exciting new support.

CAPITALIZATION OF COOPERATIVES

A major challenge facing many cooperatives today is how the owner-members will finance their cooperative. The revolving fund financing concept discussed earlier in this chapter has served cooperatives well by providing a mechanism through which users can finance cooperative growth by retaining earnings. But economic pressures on cooperatives have been so severe in recent years that many have been unable to "rotate" or return members' stock—that is, they have not been financially able to pay members on any regular basis for stock they have accumulated through their patronage over the years. It has been common for cooperatives to allow members to cash in their stock only upon retirement or upon death.

But today, many cooperatives face a situation in which a large number of their owners will be retiring in the next few years. This is likely to place a great deal of financial pressure on many already weakened cooperatives. The inability of a cooperative to cash a farmer out, at least on retirement or to his estate, renders its stock worthless in the eyes of many farmers.

There is also a strong opinion among many farmers that cooperative stock should be held by those who are currently using the cooperative, not those who are retired or who have left farming.

Cooperatives today are struggling with these issues.

Opportunities for the Future

Agricultural cooperatives are a unique form of business organization and an important part of the American free enterprise system. Their unique philosophy guarantees that first and foremost they will seek to provide necessary services to the farmer. They are member owned and member controlled, which creates both unique operating problems and unique opportunities.

Today, agricultural cooperatives face new and unprecedented challenges. The success of cooperatives has generated growth that they are just now learning to live with. The role that many cooperatives play as major forces in the market produces much pressure and often leads opponents to reexamine the basic advantages that have traditionally been given to cooperatives to encourage their growth. Cooperatives must respond to these increasing pressures in measured and responsible ways. Today, more than ever before, cooperatives must continue to serve their member-patrons profitably. Patron-members expect the same service and quality from the cooperative, but at competitive prices. As the cost-price squeeze continues to put pressure on producers to reduce costs, cooperatives that are unable to meet noncooperative prices for input supplies or to pay existing market prices for commodities they purchase from farmers may lose a significant share of the market.

Their changing membership is also presenting cooperatives with important challenges. But in these challenges lies the opportunity for the future. By recognizing and adapting to the changing needs of farmers, cooperatives can maintain their important status in American agriculture and fulfill their basic role of providing necessary services to farmer-members.

SUMMARY

Cooperatives are business organizations owned and controlled by those who use them. Their basic purpose is to serve the needs of their members rather than to make a profit on their own. Their growth in agriculture has been encouraged by favorable government policies that are designed to help individual farmers help themselves. Today, about one-fourth of all farm inputs are supplied by cooperatives. Also, nearly one-third of all agricultural production is marketed through cooperatives. Many cooperatives even process their members' products and distribute them directly to supermarkets.

Cooperatives operate at cost, since they are obligated to return any income in excess of expenses to members in proportion to the individual member's purchases or marketing. These savings are partially refunded to members in cash and partly as additional stock. Cash refunded as stock is actually reinvested in the business. This plan, known as revolving fund financing, has been extremely important to the growth of cooperatives.

Today, cooperatives are the largest factor in many agricultural markets. Yet they face serious challenges. Noncooperative competitors who believe cooperatives are unfairly favored by certain laws and government policies are seeking to reduce this advantage. Large cooperatives are struggling with problems of bigness, and larger farmers are adding new demands on their cooperatives. Yet cooperatives are and will continue to be strong.

DISCUSSION QUESTIONS

1. List the Rochdale principles. How appropriate do you feel these principles are for today's cooperatives, and why?

2. Increasingly, cooperatives are being pressured to move away from the one person, one vote concept. Why do you suppose this is so? What impact do you think it might have on cooperatives?

3. List the advantages and disadvantages of cooperative agribusinesses as opposed to noncooperative agribusinesses.

4. Which type of regional cooperative has the greatest control over local cooperative outlets? Is this always an advantage? Why or why not?

5. List several problems facing cooperatives today. Which of these do you believe are the most significant, and why?

BLUEBERRY GROWERS' DILEMMA

Several blueberry growers in the state have been continually frustrated by their inability to market their blueberries effectively. The growers are scattered over a 300-mile area. Most are small growers with only small patches, but a few of the growers have larger acreages. Some of the smaller patches use "you-pick"-type market operations, while the larger growers hire migrant labor and harvest for food processors in the area. All are faced with complicated insect problems and have relied on local chemical-fertilizer plants to advise them, with varying degrees of success.

Lately some of the growers have been considering developing a cooperative to serve their needs. They have asked you to help them think through some of the problems and opportunities that might result from establishing the cooperative.

QUESTIONS

1. Explain to the growers what basic cooperative principles they would have to adhere to.

2. What are some of the specific advantages that might be gained from organizing such a cooperative?

3. What problems might you expect the new cooperative to encounter?

4. What additional information would you need before advising the growers whether or not to form a cooperative?

FINANCIAL MANAGEMENT
AND CONTROL
OF THE AGRIBUSINESS

OBJECTIVES

•   Decide which principles our economy uses to allocate its resources

•   Explain how our modified free market system encourages consumers to allocate scarce resources by "voting with their dollars"

•   Describe how profit and the accumulation of wealth provide the primary incentive for efficiency

•   Relate opportunity cost to economic profit

•   Identify the three important "marginal" principles of economics

•   Summarize the effect of supply and demand on producers and consumers as they respond to price levels

•   Define market equilibrium

•   Explain the concept of elasticity and its relationship to supply and demand

Our economic system allocates scarce resources to meet consumer needs.
A. Cattle on feed
B. Market in action
C. Supply-demand curve
D. Processing meat
E. Meeting consumer needs

YOU CAN MAKE EVEN A PARROT
INTO A LEARNED ECONOMIST—ALL
HE MUST LEARN ARE THE TWO
WORDS "SUPPLY" AND
"DEMAND."   —Paul A. Samuelson

5

ECONOMICS FOR MANAGERS

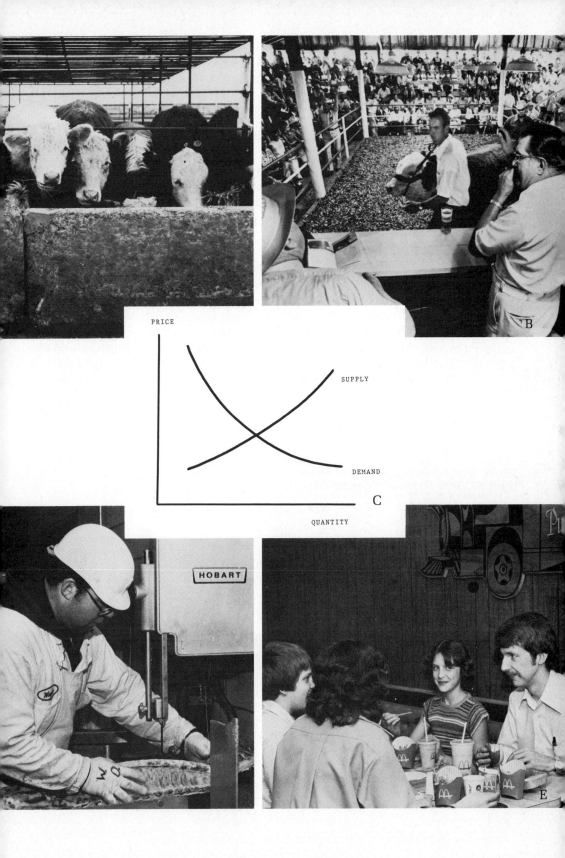

PRICE

SUPPLY

DEMAND

C

QUANTITY

HOBART

B

E

THE AMERICAN ECONOMIC SYSTEM

We inhabit a world that is saddled with the twin problem of limited resources and unlimited wants. Deciding how to allocate relatively scarce resources is the basic task of economics. *Economics* is the study of how resources (land, labor, and capital) are combined to meet the needs of people, and how these needs dictate the distribution of production capabilities.

Every society must develop a system for making production and distribution decisions. In some countries the decisions are made centrally by the government. Our society, on the other hand, has chosen the free enterprise or free market system to make these decisions.

Free Market System

In a free market system, consumer wants are expressed directly in the marketplace and become the basis for the allocation of scarce resources (see Figure 5-1). Consumers make their wants known by "voting" with their dollars, effectively "bidding" the price up on whatever scarce items they may want. Businesses constantly monitor changing consumer wants as they offer various alternatives, respond to changing prices, and make adjustments in the production process. Producers are keenly aware of the changing availability of limited and costly resources. They continually search for ways to combine resources more and more efficiently in order to attract the consumer's dollar with more desirable goods and

**Figure 5-1 The United States economic system.
In the American free-enterprise capitalistic
economy, business organizations working within
the market system combine and allocate limited
resources to satisfy unlimited wants of the
consumer.**

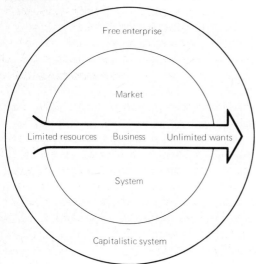

FINANCIAL MANAGEMENT AND CONTROL OF THE AGRIBUSINESS

services. The single most important aspect of the free market system is its orientation toward the consumer's desires. In the free market system, "the consumer rules."

When consumers want more shrimp than is available on the market, restaurant owners and food brokers bid up the price. As menu prices reflect the shortage, fewer and fewer consumers can afford the shrimp. But, at the same time, the higher market price encourages Gulf Coast and Pacific Northwest fishers and canners to spend more hours harvesting and processing the precious delicacy. And if the situation persists over a long enough period of time, fishers may even be encouraged to invest in more shrimp trawlers. Shrimp prices then begin to fall as shrimp availability is brought into line with declining consumer wants; as prices begin to fall, quantity demanded by consumers may gradually increase again.

Such adjustments are often referred to as the *invisible hand* by which the free market system guides economic decisions. This well-known phrase was coined by economist Adam Smith in his famous book, *Wealth of Nations*, in 1776. Smith believed that the interests of consumers would be best served if individual businesses were free to act according to their own selfish interests without artificial or government restrictions, as long as there are sufficient numbers of buyers and sellers, and as long as the activity of each is limited enough to prevent one individual from unduly influencing the market price. According to his theory, the greater the extent of a perfectly competitive situation among businesses, the more effectively the invisible hand will guide economic decisions for the good of all. This system of little government intervention in the market system is often referred to as a *laissez-faire* or *hands-off policy*.

Many people believe that production agriculture is one of the best examples of perfect competition. The large numbers of agricultural producers, the uniform nature of most agricultural commodities, and the large numbers of buyers of agricultural products all converge to produce a successful free market situation. The market quickly transmits news of changing consumer wants to agricultural producers, who then respond accordingly.

Capitalistic System

The United States free market is a capitalistic system. *Capitalism* is a system in which property is owned and controlled by private citizens. Any profits that can be generated by the use of that private property belong to the owner. The profit motive, along with the corresponding possibility of accumulating wealth, is thought by many to be the greatest single factor in the unparalleled economic success of our country.

Business is the organization that private property owners create in order to coordinate and manage their property to generate a profit. In a larger sense, business is the vehicle of the free enterprise system. Private property owners may delegate the control of their property to professional managers, but those owners maintain ultimate control over their own property. The concept of private property, coupled with the free market system, is at the very heart of the United States economy.

Imperfections in the System

Of course, no system is perfect. A completely free market capitalistic system is geared to react only to economic pressures, and so can cause individuals a great deal of pain while it is in the process of making its adjustments. The unrestricted free enterprise system does not heed the anguished cries of coal miners who lose their jobs when the coal has run out; nor does it have an easy answer for the 55-year-old grain elevator owner who loses a lifetime investment when the railroad near the elevator is abandoned; nor does the system immediately respond to public environmental problems.

Opponents of the free enterprise system also point to "unnecessary duplication" of facilities in competitive situations. Why should there be seven separate fertilizer plants serving the same farm community, with all needlessly "squandering" money on advertising to promote their own businesses? Free enterprise supporters concede that a single larger operation might occasionally realize economic efficiencies as a result of its size, but they argue that the resulting lack of competition would foster inefficient activities and sloppy management. They say that strong competition assures the consumer of a consistently better and more creative choice of services, since competitors will have to struggle mightily to attract the consumer's dollar.

Mixed Free Enterprise System

American society has chosen to place some restrictions on the free enterprise system in order to lessen the hardships imposed on individuals as adjustments are made in the allocation process. As a result, the particular type of economic system in the United States is often referred to as a *mixed free enterprise system*. Because Americans are not satisfied with the consequences of the free market system, they have artificially supported the prices of some farm crops, such as peanuts and sugar beets, through government programs. Increasingly, the government imposes restrictions on the use of pesticides in order to protect the health and well-being of citizens. And government occupational health and safety regulations have made sweeping changes in many agribusinesses. In each case the intervention occurs because the free market mechanism reacts too slowly or painfully to be acceptable to our society at large.

Although some argue that imposed restrictions have seriously undermined the delicate workings of the free market system, that system continues to transmit its feedback on consumer preferences to businesses rather quickly and decisively. The free enterprise system does exhibit some inefficiency and may cause some temporary hardships, but it has proved the most effective and efficient economic system ever devised. It produces more food and fiber far more efficiently than any other system in the world.

Profits in a Mixed Economy

In a perfectly competitive free market system, profits should not exist. The theory goes that many firms will be attracted into any market that is potentially profitable; once this happens, production will increase, prices will drop as a result, and profits will eventually fall back to zero. Even in cases in which there are fewer firms involved, if the firms produce too much product they will lose money because of the cost of storing the surplus combined with the low market price. Once this happens, some firms will exit from the market, thereby reducing the supply and driving the price upward until losses are reversed and profits are again at zero or higher.

But in the real world profits do exist. And the possibility of earning profit is the motivating force behind most business decisions. While it is true that some businesses also have nonprofit objectives, the profit goal remains the primary objective of essentially all businesses.

Why Profits Exist   There are several explanations for profit. First, profit is the reward for taking a risk in a business. When a private property owner commits personal resources to a business project, there are no guarantees of a return on investment. There is always some possibility that the project will fail and that all or part of the investment will be lost. The greater the risk involved, the greater the potential profit for successful ventures. In fact, the anticipation of higher profits is the motivating force behind extremely risky ventures.

Second, profits result from the control of scarce resources. In our system nearly all property is owned and controlled by private citizens. When a citizen owns a resource that others want, the others will bid the price up, which generates a profit for its owner. The greater the demand for a resource, the higher its price will be, and the greater the profit reward to its owner or owners.

Third, profits exist because some people have access to information that is not widespread. Resource owners who have special knowledge, such as secret processes, formulas, and recipes, can use this information exclusively and can thereby maintain significant advantages over their competition. The whole concept of patents and copyrights evolved as part of a formal attempt to encourage creativity by ensuring that the creator profits from his or her ideas.

Fourth, profits exist simply because some businesses are managed more effectively than others. The managers of such businesses are often creative planners and thinkers whose day-to-day organization is extremely efficient. The reward for doing the job is usually profit.

The profit motive is the spark plug of the free market capitalistic system. The prospect of earning and keeping a profit serves as the incentive for creativity and efficiency among people. It stimulates risky ventures and drives people to develop ways of cutting costs and improving techniques, always in an effort to satisfy consumers' interests.

Macroeconomics: The Big Picture

Agribusinesses are greatly affected by macroeconomics because worldwide consumer demand for various food and fiber products is constantly changing. Economic conditions are influenced dramatically by such factors as weather conditions, government policies, and international developments. Macroeconomics is concerned with how the different elements of the total economy interact. Skill at anticipating and interpreting the macroeconomic environment is critical to the success of any agribusiness manager.

A grain embargo that forbids American wheat sales to Communist bloc countries has far-reaching effects for agribusinesses. Fertilizer and chemical manufacturers, distributors, and dealers are careful students of such trends because the trends will greatly influence the demand for their products. Crop failures in many parts of the world in the early 1970s set the stage for corn and wheat prices to rise sharply. Fertilizer demand soared as farmers scrambled for enough fertilizer to increase production. The result was a temporary, but severe, fertilizer shortage that caused prices of some types of nitrogen fertilizer to triple in a few months. Fertilizer manufacturers responded by announcing plans for new production facilities. Just a few years later this new production capacity, coupled with more normal weather and yield, created a surplus of nitrogen. Fertilizer prices quickly reverted to their earlier levels or even lower, thus relegating some companies to a loss position.

Agribusiness is an integral part of the macroeconomic system. This is because the role it plays—allocating scarce natural and financial resources to meet the critical food and fiber needs of the world's population—is a key one. Agribusiness is in direct competition with other sectors of the economy for limited resources and so is greatly affected by wider economic pressures and trends.

Our total economic structure is intricately interrelated. When steelworkers strike for several weeks and ultimately negotiate significant wage increases, agribusiness, which is a major user of steel products in all types of agricultural equipment, is likely to feel an immediate shortage during the strike and the pinch of higher prices later. When government policy directly affects interest rates, agribusinesses, which depend heavily on borrowed money to finance production, inventory, and accounts receivable, are greatly affected. Understanding and interpreting macroeconomic pressures are indeed crucial responsibilities for agribusiness managers.

Microeconomics: Economics Within the Firm

Microeconomics is the application of basic economic principles to decisions within the firm. Every agribusiness faces tough questions when it comes to allocating its limited resources. Managers must decide the best way to use physical, human, and financial resources in the production and marketing of goods and services to meet customers' needs and generate a profit. Tools of economic analysis are essential to the manager who must make daily business decisions. In fact, most of the management tools developed in this book are based on fundamental economic concepts.

BASIC ECONOMIC CONCEPTS

Profit and Opportunity Cost

Both accountants and economists talk about profits, but each tends to view profits somewhat differently. The accountant looks at profits as income left over after all actual measurable costs are subtracted (see Chapter 6). Economists, however, determine profit by examining alternative uses for resources within the firm.

Opportunity cost is the income given up by *not* choosing the next best alternative for the use of resources. It represents the amount that the business forfeits by not choosing an alternative course of action. Since an opportunity cost is never actually incurred, the accountant cannot measure it precisely. But economists argue that from the standpoint of making economic decisions, an accurate determination of the cost involved in choosing one alternative must include the amount that is lost by not selecting the next best alternative.

Economic Profit

Economic profit is defined as accounting profit less opportunity cost. Economic profit, then, forces an examination of alternative uses of resources. Focusing on the opportunity costs helps in analyzing various economic alternatives.

Sam Petrocelli owns and operates his own bulk fertilizer plant. He is 40 years old, has a college degree, and has been quite satisfied with his business. He currently has $600,000 of his own money invested in the business. Sam draws an annual salary of $30,000. Last year his books showed that the business made a profit of $80,000. How well he is doing can be evaluated in the following way.

Start with the accounting profit of $80,000 and add his $30,000 salary; the result shows that Sam realized $110,000 from his business last year. Then consider the appropriate opportunity cost. This requires determining what alternative uses there might be for Sam's resources. First, Sam's resources include his own time and talent. He figures that he could sell his business and go to work for someone else for a salary of approximately $30,000 annually, given his experience and contacts. This is an opportunity cost that takes into account Sam's time and management abilities. Then Sam must consider his own investment of $600,000. What are some of its alternative uses? Assume, for example, that he could: (1) put it into a savings account at 8 percent; (2) buy government bonds at 9 percent; or (3) invest in corporate bonds at 10 percent. The opportunity cost would be 10 percent of $600,000, or $60,000 each year, because that is the most profitable alternative use for Sam's money. Thus, Sam's economic profit would be

Accounting profit	$ 80,000
Salary withdrawal	30,000
Total accounting profit realized by Sam	110,000
Less opportunity cost:	
1. Other job	30,000
2. Best investment alternative, $600,000 × 10%	60,000
Total opportunity cost	90,000
Economic profit realized by Sam	$ 20,000

This $20,000 economic profit represents the real financial reward that Sam received for risking his own resources in the business. It is sometimes called pure economic profit. As long as the amount is on the plus side, it suggests that the decision to commit the resources to the business is a good one. But what happens when Sam has a bad year and shows an accounting profit of only $25,000? Assuming that opportunity cost is the same, economic profit slips to the minus side ($25,000 + $30,000 − $30,000 − $60,000 = −$35,000), which indicates that, had it been pursued, the lost opportunity to invest the capital in corporate bonds would have yielded higher returns than the business.

Even though the accounting profit would still be positive, the negative economic profit clearly indicates problems. Should this trend continue, it would make sense for Sam to sell out, unless, of course, Sam considers the freedom and psychological rewards from running his own business important enough to offset the negative economic profit.

Use of Economic Profit   Before investing sums of money in specific alternatives, managers must be able to estimate opportunity costs. This estimate helps managers to decide whether any given use for their resources of time and money is the very best opportunity available.

However, some shortcomings of the economic profit concept should be recognized.

1.   There are many "imputed" values that in reality are hard to estimate. In the case of Sam Petrocelli, what interest figure will yield the "correct" opportunity cost for the situation? For some people the 10 percent rate will apply, but many investors have the know-how and time to research other possibilities and invest at rates of 12 percent or higher. The same argument applies to the salary figure specified: this may or may not be realistic, depending on the situation.

2.   A possibly faulty assumption is made that employment in industry would be currently available for Sam. Furthermore, a change in employment might cause personal or family problems. Weighing "adjustments" of this kind in dollar terms can be extremely difficult, if not impossible.

FINANCIAL MANAGEMENT AND CONTROL OF THE AGRIBUSINESS

3. Finally, different types of investments may be difficult to directly compare with one another in a way that will satisfy the opportunity cost concept. For example, investment in "blue-chip" or high-quality stocks cannot be directly compared with speculative ventures like oil drilling, since the two kinds of investments involve two different classes of risks.

Economic Principles to Maximize Profits

There are three basic microeconomic principles that relate to profit maximization for the individual firm. These principles and the questions they answer are:

1. Marginal cost = marginal revenue. This concept answers the question, "How much to produce?" You should continue adding inputs to the point at which the extra cost of producing the last unit of output is just equal to the extra revenue received from that unit.

2. Marginal rate of substitution = inverse price ratio. This production principle deals with the question, "What is the least-cost combination of inputs?" You should substitute input X for input Y to the point at which the marginal rate of substitution of X for Y is just equal to the inverse price ratio, i.e., the price of Y divided by the price of X.

3. Equal marginal returns. The final production principle relates to utilizing one variable input of limited quantity over several possible production enterprises. This answers the question, "What to produce, or how should a limited input be allocated?" You should spread the variable input among the enterprises until you receive equal marginal returns from the last unit of input invested in each production enterprise or until you employ inputs in the enterprises with the highest marginal returns.

Marginal Cost/Marginal Revenue

Marginality is an economic concept designed to help managers maximize profits. It focuses attention on the changing input-output relationships in a business. Economists have noted that the cost of producing additional units once production has been increased will differ from the costs of units before the production increases. The additional cost incurred from producing one more unit is called *marginal cost*. Usually, the marginal cost decreases as more product is produced and sold—up to a point. Then, as the limits of production capacity are tested, it becomes more and more difficult to keep increasing production. Marginal costs gradually begin to increase as the strain on production capabilities becomes greater.

    Marginal revenue, on the other hand, represents the additional income generated by selling one more unit of product. For small producers in a large market, marginal revenue is constant at the market price because it is always possible to sell the additional product for the same price. But for larger producers in a smaller market, producing more may affect the market price adversely. In that case, marginal revenue may fall as more is produced and sold, because the supply exceeds the demand for the product.

A basic principle of economics is that profits will be maximized by increasing production until marginal cost (cost of producing one more unit) just about equals marginal revenue (income generated by selling one more unit).

$$MC = MR$$

The idea is that inputs should be added to the production process only until the point at which their costs are just offset by the additional revenue generated by the resulting outputs.

To illustrate: a few years ago, Roberta Sutton, Manager of Riverside Orchards, Inc., was confronted with a problem. Although her apple trees were very healthy and most were in their prime years of production, apple output had been steadily declining. The manager knew that weather had not been a problem. After consultation with extension horticulturists, Roberta decided that the trees were probably not being pollinated as well as they might be, so she settled on the plan of adding beehives to the orchard. These two enterprises seemed to complement each other. The bees would help to pollinate the trees and therefore to increase apple production, and with a little luck they might also produce some honey to sell with the apples.

The main problem confronting Roberta at this point was to decide the optimum number of beehives. She decided to experiment on a 1-acre plot of apple trees that was separated from the rest of the orchard. Through experiments she found that an increase in bees tended to correlate well with an increase in apple production. But gradually, as more hives were added, increases in apple production tapered off. Finally, the addition of more hives did not increase apple production at all. Using bees as the only *variable* "input" and apples as the only output, Roberta plotted the relationship noted in Table 5-1.

As more hives were added, output of apples increased, up to the

TABLE 5-1 Relationship between Input (Bees) and Production of Apples at Riverside Orchards

BEES (INPUT)	APPLES (OUTPUT)
Hives	Bushels
0	200
1	220
2	228
3	234
4	237
5	236

level of four hives. Even before knowing anything about costs and revenues it is apparent that the manager would not want to add the fifth hive, since output actually declined at that point. Apparently, adding the fifth hive put so many bees in the orchard that they produced some sort of adverse reaction (perhaps they scared off the pickers!). Even if bees came absolutely free of charge, Roberta would be better off holding input to a maximum of four units. Now that the maximum number of hives that could possibly prove useful is known, the important question becomes exactly how many hives should be added to the 1-acre tract of trees if we are looking for a good investment (whereby marginal cost will about equal marginal revenue). To discover the solution, study the costs and income flow presented in Table 5-2.

Total Variable Cost (3)   *Total variable cost* equals the units of variable input multiplied by the cost of the input. In this example, a hive of bees costs $30. Column 3, then, is simply the number of beehives in column 1 multiplied by the $30 cost per hive. (In this example, it is assumed that all other inputs necessary for the production of apples are held constant. Thus the effects on profitability of adding more and more of the single variable input can be examined.)

Total Fixed Cost (4)   *Total fixed cost* is constant. Fixed costs do not vary with the level of production. These costs must be paid at this point regardless of how many beehives are used. Here fixed costs include all the other expenses of producing apples. These costs were estimated by the manager to amount to $1000 for the 1-acre tract.

Total Cost (5)   Column 5 is *total cost*. This is the sum of columns 3 and 4.

Marginal Cost (6)   *Marginal cost* is defined as the extra cost incurred in producing one more unit of output. As the name implies, marginal cost involves a change in cost between two successive output levels. Marginal cost represents the change in total cost divided by the change in output. For example ($1030 − $1000) ÷ (220 bushels − 200 bushels) = $1.50/bushel.

Total Revenue (7)   *Total revenue* is equal to the number of units sold multiplied by their selling price. In this case, apples are worth $6 per bushel; the total revenue column is equal to column 2 multiplied by $6.

Marginal Revenue (8)   *Marginal revenue* is the amount of additional income generated by selling one more bushel of apples. Marginal revenue equals the change in total revenue divided by the change in output. Again, note the importance of *change* in the analysis. In this example, marginal revenue is constant at $6 because changes in production do not affect price in this particular market.

   An important production principle can now be applied by utiliz-

TABLE 5-2 Costs and Revenues for Bee-Apple Relationship

BEEHIVES (INPUT) (1)	BUSHELS OF APPLES (OUTPUT) (2)	TOTAL VARIABLE COST (3)	TOTAL FIXED COST (4)	TOTAL COST (5)	MARGINAL COST (6)	TOTAL REVENUE (7)	MARGINAL REVENUE (8)
0	200	$ 0	$1,000	$1,000	—	$1,200	—
1	220	30	1,000	1,030	$ 1.50	1,320	$6.00
2	228	60	1,000	1,060	3.75	1,368	6.00
3	234	90	1,000	1,090	5.00	1,404	6.00
4	237	120	1,000	1,120	10.00	1,422	6.00
5	236	150	1,000	1,150	X	1,416	6.00

ing data from Table 5-2. *Produce to the point at which marginal cost most nearly equals marginal revenue without exceeding it.* One should continue adding input to increase the level of output only until the point at which the extra cost of producing the last unit of output is just equal to the extra revenue that the last unit of output produces.

What level of production should the manager employ in this example? Using the principle of MC = MR, an input level of three hives should produce the maximum level of profit. At this point the extra cost of producing one more bushel of apples is $5, while the selling value of that extra bushel is $6. This situation would be economical. Thus profit is maximized in this case at three hives and 234 bushels of production.

Marginal Rate of Substitution/Inverse Price Ratio

Often in any business enterprise several different combinations of inputs may produce the same level of output. Thus, a producer who is intent on maximizing profit would be interested in the least-cost combination of inputs that will produce that same level of output. The concept introduced earlier in this section suggested that a producer should substitute inputs to the point at which

MRS = IPR

Again, an example is included to illustrate this concept. Joe Brown feeds cattle and is interested in substituting more hay for corn in the feed ration that he currently uses. Based on past feeding trials, he believes that the following combinations of hay and corn will all produce an 1100-pound steer.

From Table 5-3, the marginal rate of substitution of hay for corn can be calculated as

$$MRS_{\substack{hay\ for \\ corn}} = \frac{change\ in\ amount\ of\ corn}{change\ in\ amount\ of\ hay}$$

while the inverse price ratio is

$$IPR = \frac{price\ of\ hay}{price\ of\ corn}$$

Combinations of Inputs to Produce 1100-Pound Steer

TABLE 5-3

HAY (POUNDS)	CORN (POUNDS)	MRS	TOTAL RATION COST
500	1300		$80.00
600	1200	1.00	78.00
700	1125	.75	77.25
800	1075	.50	77.75
900	1050	.25	79.50

Assume that the price of corn is 5 cents/pound and hay is 3 cents/pound.

Utilizing the production principle of MRS = IPR, the ration of 700 pounds of hay and 1125 pounds of corn should be selected. To select the least-cost ration, you should continue substituting hay for corn until the marginal rate of substitution is just above or equal to the inverse price ratio. As a check on the solution, the total ration cost at each input level of corn and hay has been included in Table 5-3. The minimum-cost ration is $77.25, the one selected by our production principle.

Equal Marginal Returns

Another important production decision criterion relates to what should be produced. Often the firm can produce many different products, but inputs are limited or a budget for production expenses must be followed. This final production principle says that you should produce among different enterprises to the point at which there are equal marginal returns from these enterprises, or variable inputs should be used in their highest marginal use to the point at which there are equal returns.

Suppose that Jane Henry is a student preparing for final exams. Her finals include exams in History, English, Marketing, and Agribusiness Management. Jane has only 30 hours of study time to devote to these four subjects and would like to maximize her grade point average. What should she do, given the estimates of hours studied and final exam grade in Table 5-4?

TABLE 5-4 Study Time and Estimated Final Grade

HOURS OF STUDY	HISTORY		ENGLISH		MARKETING		AGRIBUSINESS	
	SCORE	MR	SCORE	MR	SCORE	MR	SCORE	MR
0	60	—	75	—	80	—	65	—
5	70	10	82	7	85	5	75	10
10	76	6	88	6	89	4	84	7
15	81	5	92	4	92	3	87	5
20	84	3	94	2	93	1	90	3
25	85	1	95	1	93	0	92	2
30	85	0	95	0	93	0	93	1

Jane allocates her study time in blocks of 5 hours and has estimated the increased exam scores she will receive in each subject if she spends an additional 5 hours of time studying that subject. Thus, if Jane were to spend all her study time on History, her exam score in History would be maximized, but her other subject grades would suffer.

If Jane utilizes the equal marginal returns principle, she will spend 10 hours of study time each on History, English, and Agribusiness and not study for the Marketing final. No other combination of study time can give Jane a higher overall average on her exams.

Supply: The Producer Side of the Market

Supply, from an economic viewpoint, respresents the relationship between two variables: price and quantity supplied. *Supply* may be defined as the quantities that producers are willing and able to put on the
market at different prices. Supply reflects the direct relationship between price and quantity. The law of supply suggests that as price increases, producers are willing to put more on the market. Even though
their marginal cost may increase, the higher price increases marginal
revenue and thus makes increased production profitable. The supply
curve or function shown in Figure 5-2 depicts a price-quantity relationship. If the price were $20, producers would be willing to supply 290
units. If the price were $40, producers would supply 600 units. Of
course, a single market price is all that is possible at a given point. The
supply curve simply shows what producers would be *willing* to produce
at various prices.

The supply curve can shift or change position over a period of
time. When supply increases, the *entire* curve shifts to the right. In this
case, the same quantity is offered at a lower price or a greater quantity
is offered at the same price. Figure 5-3 illustrates an increase in supply.
The opposite movement in the curve, that is, a move to the left, would
denote a decrease in supply.

Several different factors can cause a firm's supply curve to shift.
Since the amount of product that a company is willing to supply depends heavily on its marginal cost and marginal revenue relationships,
anything that changes the basic cost structure of a firm can shift its supply curve. Some factors include the following.

1. *Change in technology:* Improved efficiency shifts the supply curve
    to the right.

2. *Change in the price of inputs:* A price increase shifts the supply
    curve to the left.

3. *Weather:* Poor weather conditions can shift the supply curve to
    the left.

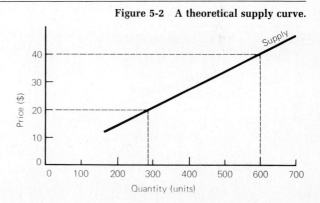

Figure 5-2   A theoretical supply curve.

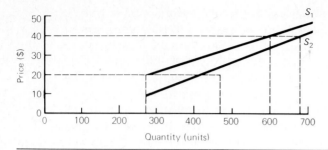

Figure 5-3   Shift in supply.

The supply curve is based on the cost curves for the individual producer. Thus, most factors that shift supply curves relate to direct changes in costs that cause the curve to shift to the right or left. For example, a cattle producer will decrease the supply of cattle when the price of corn goes up. Why? Corn is an input in cattle production; as the price of corn goes up, the extra cost of producing cattle goes up. Thus, the supply curve is actually the marginal cost curve.

In addition, there are short-run and long-run supply curves for the producer. In the short run the producer will continue producing as long as variable costs can be covered. In the long run the producer must cover all costs of production—both fixed and variable. Hence,

- Short-run supply = MC above AVC
- Long-run supply = MC above ATC

Demand: Consumer Side of the Market

The consumer side of the market is represented by the demand curve. *Demand*, in economic terms, is the amount that consumers are willing and able to buy in the market at various prices. As with the concept of supply, we are concerned with a price-quantity relationship. The law of demand states that there is an inverse relationship between price and quantity; that is, as price increases, consumers are less willing to buy. The demand curve that is depicted in Figure 5-4 illustrates a typical

Figure 5-4   A theoretical demand curve.

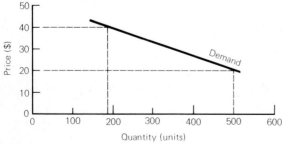

FINANCIAL MANAGEMENT AND CONTROL OF THE AGRIBUSINESS

series of price-quantity relationships. If the price were $20, consumers would be willing to buy 500 units. But if the price were $40, consumers would be willing to purchase only 180 units. Of course, only a single price can exist in the market at any time. The demand curve simply shows the amounts that consumers would be willing to buy at each of the various possible prices.

A demand curve can also shift or change position over a period of time. Demand increases when consumers want to buy more at the same price; at such times, the demand curve shifts to the right. Figure 5-5 illustrates an increase in demand.

Several important factors can cause a demand curve to shift. Since shifts in demands are totally dependent on the consumer, the reasons for shifts are heavily influenced by psychological and emotional factors, and can be quite complex. Some of these factors include the following.

1. *Income:* As their incomes increase, consumers can afford to buy more, and this shifts the demand curve to the right.

2. *Tastes and preferences:* Emotional and psychological wants can shift demand in either direction.

3. *Expectations:* When consumers expect the price to fall, they may postpone purchases, thereby causing the demand curve to shift to the left.

4. *Population:* Sheer increases in number of consumers can shift the demand to the right.

5. *Price of substitutes:* A decrease in the price of a close substitute product may shift the demand curve to the left.

The concept of demand is based on the law of diminishing marginal utility, which states that as more and more of a product is consumed, the extra satisfaction of consuming an additional unit actually declines. This translates directly into the negative slope of the demand curve and the inverse relationship between price and the quantity consumed. At higher and higher prices, consumers tend to consume less and less of a given product. At higher prices some goods have substitutes

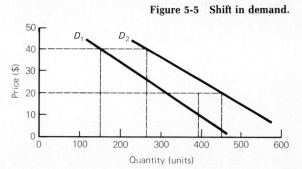

Figure 5-5   Shift in demand.

which the consumer would switch to, while at other, even higher, price levels, the consumer may give up consumption of that product altogether.

Derived Demand   The demand for most agricultural products, particularly farm supplies, is a *derived demand*. Derived demand is not based directly on general consumer demand, but rather on the need for a product that indirectly relates to consumer demand. For example, the farmer's demand for fertilizer is derived from the consumer's demand for corn. When export demand for corn increases substantially, the price of corn increases. This also increases the demand for fertilizer, since when the price is higher farmers desire to produce more corn. This is one reason why agribusiness managers and marketing experts are so concerned about general economic trends. Anything that significantly affects consumer demand for agricultural products is bound to have an impact on the demand for farm supplies, through the process of derived demand.

Market Equilibrium and Price Discovery

As producers and consumers meet in the marketplace, the equilibrium of quantity and price is determined. This process is called *price discovery*. There is actually one price and quantity that will "clear the market" at a given point. At this point everything that producers are willing to sell will equal everything that consumers want to buy. Figure 5-6 illustrates the market-clearing conditions of equilibrium. Here there is a single price, Pe, and quantity, Qe. (In the real world, demand and supply are not static, but are in a constant state of fluctuation.) At any point, "price" represents the market's best guess of the *current* supply-demand situation. Because conditions are based on buyers' and sellers' judgments of the actual supply and demand, the situation is extremely volatile and can change both rapidly and frequently. This is why market prices for a great many agricultural products and supplies change throughout the day.

  The supply and demand curves represent a theoretical relationship between price and quantity at given points. The curves here have

Figure 5-6   Supply and demand for tractors, 1984.

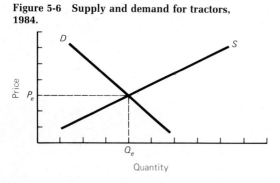

FINANCIAL MANAGEMENT AND CONTROL OF THE AGRIBUSINESS

been illustrated by straight-line functions. This was done to facilitate explanation of the curves; but most curves are actually curvilinear over some range of price and quantity, and may be quite complex. Agricultural economists spend considerable time and effort attempting to identify specific curves.

Use of the Supply-Demand Model

Suppose that for four-wheel-drive tractors in 1984, agricultural economists determined the price-quantity relationships for supply and demand to be those shown in Figure 5-6.

This means that for 1984 Qe tractors were sold at a price of Pe. Now suppose that 1984–1985 was a bad year for farmers, and farm income was reduced by 15 percent. What would the new supply-demand relationship look like? Figure 5-7 illustrates both the 1984 and 1985 relationships.

Elasticity

Managers are often concerned with predicting the degree of customer reaction to a change in price. *Elasticity* is a good way to measure consumer response. Elasticity of demand reflects the percentage change in the quantity demanded when the price changes by 1 percent. If the demand for bluegrass seed increases by 1 percent when its price decreases by 1 percent, the demand elasticity for bluegrass seed is 1.0. The formula for elasticity is:

$$\text{Elasticity} = \frac{\% \text{ change in quantity}}{\% \text{ change in price}}$$

or

$$= \frac{\text{new quantity} - \text{old quantity}}{\text{new quantity} + \text{old quantity}} \times \frac{\text{new price} + \text{old price}}{\text{new price} - \text{old price}}$$

Figure 5-7 Changes in market equilibrium.

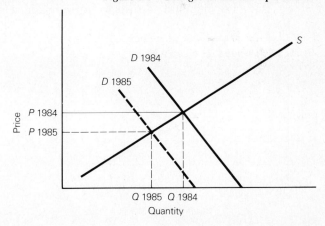

Q 1985 Q 1984

Quantity

As Figure 5-8 shows, if the price of bluegrass seed were to fall from $40 to $30, the quantity demanded would increase from 100 to 200 bushels.

$$\text{Elasticity} = \frac{200 - 100}{200 + 100} \times \frac{30 + 40}{30 - 40} = \frac{100}{300} \times \frac{70}{-10} = -2.33$$

This means that when the price drops by 1 percent, the quantity demanded increases by 2.33 percent. But if the price were to fall from $20 to $10, quantity would increase from 300 to 400 bushels. On a percentage basis, demand is less responsive at this level.

$$\text{Elasticity} = \frac{400 - 300}{400 + 300} \times \frac{10 + 20}{10 - 20} = \frac{100}{700} \times \frac{30}{-10} = -0.43$$

These demand elasticities utilize the formula for arc elasticity of demand. This measures the percentage change over a segment of the demand curve rather than evaluating change at a specific point on the curve. The coefficient for elasticity of demand should always be negative, since change is measured along the demand curve. As price increases, quantity demanded decreases, or vice versa; thus demand elasticities will always be negative.

There are three types of demand elasticities. To evaluate the elasticity of demand coefficient, one should take the absolute value, i.e., ignore the negative sign, and fit the coefficient into one of three categories:

$|e| > 1.0$ Elastic
$|e| = 1.0$ Unitary
$|e| < 1.0$ Inelastic

Thus, if demand elasticity, in absolute terms, is greater than 1.0, demand is elastic. This means that a small change in price will result in a relatively large change in the quantity demanded. Types of products for which demand is elastic are: products for which there are many close substitutes, luxury goods, and products that make up a large portion of the consumer's budget.

Alternatively, if the absolute value of demand elasticity is less than 1.0, demand is said to be inelastic. Here a change in price has a

Figure 5-8   Demand for bluegrass seed.

relatively small impact upon the quantity demanded. Goods that fit into this category are typically necessities, products that account for a very small part of the consumer's budget, or products that have no close substitutes. The demand for natural gas to run and heat a large production facility is fairly inelastic—it is essential to the efficient production process and, at least in the short run, it has no substitutes. Thus, this production facility may have no option but to pay higher natural gas bills this winter to maintain the facility. However, over the longer term, the firm may switch from gas to oil or electricity. So the period of time under consideration also affects the type of elasticity present.

Supply elasticity can be calculated in a way that is similar to the calculation of demand elasticity. Supply elasticity is always positive, since changes in price cause the quantity supplied to change in the same direction. It can be less than, equal to, or greater than 1, depending on whether quantity supplied changes proportionately less, equal to, or more than the change in price.

ECONOMICS AND THE MANAGER

Increasingly, agribusiness managers must understand the economic world in which they operate. Not only are economic principles useful in predicting business trends, but those same principles serve as the basis for many management decisions. This chapter has barely scratched the surface of economics. Professionally trained managers should undergird themselves with basic economics through both formal and informal study.

SUMMARY

Economics involves the allocation of scarce resources, that is, land, labor, capital, and management, to meet the needs of people. Throughout the United States, the free enterprise market system, modified by some governmental restraints, is used to make these allocations. The profit motive is used as an incentive that guides businesses in fulfilling consumer wants as consumers express these wants in the marketplace with their dollars. Agribusinesses are an integral part of this system.

Agribusiness managers use a great many economic principles to make important business decisions. The marginal cost–marginal revenue concept suggests the most profitable level of production. The opportunity cost concept is critical in assessing various decision alternatives. And applying supply and demand principles to agricultural supplies and farm products is basic to almost all agribusiness plans.

DISCUSSION QUESTIONS

1. What are the primary differences between our economic system and socialistic economic systems? Which system do you prefer, and why?

2. What is the role of profits in a free market economic system?

3.   List five ways in which our society restricts the free market system. In your judgment, is this good or bad? Why?

4.   Explain why profits theoretically fall to zero in a perfectly competitive market. Why do profits exist in the real world?

5.   Why should agribusiness managers be interested in macroeconomics?

6.   What are the opportunity costs associated with attending college?

7.   The variable cost of manufacturing farm gates is $100 per gate; in order to sell one more and maximize the firm's profit, the additional gate will have to be sold at $110. What is the marginal cost? The marginal revenue? Should the manager produce at this level? Why or why not?

CASE PROBLEM: COMFORT CABS, INC.

Comfort Cabs, Inc., manufactures and sells all-weather cabs to be installed on farm tractors. Comfort Cabs are high quality, easily installed, and somewhat unique in the industry. The combination air-conditioner–heating unit is quite dependable and requires little maintenance.

Comfort can product up to 1000 cabs quite easily, but producing more cabs causes increasing pressure on production facilities and requires overtime labor. Consequently, production costs are forced upward at higher levels of production.

Comfort's cost accountants and marketing research department have estimated the following consumer demand and production costs at various price levels.

PRICE LEVEL, $/CAB	NUMBER OF CABS PRODUCED	POSSIBLE SALES
1,000	1,000	3,100
1,100	1,500	2,200
1,200	1,800	1,800
1,300	2,050	1,500
1,400	2,200	1,300
1,500	2,300	1,200
1,600	2,350	1,100

QUESTIONS

1.   Using graph paper, plot Comfort's supply and demand curves. At what price and quantity will Comfort sell all it produces?

2.   What would happen if Comfort were to raise prices to $1300? Ex-

plain the mechanism that would tend to bring the market back into equilibrium.

3. Using these curves, show what might happen if grain prices were to strengthen gradually over a period of months.

4. When prices change from $1500 to $1600, what is the elasticity of demand? What does this mean? When the price changes from $1000 to $1100, what is the elasticity? In which case will total revenue change more?

OBJECTIVES

- Describe the necessity for a good financial information system in any agribusiness

- Discover the way in which basic financial information is assimilated into an agribusiness

- Define the balance sheet and describe how it is used by the agribusiness manager

- Define the profit and loss statement and describe how it is used by the agribusiness manager

- Summarize financial statement terminology as it is used by the agribusiness manager

- Develop a working knowledge of how financial statements aid the agribusiness manager's decision-making process

Keeping financial records is fundamental to managing the agribusiness.
A. Keeping records
B. Reviewing financial statements

THE BOTTOM LINE: HISTORIAN OF THE PAST, ARCHITECT OF THE FUTURE

UNDERSTANDING FINANCIAL STATEMENTS

A.

B.

THE BOTTOM LINE

Among managers, no term is used so often as the *bottom line*. For any business the bottom line is the last figure on the financial statement, and because it indicates profit or loss, it is absolutely crucial. Without profits a business cannot exist for any extended period of time. The bottom line measures managers' success or failure in controlling the resources of the agribusiness. It provides historical evidence of the skill and ability demonstrated by the decision makers, or those people to whom the firm has entrusted the employees, money, and materials at its command. Even more importantly, the bottom line defines the potential of the firm. It is the architect of the company's future in terms of growth, modernization, new product development, and rewards both for employees and for investors.

The bottom line is of great importance in itself, but other aspects of financial data are also important. The successful agribusiness manager must know how and why the bottom line of a particular agribusiness evolved the way it has. That is what the study of financial management is all about. The successful manager understands the financial operations of the firm well enough to use them as tools for creating the best possible bottom line in the future.

THE IMPORTANCE OF FINANCIAL STATEMENTS

Financial management requires the highest degree of specialized know-how in interpreting financial information from a firm's records. Without this know-how, agribusiness managers at any level find it difficult to implement the goals and objectives of the organization. Each agribusiness enterprise therefore must accumulate the records, knowledge, and information that are vital for its success. The importance of financial information and records is evidenced by the tons of paper, the billions of forms, the millions of business machines, the thousands of electronic data processors and computers, and the thousands and thousands of people who are employed in recording business activities throughout the country.

Modern financial recordkeeping had its beginning some six centuries ago in Italy. The growth of commerce in Venice and Genoa, which were great commercial centers, created an accompanying need for business records. As a response to this need, a system of records and bookkeeping was developed that is used widely throughout the world to this day. This system summarizes the records of a firm by dividing them into two basic documents. These documents are called the *balance sheet* and the *profit and loss statement*. Together they make up the financial statements of the firm. The remainder of this chapter will relate to the importance and use of these financial statements for agribusiness managers.

THE WHY OF RECORDKEEPING

Agribusinesses seek to generate the greatest possible returns from the resources they possess. Associated with the profit objective are several other objectives, such as the desire to produce a quality product or ser-

FINANCIAL MANAGEMENT AND CONTROL OF THE AGRIBUSINESS

vice, the desire to reward the employees of the business, the desire to help the business grow, and the desire for a good public image as a "citizen" of the community. These kinds of objectives are common to all business organizations, from a huge implement manufacturer to a local small-town feed dealer. Such objectives are usually not accomplished by means of a single, brilliant tactical maneuver, but rather through the consistent use of resources to their greatest potential over a long period of time. To achieve this consistent use of resources, managers need the right kind of information or records. Business records are tools to help managers guide the operation of the business intelligently and make good management decisions that are in line with the needs, objectives, and goals of the company.

Every agribusiness must keep track of sales, purchases, expenses, and profit or loss. Records that demonstrate these factors are necessary to meet the requirements of governmental units, financial lending institutions, investors, employees, and suppliers of the business. Even more importantly, the records of the company should furnish the fuel for all financial planning and management decisions. The records system should provide knowledge that meets the following criteria:

1. It should be simple and easy to understand.

2. It should be reliable, accurate, consistent, and timely.

3. It should be based on the uniqueness of the particular business.

When designing the records system for an agribusiness, it is usually advisable to secure the services of competent professional advisers or consultants who are not members of the firm. These professionals can help to determine objectively which system of records best fits the firm's needs. In addition, most agribusinesses need trained and competent bookkeepers or accountants to maintain the internal system.

MANAGING AN ACCOUNTING SYSTEM

The accounting system also functions to prevent errors and to safeguard an agribusiness's assets. To do this, it must be maintained accurately and honestly by competent personnel. As the business grows larger, a system of checks and balances should be instituted to ensure that no one person has complete control over any transaction. Employees who are working as cashiers or collecting monies should not be engaged in bookkeeping. The person who is performing purchasing duties should not be keeping the books or writing the checks.

Whenever and wherever possible, the responsibilities of records, reports, and controls should rest with at least two people. A retail salesperson normally has any customer cash refunds verified by another employee. Managers often hire outside auditors to verify the accuracy and integrity of the organization's financial records. All this is not to imply dishonesty so much as to confirm the credibility and integrity of all involved, and to verify that records are being kept properly. When proper checks are built into an accounting system, there is little reason to suspect improprieties.

Good financial records should provide the basis for:

1. Determining the success of the business in terms of profitability during specific time periods or cycles

2. Determining the general financial condition or health of the enterprise at a given moment

3. Predicting the future ability of the business to meet the demands of creditors, of change, and of expansion

4. Analyzing the trends in performance as they relate to management's abilities and to the success or failure of past decisions and achievements

5. Choosing among the various possible alternatives for the future use of resources

Working with Accountants and Bookkeepers

Many agribusiness managers, such as Ray Whyth, the owner and president of a sizable farm-building construction company, confess to a fear of financial management and accounting simply because they are unfamiliar with the way the system works. Ray's unfamiliarity stems from the fact that his company started small, and he simply has not grown financially with the company. Many other managers have come up through the ranks in larger companies from the area of sales, production, and operations, and they also have not been exposed to the records systems. It is not necessary for the manager to know how to do the accounting personally or to maintain the records of an organization. Instead, the agribusiness manager should concentrate on understanding how the system works and what information the recordkeeping process produces for use in decision making.

The agribusiness manager who works with comptrollers, accountants, and bookkeepers is likely to find many who view the world about them in a conceptual and abstract manner. For such people the books, records, and figures become a reason unto themselves for their own existence. The approach of such specialists can produce information which, though accurate and interesting, may not be understandable or meaningful to those controlling and managing the organization. Determining which information is needed and what form it should take is the responsibility of the manager.

Each manager reviews the information supplied by the records of the organization, testing it against the criteria of the five points provided previously. He or she must ask such questions as "Will this information or data allow management to make wiser decisions?" "Is the information prepared in such a way that managers can easily understand and interpret it?" "Is it information that the particular agribusiness truly needs?"

Records that do not meet these tests should be altered or dropped, unless they are required by law or by government agencies.

THE ACCOUNTING PROCESS

The recordkeeping process derives largely from the original documents of the organization. These documents include such things as sales slips, receiving tickets, checks, invoices, employee time cards, and bills. One could say that such original documents are the building blocks for the entire recordkeeping system. If we look closely at Ray Whyth's farm-building construction business, we will see that each day the firm incurs more expenses and acquires more income. These day-to-day transactions are recorded in a book called the *journal*. The journal is also referred to as the book of original entry for the business. Here are recorded, in chronological order, all the transactions of the business. The journal, then, provides a running account of the day-to-day transactions or activities of the business. In a small business there may be only one book or general journal in which all the transactions of the business are recorded. As a business such as Ray Whyth's grows larger in size, it is necessary to have several specialized journals for particular areas of the business to record such separate categories as sales, purchases, and available cash. While the journal records the transactions or activities of the business chronologically, it does not put them into any meaningful form by which the manager can interpret or use the information presented.

BUSINESS INFORMATION MUST BE ORGANIZED

In looking at Ray Whyth's farm construction business, it is apparent that he should have a record of its property or assets. *Assets* are those things of value that are at a business's command. Those who are interested in a particular agribusiness require such information as the amount of available cash, the amount of money that customers owe to the business, the amount of stock or merchandise available, and the equipment needed to carry on business activities, including buildings, land, office and sales space, and trucks.

Those who are interested in the business are also concerned with the liabilities of that business. *Liabilities* are the sums of money that have to be paid to creditors at specified dates in the future. To put it another way, liabilities represent the sums that are owed to people outside the business.

In addition to information about assets and liabilities, the full financial picture requires information about the amount of money that the owners have invested in that business. This sum is called *net worth*.

Then, too, there is the need for records that detail income and expenses in such a way that the success of the business, in terms of income or loss, may be meaningfully measured by the manager for decision-making purposes and by the government for tax purposes.

To provide the aforementioned information, the records that are kept in the journal have to be transferred to another book or series of books called the *ledger* (Figure 6-1). The transferring of information from the journal to the ledger is known as *posting*. The ledger is composed of a series of records called accounts. Each *account* is a separate recording for one of the information categories previously mentioned. An account will categorize each separate kind of asset and will list the amount of said asset in terms of money. There will be an account for each of the creditors of the business to indicate the amount of money, or liability, that each creditor is owed by the business. There will be an account that lists the amount of money or capital that the owner or owners of the business have invested. There also will be accounts for each kind of income and for each kind of expense. Ledger accounts, then, provide for the separating, categorizing, and recording of related transactions or activities within the business, and they do so in an organized manner. Maintaining financial information in separate ledger accounts not only makes it more usable but provides information that is more easily understood by the agribusiness manager.

Figure 6-1   Example of a ledger page.

GENERAL LEDGER POSTING

079   LAFAYETTE CO-OP ELEVAT   50   STOCKWELL

DATE		SOURCE DOC	CUSTOMER		D E P T	ACCOUNT CODE			QUANTITY	AMOUNT	BALANCE
MO DAY	YR	JR ID NO.	ACCT NO.	DOC NO.		MAJ	MIN	SUPPL			
0401 9					5	7250			COMP & BOND INSURANCE		
0430 9	57	405			5	7250				336.00 *	
0430 9					5	7250				48.00	
			48 MT	Y			48	MB	40 MLY		384.00
						7299			ALLOC--EMPLOYEE COSTS		
0401 9					5	7299				3,093.03 *	
0430 9	56	402			5	7299				498.02	
0430 9	56	403			5	7299				95.55-	
0430 9	56	403			5	7299				78.49-	
0430 9					5	7299					3,417.01
			323 MT	Y			493	MB	252 MLY		
						7300			REPAIRS & MAINTENANCE		
0401 9					5	7300				761.96 *	
0401 9	11	325			5	7300				19.12-	
0430 9	50	50999			5	7300				28.12	
0430 9	52	27301			5	7300				19.12	
0430 9	58	431			5	7300				8.81	
0430 9					5	7300					798.89
			36 MT	Y			208	MB	38 MLY		
						7330			SUPPLIES		
0401 9					5	7330				794.10 *	
0430 9	51	41179			5	7330				27.00-	
0430 9	51	65587			5	7330				8.00	
0430 9	51	65845			5	7330				4.00	
0430 9	51	66153			5	7330				4.00	
0430 9	51	66487			5	7330				20.00	
0430 9	52	27392			5	7330				23.57	
0430 9	52	27493			5	7330				188.63	
0430 9	52	27493			5	7330				7.55	
0430 9	55	2187			5	7330				24.00	
0430 9	58	432			5	7330				26.57	
0430 9					5	7330					1,073.42
			279 MT	Y			150	MB	100 MLY		
						7340			POSTAGE & MAILING		

F9 2004 (1-72)

The accounts in the ledger are summarized on a predetermined regular basis called the *accounting period*. Usually, the accounting period will consist of 1 month for all but the very smallest or simplest business. Summaries of the accounts in the ledger are termed the *financial statements* of the organization.

FINANCIAL STATEMENTS

Financial statements usually consist of the balance sheet and the profit and loss statement. Essentially, a *balance sheet* shows what a business owns, what it owes, and what investment the owners have in the business. It can be likened to a snapshot that shows the financial makeup and condition of the business at a *specific point*. The *profit and loss statement*, on the other hand, is a summary of business operations over a certain period, usually the period between the dates of two balance sheets. It can be seen as a moving picture that details the business activities as they occur over a period of time. Generally, the balance sheet tells exactly where the business is, and the profit and loss statement demonstrates how it got there since the last time a balance sheet was prepared. The profit and loss statement is also known as the operating statement, the income statement, or simply the P & L statement.

The length of the accounting period and the dates of issuing financial statements are particularly important in agribusinesses that are of a highly seasonal nature. Hilltop Fertilizer, Inc. (Exhibits 6-1 and 6-2) is an excellent example. In most parts of the country, fertilizer and chemical operations conduct a very large portion of their annual business in the 2 to 3 months of the planting season. For example, the balance sheet drawn up just prior to the rush season is likely to show large amounts of fertilizer on hand and little money owed by customers. If the sheet is drawn up just after the busy season, it is likely to show less fertilizer in storage and larger amounts of money owed by customers. Such financial statements can be very misleading. Consequently, the agribusiness manager must understand why variations in financial statements are inescapable in highly seasonal agribusinesses. Previous years' financial statements often provide a more valid comparison than a simple month-by-month comparison.

Hilltop Fertilizer Co., Inc.: An Example

Hilltop Fertilizer Co., Inc. (Figure 6-2) is a good example of an agribusiness. Hilltop is an actual retail fertilizer plant located in the Midwest. It sells a wide range of dry-blended fertilizers, anhydrous ammonia, and agricultural chemicals. It also provides custom application services to its customers within a 15- to 20-mile radius. Annual sales total about 5000 tons of fertilizer, with about 60 percent of the business occurring between April and June. It purchases fertilizer from national manufacturers and blends it to the individual farmer's needs. Exhibits 6-1 and 6-2 summarize Hilltop's operations during a recent year. To simplify the illustration, the exact figures have been rounded to the nearest $1000.

Hilltop Fertilizer, Inc. Balance Sheet December 31, 1984

(a)	Assets		
(b)	Current assets:		
(c)	Cash		$ 50,000
(d)	Accounts receivable		150,000
(e)	Inventory		80,000
(f)	Prepaid expenses		10,000
(g)	Other		10,000
(h)	Total current assets		300,000
(i)	Fixed assets:		
(j)	Land	20,000	
(k)	Buildings	100,000	
(l)	Less: Accumulated depreciation	50,000	
(m)		70,000	
(n)	Equipment	250,000	
(o)	Less: Accumulated depreciation	130,000	
(p)		120,000	
(q)	Total fixed assets	190,000	
(r)	Other assets	10,000	
(s)	Total assets		$500,000
(aa)	Liabilities		
(bb)	Current liabilities:		
(cc)	Accounts payable	43,000	
(dd)	Notes payable	100,000	
(ee)	Taxes payable	5,000	
(ff)	Wages payable	2,000	
(gg)	Total current liabilities		150,000
(hh)	Long-term liabilities:		
(ii)	Mortgages	40,000	
(jj)	Other	10,000	
(kk)	Total long-term liabilities	50,000	
(ll)	Total liabilities		200,000
(mm)	Net worth		
(nn)	Owner-invested capital:		
(oo)	Common stock	200,000	
(pp)	Retained earnings	100,000	
(qq)	Total net worth	300,000	
(rr)	Total liabilities and net worth		$500,000

THE BALANCE SHEET

As was already mentioned, the balance sheet is a summary of what the
business owns and owes and of the investment that the owners have
made in the business (Exhibit 6-1). The possessions that have monetary

Hilltop Fertilizer, Inc. Profit and Loss Statement Year Ending
December 31, 1984

(a)	Sales		$1,000,000
(b)	Cost of goods sold		750,000
(c)	Gross margin		250,000
(d)	Operating expenses		
(e)	Salary and wages, including benefits	75,000	
(f)	Local taxes, licenses	5,000	
(g)	Insurance	6,000	
(h)	Depreciation	20,000	
(i)	Rent and lease	7,000	
(j)	Advertising and promotion	5,000	
(k)	Office expense	2,000	
(l)	Utilities	3,000	
(m)	Maintenance and repair	17,000	
(n)	Bad-debt loss	2,000	
(o)	Supplies	4,000	
(p)	Other	4,000	
(q)	Total operating expense		150,000
(r)	Net operating profit	100,000	
(s)	Interest expense	15,000	
(t)	Other nonoperating income	5,000	
(u)	Net profit before taxes		90,000
(v)	Profit taxes		40,000
(w)	Net profit after taxes		$ 50,000

value are called *assets* (a). Assets are usually listed at the top or on the left-hand side of the balance sheet (Exhibit 6-1, *a* to *s*). The amount that the business owes to creditors is called *liabilities* (aa). Liabilities are generally located in the middle section or on the right-hand side of the balance sheet (Exhibit 6-1, *aa* to *ll*). Legally, the creditors of the business would have first claim against any of its assets. The value of the assets over and above the liabilities can justifiably be called the owner's claim against the assets, or *owner's equity*. Owner's equity is often referred to as *net worth* (mm). The net worth section usually appears just below the liability section.

This brings us to the *dual-aspect* concept of the balance sheet. The balance sheet is set up to portray two aspects of each entry or event recorded on it. For each thing of value, or asset, there is an offsetting claim against that asset. The recognition of this concept leads to the balance sheet formula:

Assets = liabilities + owner's equity

An examination of the following case will clarify this concept.

Figure 6-2   Hilltop Fertilizer, Inc.

When Ray Whyth decided to start his farm-building business, he deposited $2000 in cash in the bank. This sum represented an investment of $1000 from his own funds and $1000 that he had borrowed from the bank. If he had drawn up a balance sheet at that time, it would have shown assets of $2000 cash balanced against a liability claim of $1000 and an owner's claim of $1000, using the balance sheet formula:

Assets = liabilities + owner's equity
$2000 = $1000 + $1000

As this formula indicates, there will always be a balance between assets and the claims against them (liabilities + owner's equity). The balance sheet is well named because it always balances, unless there has been a clerical error.

Assets (a)

It was stated earlier that assets are things of value that are at a business's command. Of course, the business does not legally own anything unless it is organized as a corporation (see Chapter 3). But regardless of whether the business is organized as a proprietorship, a partnership, or a corporation, all business bookkeeping should be reckoned and accounted as a separate entity from the personal funds and assets of its owner or owners. Small agribusinesses where personal and business assets are mixed have difficulty in sharply defining genuine business performance. Business assets are typically classified in three categories: current assets *(b)*, fixed assets *(i)*, and other assets *(r)*.

Current Assets *(b)*   For bookkeeping purposes the term *current assets* is used to designate actual cash or assets that can be converted to cash during one normal operating cycle of the business (usually 1 year). The distinction between current assets and noncurrent assets is important because lenders and others pay much attention to the total value of current assets.

The value of current assets bears a significant relationship to the stability of the business because it represents the amount of cash that might be raised quickly to meet current obligations. When a firm called the Lincoln Nursery discovered that it was necessary to fumigate a large acreage prior to planting nursery stock, its owners experienced great difficulty raising the funds for the emergency because their current assets were limited.

The major current asset items may include the following.

CASH *(c)*   Cash funds are those that are immediately available for use without restriction. These funds are usually in the form of checking account deposits in banks, cash register money, and petty cash. Cash amounts should be large enough to meet any obligations that fall due immediately. Hilltop has cash balances of only $50,000 as of December 31 (see Exhibit 6-1). As carloads of fertilizer arrive soon after the first of the year, Hilltop may have to borrow added short-term funds to meet its purchasing obligations.

ACCOUNTS RECEIVABLE *(d)*   Accounts receivable represent the total amount owed to the company as payment for purchases. Essentially, these accounts result from the granting of credit to customers. They may take the form of charge accounts on which no interest or service charge is made, or they may be of an interest-bearing nature. In either case, they are a drain on the cash position. The larger the outstanding amount in accounts receivable, the less money the company will have available to meet current needs, such as fertilizer deliveries. The amount of money in this category depends on the firm's credit policy; that is, how much credit is extended to customers and how efficient the business is at collecting outstanding accounts.

Some agribusinesses depend heavily on credit as a selling tool. Much of farming is seasonal, and many customers prefer to postpone payment until after the harvest and/or the selling of crops. Hilltop Fertilizer is in a businesss in which selling on credit is common. As Exhibit 6-1 indicates, on December 31 Hilltop's customers still owed a total of $150,000. This is a figure that Hilltop's management *and* creditors will watch closely, since borrowing money to pay the firm's obligations is an added expense that reduces the business's profitability. The trick is for Hilltop to offer enough credit so as not to hurt sales, while at the same time keeping its credit tight enough not to jeopardize its own cash-flow position. (More on this in Chapter 9.)

INVENTORY (e)   *Inventory* is defined as those items that are held for sale in the ordinary course of business or that are to be consumed in the process of producing goods and services to be sold. Inventory items are usually valued at cost (actual funds expended) or market value (what they are worth), whichever is lower. Hilltop has $80,000 worth of fertilizer and chemicals as of December 31. The firm may already be building some inventory for spring sales. The objective of its managers is to keep inventory as low as possible, in order to minimize the cash investment while still maintaining an adequate supply of fertilizer to meet the customers' needs. Control of inventory and inventory expenses is one of management's most important jobs, particularly for retailers. Good bookkeeping records are particularly useful in controlling inventory. The better Hilltop is at matching supplies of fertilizer with customers' demands, the more profit the firm will make.

PREPAID EXPENSES (f)   Prepaid expenses represent assets that have been paid for in advance; usually, their usefulness is due to end after a short time. A good example would be prepaid insurance. A business often pays for insurance protection for as much as 3 to 5 months in advance. The right to this protection is a thing of value (an asset), and the prepaid or unused portion can be refunded or converted to cash. Hilltop has $10,000 in prepaid insurance.

OTHER CURRENT ASSETS (g)   A firm may have various other assets that can easily be converted into cash. For example, Hilltop has $10,000 in "marketable securities." This term indicates an outside investment in another company's stocks and bonds, an investment that can be cashed in during the accounting year.

Fixed Assets (i)   *Fixed assets* are those items that the business owns that have a relatively long life. Fixed assets are usually used to produce or sell other goods and services. If they were to be held for resale, they would have to be classified as inventory (current assets), even though the assets might be long-lived. Normally, fixed assets comprise land, buildings, and equipment. Some companies lump all their fixed assets into one entry on their balance sheets. More information can be gained and more control exercised over these assets, however, if they are listed separately on the balance sheet. Some managers may even wish to list types of equipment separately.

Hilltop Fertilizer's balance sheet would be clear if its equipment (n) were broken into the two main categories: fertilizer mixing equipment and rolling stock (trucks, spreaders, etc.). Some fertilizer companies even list large, especially expensive equipment, such as "floaters" (self-propelled fertilizer applicators with large floater tires, which may cost $40,000 to $50,000), as separate entries on the balance sheet.

One other aspect of the fixed-assets bookkeeping that should be considered is depreciation (*l* and *o*). Generally, all fixed assets, with the exception of land, *depreciate* (decrease in value) over time. For example, Hilltop's largest floater, which is 3 years old and showing wear, may be worth only $20,000, much less than its original $40,000 purchase cost. For a balance sheet to show the true value of the company's assets, it must reflect the assets' loss in value.

Theoretically, the net fixed-asset value on the balance sheet reflects the actual value of the asset in its present state. However, the real value of fixed assets may be considerably different. The actual market value could be accurately established only by selling the asset, but an ongoing business cannot sell its assets.

Several methods may be used to determine the amount of depreciation. Annual depreciation is allowed as an expense item on the profit and loss statement (discussed later), and so it significantly affects total expenses, profits, and, consequently, taxes. Internal Revenue Service regulations greatly affect the method used to calculate depreciation.[1] But for both tax and accounting purposes the business can deduct the loss in the value of an asset each year during the useful life of the asset, until it reaches the point where the total cost has been deducted.

Land is usually entered at its purchase cost, even though its current value may be much greater. Accountants argue that because it is impossible to accurately determine its real market value without selling the land, the balance sheet should reflect its original purchase cost so as not to overstate the value and mislead the reader. Obviously, when agribusiness firms have significant land assets whose value has increased greatly, the balance sheet may vastly understate the real market value. For example, Ray Whyth's construction business is located on 10 acres of land that he purchased in 1941 for $10,000. A short time ago a large chain offered him $300,000 for the same 10 acres. If Ray could revalue his land, his net worth would be shown as being much greater. Accountants are working on new methods of reporting fixed assets whose value has been drastically increased by rapid inflation, but most businesses still report the purchase cost, unless otherwise noted.

Other Assets *(r)* A miscellaneous category called *other assets* accounts for any investment of the firm in securities, such as stock in other private companies and bonds. The category also includes intangible assets, such as patents, franchise costs, and goodwill. Goodwill is the extent to which price paid for an asset exceeds the asset's physical market value, usually because of the value of the reputation established in the market area by the previous owner. Items in the other assets category usually have a longer life than current asset items and are generally nondepreciable in nature. In many cases, they cannot easily be sold within the operating year or without incurring considerable loss in value.

---

[1]Publication 534, *Depreciation*, is available free of charge through your Internal Revenue Service (IRS) Forms Distribution Center. A more general guide is IRS Publication 334, *Tax Guide for Small Business*, also available through the IRS Forms Distribution Center.

Liabilities *(aa)*

Liabilities consist of money that the business *owes* to other people (other than capital invested by the owners). Liabilities are claims against the business's assets, but they may not be claims against any specific asset, except in the cases of some mortgages and equipment liens. This means that unless a creditor holds a lien or mortgage (legal claim) against a specific fertilizer truck, spreader, or land, that creditor has no claims against individual assets; his or her only claim is against a specific dollar portion of the total value of the company's assets. Essentially, liabilities are divided into two classes: current liabilities and long-term liabilities.

Current Liabilities *(bb)*   The term *current liabilities* describes those outsiders' claims on the business that will fall due within one normal operating cycle, usually 1 year. Some of the more important current liabilities entered on the balance sheet are the following.

ACCOUNTS PAYABLE *(cc)*   Accounts payable represent the amount that Hilltop owes to vendors, wholesalers, and other suppliers from whom the business has bought items on account. This category also includes any items of inventory, supplies, or capital equipment that have been purchased on credit and for which payment is expected in less than 1 year. When Hilltop purchases 100 tons of potash from their supplier on short-term credit at $100 per ton, or $10,000, accounts payable immediately increases by $10,000.

NOTES PAYABLE *(dd)*   Notes payable are sometimes labeled as short-term loans or liabilities. The category represents those loans from individuals, banks, or other lending institutions that fall due within a year. Also included in this category is the specific portion of any long-term debt that will come due within a year.

In highly seasonal agribusinesses, short-term loans are a very important part of financial management (see Chapter 8). Cash needs intensify during the peak season, when the agribusiness must pay for increased inventory and for financing accounts receivable. This situation requires careful money management. Hilltop shows $100,000 in short-term credit as of December 31.

ACCRUALS   Taxes payable *(ee)* and wages payable *(ff)* are often called *accrued expenses* or *accruals*. They include those obligations that the business has incurred for which there has been no formal bill or invoice. An example of this would be accrued taxes. Hilltop knows that the business has the obligation to pay $5000 in taxes, an amount that is accruing or accumulating each day. The fact that the taxes do not have to be paid until a later date in the operating year does not diminish the daily obligation. Another example of accrued expenses would be Hilltop's wages of $2000. Although they are paid weekly and monthly, they are being earned daily or even hourly, and they constitute a valid claim against Hilltop's assets. An accurate balance sheet reflects these obligations.

Long-Term Liabilities *(hh)* Outsiders' claims against the business that do not come due within 1 year are called *long-term liabilities* or simply *other liabilities*. Included in this category are bonded indebtedness, mortgages, and long-term loans from individuals, banks, or others. Any part of a long-term debt that falls due within 1 year from the date of the balance sheet is recorded as part of the current liabilities of the business. Hilltop has both a mortgage *(ii)* and other long-term debt *(jj)*.

Net Worth *(mm)*

The *net worth* or owner's equity section *(mm)* details the claims of the owners against the business's assets. Essentially, this is a balancing figure; that is, the owners receive whatever assets are left after the liability claims have been recognized. This is an obvious definition if one remembers the balance sheet formula. Transposing the formula, it becomes

Assets − liabilities = owner's equity

In an incorporated business the owners' original or contributed investment to the business is listed as a separate entry called *common stock (oo)*. This does not necessarily represent the current market value of the common stock, but rather its original value. (Market value of stock is a totally separate issue, determined solely by buyers' and sellers' perceptions of the value of the business.)

The category of *retained earnings (pp)* represents the net gain on the owners' original investment. If no profits were ever drawn from the business, the retained earnings figure would reflect the total amount of profit that the business has made since its inception. Of course, most owners expect to remove profits regularly from the business as a return on their investment. Thus retained earnings represent whatever net profits the owners have chosen to leave in the business as additional contributed capital.

Hilltop owners have left $100,000 of earned profits in the business to combine with their original $200,000 investment. For most companies, retained earnings are an important source of capital for growth.

When the business is a sole proprietorship or partnership (see Chapter 3), it is customary to show owner's equity as one entry with no distinction between the owners' initial investment and the accumulated retained earnings of the business. However, in the case of the incorporated business there are entries for stockholders' claims and also for earnings that have been accumulated and retained in the business.

Of course, if the business has been consistently operating at a loss, the owners' claims may be less than the initial investment; and, in the case of a corporation, the balancing account could be an operating deficit rather than retained earnings.

The complete combination of all the entries we have been discussing creates a full balance sheet. This sheet provides a great deal of information. It tells just what the business owns and what claims exist against it. Managers need this information to help them decide what actions they should take in running their businesses.

PROFIT AND LOSS STATEMENT

The profit and loss statement (Exhibit 6-2) summarizes income and expenses during a specific period of time and demonstrates the profit or loss that results from the combination of income and expenses. For these reasons, it is most commonly known as the profit and loss statement.

The profit and loss statement is the primary measure of management efficiency; therefore, it is a key financial statement for operating managers. Its very format emphasizes the basic profit formula, and so holds the key to many operating management problems.

> Sales
> − Cost of goods sold
> ──────────────
> Gross margin
> − Expenses
> ──────────────
> Profit

Because this financial record summarizes the activities of the company over a specific period of time, it lists only those activities that can be expressed in terms of dollars. While the balance sheet analysis indicates the change in the position of the company at the end of a particular accounting period, the profit and loss statement details how the change took place during that accounting period.

The profit and loss statement identifies the dollar volume of business during a specific period and then matches to it, as precisely as possible, the expenses incurred to perform that business. Not all the cash expenditures (sums spent) during an accounting period can be attributed to business transacted during that period. Hilltop may purchase a truck one year but use it for several years. It would be misleading to charge the entire cost of the truck (an expenditure) to the business during the year in which it was purchased, since the truck will last for several years; therefore, only that part that is used during the operating period is reported as an expense (previously referred to as depreciation). This loss in value is reported on the balance sheet (Exhibit 6-1, l and o). Similarly, Hilltop could have purchased fertilizer (inventory) near the end of an accounting period without selling it until the following period.

Therefore, only as an asset is used up or sold does it become an *expense* to the business because it has to be replaced. That is, as any asset becomes part of the operation and is directly or indirectly sold to a customer, it becomes an expense. As the Hilltop truck is used, it wears out. For business purposes, one might even say that it is being sold to customers bit by bit as the wearing-out process occurs; this is why it is listed as a depreciation expense.

The primary purpose of the operating statement (profit and loss) is to match precisely the expenses and the income from the business generated during that period so that management can accurately measure business profits.

The accounting process helps in distinguishing between expenses and expenditures. An *expenditure* is incurred whenever the business acquires an asset, such as a truck, building, or fertilizer, whether it is used immediately or years later. *Expenses* are expenditures that are incurred by the business during the accounting period being reported. Expenses directly affect net worth—higher expenses mean lower profit, which, in turn, dictates a lower addition to the firm's net worth. Whenever an asset is acquired, the business must make arrangements to pay for it, either immediately or later. Date of payment is extremely important to the firm's cash flow, but it has little to do directly with profits or losses.

Profit and Loss Statement Format

The format of a profit and loss statement varies somewhat from business to business, but such statements generally begin with sales and subtract the appropriate expenses, with profit showing as a remainder.

Sales *(a)* *Sales* represent the dollar value of all the products and services that have been sold during the period specified on the profit and loss statement. These may be either cash or credit sales. Sometimes customers return products after the products have already been purchased. The dollar value of all returns is usually subtracted from the dollar value of all sales. Sometimes the returns are shown as a separate entry. Some customers may be given discount prices for the goods or services they buy. Either the discounted price or the full price may be shown on the profit and loss statement, with a special entry indicating how much discount has been given.

> Sales
> — Returns
> — Discounts and allowances
> Net sales

Cost of Goods Sold *(b)* *Cost of goods sold* represents the total cost to the agribusiness of goods that were actually sold during the specified period. In the case of retail firms, whose purpose is to resell a previously purchased product, this category is a rather straightforward accounting of the actual purchases plus any additional freight charges. In Hilltop's case, the fertilizer and chemicals that were purchased and resold during the year actually cost the firm $750,000.

Many types of agribusiness firms are involved in processing or manufacturing. In these cases, determining the cost of goods sold is considerably more complicated because it involves not only the costs for raw materials but the many internal, direct manufacturing costs. In such cases, the cost-of-goods-sold section becomes more complex, and it is recommended that the cost of manufactured goods be detailed to show important cost breakdowns.

To provide an accurate cost-of-goods-sold figure, current inventories of raw and finished products must be balanced against those of the previous accounting period. In a manufacturing or processing business, the cost of the raw materials and direct labor that have been used during the accounting period are usually included in the cost of goods sold, and are subtracted from sales to establish the gross margin. Decreases or increases in inventories from one accounting period to another reflect consumption of or additions to inventories, so that the balancing of changes in inventory is intended to reflect the actual costs incurred during the current accounting period. For example, if a firm consumed a large amount of raw materials, which naturally would decrease inventories from the previous accounting period, the net change in inventory would be reflected in the cost of goods sold. Hilltop had a fertilizer inventory of $100,000 in the previous period; now it shows an inventory of $80,000. The decrease in fertilizer inventory of $20,000 would have to be added to new purchases of $730,000 to equal the total cost of goods sold of $750,000 (b). The formula is:

Beginning inventory	$100,000
− Ending inventory	− 80,000
Net inventory change	= 20,000
+ Purchases	+ 730,000
= Cost of goods sold	$750,000

In addition, if Hilltop paid any freight or transportation expense in receiving inventory at their facility, this expense would also be included as a part of cost of goods sold.

Gross Margin (c) *Gross margin* represents the difference between total sales and the cost of goods sold. The gross margin is the money that is available to cover the operating expenses and still leave a profit. If the gross margin is not large enough to cover operating expenses of the business, losses and not profits will be the result.

Gross margins are particularly important to retail agribusinesses because such businesses have relatively little control over cost of goods sold. The prices of the goods that an agribusiness purchases are the most critical factor affecting its gross margin. Different products usually have different individual gross margins, so the total gross margin for the business will also depend on the particular combination or mix of products and their sources. Often management can affect the cost of goods sold through careful purchasing. Hilltop Fertilizer has a gross margin of $250,000, which is enough to cover its expenses and still leave a profit.

To demonstrate the importance of pricing on gross margin profit, let us assume that Hilltop was able to raise its price by 1 percent on $1 million in sales. This would have increased sales to $1.01 million. With the cost of goods sold remaining constant, gross margin would have increased to $260,000; but after expenses had been subtracted, operating profit would have increased by 10 percent to $110,000, and net profits would have increased by over 10 percent. The same kind of effect on the bottom line would be seen if the cost of purchased fertilizer (cost of goods sold) were reduced slightly. This points up the fact that business success is largely centered around relatively small but important changes, and illustrates the tremendous importance of relevant financial data.

Operating Expenses *(d)* *Operating expenses* represent the costs that are associated with the specific sales transacted during the time period designated on the profit and loss statement. It is easier to interpret these expenses if they have been divided into major divisions, such as marketing expenses, including:

> sales, wages, salaries, and commissions
>
> transportation
>
> advertising and promotion

administrative expenses, including:

> auditing fees
>
> directors' fees
>
> management salary
>
> office expenses
>
> travel expenses

general expenses (overhead), including:

> depreciation
>
> insurance
>
> taxes (net profits taxes)
>
> rent
>
> repairs
>
> utilities

(Manufacturing costs, where incurred, are included in cost of goods sold.)

In Hilltop Fertilizer's profit and loss statement, the various expense categories are simply listed (e through p). The returns and allowances have already been excluded. Net sales for the year ending December 31 were $1 million. If Hilltop had detailed its expenses in the categories suggested, it would have been much easier for its managers to analyze and interpret the valuable financial information that the profit and loss statement can provide.

Net Operating Profit *(r)* Also called the *net operating margin*, the *net operating profit* is the amount left over when operating expenses *(q)* are

123

subtracted from the gross margin *(c)*. It is affected by the same factors that influence gross margins, plus the factors of associated business expenses.

Net Profit before Taxes *(u)*   Net profit before taxes is the amount that remains after taking into account any nonoperating income or expenses. Nonoperating income would include any income derived from other sources, such as interest or dividends earned on outside investments *(t)*. Local cooperatives may include patronage refunds from their regional cooperative in other income. Hilltop generated $5000 in other nonoperating income from interest on investments and the sale of some very old equipment. On the other hand, Hilltop incurred nonoperating interest expenses of $15,000. This $15,000 is interest on money that Hilltop had borrowed from various sources (as they appeared on the balance sheet), and so is not directly part of the operations. Some operating statements list interest expense as an operating expense. It can be correctly treated either way.

Net Profit after Taxes *(w)*   Net profit after taxes, or net income as it is sometimes called, simply takes into account the federal business profits tax *(v)*. The rate of tax depends on many factors, including the size of the profits, profit levels in previous years, type of business organization, and several complicated tax regulations. In larger corporate organizations, tax rates often reach nearly 50 percent of the profits. In the case of proprietorships and partnerships, federal profits taxes are not levied against the businesses themselves, but are assessed against the individual owners. Profits are taxed as personal income (see Chapter 3). Cooperative businesses often have no entries either for taxes or for after-tax profits.

SOME IMPORTANT ACCOUNTING PRINCIPLES
It is important that agribusiness managers understand the following principles and ideas about financial accounting.

1. Only facts that can be recorded in *monetary terms* are reported.

2. Records or accounts are kept only for the business entities, with personal and business transactions carefully separated.

3. Accounting methods assume that the business will continue to operate indefinitely.

4. Valuable things (called assets) at the command of a business are ordinarily recorded at the price paid to acquire them. This practice is called the *cost basis of valuation*. The amounts listed on the financial statement do not necessarily reflect what the asset could be sold for at any given moment.

5. Every accounting event is composed of two transactions: changes in assets and changes in equities (*equity* means ownership). All assets are claimed by someone; therefore, claims must equal as-

124

sets. These claims can be found among owners, stockholders, banks, suppliers, etc.

6. Most accounting is handled on the *accrual basis of reporting*. The objective of the accrual method is to report revenue (income) in the statement of operations for the period during which it is *earned* (regardless of when it is collected), and to report an expense in the period when it is *incurred* (regardless of when the cash disbursement is made). This procedure clearly indicates the real profits of the business.

7. The format for the operating statement must reflect the unique needs of the organization. To do this requires the continued help of competent professional bookkeepers and accountants.

8. Once a format is developed, it is not sacred and should be changed as necessary to meet changing conditions. But a degree of continuity should also be maintained to allow comparison on a historical basis.

9. Finally, one of the major purposes of records and financial information is to provide the necessary fuel for informed decision making on the part of agribusiness managers.

SOURCE-USE STATEMENT ANALYSIS: A CASE STUDY

The Aggieland Company provides landscaping services to a wide region of east central Texas. This company has done reasonably well since its inception in 1974. However, the owner, Ted Blank, has a problem. He has recently refused to bid on several sizable projects because his crews are working full time and he doesn't have the necessary equipment to do more jobs. Thus, Ted has visited his banker and discussed the possibility of a sizable loan to expand his business. Ted had considered equity capital for part of this expansion, but concluded that he was already investing most of the profit from operations back into the business, and, he needed the rest for living expenses.

Ted constructed the following balance sheet for the visit to his banker:

Balance Sheet for Aggieland Agribusiness Company

Assets		Liabilities	
Current assets:		Current liabilities	
Cash	5,000	Accounts payable	5,000
Accounts receivable	14,000	Accrued expenses	2,000
Inventory	21,000	Current portion of long-term debt	10,000
Fixed assets:		Long-term liabilities	
Equipment	175,000	Long-term debt	90,000
Buildings	45,000		
Other assets:		Net worth	157,000
Investments	4,000		
Total assets	$264,000	Total equities	$264,000

125

The Source-Use Statement

This statement is basically a way of accounting for changes in asset, liability, and net worth accounts from one period to the next. It can be tabulated at the end of the period, like the balance sheet and income statement, to help interested parties see what happened, or, more importantly, it can be constructed at the beginning of the period in an attempt to budget appropriate changes over the period.

The source-use statement, like the balance sheet, always balances, i.e., sources of funds (dollars flowing into the business) always equal uses of funds (dollars flowing out of the business) over the period.

Sources of funds include:	Uses of funds include:
Beginning cash balance	Ending cash balance
Increase in liabilities	Decrease in liabilities
Decrease in assets	Increase in assets
Depreciation	Losses
Profits	

Ted, after a discussion with his banker, decided that he would purchase an additional $100,000 worth of equipment in order to be able to handle more business. He anticipates that the additional equipment will allow him to add two new crews and over period of a year add approximately 20 percent to his net profit figure. (Last year's profit was $40,000.) Ted wants to estimate the impact this will have on his firm in the short run, so he wants to estimate a source-use statement for his firm. He believes that the expansion will cause the inventory and accrued expense accounts to increase 30 percent, while most other accounts will stay the same. Depreciation will increase from $12,000 to $19,000 per year. In addition, during the year Ted has payments of $10,000 to make toward his existing long-term debt.

Ted can now estimate how much his source-use statement will be affected over the next period and can construct a pro forma balance sheet as follows:

Sources		Uses	
Beginning cash	$ 5,000	Ending cash	$ 5,000
Increase in accrued expenses	600	Decrease in long-term debt	10,000
New loan	????	New equipment	100,000
Depreciation	19,000	Increase in inventory	6,300
Profits	48,000		

Total uses:	$121,300
Total sources w/o loan:	72,600
New loan:	48,700

Pro Forma Balance Sheet for Aggieland

Assets			Liabilities	
Current assets:			Current liabilities	
Cash		$ 5,000	Accounts payable	$ 5,000
Accounts receivable		14,000	Accrued expenses	2,600
			Current portion of	
Inventory		27,300	long-term debt	10,000
Fixed assets:			Long-term liabilities:	
Equipment	275,000		Long-term debt	128,700
Buildings	45,000			
– depreciation	19,000		Net worth	205,000
Net buildings and equipment		301,000		
Other assets:				
Investments		4,000		
Total assets		$351,300	Total equities	$351,300

Thus, Ted's estimated source-use statement balances if he requests a loan of $48,700 from his banker. This is an absolute minimum for the loan request, however. Ted will need some of the profits for personal living expenses, and he has made no allowance for contingencies. In addition, at the end of the period the first payment on the new loan will be due. In reality, Ted's request to the bank must be a figure that both he and the banker can live with. A conservative approach to estimating profits and other relevant changes that this expansion will make in the firm's financial statements is probably the best approach.

SUMMARY
Profit is the focal point of any business, but it is the net result of many factors, many of which are reflected by financial statements. Agribusiness managers rely on basic financial statements to interpret how the business is doing and to suggest the direction it should take.

All financial statements rely on a systematic record-keeping system. Accountants have developed highly refined sets of rules for handling every conceivable financial transaction. The daily transactions are summarized in balance sheets, profit and loss statements, and other financial reports for owners, managers, and other concerned parties.

A balance sheet shows assets, or what the business owns at a certain point. It also shows liabilities, or claims of creditors against those assets, and the value of owners' claims against the assets. Assets always equal liabilities plus net worth; the latter is included because all the assets must be claimed. Both assets and liabilities are broken down into several categories to provide a useful financial picture of the business.

The profit and loss statement summarizes the income over a period of time and then carefully matches the appropriate expenses incurred in generating the sales revenue. Any excess of income over expense is profit. The format of the profit and loss statement emphasizes the gross margin, or income left after the cost of goods sold has been covered. The gross margin is dollars left to cover operating expenses, which are generally itemized on this report.

Agribusiness managers must be familiar with the intricacies of these statements, since they become the core of many management decisions.

DISCUSSION QUESTIONS

1.   List and discuss the five major purposes of the agribusiness financial records system.

2.   Trace the steps of the financial records system from beginning to end, and explain the reason for and function of each step.

3.   List and define the major sections of the balance sheet.

4.   Draw a diagram of the balance sheet formula.

5.   List and define the major parts of the profit and loss statement. What other terms are sometimes used instead of the profit and loss statement?

6.   Why are current assets so important to the agribusiness?

7.   Discuss the meaning of depreciation and describe how it is treated on the financial statement.

8.   Define the difference between short-term and long-term liabilities.

9.   Define the difference between an expenditure and an expense from an accounting point of view.

10.   Discuss why inventory adjustments are necessary to determine the cost of goods sold.

11.   What is the difference between gross margin and net profit, and how are they related?

12.   Why do accountants usually value assets at their original cost?

THE CASE OF DONNA ROWE

Donna Rowe graduated from Plymouth High School 8 years ago with a background in vocational agriculture. Donna had worked for the Ford Motor Company as a truck driver until a year ago, when she decided to start her own business. Her father was an established poultry farmer, and through him she had learned that the Kroger Company was looking for someone to haul eggs to their egg processing plant. Donna had saved $6000, but the refrigerated truck that she needed cost $12,000. The truck was 2 years old, and she estimated that it would last for another 5 years. She also wanted to buy her own gas supply tank so that she could save on fuel for the truck, and this cost her another $500. She estimated that she would need another $500 for gas, possible repairs, small supplies, and miscellaneous expenses. Donna calculated that she needed at least $500 to make ends meet before the first check from Kroger came in. (Kroger paid for hauling eggs on a monthly basis.) Donna decided that she would be able to invest $5000 of her own money, while saving $1000 for living expenses and emergencies. Her sister agreed to keep the books, and Donna remodeled the family garage for an office at a cost of $800. She also installed a phone, a used file, a desk, a typewriter, and an adding machine, all for another $350. Her father was willing to lend her $4000 for 18 months at 8 percent interest, and the Plymouth National Bank agreed to lend her the balance. The loan was to be repaid in five equal payments of the principal, with interest charged at an annual rate of 10 percent.

At the end of the first year Donna's expenses were as follows: gas and oil $1900; repairs and tires $2100; telephone $200; office supplies and stamps $165; utilities $175; and miscellaneous supplies and costs $150. Her income from the business was $29,500. She had been making $14,000 per year when working for Ford, and she calculated that she should make at least that much to justify the time spent in the business. Her sister spent about 1 day a week in doing the office work, and Donna felt that she should be reimbursed at a rate of at least $25 a day for her efforts. Assume that her tax rate is 25 percent.

QUESTIONS

1. How much money did Donna Rowe have to borrow from the bank?

2. Draw up a balance sheet and profit and loss statement for Donna's business at the end of the first year of operation. Make whatever assumptions are needed, but be prepared to justify them.

3. Donna has a chance to buy another route for $12,000, a deal that includes a 1-year-old truck. She has a friend who is willing to drive the truck for a salary of $12,000 per year. Should Donna buy this additional route? Please explain why or why not.

• Identify the different perspectives of agribusiness financial statements as seen by owners, managers, lenders, and the government

• Explain the value of comparative data and ratio analysis in analyzing financial statements

• Interpret the different kinds of financial ratios and their use

• Understand the use of financial analysis and ratios in the decision-making process

• Summarize the value and use of ROI (return on investment) or earning-power analysis

• Describe the limitations of financial analysis

Agribusiness managers rely on financial analysis to aid their decision making.
A. Evaluating with ratios
B. Profitability analysis

INFORMATION BECOMES
KNOWLEDGE ONLY WHEN IT IS
USED

7

ANALYZING
FINANCIAL STATEMENTS

A.

B.

FINANCIAL STATEMENTS AS KNOWLEDGE

The financial statements of any agribusiness provide a wealth of information for managers, owners, lending institutions, and government. Some of this information requires little interpretation, but much of it is meaningless unless it is put into proper perspective. Many persons who look at a financial statement are like the explorer who sees an iceberg for the first time and fails to realize that what is seen is only the tip and that 90 percent of the iceberg is hidden under water. Real knowledge can be found in the financial statement, but it is not apparent to the casual observer. Without analysis, financial statements can be almost meaningless scraps of paper.

Financial analysis might be compared to a person's medical checkup, where much more is expected than a superficial glance from the doctor. For doctors to report accurately what they see, a series of tests must be performed and many questions must be asked. Those who are interested in the financial well-being and progress of the business must follow the same procedure. The business that survives and prospers will have managers who use the tools of financial analysis to check the vital financial functions and health of the firm and then prescribe the changes needed to make the business even more viable in the future. Methods by which those who are interested in the business can use financial analysis to determine how successful the business performance has been, what problems or opportunities exist, and what alternative or remedial courses of action might improve performance in the future are all discussed in this chapter.

The financial statements of an organization, because they can be interpreted from differing points of view, should provide enough perspectives to satisfy all interested parties. The community looks at what the agribusiness is spending on being a good citizen, employees are interested in their share of the revenue, the cooperative member is interested in the efficiency and savings that result from patronage, the supplier is interested in the firm's ability to market and pay for its products, and the board of directors is interested in the effectiveness of the management team in using the firm's assets and resources.

A manager such as Beryl Johnson, president of the Johnson Cattle Co., is inclined to approach the business financial statements primarily from two points of view: the ways in which the business has performed, and the ways in which financial information can improve decision making in the future. Profit is the primary gauge for success or failure. The manager must also bear in mind that the financial statements and their analysis should provide good, accurate information for lenders, investors, and government, since success requires the satisfaction of these interested parties.

When Pilar Ramorez invested in Monsanto, she had a high degree of interest in the business's profits and general health. However, her primary interest was centered on the rate of return for the funds she had invested. She expected her investment to equal or surpass alternative investment opportunities with similar risks. Members of cooperatives, on the other hand, concentrate their interest on the efficiency of the firm and the savings accruing to them through their patronage.

Meanwhile, Craig DeWitt, who heads the commercial loan department of Farmers' Bank & Trust, is interested in a firm's profits, because it is an important barometer of the firm's ability to repay loans. Because he is interested in protecting the loan against loss, the firm's assets versus liabilities are a primary focus for him, as for all lenders.

Governmental units are interested in financial statements from several points of view, depending on their particular needs. For example, the Internal Revenue Service is interested in profits, the tax assessor is interested in asset valuation, and the Labor Department is interested in wages. Each of the many governmental units will require certain kinds of information, and supplying it in proper form is mandatory for the business.

The agribusiness manager must be aware of each of the perspectives in designing and analyzing the financial statement of the business.

How Often Should Financial Statements Be Analyzed?
A successful business operation depends greatly on managerial planning. However, since planning involves the consideration of an uncertain future, even the best management plans have gone astray. Therefore, the management team requires a continuous reading of the firm's progress, or lack of it, toward previously established goals. Many businesses fail because management discovered too late that plans were going wrong. Through continual evaluation of financial records, management might have recognized the problem as it was developing, which would have allowed sufficient time for corrective action.

An analogy might be taken from an automobile's oil supply. There is a pressure gauge to indicate when the oil level is dangerously low; however, the sensible motorist will have the oil checked periodically when getting gas to forewarn of potential problems. It is the same with business records. These records should be timely enough to prevent serious problems from developing. A spot-check of the business's health should be taken at regular intervals. In most businesses, the financial statements should be prepared and analyzed on a monthly basis, or at the very least on a quarterly basis, so that problems or opportunities can be determined before they develop or pass by. Only very small and simple businesses can depend on the annual preparation and analysis of financial statements. The cost of the process is small compared to the risk of discovering too late that problems or opportunities have been missed.

What Areas Require Analysis?
The collection of data can become an unending process with increasing costs and diminishing returns. Generally, data not relevant to the decision-making process are useless as far as management is concerned.

Business managers require information on:

1. The firm's cash position; that is, its abaility to meet current commitments, such as payrolls and supply purchases (liquidity)

2. The firm's ability to repay long-term loans and debts (solvency)

3. Trends in revenues and costs, such as production costs, sales, overhead costs, and wages

4. Trends in production and performance, measured in accordance with previously established standards of efficiency

5. The firm's capital structure; data on sources and uses of funds and the firm's ability to meet future change and expansion

6. The firm's success in terms of actual profitability and also in terms of trends in profitability

7. The firm's use of such resources as assets, return on investments, and return to present and future investors

8. The competency of management teams in terms of their use of the resources of the firm

Begin by Establishing Bench Marks

The interpretation of financial information need not be a complex process. It is centered largely around developing bench marks or points of reference. Much information can be secured by very simple procedures. One of the easiest ways to determine trends and identify problems or opportunities is simply to compare the current period with similar periods from the past: last year with this year or with an average figure, for example.

At this point, a most important concept should be noted. Financial analysis and records do *not* solve problems or create opportunities— people do. All analysis of records can do is to help define and identify problems and opportunities. Alternative courses of action or restraints may be suggested, but these records do not have a cognitive value.

Suppose that David Hill, comptroller of the Paramont Canning Company, notes that accounts receivable for December stands at $358,000. That figure in and of itself may have little significance. However, if he notes that last year's December accounts receivable was $260,000, he can be alerted to a potential problem or opportunity (see Exhibit 7-1).

Many reasons could account for the change. More questions and answers may well be needed to provide sufficient information for the manager. Product prices could simply have gone up 25 percent, thereby raising the value of accounts receivable, or the total number of sales could have been 25 percent higher.

The critical issue is that a simple comparison with a past period gave the figure on the page added significance. This simple and easily

PARAMONT CANNING COMPANY
BALANCE SHEET
DECEMBER 31, 1984

ASSETS	DECEMBER 31, 1984	DECEMBER 31, 1983
Current assets:		
Cash	$ 265,000	$ 202,000
Marketable securities	350,000	380,000
Accounts receivable	358,000	260,000
Inventory	545,000	590,000
Total current assets	$1,518,000	$1,432,000

prepared comparison is one of the best methods for identifying points where questions should be raised by the manager (see Exhibit 7-1).

Another excellent comparison is provided by the financial statement and the budgeted forecasts. This is particularly true if the former is a profit and loss statement. Management of Somane Farm & Home Store can compare actual operating results with the budget and with last year's performance figures. Analysis indicates significant gross-margin problems (see Exhibit 7-2).

COMMON-SIZE STATEMENTS
Common-size statements are another useful method of analysis. Again, their greatest functional benefit is to put things in perspective. *Common-size analysis* simply expresses the profit and loss and balance sheet figures as percentages of some key base figure, which could be derived from similar businesses or from the firm's own total sales, total assets, budgets, or forecasts. They provide the manager with bench marks that give figures added dimension.

For example, the Somane Farm and Home Store (Exhibit 7-2) may show a figure of $5350 for sales promotion in the "This year to date" column. When one realizes that this accounts for 3 percent of gross sales, the magnitude of the sales promotion figure takes form. Comparison with similar figures from the past yields even more meaning. Realization that last year's promotion expense was only $4500 might elicit a hazy reaction, but a comparison with a promotion expense last year that constituted only 2.6 percent of gross sales will trigger an immediate response. When Jerry Holmes, the sales manager, looks at this comparison, he can see that promotion expenses have increased by 16 percent, and that the figure is already substantially over the budgeted amount for the entire year. Action, or at least investigation, is called for at this point.

Common-size analysis should include raw figures from the statement to prevent distortion or masking. This is particularly true when

EXHIBIT Somane Farm & Home Store Can Compare Actual Operating Results to the Budget and to Last Year's Forecast
7-2

EXPENSE BUDGET AND CONTROL REPORT
FARM & HOME STORE, SOMANE, N.Y.

	Last year to date (actual)		This year to date (budget)		This year to date (actual)		90-day (budget)		90-day (actual)	
	DOLLARS	PERCENT OF SALES	DOLLARS	PERCENT OF SALES	DOLLARS	PERCENT OF SALES	DOLLARS	PERCENT OF SALES	DOLLARS	SALES
Net sales	175,502	100.0	180,000	100.0	178,406	100.0	81,889	100.0	——	——
Cost of goods sold	131,566	76.8	135,000	75.0	136,301	76.4	62,889	76.8	——	——
Gross margin	44,639	24.1	46,500	25.8	42,105	23.6	19,704	24.1	——	——
Full-time labor	19,764	11.3	20,500	11.4	19,764	11.1	9,882	12.1	——	——
Part-time labor	4,392	2.5	5,000	2.8	4,392	2.5	2,196	2.7	——	——
Overtime labor	0	0	0	0	0	0	0	0	——	——
Management fee	4,500	2.6	4,500	2.5	4,569	2.6	2,000	2.4	——	——
Total property expenses	1,800	1.0	1,800	1.0	1,800	1.0	900	1.1	——	——
Warehouse expenses	550	.3	500	.3	580	.3	250	.3	——	——
Advance and sales promotion	4,500	2.6	4,500	2.5	5,350	3.0	2,000	2.4	——	——
Interest	3,750	2.1	3,750	2.1	3,583	2.0	1,875	2.3	——	——
Other general expenses	365	.2	500	.3	1,244	.7	165	.2	——	——
Total expenses	39,621	22.6	41,050	22.8	41,282	23.1	19,268	23.5	——	——
Operating margin	5,018	2.9	3,950	2.2	823	.5	436	.5	——	——

comparing percentages with those of firms with a similar nature. One firm may be very large and have sales in the millions, while a smaller firm's sales might be in the thousands. Figures would help amplify and clarify differences.

RATIO ANALYSES

Great strides have been made in the use of ratios to analyze financial statements. The strength of financial ratio analyses lies in the fact that they eliminate the weaknesses of dollar differences, which are sometimes not only confusing but may be misleading.

For example, we may consider the following table:

	COMPANY A	COMPANY B
Current assets	$200,000	$1,000,000
Current liabilities	100,000	900,000
Excess of current assets (margin)	$100,000	$ 100,000

Both companies have the same dollar margin of $100,000 current assets over current liabilities. However, Company A, all things being equal, is in a healthier financial condition than Company B. In this case, it is the ratio of current assets to current liabilities that provides the most accurate reading of the situation. The figures are, of course, so obvious that to calculate the exact ratio is hardly necessary.

Agribusiness managers and analysts are likely to develop their own favorite set of financial indicators. It would not be productive to present either an exhaustive set of ratios to consider or a selective set of indicators that are crucial, or even all that are useful in every possible situation, since agribusinesses vary so greatly in size and kind.

Why Use Financial Ratio Analysis?

Financial ratio analysis is often used to measure the performance of the many facets of the business mentioned previously. When properly used (with its limitations understood), it can be a very helpful management aid. More and more agribusiness managers are using ratio analysis extensively because it not only provides better indicators for managerial decisions but also is useful in the following ways:

1. *Easy to calculate:* Most ratios compare two statistics that are normally provided in the profit and loss statement or on the balance sheet. Because these data are readily available at a more or less fixed cost, not much time or expense is required to compute a ratio.

2. *Easy to make comparisons with:* They allow comparison of past with present performance, as well as comparisons with firms of a similar nature. They are of particular value to boards of directors of the corporate firm.

3. *Easily understood:* Not all members of the management team are financial sophisticates, and ratios provide overview information simply and clearly for all management personnel.

4. *Able to communicate a firm's financial position to interested parties outside management:* For example, financial authorities and stockholders, cooperative patrons, or investors may rely on ratios to determine a firm's creditworthiness and success in the use of its resources.

Limitations of Financial Ratio Analysis

Because financial ratio analysis is being used extensively nowadays, there is a potential for more and more misuse of the technique. In spite of their advantages, financial ratios are merely indicators. If a particular facet of the business is headed for trouble, a change in a ratio can only sound a warning. Even a drastic change in a given ratio may not isolate and identify the actual cause of the problem. More often than not, additional analysis is required before the appropriate corrective action can be taken. Care must be taken to ensure that all comparisons are between elements that are genuinely similar in nature.

Changes in the accounting methods of the agribusiness itself, or differences between the firm's accounting methods and those of similar firms, may limit the use of ratios. If Hilltop Fertilizer were to change the way it values inventory, assets, and depreciation method, comparisons of its ratios with previous ratios would lose their validity. Time factors also pose a significant restraint on ratio analysis. Financial statements are indicative of one period of time. Comparing one monthly period with another or one yearly statement with another can present a distorted view of the business. Comparing Hilltop's May inventory with July accounts receivable would provide a ratio that was virtually useless. Bad information or analysis can be worse than no information at all.

Selecting the Proper Ratios

Agribusiness managers should exercise care in selecting those periodic ratios that provide fuel for decision making in their own unique businesses. Professional advice from outside the business can often be of great help. The first consideration to be made in selecting critical ratios is whether the ratios cover those areas of the business where knowledge is critical to its very existence. Hilltop would have a high degree of interest in accounts receivable and inventory because its fertilizer business is so seasonal. Loss of control over either of these important sectors could be fatal to maintaining its liquidity. Large variations in different periods are therefore an important criterion for analyzing accounts. Another factor is the sheer size of the account. A food processor like Paramont Canning Company would be extremely aware of changes in costs for direct labor, raw materials, and supplies, because they account for the major portion of the production costs. Agribusiness managers must study their own operations and use those financial ratios that are best for the unique business involved.

Most agribusiness managers will want ratios to help monitor profitability, liquidity, solvency, and resource use. Just a few of the more commonly used and most helpful agribusiness ratio analyses are discussed. These ratios will be related to the balance sheet and the profit and loss statement for Hilltop Fertilizer, Inc. (review Exhibits 6-1 and 6-2 in Chapter 6). From a management point of view, these ratios can be presented under the following headings:

1. Profitability indexes or ratios

2. Liquidity indexes or ratios

3. Solvency indexes or ratios

4. Operational efficiency indexes or ratios

We will discuss them in that order.

Profitability Ratios   The term *profitability ratios* refers to several separate indicators or ratios that help determine a firm's profitability and performance record.

The relationship between kinds or amounts of earnings[1] that Hilltop generated and sales *(the earnings on sales ratio)* is shown here:

Earnings ÷ sales = EOS (earnings on sales)
$100,000 ÷ $1,000,000 = 0.10 or 10%
(From profit and loss, r and a)

The earnings on sales ratio (Equation 1) brings us face-to-face with management decisions that reflect operative efficiency and pricing policy. Earnings may be increased by changes in pricing policy. Low prices may generate increased sales, but could produce zero profits, while higher prices might reduce sales significantly. The pricing strategy must be developed by careful consideration of the competitive environment. Sales forecasts can be helpful in this area, and ratios give a good reading on sales projections.

On the cost side, Hilltop can attempt, by management decisions, to reduce such things as labor, administrative expenses, and selling costs.

Managers often find it helpful to look at income after all business costs of interest and taxes have been added, or the *profit on sales ratio*:

Net profit ÷ sales = POS (profit on sales)
$50,000 ÷ $1,000,000 = 0.05 or 5%   (2)
(From profit and loss, w and a)

Equation 1 indicates Hilltop's ability to pay interest on its investment and to develop helpful information for decisions as to owner equity and borrowed capital alternatives. Equation 2, on the other hand, indicates how well Hilltop fared on profits returned when all costs and

[1]Earnings are net operating profit without nonoperating costs or income.

other income of the business had been included and compared to overall sales. This ratio is one on which all those interested in Hilltop will place a priority, and changes will be monitored carefully.

Usually, the assets of a firm are not owned entirely by the investors. A *common ratio,* which determines the return on investor ownership, is particularly valued by owners:

Net profit ÷ net worth = POEC (Profit on equity capital)
$50,000 ÷ $300,000 = 0.167 or 16.7%   (3)
(from profit and loss, w; balance sheet, qq)

This ratio is helpful in determining the wisdom of investment in Hilltop's assets. It can be invaluable in encouraging additional investment of equity capital if greater cash flow is needed in the business. Stockholders also use this ratio as an indicator of the value of their stock.

Another commonly used ratio is the *gross margin,* which is total sales less cost of goods sold divided by total sales. These are the funds Hilltop has left to pay the operational and other outside business costs.

(Sales − cost of goods sold) ÷ sales = GM (gross margin)
($1,000,000 − $750,000) ÷ $1,000,000 = 0.25 or 25%   (4)
(From profit and loss, a and b)

Here Hilltop reveals prices received for merchandise sold, and in particular the *product mix* (combination of products sold). More detailed analysis may be indicated here if the gross margin is too low. Costs of goods or raw product and leakage are pinpointed for further study. This ratio is crucial. Any drop in gross margin is a signal for immediate managerial action. Small changes here have a great effect on profits.

Liquidity Ratios   Now we will analyze some of the most common liquidity ratios that are helpful in determining Hilltop's ability to meet its short-run obligations. The most popular liquidity ratio is called the *current ratio:*

Total current assets ÷ total current liabilities = CR (current ratio)
$300,000 ÷ $150,000 = 2   (5)
(From balance sheet, h and gg)

This ratio indicates Hilltop's ability to meet current bills and obligations. There is considerable thought that this may not be a positive enough indication of a firm's real ability to meet current needs. The need to quickly liquidate inventories, accounts receivable, marketable securities, etc., may cause a sharp decrease in their value. Therefore, managers use a second ratio that more clearly delineates a firm's ability to meet immediate cash needs. This is called the *acid ratio:*

(Cash + marketable securities + accounts receivable)
÷ total current liabilities = AR (acid ratio)   (6)
($50,000 + $150,000) ÷ $150,000 = 1.33
(From balance sheet, c, d, and gg)

While at first glance Hilltop would appear to be in good shape, difficulty in collecting accounts receivable could cause problems if there were a sudden drain on cash.

This ratio is of great interest to lenders of short-term funds in particular. These funds may require modification of marketable securities and accounts receivable, because the immediate cash value may be lower than the ratio indicates.

A new or rapidly growing firm with immediate cash needs for labor, supplies, and goods must be more aware of this ratio than older, more established businesses. The ease of converting inventory to cash must also be considered. It is possible for a firm to be making a profit, and have a strong net worth position in relation to total assets, and still be so starved for available working capital that it is unable to take advantage of discounts or quantity buying, meet emergencies, or even pay current bills.

Solvency Ratios   A third challenge to management is keeping the firm solvent. *Solvency* is related primarily to a firm's ability to meet long-run claims or debts. These ratios pinpoint the portion of a business's capital requirements that is being furnished by owners. Solvency measures the kinds of problems that lenders will incur in recovering their money in the event of business failure. These ratios can have a real effect on the amount of long-term money a firm can borrow. They also affect alternative sources of outside capital. Since creditors supply a greater portion of the capital and assume a greater share of the risk, they normally demand more control over management's decision prerogative or independence. These ratios can also indicate when a firm should consider borrowing more of its capital needs, with consequent opportunity for increasing its return on its own investment. The first solvency ratio (Equation 7) indicates the relationship of Hilltop's net worth to the total debts of the firm:

$$\text{Total liabilities} \div \text{net worth} = \text{solvency ratio}$$
$$\$200,000 \div \$300,000 = 0.667 \tag{7}$$
(From balance sheet, ll and qq)

In Hilltop, we find a ratio of 0.667 to 1, or total liabilities that are equal to 66.7 percent of owner equity.

Here we can see the ownership interest in contrast to the creditor interest in the firm. Many lenders require a 1 to 1 ratio as the absolute lower limit. Changes in this ratio over a period of time can be of great significance in planning long-range financial programs for Hilltop. Of great importance in analysis of this ratio is consideration of the liquidity aspects of current assets. Here we find Hilltop having a large percentage of its current assets in accounts receivable and inventory, which could be of questionable value without further investigation. Lenders therefore may tend to discount Hilltop's relatively good ratio.

Another solvency ratio (Equation 8) involves the relationship between what the owners are contributing toward supporting the firm and the total net assets of the firm.

$$\text{Net worth} \div \text{total net assets}^2 = \text{solvency}$$
$$\$300,000 \div \$290,000 = 1.04 \tag{8}$$
(From balance sheet, qq, h, gg, q, and kk)

Again, there is no exact standard for every business, but usually if less than 50 percent of the total net assets of a firm is contributed by owners, one is apt to find solvency problems developing and to experience difficulty in securing more long- and short-term credit.

A third solvency ratio determines the percentage that lenders are contributing to the permanent or long-term investor capital of the firm:

$$\text{Long-term debt} \div \text{net worth} = \text{solvency}$$
$$\$50,000 \div \$300,000 = 0.167 \tag{9}$$
(From balance sheet, kk and qq)

Changes in this ratio can signal danger if the lenders' portion becomes excessively high. By the same token, a low percentage invested by lenders could signal the opportunity for expansion or additional borrowing potential. It would appear from this ratio that Hilltop could expand its long-term debt and replace some of its short-term debt if it so desired. Expansion plans and current interest rates would be important factors in making this decision.

Efficiency Ratios The final management challenge to be discussed in relation to ratio use is in the area of firm efficiency. This area, in particular, offers the greatest opportunity for Hilltop management to develop unique, meaningful ratios that will be of greatest value to its business in the efficiency or operations area.

The *turnover ratio* can be used to determine the intensity with which Hilltop's assets are used, as measured by the number of times assets turn over in a period:

$$\text{Total sales} \div \text{total assets} = \text{turnover}$$
$$\$1,000,000 \div \$500,000 = 2 \tag{10}$$
(From profit and loss, a; balance sheet, s)

This figure shows that Hilltop turned its assets twice during the year. For this ratio to take on meaning, Hilltop managers would have to compare it with the situation in previous years and to the turnover ratio in similar businesses. If last year's turnover ratio had been only 1.8, Hilltop would know that it is moving in the right direction. A retail grocer would be very unhappy with this ratio because of the necessity for rapid turnover in that kind of business, while a storage company would be extremely happy with this ratio, since it uses a huge amount of assets as compared with sales.

---

[2]Net working capital + net fixed assets = total net assets: (h − gg) + (q − kk) = total net assets. Net working capital is figured by subtracting current liabilities from current assets, and net fixed assets are figured by subtracting long-term liabilities from fixed assets.

The turnover ratio (Equation 10) suggests that the more Hilltop can sell with a given set of assets, the higher its return on investments will be. Many large agribusiness firms use this as a primary measure of effectiveness in the management team. Management alternatives that affect this rate are primarily based on increasing sales volume by using assets more effectively, by increasing prices, by reducing ineffectively used assets, by reducing accounts receivable, or by choosing better alternatives for use of available cash.

In most firms, the *inventory turnover ratio* is of great concern. One's whole business policy can be influenced by this measure of efficiency or some variable thereof:

Sales ÷ ending inventory = rate of turnover
$1,000,000 ÷ $80,000 = 12.5   (11)
(From profit and loss, a; balance sheet, e)

Here, caution must be used, since the inventory must be meaningful. This is a static reading that is taken. In Hilltop, with an extremely seasonal business, the ending inventory is not representative, and could provide a meaningless figure. The manager may need to take beginning and ending inventory and average them; he or she may also take monthly or estimated average inventories to gain an acceptable figure. In a firm like Hilltop, the typical monthly average would probably be a valid figure to use in analyses. A comparison between the firm's sales level and inventory level, must utilize the correct figures. If, for example, the firm values inventory "at retail or shelf price" in making comparisons, then the sales figure must be net sales. However, many firms value inventory on an at-cost basis, and it would be misleading to compare this to net sales. The correct figure for comparison in this case would be cost of goods sold.

The rate of turnover indicates how successfully working capital has been managed. If capital is being tied up in inventory, a higher margin will be required on sales, because too much stock is on hand. It can also add a severe burden of interest on inventory investment if short-term financing at high interest rates is being used. Too high a rate of turnover could indicate a lost opportunity for sales because of out-of-date stock or inability to meet delivery requirements. Agribusiness managers must also consider discounts for early delivery and match these against current interest rates. If Hilltop has storage facilities for fertilizer and the discount is greater than its interest rate, available profits can be enhanced by the large inventory.

Another measure of efficiency is found in the average collection period of accounts receivable. An extended period for collection of accounts receivable could indicate that profits might be reduced because of added collection costs, interest on funds needed to support the account, and bad-debt losses. On the other hand, too low a figure could indicate that overly strict credit policies were causing lost sales. Two important criteria should be used; generally, the amount of the period of collections (1) should match that of others in the industry, and (2) should be at least equal to the time extended by suppliers or vendors of the firm. All this can be checked by means of the *receivables ratio:*

(Receivables ÷ sales) × 360 days = days sales in receivables
($150,000 ÷ $1,000,000) × 360 = 53.6 days   (12)
(From balance sheet, d; profit and loss, a)

A firm's credit policy and standing in relationship to creditors, as well as changes or trends, should be indicators of efficiency in managing working capital. One of the best rules of thumb in relation to the receivables ratio is that the collection period should not exceed the regular payment period by more than one-third. If, for example, the credit policy states that accounts are due in 30 days, the calculated collection period should not exceed 40 days.

We must use caution in determining the most efficient receivables ratio. Accounts receivable may vary from time to time or seasonally in a firm because of the nature of its business, and this factor should always be taken into consideration.

A whole gamut of efficiency ratios can be developed by management in relationship to costs and sales. These should be unique and meaningful to the individual business and to the type of industry. In this area, management should be operating on predetermined control standards of efficiency. We shall examine only one specialized efficiency ratio, but the wage efficiency ratio (Equation 13) will clearly indicate the possibilities that exist:

Labor cost ÷ total sales = percentage of labor cost
$75,000 ÷ $1,000,000 = 0.075 or 7.5%   (13)
(From profit and loss, e and a)

It is particularly important for management to monitor labor costs, especially if new operations or equipment is being considered.

Summary of Ratio Analyses

1. Some ratios are expressed in reverse order; that is, "sales to receivables" to one person may be "receivables to sales" to another. Either is correct, but the interpretation should also be reversed.

2. All ratio comparisons should be based on similar data from similar businesses; to compare the "sales to fixed assets" ratio of a steel manufacturing plant with the same ratio for a small farm supply business would be ridiculous.

3. In addition to comparisons of ratios between companies, comparisons of ratios from period to period in the same agribusiness are justified.

4. Trend is an important feature of financial ratio analysis; for example, gradually improving ratios are more impressive than declining ratios.

5. The development and use of a large number of financial ratios may add confusion to chaos; hence, ratios should be specifically selected with regard to the nature of the problems for which solutions are desired.

6. In addition to financial ratios, ratios related to other phases of a business are often used as measures of efficiency; for example, inventory turnover ratios. These may be called management ratios, physical ratios, efficiency ratios, or industrial ratios.

7. Faith in financial ratio analysis often becomes so strong with some people that it becomes their only basis for decision making. At their best, ratios are aids to sound decision making, not substitutes for it.

FUNDAMENTAL PROFITABILITY AND PERFORMANCE MEASURES

Three fundamental measures of how well the business is being managed are (1) profits on sales, (2) return on assets, and (3) leverage. The combination of these very important aspects into a single index or ratio provides one of the most useful management ratios available to measure the performance of the agribusiness and the skill and ability of the management team. Many sophisticated managers, bankers, investors, and boards of directors depend on this conceptual measure as the primary gauge of a business's success. The combination of these three factors or measures into a single ratio is called ROI (return on investment), that is, earning power of the firm.

ROI in Perspective

Figure 7-1 shows the step-by-step process of developing a ROI analysis system. ROI is measured here in terms of return on net worth, or RONW. The chart illustrates the three key component ratios which individually and together affect RONW. Management can use this chart as a tracking system or "early warning" system to determine when action is needed if the firm is to continue to move toward its profit and ROI goals.

Figure 7-1 indicates that ROI is directly affected by (1) the earnings which the firm is able to generate from sales (net profit divided by sales), (2) the intensity with which the assets of the firm are used, measured by asset turnover (total sales divided by total assets), and (3) the use of outsiders' funds to expand the business, measured by the leverage ratio (total assets divided by net worth).

Each of these factors is important to reaching the firm's profit goal, and should be carefully considered. The top part of Figure 7-1 relates to the earnings picture and brings the manager face to face with problems related to personnel, pricing, product mix, etc. Careful control of expenses is essential, and monitoring systems must be implemented to deal with internal as well as external changes over time, i.e., personnel and management decisions versus competitive decisions that must be made.

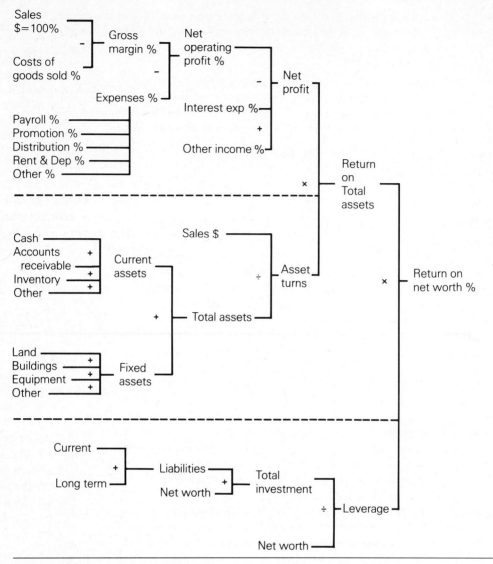

Figure 7-1 The step-by-step process that produces an ROI.

The asset turnover concept suggests that the higher the sales volume produced with a given set of assets, the higher the firm's ROI will be. For example, as more milk is processed through a dairy plant of a given size, the associated assets are being utilized more effectively, up to a point. A firm may attempt to push volume to a level at which physical processing or handling capacity is reached. However, the cost of squeezing out the marginal volume may be prohibitive.

As a practical matter, most agribusiness firms have some "slack" in this regard and are typically struggling to maintain or increase volume

FINANCIAL MANAGEMENT AND CONTROL OF THE AGRIBUSINESS

through their facilities. For example, the Payment-in-Kind program of 1983 led to a great deal of excess capacity in many Midwestern grain elevators. Managers adopted strategies, some successful and some not, to attract scarce grain supplies to their facilities.

In the asset utilization area, managers must frequently evaluate their investment in assets: when equipment should be replaced, what fixed facilities are needed and what should be rented, whether inventories can be reduced without decreasing sales, how extra cash should be invested, etc. All of these decisions relate directly to asset efficiency and indirectly back to the earnings ratio.

The third critical area of the profitability analysis system relates to solvency. Should the firm expand, given an acceptable solvency ratio? What implications does expansion have for the firm's future earnings? Can a larger firm be managed as efficiently? Obviously these are all tough questions faced by management, stockholders, bankers, etc. However, proper evaluation of the "correct" solvency relationship for the firm can have a dramatic impact on return on net worth.

Improvements in any of the three individual ratios will improve profitability as measured by RONW. It is important for the manager to understand that these ratios are interrelated; changes in one may affect performance in the others. Thus, the final impact of a given change in the firm's RONW must be viewed as a dynamic relationship among these three separate ratios.

Price Is an Important Consideration
When a price increases, some customers will shift to other firms and some will remain. If it is foreseen that most customers would stay despite the price increase, the earning power would rise because any decrease in turnover would be offset by an increase in the sales margin.

If the firm lowered prices, hopefully an increase in the turnover would offset the decline in the sales margin. But the question is, how much will sales be increased, or what is the "elasticity" of demand?

Successful use of a low sales margin and high turnover is evident in the rapid increase in the number and patronage of discount houses. Generally, businesses with a low turnover will have a high margin, and firms with a high turnover will have a low margin, which is the case with the discount house.

ROI, or the earning power of the business, offers the advantage of bringing together in a single figure the complex relationship of turnover and margin, and allows managers to improve their knowledge of how decisions and changes made in either area affect the other. Decision making in agribusiness does not occur in a vacuum. An attempt to control inventory or reduce assets is likely to affect sales. Certain items may be out of stock, for instance, and some sales or turnover will be lost. ROI will help the agribusiness manager gauge the effects of such decisions on overall earning power.

While ROI is certainly not a ratio that can be compared from agribusiness to agribusiness on an unqualified basis, it does offer a more easily compared measure of different firms' resources than almost any other ratio. For this reason, ROI is considered the most accurate measure of effective resource use by managers, boards of directors, lending institutions, investors, and others interested in the business. The ROI is sensitive enough so that even small changes in trends should cause the manager to be elated (if it is improving) and try more of the same, or to be concerned (if it is declining) and begin searching for methods of improvement. Changes in figures on the turnover, earnings, or solvency can also point to or help identify places where problems or opportunities arise. For example, if Hilltop Fertilizer were to note a drop in its ROI figure and see that the turnover figure was up slightly, but the earnings side was down somewhat, it could concentrate its management efforts in such areas as expenses involved in sales or administration or price. Careful use of ROI can be the single most helpful indicator of complete firm performance available to the agribusiness manager for classifying expenses into categories on the profit and loss statement (sales, administration, etc.) so that the problems and opportunities can be more easily located to remedial reasons.

GRAPHING TO INCREASE UNDERSTANDING

Simple graphs of financial ratios often enhance the ability of managers to interpret data and information. Graphing of important ratios, for example, allows many more periods and time spans to be compared; the more time or periods or ways in which something can be compared, the more meaningful data become (see Figure 7-2).

The graph could illustrate the competitive pricing war Hilltop was waging with local fertilizer companies. As Hilltop lowered prices, sales volume or turnover increased, but at the same time, earnings on sales decreased as a percentage. If a further factor, net operating profit, were compared, Hilltop could measure visually the net effect of price changes,

Figure 7-2 Simple graphs of financial ratios often enhance the ability of managers to interpret.

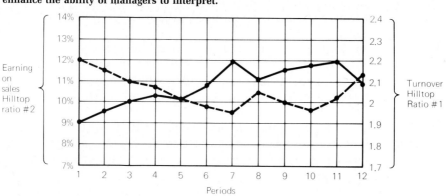

FINANCIAL MANAGEMENT AND CONTROL OF THE AGRIBUSINESS

and plan its sales strategy accordingly. Monthly reassessment by means of these ratios would allow Hilltop to see whether its plans were still on target.

Graphing increases comprehension by presenting a visual picture, and it allows for comparison of separate aspects of financial information in a very clear illustration. A graph also can be widely distributed to less sophisticated members of the management team for use in decision making, since it is easier to conceptualize than a set of numbers.

SUMMARY

Financial statements provide a wealth of information for a variety of persons and organizations interested in evaluating the agribusiness. Owners, managers, lenders, and government agencies all look at financial statements from a different perspective.

Analysis of financial statements is often comparative, over time, against budget, or with similar firms. Ratios show important financial relationships in the business. These ratios must be understood and used carefully or they will be misleading; used properly, they are indicators of strengths and weaknesses in the business.

Ratios generally measure profitability, liquidity, solvency, or efficiency. Return on the owners' investment is the most fundamental measure of profit. The ROI chart shows the relationship of sales and expenses with assets. Sometimes graphing financial ratios over time is a highly valuable management tool.

Financial analysis is a fundamental management tool for the agribusiness manager. Although it is not a substitute for human judgment, financial analysis gives the manager important insights for decisions.

DISCUSSION QUESTIONS

1. Discuss the major value of financial analysis to agribusiness managers.

2. Describe the major interest taken in an agribusiness by a general manager, the president of its bank, a prospective investor, and a government official.

3. Name some of the reasons why an agribusiness firm should have a monthly financial statement. Under what circumstances would a less frequent financial statement be sufficient?

4. List the advantages of ratio analysis for the agribusiness manager.

5. List the limitations of ratio analysis for the agribusiness manager.

6. Discuss the value of common-size statements to the agribusiness manager.

7. What criteria should the agribusiness manager use to select ratios needed by the business?

8. What major areas of the agribusiness are usually covered by ratio analysis?

9. Discuss the major reason for each of the four areas of ratio analysis and what they illustrate to those who are interested in the firm.

10. What are the advantages of ROI as a tool of analysis for agribusiness managers?

11. What specific measures might agribusiness managers take if the earnings side of the ROI were down? If the turnover side were down?

12. Discuss the merits of graphing ratios; use the Hilltop ratios to develop a graph.

THE CASE OF MILLER DAIRY
Use the following condensed financial statement from Miller Dairy, Inc., to draw up an ROI for the company.

QUESTIONS
1. Follow the step-by-step formula given in Figure 7-1 as a guide.

2. When finished, develop at least one solvency, liquidity, profitability, and efficiency ratio, using the same information.

CONDENSED FINANCIAL STATEMENT
MILLER DAIRY COMPANY

BALANCE SHEET		PROFIT & LOSS STATEMENT	
Current assets		Sales	$1,500,000
Cash	$ 70,000	Cost of goods sold	1,250,000
Accounts receivable	240,000	Gross margin	$ 250,000
Inventory	250,000		
	$560,000	Sales expenses	$ 50,000
Net fixed assets	$250,000	Administrative	
Total assets	$810,000	expenses	25,000
Current liabilities		Other expenses	25,000
Accounts payable	$210,000	Total expenses	$ 100,000
Notes payable	125,000	Operating profit	$ 150,000
	$335,000	Interest expense	10,000
Long-term liabilities	$115,000	Income tax	50,000
Total liabilities	$450,000	Net income	$ 90,000
Owners equity	$200,000	Dividend paid	$ 10,000
Retained earnings	$160,000	Retained earnings	$ 80,000
Total liabilities and net worth	$810,000		

OBJECTIVES

• List the reasons for increasing an agribusiness's financial resources, and the questions to ask before doing so

• Describe the kinds of capital available to the agribusiness

• Describe the various kinds of loans, funds, and other capital available

• Calculate the cost of different kinds of borrowing

• Determine the amount that an agribusiness should borrow

• Utilize cash budgets and pro forma financial statements in financial planning

• Be able to choose a lending institution and prepare to seek the loan

• Describe means of generating capital funds internally

Agribusinesses rely on a variety of sources to finance their businesses.
A. Cooperative banks
B. Commercial lenders
C. Borrower-lender relationship

THE AGRIBUSINESS MANAGER MUST
HAVE THE "MIDAS TOUCH"

FINANCING THE AGRIBUSINESS

A.

B.

C.

THE GOLDEN TOUCH

Money is the lifeblood of any agribusiness. It is needed for financing such assets as machinery and equipment, accounts receivable, labor, materials, supplies, and taxes. This is why the managers of an agribusiness are expected to be "King Midas." Everything that they touch must turn to gold, in order to repay those who favor the business with the use of their money. Whenever and wherever financial resources are secured, money is siphoned into the enterprise with the full expectation that it will be returned with a profit. This "golden" or profit-making touch is not a myth, and the manager who lacks it will find the agribusiness hard pressed for funds. There are three sources from which the manager may raise the funds needed to operate an agribusiness: (1) investment by owners, (2) borrowing, or (3) funds generated by profits and depreciation. A study by Gorman and Shea shows that the major source of funds for businesses (over 50 percent) is the net worth of the firm (also called "owned capital"). The larger a company is, the more it depends on net worth as a source of funds. One major reason for this is that larger companies usually enjoy access to public offerings of their stocks or equity, along with the ability to attract investors to them, a situation that is not shared by smaller companies. Whatever the kind or size of a business, its ability to generate profits will ultimately determine the amount of funds that are made available for its use. That is why managers need the "King Midas Touch."

REASONS FOR INCREASING FINANCIAL RESOURCES

The ultimate reason for increasing the financial resources of an agribusiness is to increase its revenues and profits by generating additional business. Extra funds are used for general purposes, to increase liquidity or cash position, or for expansion and growth. An agribusiness may find that its funds are tied up in fixed or current assets and that it is unable to meet its day-to-day obligations. Bills cannot be paid with such nonliquid assets as accounts receivable, inventory, new orders, or a piece of equipment. Consequently, an agribusiness requires working cash. The principal source of working cash must be the income generated by the business itself, but in short-term situations additional cash may be required to meet the day-to-day obligations of the business. This is particularly true if the agribusiness is seasonal in nature, as so many of them are. In that case, cash funds can become tied up in inventory and in accounts receivable, which will not translate to cash until sometime later. As a rule, most agribusinesses find it advisable to keep on hand enough cash to equal 20 to 25 percent of the amount represented by their current liabilities. This ensures the payment of short-term and unexpected obligations.

The most important use for additional financial resources is for expansion. Expansion can require either short- or long-range commitment of funds. Short-range expansion involves such factors as increased labor, increased inventories, and increased accounts receivable. Long-run expansion encourages more ambitious projects, such as the purchase of new equipment, land, and buildings.

The objective of increasing the capital of an agribusiness is to multiply its sales volume and revenues, and consequently its profit, through the shrewd application of increased assets. *Capital,* or the financial resources of a business, comprises in its broadest sense all the assets of that business, and represents both owned and borrowed amounts.

DETERMINING WHEN FINANCIAL RESOURCES SHOULD BE INCREASED

As an agribusiness manager considers the possibility of acquiring additional financial resources, several questions should be asked and carefully answered.

1. Are additional funds really needed in the agribusiness?

2. Why are additional funds needed?

3. What increases in revenue and/or profit will be generated by additional funds?

4. When will these additional funds be needed?

5. For how long a period will these additional funds be needed?

6. How much is needed in the way of additional financial resources?

7. Where can these additional funds be obtained?

8. How much will these additional funds cost the agribusiness?

9. If the funds are borrowed, how will the indebtedness be repaid?

The manager who is seeking additional financial resources for the agribusiness should use the foregoing as a checklist to select the one alternative that is most likely to be profitable.

RAY WHYTH REVISITED

A previous chapter contained the example of Ray Whyth starting his farm-building construction company some 17 years ago with $1000 in cash that he had saved plus $1000 that he had borrowed from the bank. Today, Ray's company is a corporation that is owned primarily by members of the family. Tracing the factors involved as Ray Whyth investigated an expansion opportunity will serve to illustrate the principle of financing an agribusiness.

Ray's present annual sales exceed $1 million, and although he now erects some commercial buildings and silos, his major source of revenue remains farm buildings of various kinds. His work force often exceeds fifty people. Recently, Ray was offered the opportunity of purchasing a small lumberyard in Ashley, a town of 6500 people. The yard had a yearly gross of over $750,000 and was earning 15 percent on owner equity and 5 percent of sales in net after-tax profits. Ray had used the financial tools discussed in previous chapters to analyze the business, and felt that the lumberyard would be a great opportunity to expand his own business. He knew that he had two expansion alternatives: either to expand his current operation or to diversify his business. He saw the lumberyard as an opportunity to do both at once.

Ray analyzed a number of advantages. His analysis of the lumberyard revealed that it could use an increase in turnover. By combining his building company's needs for lumber with the lumberyard's need for increased sales, he could increase the sales volume of the lumberyard by about 70 percent. The added purchasing volume for the construction company would allow him to buy lumber more cheaply because he could buy it in greater quantities and in full carloads. He could also consolidate his storage and handling operations and operate more efficiently because he would be located on a rail siding. His offices and entire operation could be moved to one location, and he figured that combining the operation would result in lower administrative costs. With savings in cost of goods sold and administrative expenses, along with more operational efficiency, he foresaw the potential of lowering the prices for both businesses and being more competitive in both marketplaces. His figures showed that even if he lowered prices by 5 percent and assumed the same sales volume, he could maintain the existing gross margins; but he hoped that sales would eventually climb as much as 50 to 100 percent because of his strongly competitive price position. At this point, the future looked very bright to Ray and his family. They felt they had successfully addressed questions 1 and 2: "Are additional funds needed?" and "Why are they needed?" While Ray's own company was in a very comfortable position financially, he knew that he would have to secure added financial resources to purchase and operate the lumberyard. The balance of this chapter will relate to the principal tools and alternatives that Ray Whyth had to consider.

KINDS OF CAPITAL AND LOANS

The next question that Ray had to ask himself was, "What kind of capital do I need?" Basically, there are four types of capital:

1. Short-term loans: 1 year or less

2. Intermediate-term loans: 1 to 5 years

3. Long-term loans: 5 years or more

4. Equity capital: no due date

Short-Term Loans

Short-term loans are generally defined as loans for 1 year or less, and they are used whenever the requirement for additional funds is temporary. Ray Whyth recognized the need for funds to build inventory for the spring and summer, when the building business is at its seasonal peak. Some of these funds would also be needed to support accounts receivable as inventory was sold to customers. An important characteristic of short-term loans is that they are usually self-liquidating, that is, they often start a chain reaction process that results in their repayment.

Loan⇒inventories⇒receivables⇒cash⇒repay loan

While short-term loans may be made on an unsecured basis to firms that are well established, there is often a requirement for *collateral*, or for the loan to be secured by some of the firm's assets. Collateral can take many forms, but for short-term loans it most often takes the form of current assets. Some of the most common kinds of collateral are inventory, accounts receivable, warehouse receipts, and marketable securities. A personal guarantee of the loan by the owners is also common. (In other words, the owner or owners endorse the note and become personally liable if the firm is unable to meet the payment.) Short-term loans may be regular-term notes, with a specific amount due at a specific time, or they may be revolving or line of credit loans. Managers who anticipate a need for short-term funds often apply for a line of credit in advance of their needs. A *line of credit* is a commitment by the lender to make available a certain sum of money to the firm, usually for a 1-year period and at a specified rate of interest, at whatever time the firm needs the loan. Usually, the loan must be repaid during the operating year of the firm. With a line of credit a manager is assured of protection in the form of cash that is available as it is needed; there is also the added advantage of not incurring interest on the borrowed funds until they are actually used. Lenders who make a line of credit available to an agribusiness often require that a monthly copy of the firm's financial statement be furnished to them so that they can monitor the financial health of the firm. Ray Whyth wanted to avail himself of a line of credit for his short-term cash needs for seasonal purposes. He did not feel that he would have a problem securing these funds because he could pledge his inventory and accounts receivable as collateral against any outstanding loans.

It is important for the agribusiness manager to recognize that short-term borrowing is only appropriate for temporary uses. When, for example, funds are borrowed to increase inventories in order to accommodate increased sales volumes, and the loan is expected to remain in force for some time, a more permanent form of funds is needed. This will increase the total working capital of the firm.

Intermediate-Term Loans

Intermediate-term loans are usually used to provide capital for from 1 to 5 years. Such a loan is almost always *amortized*, that is, paid back in installments over the life of the loan. The purpose of the intermediate-term loan is to provide the agribusiness with a source of capital that will allow growth or modernization without forcing the "owners" to surrender control of the business. These loans provide for additional working capital, which can be used to increase revenues and sales; the funds generated by the increased revenues will, in turn, help to retire the loan.

In many respects the intermediate-term loan is similar to the short-term loan. Most require some sort of collateral and/or security against fixed assets, if that is the purpose of the loan. Intermediate-term loans provide permanent increases in capital for the agribusiness whenever larger inventories, larger accounts receivable, new equipment, and/or modernization are essential to the growth and profitability of the firm. Ray Whyth foresaw a need for an intermediate-term loan. He wanted to increase both his accounts receivable and his inventory as he acquired the lumberyard. He also needed funds to pay for moving and consolidating his operation at the new central site.

Long-Term Loans

In general, long-term loans have a duration of more than 5 years. The time distinctions among these loans are somewhat arbitrary, and there is some overlap in the functions of intermediate- and long-term loans, depending on the philosophies and policies of lender and borrower. But the real difference between intermediate- and long-term loans usually rests with the planned use for the funds, as well as with the long-term prospects for the existence of the firm and its solvency. The purpose of the loan is most often for real estate, that is, for land and buildings. As the lender examines requests for long-term loans, he or she becomes deeply concerned with evaluating the past track record of the firm, the skill and ability of the management team, and the stability of the business enterprise. The security for long-term loans is usually a mortgage or claim on the fixed assets of the firm, and the longer the period of the loan, the riskier it becomes for the lender. There is always the chance that an unstable enterprise will be forced to dispose of fixed assets in a forced sale, where these assets may bring only a fraction of their true value.

Usually, long-term loans also lock a lender's money into a fixed interest rate, or rate of return. As conditions change, money can increase in value, and the lender can be stuck with a relatively low return on the funds. Long-term loans are nearly always amortized equally over the loan period and secured by a mortgage or claim on a specific fixed asset. Sometimes bonds are used to secure long-term capital, but a small firm seldom has the size or strength to sell a bond issue. Because Ray Whyth plans to build new storage facilities at his new site as well as enlarging the office building to accommodate the consolidated business, he will also need a long-term loan.

Equity Capital

If the agribusiness is not solid enough (solvency is discussed in Chapter 7) or cannot meet the stiff collateral requirements of lenders, it may have to turn to equity capital to meet its long-term needs. *Equity capital* can be used for the same purpose as borrowed funds, but there is an important difference: equity capital does not have to be repaid. It becomes a permanent part of the capital of the business. Equity capital is secured either by reinvesting profits from the business or by finding investors who are willing to risk adding their money to the business.

Lenders pay particular attention to equity when they are making long-term loan commitments, and they may insist that a larger percentage of the owner's money be invested in the capital of the agribusiness. This is particularly true of new businesses, where risks are harder to calculate. Some owners do not wish to increase their equity for various reasons, but it may be the only prudent way of securing long-term capital funds. Ray Whyth will strongly consider expanding his equity base. Inasmuch as his business is already organized as a corporation, it will be easier for him to make the move should he so desire. (A more detailed analysis will appear later in the chapter.)

THE COST OF CAPITAL
When a business borrows money, it incurs special costs that are paid to the lender. One of these is *interest*, but interest is not the only cost of borrowing money. Several other factors affect the net cost of borrowed capital:

1. Repayment terms and conditions
2. Loss of control; that is, compensatory balances, points, and stock investments
3. The income tax bracket of the firm

Repayment Terms
The repayment terms and conditions directly affect the rate of interest that is actually paid. If Ray Whyth borrowed $50,000 for 1 year at a simple interest of 8 percent, his interest cost would be $4000. At the end of the year Ray would pay the lender $54,000, and his real interest rate would have been 8 percent. The formula for simple interest is:

$ Interest paid ÷ amount borrowed = annual interest rate
$4000 ÷ $50,000 = 8%

Sometimes, however, loans are *discounted*, which means that the amount of interest to be paid is deducted from the sum of capital at the time it is borrowed. If this method had been used in Ray's case, the $4000 interest to be paid, or 8% × $50,000, would have been deducted from the loan, and Ray would have had the use of only $46,000 in capital. The discounted loan formula is as follows:

Amount of loan − amount of interest paid = sum of available capital

At the end of the year, $50,000 would have been repaid to the lender; but because Ray had the use of only $46,000, the interest was:

Cost of loan ÷ amount of capital available = rate of interest
$4000 ÷ $46,000 = 8.7%

The real cost of interest on this discounted loan was 8.7 percent.

If the loan were repaid in installments, the real rate of interest would increase substantially. The formula for figuring the real rate of interest on an installment loan is as follows:

$$APR = \frac{2 \times P \times F}{B \times (T + 1)}$$

where APR = annual real percentage rate of interest
          P = payments per year
          F = dollars paid in interest
          B = amount of capital borrowed
          T = total number of payments

$$APR = \frac{2 \times 12 \times \$4000}{\$50,000 \times (12 + 1)}$$

$$APR = \frac{\$96,000}{\$650,000} = 14.8\%$$

Banks often require that borrowers have a compensatory balance in their accounts at the lending bank. To obtain a $50,000 loan, Ray might be required to maintain a minimum balance of $10,000 in his company bank account while the loan is outstanding. This means that he would have the use of only $40,000 in additional capital from the loan. The formula for figuring the real rate of interest in this case is:

Sum paid in interest ÷ actual capital available = real rate of interest
$4000 ÷ $40,000 = 10%

If Ray normally carries a cash balance, this amount could be deducted from the compensatory balance to lessen the impact of the real interest cost. Sometimes lending institutions require that a certain amount of *points* (service charges based on the face value of the loan) be paid to secure the loan. These charges for risk and for loan servicing are made in advance, and the amounts so charged are usually deducted from the total capital at the time the loan is made. Another demand that lenders sometimes make is that the borrower purchase a certain amount of stock in the lending institution, an amount that is determined by the value of the loan. The lender might require the purchase of one share of stock, valued at $10, for each $1000 that the borrower borrows. In reality, this is a form of discounting that can be used to determine the real cost of the loan. Actual or real interest rates must be revealed to individual borrowers by commercial lenders under federal truth-in-lending laws, but this law applies to consumer loans and time purchases. It does not apply to most commercial or business transactions.

Other Restrictions
Lenders will often place restrictions on the management prerogatives of an agribusiness during the loan period. These restrictions vary from requiring monthly and annual financial statements or other financial information regarding inventories and accounts payable to actual restrictions

on expending capital funds without the approval of the lender. Agribusiness managers must be sure that they can live comfortably with these restrictions before they agree to them. Otherwise, they may find themselves severely handicapped in decision making and in using business flexibility to meet changing conditions and new opportunities.

Interest Rates and Taxes

One of the things that agribusiness managers often overlook is that they can deduct from the business's taxable profits every dollar of interest paid, because the interest is a business expense. To know the real cost of borrowing capital funds, then, the manager must know what the after-tax cost of interest is. The effect of this can best be seen by looking at net profits after taxes, before and after borrowing from the bank. Using Ray Whyth's company (a corporation) and assuming that he had borrowed the $50,000 at 8 percent interest, consider the following tabular information.

	BEFORE LOAN	AFTER LOAN
Operating profit	$50,000	$50,000
Interest charges	-0-	−$ 4,000
Profit before taxes	$50,000	$46,000
Income tax (assume 25% rate)	−$12,500	−$11,500
Net profit after taxes	$37,500	$34,500

The difference between the two situations is $3000. The real interest rate for decision-making purposes is then only 6 percent. The formula is:

After-tax cost = before-tax cost × (1.0 − marginal tax rate)
After-tax cost = 8% × (1.0 − 0.25) = 6%

The marginal income tax rate mentioned is the rate of income tax paid on the last increment of taxable income. Proprietorships and partnerships (see Chapter 3) must also be aware of this cost as they decide between investing their own funds and borrowing capital funds for their businesses.

THE LEVERAGE PRINCIPLE

Leverage is the concept of financing through long-term debt in place of residual equity capital. Many managers like to use debt as a lever against equity as much as possible so that they can maximize the amount of assets or capital at their disposal. Several factors affect the leverage principle. First, it must be remembered that as the proportion of debt to equity increases, lenders are likely to increase the cost of supplying capital funds because of the decrease in solvency and the resulting increase in risk. It must be borne in mind that risks for equity holders also increase as debt increases, because they hold a last-place claim on the firm's assets in the event that all does not go well. Leverage, or increasing the proportion of debt to equity, can be either a profitable or an unprofitable decision.

As a rule of thumb, the after-tax rate of return on the capital of the agribusiness must exceed the after-tax cost of the debt undertaken to increase profits. For example, if the firm's overall ability is to return 10 percent on capital and the after-tax cost of borrowing money is 6 percent, borrowing more money should increase profits.

DETERMINING HOW MUCH THE AGRIBUSINESS SHOULD BORROW

The question of how much an agribusiness should borrow is one that agribusiness managers frequently ask. Some answer by saying, "All I can get," while others say, "Let's pay off the mortgage." These philosophical generalizations will not pay off on the bottom line. The good manager always establishes criteria and a frame of reference for such decisions. This section will deal primarily with intermediate and long-term debt, since it is assumed that short-term debt will be paid off from conversion of current assets to cash.

The amount of debt that is most desirable depends on several factors, some of which have already been discussed. Many of these factors are easy to measure, but others are much more difficult.

The first factor to consider is the amount that the agribusiness will be able to generate for debt servicing (repayment of the loan). While available funds can be calculated from all sources of cash flow (see Chapter 10), generally two factors are considered the primary inputs for debt servicing; (1) net margins for the year, and (2) depreciation. Net margins or operating profits must be further reduced by any interest that is due, income tax to be paid, dividends owed on owner equity, or patronage refunds in the case of a cooperative (see Chapter 4).

For example, if Ray Whyth has an operating profit of $50,000 and depreciation of $25,000, he has a preliminary total of $75,000. For debt servicing purposes, we would have to deduct $5000 in interest expense, $25,000 in taxes, and $5000 for stock dividends, which would leave the firm with only $40,000 for debt servicing.

Operating margin		$50,000	
Depreciation		+$25,000	
	Total	$75,000	$75,000
Interest		−$ 5,000	
Income tax		−$25,000	
Dividends		−$ 5,000	$35,000
	Total	$35,000	$40,000 for debt servicing

Ray would also have to consider other possible needs for these funds, such as boosting working capital, returning capital equities, and increasing stockholder dividends.

When lending institutions look at these debt servicing figures, many use the rule that no more than 50 to 60 percent of the total should actually be counted on as available for debt servicing, because of the possibility of change or emergency situations.

If the additional capital that is to be borrowed will increase revenues and profits, thereby increasing debt servicing potential, then the amount borrowed can be increased accordingly. Forecasting such new earnings accurately is crucial. Many managers tend to be overly optimistic, especially in the short run. Remember Murphy's law in this regard: "If anything can possibly go wrong, it will." The risk can be lessened considerably if the manager's profit forecast is understated. For example, if Ray feels that he will add $10,000 to his debt servicing capability through the loan, for the first year, at least, he would be advised to actually figure on only half this amount, or $5000, as available for debt servicing.

Several other factors must be considered as Ray analyzes the amount of money he should borrow. Debt servicing costs can be extended to the upper limits if there are:

1. Investors who are willing not to withdraw should things get tough

2. A firm with a favorable net-worth-to-debt ratio (solvency), or large amounts of working capital

3. A firm with fixed assets that can readily be converted to cash without incurring large losses

4. Redundant fixed assets that can be sold

5. A low risk on the asset purchased, as, for example, with a new piece of equipment that is improved and that will save labor

If accelerated depreciation or special depreciation measures are used to increase the speed of depreciation, then the amounts available for debt servicing must be considered in that perspective, and the manager may want to reduce the amount of this particular contribution to debt servicing.

Finally, the manager will want to take a long, hard look at the overall stability and success of the firm and of its management team; such factors as profits, control of inventories, accounts receivable, turnover, and efficiency will be the final elements in determining the amount of capital that the firm should borrow.

SOME OTHER TOOLS

Two other techniques, or tools, play an important part in financing the agribusiness firm. These are the cash budget and pro forma financial statements, both of which can help the agribusiness manager to look ahead intelligently and can aid the decision-making process immeasurably.

Cash Budget

A *cash budget* is really a projection of the firm's cash needs and income in a future time setting (see Exhibit 8-1). It allows the manager to estimate the cash funds needed to take advantage of cash discounts, to finance seasonal demands, to develop sound borrowing programs, to expand, and to make plans for debt servicing.

EXHIBIT 8-1 A Cash Budget Is a Projection of the Firm's Cash Needs and Income in a Future Setting

CASH BUDGET
For Three Months, Ending

	January		February		March	
	Budget	Actual	Budget	Actual	Budget	Actual
Expected cash receipts:						
1. Cash sales						
2. Collections on accounts receivable						
3. Other income, investments called						
4. Total cash receipts						
Expected cash payments:						
5. Raw materials						
6. Payroll						
7. Other factory expenses (including maintenance)						
8. Advertising						
9. Selling expense						
10. Administrative expense (including salary of owner-manager)						
11. New plant and equipment						
12. Other payments (taxes, including estimated income tax; repayment of loans; interest; etc.)						
13. Total cash payments						
14. Expected cash balance at beginning of the month						
15. Cash increase or decrease (item 4 minus item 13)						
16. Expected cash balance at end of month (item 14 plus item 15)						
17. Desired working cash balance						
18. Short-term loans needed (item 17 minus item 16, if item 17 is larger)						

FINANCIAL MANAGEMENT AND CONTROL OF THE AGRIBUSINESS

	January		February		March	
	Budget	Actual	Budget	Actual	Budget	Actual
19. Cash available for dividends, capital cash expenditures, and/or short-term investments (item 16 minus item 17, if item 16 is larger than item 17)						
Capital cash:						
20. Cash available (item 19 after deducting dividends, etc.)						
21. Desired capital cash (item 11, new plant equipment)						
22. Long-term loans needed (item 21 less item 20, if item 21 is larger than item 20)						

The length of time covered by a cash budget depends on the unique nature of the agribusiness. The primary considerations are how ample supplies of cash are currently, and how regularly or irregularly cash flows into the business. Highly seasonal agribusinesses will need to prepare their cash budgets over longer periods of time than those whose business activity is fairly constant.

When Ray Whyth prepares his cash budget, he will follow the steps outlined in Chapter 9. With the help of his planning committee, he will estimate, from both his existing business and the one he hopes to acquire, his cash receipts and cash payments. These estimates in reality become goals, so careful and honest input is needed. Both cash receipts and expenditures are recorded on a month-to-month basis during the budget period, the end result being the cash balance at the end of the budget period.

A goal must be set to determine whether the amount is sufficient (see Chapter 2). For example, Ray might decide that the cash equivalent of a certain number of days' sales, or a certain percentage of current liabilities, would be the bench mark or goal.

If the cash balance is short, then short-term borrowing or other adjustments might be called for. If it is larger than needed, the excess can be invested temporarily in marketable securities or in other income-producing ways. The cash budget can help the manager to decide whether there is a need for short-, intermediate-, or long-term loans or equity capital. If the cash amounts are ample at certain times and short at others, short-term capital is needed. If there is a persistent trend on the short side, intermediate or long-term capital is needed.

Pro Forma Financial Statements

Because the cash budget deals with only one account, cash, it is wise to go one step further and prepare a pro forma profit and loss statement and balance sheet. These statements really just project the best estimates of what the business will look like in the future (see Exhibits 8-2 and 8-3). The pro forma financial statements should be prepared on at least a quarterly basis for an operating year. Again, the more seasonal an agribusiness is, the more frequently it needs the pro forma statements.

The *pro forma financial statements* will provide a look into the future of the business and will help the manager judge what the financial needs of the business will be during and at the end of the operating period. If Ray fails to use this tool, he may not recognize problems until they actually arise, and then it may be too late to take corrective action. The most important figure in the preparation of these pro forma statements is *estimated sales*. This is where as many well-informed people as possible should become involved. Ray might well involve his family, the bookkeeper for the lumberyard, salespeople from both firms, supplier representatives, and his banker, to name some. Past experience and future price trends are key ingredients, along with factors of competition from other firms in the area.

It is vital that these two tools be based on solid goals in the areas of cash balances, inventory turnover, accounts receivable collection periods, expenses, and revenues.

With solid goals, management can use the interim cash budget and financial statements to check their progress against their estimates and assumptions. If actual and planned performance vary widely at any

EXHIBIT 8-2 Projected Profit and Loss Statement for One Month

PROJECTED PROFIT AND LOSS STATEMENT
For the Month Ending

	FIGURES BASED ON:
Revenue from sales	Sales budget for the month
Cost of sales	Experience
Gross margin	
Operating expenses:	
Selling expenses	Budget for the month
General expenses	Experience
Total operating expenses	
Net income from operations	
Other expense:	
Interest expense	Outstanding debt
	Expected additional debt
Net profit before taxes	
Income taxes	Tax rate of _____ percent
Net profit after taxes	
Earnings withdrawn	Owner's intention
Retained earnings	

PROJECTED BALANCE SHEET

ASSETS	**FIGURES BASED ON:**
Current assets:	
Cash	Desired cash balance
Accounts receivable	Average collection period of _____ days' sales
Inventory	Monthly turnover of _____ during this season
Total current assets	
Fixed assets	Present figure adjusted for period's depreciation
Total assets	
LIABILITIES	
Current liabilities:	
Notes payable	Amount of borrowed funds needed to balance assets with equities
Accounts payable	Expectation of _____ days' purchases on the books
Accrued liabilities	Same as preceding period
Total current liabilities	
Long-term debt	Expected and additional borrowings
Total liabilities	
EQUITY	
Paid-in capital	
Retained earnings	Present amount plus period earnings to be retained
Total equity	
Total liabilities and equity	

point, the reason can be sought and the weaknesses corrected. As a professional manager, Ray Whyth will avail himself of all these financial tools as he progresses in his new venture, prepared and as ready as anyone can be for the future.

EXTERNAL SOURCES OF FINANCING

There are a multitude of sources of capital available to any agribusiness. Some of these sources are unusual or rare, while others are rather common. The most important sources of financing for the agribusiness will be discussed in the following sections.

Commercial Banks

Commercial banks are the major source of borrowed funds for most agribusinesses. It is estimated that they provide over 80 percent of the funds loaned, excepting trade credits. Commercial banks usually offer a full line of banking services, including savings accounts, checking accounts, and loans. Banks make many kinds of loans, such as short-, intermediate-, and long-term loans, lines of credit, and special loans.

Accounts Receivable Loans   These are loans in which the bank lists a business's accounts receivable as collateral. This may be done on either a notification or nonnotification basis. *Notification* means that the bank informs the debtors that it wishes to collect the part of the money that is owed. The bank receives the payment and deducts a service charge and interest, then credits the balance against the borrower's loan. Under *nonnotification*, the borrower collects the receivables and forwards them to the bank. Recordkeeping and costs of interest are usually high, and managerial flexibility is lost, so nonnotification loans should be avoided whenever possible.

Warehouse Receipts   These are a means of using inventory as security for a loan. As inventory is stored in the warehouse, the borrower sells the inventory to the bank, then buys back the receipts from the bank. This type of loan is feasible only on nonperishable items, and allows the borrower to get along with limited working capital.

Banks also make personal unsecured loans to owners; many other kinds of secured loans, such as mortgages against real property; chattel mortgages against tools and equipment; and loans against the owner's life insurance policies, stocks and bonds, etc.

Often a bank will offer to help sell a product by buying sales installment contracts from the seller. Sales installment contracts are contracts made by the buyer to pay for the product in a specified manner. When a financial institution buys the contract, payments are made directly to that institution. The business gets its money immediately. This procedure makes it easier for the customer to finance the purchase and help the cash flow of the business. This is particularly helpful to retailers who are selling expensive items, such as farm implements and tractors.

Insurance Companies

Insurance companies are always looking for places to invest funds they have collected from policyholders. Most insurance companies are interested in intermediate- and long-term loans on fixed assets, such as equipment or real estate. They prefer large loans and mortgages for collateral. If the owners or the agribusiness itself has insurance policies with a particular company, that company will usually lend the agribusiness amounts that are equal to the cash value of the policy at very favorable interest rates.

Commercial Finance Companies

Commercial finance companies are those finance companies that specialize in business and commercial loans. They are not to be confused with personal finance companies, which make loans to individuals. Commercial finance companies often grant loans that are riskier than those that banks will accept, so commercial finance companies normally charge higher interest rates than banks. Commercial finance companies may also demand a considerable amount of control over management decisions. This is particularly true if the loan involved is high risk. Sometimes commercial finance companies will pay off all a firm's debts in order to consolidate the firm's indebtedness. This can be of particular value if cash flow presents a problem, because payment schedules can be reconstructed within the constraints of the agribusiness's cash flow.

Factors
The factor is a very specialized source of capital funds. *Factors* buy accounts receivable at a discounted price. They buy these accounts receivable without recourse; that is, they assume the risk of bad-debt losses. Except when they are convinced that the accounts are sound, they may understandably pick and choose those they buy. Their procedure is to notify the individual accounts and collect directly. Many agribusinesses do not want their customers dealing directly with the collecting factor. However, in some cases it is the only way for a business to raise quick cash.

Cooperative Borrowing
Cooperatives, of course, have all the conventional borrowing sources, but in addition agribusiness cooperatives can borrow from the Bank for Cooperatives, which is part of the Farm Credit System. This special bank is owned by its cooperative patrons, who are also its borrowers. The bank makes short-, intermediate-, and long-term loans to its members. To receive a loan, a cooperative must purchase an amount of membership stock that is equivalent to the amount of money being borrowed. This stock bears interest, and is revolved or repurchased whenever the debt is repaid and the bank has funds available for that purpose. Often the Bank for Cooperatives can offer better interest rates than some commercial banks because it is a nonprofit organization operated exclusively for its members' benefit. Because they specialize in cooperative loans, the bank's personnel are often able to offer management help and guidance to member-borrowers.

Trade Credit
One of the most neglected sources of capital is the credit advanced by suppliers and vendors of the agribusiness firm. If the agribusiness is creditworthy, most suppliers and vendors will allow credit terms. The manager can often negotiate for longer credit terms than are usually extended. For example, Ray Whyth was such a steady purchaser of treated poles that he was able to get his supplier to extend his normal 30-day credit terms to 90 days from invoicing. In Ray's case he had often collected for the farm building prior to the 90-day credit period, so in a very real sense the pole supplier also became a supplier of Ray's business capital, but without any cost to Ray. In other cases, a supplier may be willing to sell to an agribusiness on consignment. This means that the business does not have to pay for supplies until it is able to actually sell

them. The agribusiness manager should make sure that maximum terms are being extended by suppliers and vendors, and that the procedure for paying accounts payable takes every advantage of all credit terms extended.

Leasing or Renting

Leasing provides an opportunity for many agribusiness firms to extend their capital assets without having to borrow. The agribusiness can lease or rent stores, factories, warehouses, offices, equipment, or trucks, among other things. Almost any important fixed asset can be rented or leased. Leasing is the equivalent of borrowing, because it takes its place as a means of acquiring capital. Much of the money used in leasing comes from financial institutions and insurance companies. Special organizations have been set up to lease a business almost anything. Ray Whyth is seriously considering leasing trucks for his business in order to conserve his cash.

The typical lease, as would be expected, will cost more than interest on a loan. The *lessor* (person granting the lease) must charge an amount to cover profit for arranging the lease, the element of risk, interest on the capital involved, and the depreciation of the article leased. The longer the lease period, the lower the lease charges will be, which means that if Ray Whyth leases a truck for 4 years, he will pay a lower yearly rate than he would if he leased it for 2 years. In many cases, the *lessee* (person renting the property) can arrange to purchase the property at the end of the leasing period for a predetermined amount.

Advantages and Disadvantages of Leasing A business leases to avoid using its cash resources for purchasing assets. It will not have to resort to borrowing or selling equity. Many agribusinesses take the position that their funds should be used for expanding their operations rather than buying assets that can just as easily be leased. Leasing is also a deductible expense, and may be cheaper than borrowing, buying, and incurring the cost of depreciation. Another advantage is that leased assets can be turned back to the lessor and newer or better assets procured. This is of special value when change or technology is pertinent to the asset.

But leasing is not without its drawbacks. For most businesses, leasing will cost more than borrowing. Leasing also commits the business to certain payments, whereas if the asset were owned it could be sold to at least minimize the financial commitment. Finally, leased property often grows in value, and such increases in value are only of benefit to the lessor or owner.

Other Sources of Capital

The agribusiness can draw upon many other sources of capital, including bonds, debentures, and promissory notes.

Bonds Bonds are usually issued by corporations. They are an obligation by the corporation to pay a certain sum at a specified time in the future. They are issued in series and are redeemed in the order in which they are issued. Usually, bonds carry a specified rate of interest that is paid on an annual basis. They are generally used for raising long-term capital, and the date of redemption is often 20 to 30 years from date of issue. Bonds are not secured by any particular collateral other than the general assets of the firm, but they have a preferred risk; that is, they are redeemed prior to the common stock of the corporation or some other obligation of the firm. They may be traded on the stock exchanges if they qualify. As a source of funds, bonds are of most value to large corporations.

Debentures *Debenture notes*, which are issued in exchange for the loan of capital, usually create a security against the general assets of the firm, or a part of the company's stock and property, though not necessarily in the form of a mortgage or lien. Most debentures are restricted as to their sale and transfer among lenders, and usually have coupons attached to facilitate the payment of interest. They are generally issued and redeemed in a series, without any one debenture taking precedence over another.

Promissory Notes A *promissory note* is a promise by the borrower to pay to the lender a particular amount of money and a particular amount of interest after a specified period of time. Promissory notes are common to most agribusiness firms and banks, private individuals, and creditors. Agribusiness firms may also accept promissory notes from their customers. Such notes may be negotiable, that is, they can be sold by the holder and the new owner will have the same claim against the borrower as the original lender. When an agribusiness firm holding negotiable notes from customers needs cash, negotiable promissory notes can be sold to a bank or other person, usually at a discount. For example, Ray Whyth might sell a farmer some materials to build a pole barn, say $5000 worth, and accept in return a negotiable note that is due in 6 months and bears a 10 percent interest rate. In the meantime Ray might need cash, in which case he could go down to the bank and sell the note. If the farmer's credit is good, and the banker feels the interest rate is good, the note might be purchased by the bank for face value or at a very small discount that reflects a service charge. The farmer would then pay the bank when the note was due.

CHOOSING A BANKER

The selection of the *right* bank can spell the difference between success and failure for the agribusiness firm. The right bank can be a lot more than just a place to deposit funds, service a checking account, and request an occasional loan. Convenience should not be the main criterion for selecting a bank. Many agribusinesses are located in rural communities and small towns. They feel that loyalty demands they do business with banks in their community, but this feeling has merit only if the bank can meet the needs of the agribusiness. Many small banks simply do not have the facilities or requirements needed to make a growing agribusiness viable. One of the ways in which a small bank can expand its services is by facilitating working arrangements with larger banks. Here the best of both worlds can be combined; that is, the business can have the advantage of dealing locally and the advantage of having full-service banking available.

Requirements for Selecting a Bank
There are five main points to consider when selecting a bank.

1. Is the bank progressive in its attitude toward agribusiness?

2. Are the credit services offered sufficient to meet the agribusiness's needs?

3. Is the bank large enough to meet the business's capital needs?

4. Does the bank have qualified personnel who are knowledgeable about agribusiness?

5. Are the bank's management policies in line with the agribusiness's objectives and financial strategy?

Is the Bank Progressive?   The progressive agribusiness manager needs a progressive bank, one that keeps up with changing times and with the community it serves. Physical facilities do give some indication of progressive thinking, but the real test is the organization and its people. Do the employees take a friendly interest in serving the agribusiness? Are they interested in the community and do they participate in civic affairs? Does the bank have personnel who specialize in agribusiness services, and have they appointed someone to handle the firm's account? Has this person called on the firm? These are but a few of the ways to judge how progressive a bank is or will be as it serves a business.

Check Credit Services Offered   The banker should understand the unique needs of the agribusiness. Can or will the bank make loans on receivables or warehouse receipts; provide lines of credit; or make short-, intermediate-, and long-term loans? Will it honor drafts, accept negotiable notes, and the like? Will it provide credit references for potential customers, help to solve capital problems, refer customers by building the firm's image? What does the bank charge for its various services? Are rates competitive?

How Big Is Big Enough?   Size of the bank can be an important factor, especially if the agribusiness's credit needs are large or increasing. Banks are regulated by state and federal agencies that restrict the size of loans

FINANCIAL MANAGEMENT AND CONTROL OF THE AGRIBUSINESS

and the amount that a bank can lend to any one customer. Managers must make sure not to be caught in a situation where this "legal limit" will hamstring the business. If a local bank cannot meet the firm's capital requirements, the agribusiness manager should make sure that it can make arrangements with other banks to fund the balance of the credit needed. Is the bank large enough to have a separate, well-managed trust department? If the agribusiness sells on installment loans, can the bank handle a working relationship with it? Since size and prestige are often related, the agribusiness manager should make sure that the bank has a solid image in the financial community.

Qualified Personnel Agribusiness is a unique form of business. It is important for the personnel at the bank selected to know the needs of the agribusiness. An understanding of agriculture, seasonality, and the like is indispensable. Do bank personnel also understand financial information, analysis, and the tools of financial management and planning? Are the bank personnel knowledgeable enough to provide sound input knowledge? A good banker can become an important member of the management team, who is just as interested in the agribusiness's success as the business is. The banker's enlightened self-interest is to the agribusiness's advantage, too, because it leads to a healthy, growing, successful source of capital that will properly serve the business's unique needs.

The Bank Policies The agribusiness manager wants a sound, well-managed bank. Banking relationships should be more or less permanent in nature. As the bank and the agribusiness work and grow together, knowledge, experience, and personal relationships take on greater meaning. Banks can be ultraconservative or ultraliberal in their lending policies. The needs of the business dictate that a bank be found that is willing to assume a risk when it makes capital available to the firm. Some banks will not lend money unless a customer can prove he or she has a need for it, while others may lend a customer into bankruptcy. A bank that has sound policies, knowledgeable personnel, and is able to advise as well as lend money should be chosen. The agribusiness manager should look upon the banker as a partner in the business, and should do the utmost to make the relationship a profitable and satisfactory one for both of them.

Getting Ready for the Loan
Often the agribusiness manager's success in securing capital from a lending institution will depend solely on how he or she goes about it. Actually, the best guide for preparing for a loan would be the eight questions (listed earlier in the chapter) that the agribusiness manager should ask before adding capital to the firm. If the person who is negotiating the loan can answer these questions, and someone who cannot answer them should not be requesting a loan, then she or he will be well prepared.

These data should be organized and prepared clearly in a legible form. Incompleteness and vagueness are death blows, since they demonstrate the manager's ineptness and lack of financial acumen. Bankers are greatly impressed by managers who know what is going on and can prove it.

Historical evidence of performance, trends, and future plans are all important ingredients. Develop this information and organize it in the following manner:

1. Balance sheet and profit and loss statements for at least the last 3 years

2. Trends in sales, expenses, profits, etc. (ratios are helpful here)

3. Description of the market (customers), products and services, supplies

4. Information about working capital, aging accounts receivable, turnover, inventory, and so forth (again, ratio analysis and ROI are helpful)

5. Credit and character references, and the background of the management team

6. Evidence of planning for the future; that is, cash budget, expansion, pro forma financial statements

7. The applicant's personal history and that of the agribusiness

The applicant should be candid and honest. Facts should not be withheld, even those that could be damaging, since they are likely to surface anyway; damaging facts that are brought out through the manager's initiative will be less damaging than they would be if the banker felt duped.

A good question for the agribusiness manager to ask is, "If I were presented with this information, what would I think of it and would I make a loan on this basis?" Offering the banker a tour of the facility and an opportunity to meet other personnel from the agribusiness can also be beneficial in creating a favorable impression, and can be of benefit in building a better long-term relationship.

INTERNAL FINANCING FOR THE AGRIBUSINESS

One of the most important sources of capital, and one that is ignored by too many agribusiness managers, is the money obtained from retained earnings. It is not that managers lack awareness of these funds, but because they simply have not used the financial tools and techniques previously described, they have no idea how to use retained earnings to their fullest extent. Many agribusiness managers have gone to their bankers for loans, only to be told that they really would not need one if they budgeted carefully!

Equity Capital

Equity capital represents funds that are obtained by the firm through retaining the profits it has made, through the investment of more money by the owners, or through taking into the business additional people who are willing to risk their funds on it. In some small or new businesses, this may be the only alternative for securing capital funds. Some owners are not anxious to sell equity to other people. These owners feel that the loss of complete control over the business is not worth the fresh capital. Such owners should be aware that the borrowing of funds may place far more restraints on their control than the sharing of ownership. And if an owner defaults, or is slow in paying a term loan, he or she can completely lose control of the management of the business. Remember, equity capital does not have to be repaid at any certain time, and often there is no absolute need to generate funds for interest payments. Equity capital should always be considered as an alternative, and weighed against other capital sources.

Common Stock

The most prevalent form of equity capital is the kind that is secured through the sale of common stock. For the small company, this may mean selling shares of stock primarily to people who are known to the present owners. There are always people in any community who have funds to invest in a promising business venture. The firm's banker can often be helpful in suggesting interested people. Employees of the firm are also a potential source of stock purchasers, especially if the firm offers a special purchase plan that grants employees preferential prices. Common stock is usually voting stock; that is, owners of common stock have a voice in the management of the firm. Sometimes common stock is divided into classes, of which only one kind carries the voting privilege.

Ray Whyth has carefully studied the financial needs of his firm. He has decided on the particular mix of borrowed and equity funds that he thinks is optimum for the business. His intentions are to offer the lumberyard's owner, as part of the purchase price, a certain amount of stock. He also intends to offer stock to his employees and to members of the community on a limited basis. He determined this ratio of equity to borrowing by using the tools in Chapter 7 and 9 that relate to solvency.

Care must be exercised that laws relating to the sale of securities are observed when stock is offered to the public. All states have blue-sky laws, which regulate the sale of securities and stocks. In some cases, federal laws regulating the sale of stocks also apply. It is essential that a team of advisors be assembled before a public offering of stock is made. The business's banker, legal counsel, and auditor should be among those involved. If a firm wants to make a larger public offering, it will usually secure the services of an investment banker. These bankers perform a very special service by offering for sale the new stock offerings presented by companies. When an investment banker *underwrites* a stock issue, that banker makes an agreement with the corporation to market its securities by buying them and reselling them to the public. Investment bankers charge a commission of from 3 to 10 percent, depending on the difficulty of selling the stock and the quantity offered. It is unusual for even small investment bankers to underwrite less than $250,000 of stock. Present owners of the business do not necessarily have to lose control of a business by sale of its common stock. They can retain control by keeping a sufficient amount of the stocks issued themselves. Often bonds or debentures are sold as *convertible* issues. This means that they can be converted at some future time to a certain quantity of common stock. Companies offer this conversion feature as an inducement to secure buyers for their bonds and debentures, because if a company is successful its stock may appreciate in value considerably.

Preferred Stock

Preferred stock is the stock to which a corporation shows *preference*. In the event of the liquidation of the corporation, the owners of preferred stock would be repaid before holders of common stock. Most preferred stock also has a definite annual dividend rate, which means that it would pay a percentage (say 6 percent) of the face or issue value on an annual basis. Sometimes corporations will reserve the right to defer this dividend until a later date should the corporation have financial difficulties. In exchange for its preferred nature in the event of liquidation, most preferred stock does not carry with it any voting rights or control in the management affairs of the corporation.

Other Internal Financing

Partnerships may secure more capital by selling portions of their business to others who are willing to risk their money in the business. These others may be either regular or silent partners. A *regular partner* assumes the same rights and liabilities as other partners, while a *silent partner* has restricted rights and liabilities (see Chapter 3). Or an owner may simply lend money to the business just as any outside creditor would, if that owner does not wish to commit any additional funds on an equity basis.

ALL THAT GLITTERS

As the agribusiness manager strives to turn everything that he or she touches into gold, it is important to remember that not all sources of financial help are equally useful or equally applicable to all situations. Truly, the securing and managing of the financial resources of any agribusiness firm is a complex function, but careful attention to the tools, techniques, and principles given in this chapter will increase the agribusiness manager's chances of success.

The agribusiness manager needs to know the various kinds of loans, the cost of borrowing, and whether short-, intermediate-, or long-term capital is needed. The manager must explore all sources of capital to discover whether borrowing, equity financing, or some combination thereof is best for the particular agribusiness involved. But even more importantly, the manager's ability to assess the optimum amount to be borrowed, and to formulate a realistic plan for repayment, will make the agribusiness's financial strategy a firm and steady foundation for the future.

SUMMARY

Financing the agribusiness is a necessary and important management responsibility. Money must be available to finance capital purchases and operate the business on a day-in, day-out basis. There are three primary sources of capital: borrowing, funds generated from business operations, and additional investments from owners.

Borrowing can take many forms. Short-term loans of a year or less are usually used to finance seasonal business needs. Intermediate loans of 1 to 5 years are generally used to purchase equipment or finance increases in the volume of business. Long-term loans are usually for major business expansion, such as buying land and erecting buildings. Interest rates and repayment schedules vary according to a great many factors, including time, risk, amount of money, past experience, and the soundness of the firm's financial base.

Managers must consider many different sources of borrowing; for example, commercial banks, insurance companies, and finance companies, to name three. Choosing the right lender is often a critical management decision. Larger agribusinesses borrow from the public by issuing bonds or debentures through the money market.

Some agribusinesses, particularly newer ones, rely heavily on equity financing. Equity capital results from retaining profits in the business rather than distributing them to owners. Other agribusinesses sell additional stock to attract additional dollars for the business.

Each financing method has pros and cons and must be considered carefully by management.

DISCUSSION QUESTIONS

1. List the reasons why an agribusiness firm might increase its capital.

2. Discuss each of the questions a manager should ask before adding financial resources to the agribusiness.

3. Define and differentiate among the different kinds of loans, and describe the circumstances under which each should be used.

4. Discuss the issues surrounding the different costs of loans, and describe how those costs are figured.

5. What does "after-tax rate of interest" mean, and what is its significance for decision making?

6.   How should an agribusiness's financial statements be analyzed to determine the ideal amount for it to borrow?

7.   Explain the purpose of the cash budget and pro forma financial statements.

8.   What major sources of loans are available in your community? For what kinds of agribusinesses are they most appropriate?

9.   Discuss the different kinds of loans, and focus on the nature of collateral factors in each case.

10.   How would you go about selecting a banker for your agribusiness?

11.   Prepare an outline of materials that are needed when an agribusiness manager goes to a bank to secure a loan.

12.   List the major kinds of internal financing, and the advantages of this kind of capital source as compared to borrowing.

THE CASE OF JOE ALLEN

Joe Allen, the president of the Landmark Farm and Garden Company, needed to make a loan for his company. By using the tools in this chapter, he determined that his short-term loan needs for added capital to finance a larger amount of accounts receivable were $100,000. This need was largely the result of a liberalized credit policy. Assume that the income tax rate for Landmark is 30 percent, and that the interest rate is 10 percent simple annual interest. The period of the loan is 1 year. Using this information, answer the following questions. Show formulas for all examples.

QUESTIONS

1.   Figure the cost of interest for a simple annual-interest loan.

2.   Figure the amount of interest paid and the rate paid if a discounted interest is used by the lender.

3.   Figure the rate and cost of interest if a compensatory balance of $25,000 is required.

4.   Figure the rate of interest and cost of the loan if it is paid in twelve equal installments.

5.   Figure the after-tax cost of interest based on the simple annual interest rate.

OBJECTIVES

• Define control programs and explain their purpose

• Identify the areas of the agribusiness in which control programs are most often used

• Test the need for control programs against significant factors

• Describe how the control process works

• Differentiate qualitative and quantitative techniques to develop forecasts and budgets

• List the sixteen steps of developing budgets and use them as a model for control programs

• Explain "management by exception" philosophy and theory

• Develop a control program for an agribusiness

• List the reasons why credit control is such an important factor in agribusiness, and the ways in which credit can be controlled

• Compute the *real* costs of credit extension

Financial control is a necessary management responsibility in the agribusiness.
A. Cash budgeting
B. Evaluating applications
C. Extending credit

A CRISIS THAT RECURS MUST NEVER RECUR AGAIN.———Peter Drucker

TOOLS FOR CONTROLLING THE AGRIBUSINESS

THE IMPORTANCE OF CONTROL

Central to the successful management of any agribusiness firm is the ability of both managers and employees to monitor and predict their accomplishments. From a practical point of view, the general objective of the organization, to "maximize profits," does not provide the kind of guidance necessary for checking progress. No one knows what maximum profits are or can be. Progress must therefore be measured against more specific goals. Cost and revenue implications cannot be ignored, because ultimately the very existence of the business depends on its ability to make a profit. But control programs are designed to provide the agribusiness manager with the tools for monitoring and predicting accomplishment within these cost and revenue constraints.

In its simplest form, control means checking that plans are on target and on schedule, and taking remedial action as needed to ensure success. The basic control program involves three steps:

1.   Establishing predetermined goals or standards of performance

2.   Measuring performance against these predetermined goals and standards through an information-gathering system

3.   Taking action to correct deviation from goals and standards

PURPOSE OF CONTROL

Consolidate Authority and Coordinate Efforts

While managers seek to inspire the most imaginative and motivated approach from each employee, they also must prevent overlapping efforts and extension of authority beyond the limits that are sanctioned.

One of the most familiar examples of the need for control would be the purchase order and the policies and procedures that are associated with it. For instance, the Hillsdale Farmers' Cooperative once instituted the policy that all purchases above $600 had to be approved by the general manager. The control procedure required the originator to submit a request for approval to the general manager, and thence to the purchasing agent and accounting department for handling in a specified manner. In this way, the purchase order passed through many hands, but unauthorized purchases by Hillsdale employees were prevented.

Predict Trends and Results

Controls should show trends, or the direction in which the business is going. Controls sound a warning when plans or programs are heading off purpose.

Sales may be way up and inventory way down, or vice versa. Certain items may not be selling. Once this is recognized, the program can be studied and reformed. A product may have become obsolete, pricing may be wrong, or a competitor's product may be cornering the market. Without controls to alert the agribusiness manager in time, the situation could become serious or even disastrous to the business.

Provide Information for Future Planning and Goal Adjustments

The information from control programs becomes a part of the know-how of the business. An example would be the recognition that 75 percent of the sales of a certain item are made in a 3-month period. This could guide plans for future production, inventory, and storage.

Provide Information about Past Experience

Good control information will provide answers to questions such as "Under similar circumstances, what happened in the past?" or "What past experience should guide our present and future activities?" For example, "When we raised prices before, what was the reaction of our customers, our salespeople, our competitors—and what did we do about it?"

Answers based on past experience can be an invaluable part of a control-information program.

WHERE ARE CONTROL PROGRAMS FOUND?

In most agribusinesses control programs or procedures are found in the following general areas:

1. Financial and fiscal

2. Operational
   (a) Personnel and management
   (b) Production standards
   (c) Quality of product

Agribusiness managers need control programs that are based on predetermined goals or standards of performance. Without measurement criteria the information or procedure will produce nothing of value. Control programs or procedures must also be used only in separable areas of business activity where reliable records of input and output are possible.

Even the smallest organization will require control programs that are related to marketing, production of the goods or services, personnel, and records and/or finance. Though the local implement dealer needs to maintain these four basic kinds of control mechanisms, larger organizations, like the John Deere Company, would require even more complex sets of key performance areas and a much larger number of control programs. Each agricultural firm must develop the unique kinds of information and control programs necessary to its success.

KINDS OF CONTROL PROGRAMS

Control as a management function was discussed in an earlier chapter. Now, some of the tools with which the agribusiness firm can measure and predict the results of its business performance will be described.

While control programs come in a multitude of forms, such as budgets, forecasts, production standards, standard costs, personnel performance, planning programs, and financial plans, each of them has much in common with the rest. The principles for developing and using control programs are basically the same, regardless of the business area being monitored. Control programs and procedures are based upon the manager's plans, or what the manager wants or hopes will happen in the future. These programs are essentially predictive of future activities or events that implement management's decisions. They are a package tool based upon the formula in Figure 9-1.

Because the principles and steps for developing control programs are basic to all control programs, only the forecast and the budget will be presented in detail here. The agribusiness manager can adapt the principles and steps given for these most important control programs to the development of any control program.

The Relationships of Predictive Programs

What is the difference between a budget and a forecast? Though it is true that some budgets are forecasts and some forecasts are budgets, in management a forecast generally refers to the output of the business, as with sales forecasts. The budget refers to input into the business, or the cash budget. For example, the Hillsdale Farmers' Cooperative elevator would have a sales forecast or a prediction of the amount of business the organization expects to conduct during a certain period. To accompany this, Hillsdale would also develop a budget that is related to the expenditures needed to secure the projected sales. Because the survival of the organization depends on the capacity of revenues to exceed expenses, the budget and the sales forecast are inseparable.

It is important to recognize that budgets determine organizational

Figure 9-1 Control programs are predictive tools.

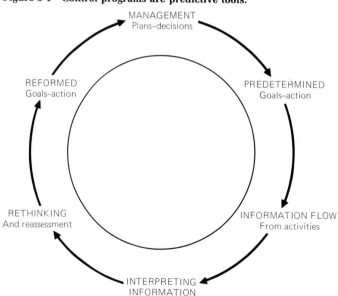

direction. Adding or subtracting resources determines the long-run form of the agribusiness in terms of growth, new products, and size. Many organizations develop budgets by simply taking last year's figures and adding or subtracting a fairly arbitrary amount. This may be better than no budget at all, but on the input side it fails to provide the flexibility and the recognition of change agents that are critical to dynamic, successful organizations. Budgets should reflect the priorities and directions or goals of the business. It is only by changing the resource input that we can change or redirect the firm's output. The budget is one of the most important vehicles for reflecting and directing this change. For example, if the management team of an Agrow fertilizer company were to decide to actively seek a larger share of the homeowner market, the input side of the budget would have to reflect this objective. The Agrow capital budget might be increased to provide either more production facilities or more bagging and packaging equipment, to produce smaller packages for homeowner use. The marketing budget might well show expanded dollar figures for more advertising and promotion, added sales personnel, and the like. The cash flow would reflect the added drain of inventory and stocking that would result from the presence of an additional product. As this discussion suggests, budget control mechanisms are a basic part of the planning process. They direct the size and kind of agribusiness and set the stage for its success over a period of time.

Quantitative Techniques in Designing the Budget
One of the most commonly used quantitative procedures is *linear projection*. To use this method, the manager first looks at past trends, then uses mathematics to project these same trends into a future time setting.

For example, if labor costs to the Hillsdale Farmers' Cooperative have increased by 5 percent during each of the past 4 years, then the agribusiness manager of that elevator might predict a 5 percent increase for each of the next 4 years. This technique can be helpful if the manager does not depend on it entirely and allows for change, whether desired or undesired.

Another quantitative technique is designing models. A *model* is an abstract presentation, usually in mathematical terms, that exhibits all the factors believed to be pertinent, and demonstrates the relative influence of each factor on the entire situation. Models also show how change in any one or group of factors affects the rest of the factors or the whole.

This may sound complex, but an example will help to clarify it. To seek a larger share of the homeowner fertilizer market, the Agrow fertilizer company might have found it necessary to add a second shift to produce the extra fertilizer. Adding a second shift would increase labor cost by a given factor, say 10 percent, since second-shift workers usually demand a wage incentive for working nights. Also to be taken into account would be the generally lower productivity of a second shift, usually 5 to 15 percent less than day-shift production. The independent variable of higher labor cost, because of a shift differential for the second shift and the lowered productivity rate of the second shift, could increase the total labor cost for the plant by 10 to 15 percent. Using this technique of budgeting a particular area of the business, we must know:

1. What are the constraints or restrictions involved here?

2. What factors or numbers should be used?

3. How are these factors related to and integrated into developing our total budget or control program?

The results must then be processed and interpreted in relationship to the total problem or goal, which in this case would be to gain a larger share of the homeowner fertilizer market. It would be necessary then to relate the model to the sales forecast to establish costs and revenues and to determine the profitability of the action being contemplated.

Finally, we have *simulation*, or a systematic trial-and-error approach to the problem. This approach is often combined with operations to provide measurable data. Simulation usually involves several possibilities that are derived from past operational experience and records. This is where industrial engineering techniques, such as standard costs and time and motion studies, become very important to a firm (see Chapter 17). The various simulations or possibilities can be run on a computer numerous times to determine what is most likely to happen in the future.

Qualitative Techniques in Budget Development

Qualitative approaches must always be part of budget development. Quantitative approaches are only as good as the information on which they are based and must still be interpreted and implemented by human beings. One qualitative technique that is currently being used successfully is consensus. In *consensus*, knowledgeable people who are associated with the business are asked separately for their opinions about a particular factor. For example, Agrow might ask the personnel manager, the operators' superintendent, a supervisor, and an outside consultant to predict the productivity of a second shift. Everyone involved shares and discusses the answer, and all then report their (possibly revised) opinions separately. The aim is to derive an answer on which all, or at least a substantial majority, can agree. The weakness of consensus is that it may simply encourage the pooling of a firm's ignorance. The technique's strength is that it provides an opportunity for people to present various points of view. Innovative ideas may result from this opportunity.

Another qualitative technique depends on the intuition and experience of the leader. The owner-manager of the small tractor or implement dealership may, over a period of time, tend to develop a consistent pattern of success or failure in anticipating the business's future. Success lies in the manager's ability to generalize the past experience into the future setting. The weakness here is that experience or intuition may be too narrowly based or out of date. If he or she is to be successful, the owner-manager of the implement dealership must be able to synthesize a large number of factors inherent to the local farm community in order to develop sound control programs. Most agribusiness managers hone this skill to a fine edge as they gain experience over the years.

Another technique is *logic,* or the combination of fact, induction, and deduction, with or without the aid of colleagues. Logic must be fortified by pertinent information and data to be successful. If a careful analysis is made, the process can be substantiated and demonstrated so that others can evaluate the procedure and possibly improve on it. The manager of the implement dealership might gather information about the competition, the general economy, the productivity of the farms in the area, and the kind of year that farmers had. These factors might form the basis for developing the budget. They could be reviewed with other people who might be able to add or subtract or modify and improve the facts or reasoning that provided the basis from which the budget was developed.

Finally, we have the use of *scenarios,* which are a series of flexible possibilities. These possibilities may vary according to such things as volumes, economic conditions, labor settlements, and so forth. The implement dealer might develop a budget and sales forecast based upon the several possible prices of grain within the marketing area. Then each scenario would be compared and modified until the best one was found. Sometimes it is helpful for the manager to develop both an optimistic, or most likely, and a pessimistic, or least likely, scenario. This would allow the budget to be modified according to the actual developments in the price of grain. This technique can be most helpful, but the manager must be careful not to use the flexible situation as a crutch to avoid using decision-making capabilities.

Whatever the methods a manager uses, certain premises or constraints will be present. The agribusiness manager must form premises or assume that certain entities will react in specific ways, that a number of forces will be present, and that certain conditions will or will not be present during the future period under consideration. The implement dealer must assume that a possible drought will or will not cause a crop failure in the coming year. Managers also operate within certain personal constraints, such as philosophies and beliefs, ethical standards, and attitudes toward people. Agribusiness managers must be sure that the premises and constraints on which they are operating are valid and do not result from their own lack of knowledge or experience, bias, or prejudice.

Budgets Vary According to the Needs of the Organization
The size and complexity of the organization will determine the kinds of budgets that are needed for success. A small business may need only an overall budget with different sections, such as sales, production, and finance. A large business may have budgets for departments, divisions,

regions, products, etc. Budgets may be either long range or short range. A *short-range budget* is generally one that will be implemented within a year, and it usually requires shorter reporting periods. A *long-range budget* is 2 or more years in implementation and is usually reported on a semiannual or annual basis. The short-range budget, therefore, becomes a component in reaching the long-range budget objectives. Budgets may also be made for specific projects; for example, constructing a new building, introducing new equipment, or introducing a new product.

The ultimate goal of budgeting is to predict and control inputs to increase the returns from resources available to the agribusiness. Preparing a budget for even a small firm is not a one-person job. Key people, advisors, and information sources should all be involved. Bankers, accountants and/or auditors, suppliers, consultants, and even customers may be involved.

Tips for Developing the Budget

Within the agricultural firm there must be a sound organization and communication system that ensures responsibility, authority, accountability, and commitment to accomplishment. A budget can be this system. The following sixteen major steps in preparing a budget, or almost any control program or system that the agribusiness manager might use, are essential to its success.

1. Set up a committee of those who are involved and schedule dates for the development process.

2. Review the organizational objectives, goals, policies, etc.

3. Review the present situation, where the business is now and how it got there.

4. Review and relate input (cost) factors to output (revenues) factors.

5. Determine why the budget is needed and the specific goals or courses of action sought.

6. Designate the budget to be developed, and list its component parts.

7. Specify how and when the budget will be used.

8. Specify the records necessary to meet the intended uses.

9. Indicate the units of measure that will be used (dollars, tons, bushels, etc.).

10. Specify the records needed to secure the desired data and information.

11. Locate the sources of information or data needed to service the program.

12. Designate and identify the budgeting period.

13. Designate the frequency of issuance, and updating, of information and data from the program.

14. Specify who is to be involved in preparing those records that are pertinent to the budget.

15. Specify who will receive the information and when they will get it.

16. Identify who is responsible for meeting the goals and standards contained in the budget. Budgets must be constantly monitored to ensure that the program is on target.

The Budgeting Process

The sixteen key factors or steps in developing a control program or budget might well serve as a general outline for our farm-implement dealer (see Exhibit 9-1).

To gain a better understanding of this process, consider the following real case (with names changed): Kalamazoo Farm & Industrial Tractor Company. This company is a partnership, with Jeff McDonald as general manager; his brother Frederick as sales manager; his daughter Elizabeth as shop manager; and Laura, Frederick's wife, as office manager. The organization is typical of many smaller agribusiness firms. As sales manager, Frederick McDonald was in charge of setting up the sales budget and forecast control programs. As he looked over the steps for developing a control program, he saw that the first step was to determine who should be involved in the development process.

He decided to select his committee from salespeople in the organization, along with his wife, who was in charge of the financial records of the firm. He also decided to involve the firm's banker, the John Deere factory representative, and even two key farmer-customers. Another source of data and information and assistance might be the county agricultural agent or an agricultural economist from the land-grant univer-

Sample Budget for Kalamazoo Farm & Industrial Tractor Company			EXHIBIT 9-1

SALES BUDGET: January–March
KALAMAZOO FARM & INDUSTRIAL TRACTOR COMPANY

SALES	BUDGET	ACTUAL	DEVIATION FROM BUDGET
Large commercial tractors	$ 270,000	————	————
Small garden tractors	70,000	————	————
Combines and harvest equipment	250,000	————	————
Tillage equipment	200,000	————	————
Farm and industrial	125,000	————	————
Total sales	$ 915,000	————	————

sity. Once Frederick had set up the committee, he wanted to work informally with some of the members on an individual basis. Others he wanted to involve in only a formal meeting. Before the meeting, Frederick reviewed and put down on paper the organization's objectives and policies regarding sales. He then reviewed the present situation and any current constraints, the records of what happened last year, and evaluations of what caused it to happen. He committed his review to paper so that he could present it to the planning committee. At this point, he also related input factors from the budget to determine the profitability of last year's program and the profit potential for the future program. Explaining the reason for developing the budget and the goals he hoped would be accomplished would be the first step in determining the committee's course of action.

When the sales-forecast committee met, Frederick presented them with the data and information he had prepared. The committee discussed all the issues involved and added new information and insights of which Frederick had not been aware.

The next thing on the agenda was to decide the parts or components of the report system. Sales were divided into large-commercial-tractor sales and small-garden-tractor sales, combines and harvesting equipment, tillage equipment, and farm and industrial sales. It was believed that this breakdown of sales would be the most meaningful one for predictive and control purposes.

Once the components of the budget had been determined, the next step was to identify how the budget was to be used and the people and parts of the organization that would benefit from the use of the sales forecast and budget. The report was then designed so that it would fill the needs of those who might be interested in using it. These included the members of the sales staff and the repair and service department. It was also most helpful to the firm's banker and to the manufacturers and suppliers of the products that Kalamazoo Farm & Industrial Tractor sells.

Then the committee determined where the information would be gathered and how it was to be tabulated. They decided that the original sales invoices to customers would provide the input information for the sales-forecast control program. The invoices would be the source, and the measure would be dollars of sales. At this point, the budget period was designated as the company's fiscal year. Sales budgets and sales forecasts are usually made for 1 year, with intermediate steps or goals on a monthly or quarterly basis. Frequent updating is necessary to make the report usable. As sales manager, Frederick would determine the frequency of review and updating based on changes and new facts. The preparation of the sales control report was assigned to the office manager, who would have the input information that would make the budget and sales forecast meaningful.

The last step was identification of the person responsible for meeting the goals and standards within the control program. As sales manager, Frederick was assigned this responsibility.

It is necessary to build into the sales forecast or budget, or any other control program, the evaluation criteria that will be used to determine whether the information prepared is actually serving the needs of the organization.

Because of the interrelationships of all budgets and the unexpected or unknown factors that can occur, budgets should be assessed or revamped whenever new facts surface. There should also be a regular planned evaluation or review period. This review permits deviations or problems to be spotted quickly and the effects, positive or negative, to be evaluated before it is too late.

All budgets and all forecast and control measures may be important to the life of the company, but the sales forecast and budget are usually developed first because sales is the basic reason for the existence of any agribusiness and affects all other aspects of the business. Those serving on the committee at Kalamazoo Farm & Industrial Tractor were able not only to add special, unique knowledge but also to assume a positive responsibility for accomplishment because they were part of the team that developed it.

Good budgets and other control programs can aid the organization in its competitive life struggle by promoting a goal-oriented team approach and by providing the specifications and controls for a successful operation.

EVALUATING CONTROL PROGRAMS

The most effective control occurs when the most attention is given to the results that are vital to the survival of the organization. Pasteur said, "Chance favors only minds which are prepared." We might rephrase this to read, "Success favors only those organizations that are prepared," in other words, those organizations that recognize and concentrate on the key performance areas.

Various management writers have called these areas KPA (key performance areas) or KI (key indicators). We shall call them SFC (significant factors of control).

Test for SFC

1. How vital is the information?

2. What will occur if the information is not known?

3. Will the information be used?

4. Will the information be accurate?

5. What is the cost (dollars and time) in relation to value?

Many control programs, when tested, are found to lack sufficient importance to justify the effort involved in maintaining them. Too many controls can render an entire control program ineffective. Too few can be fatal, so the test for significance becomes vital to the success of the enterprise. The agribusiness manager should test each new control program, as well as reviewing existing control programs on a regular basis.

MANAGEMENT BY EXCEPTION

An exciting management technique called management by exception has been introduced relatively recently. Its basic premise is that managers should not spend time on management areas that are progressing according to plan. Rather, they should concentrate on those areas in which everything is not progressing as it should. If sales are in line with the forecast, the manager can devote the bulk of his or her efforts to other areas, such as production, personnel, costs, and expansion. Consider this example of an actual agribusiness company.

On the following pages the sales forecasts for the Acme Fertilizer Company (name changed) are given. Sales are broken down into two component parts because limited production lines, bulk fertilizer and bag fertilizer, are produced at Acme. Now, referring to the sixteen steps in developing a control program, one will recall that the sales forecast is basically the predetermined course of action, or the goals, of the marketing department. These goals are essential in keeping the sales force alert and in allowing key executives to make remedial decisions related to sales performance, should the agribusiness deviate from its established goals.

This annual sales forecast for fertilizer was developed by combining all the individual salespeople's estimates of sales for the coming year. Then the marketing manager met with other key individuals, such as the executive vice president, production vice president, new products manager, and purchasing director, to determine whether anticipated input (costs) matched anticipated output (revenue). They also acted as a committee and completed the other steps in setting up a control program. The committee determined that the control program would be reported on a component basis—that is, by bag and bulk sales—and on a monthly basis with a semiannual review of other specific sales items to be made in detail as a supplement to the overall control program. The committee also decided to report the sales in dollars because this was the most meaningful alternative for all concerned.

The executive vice president and comptroller agreed that the information needed could be secured from company records, that is, the previous year's sales forecast, past actual sales, and current customer-sales invoicing. The office manager would prepare the monthly control-information report, and it would be shared with all employees of the company, as well as with the company's banker. The sales manager was given the principal responsibility for accomplishing the goals of the program.

Up to this point, the process of developing the control program was pretty much the same as that described for the Kalamazoo Farm & Industrial Tractor Company. But Josephine Drake, the sales manager of

Acme Fertilizer Company, decided that she would use a new approach for the control report: "management by exception" graphs instead of raw figures. She had decided on this reporting technique for the following reasons.

1. It allows one to ignore those management areas where goals are on target, and to concentrate on problem areas instead.

2. It allows one to see at a glance the whole situation, and the comparative data are illustrated as clearly as a picture.

3. It is simple and easy to prepare and is easily understood by anyone, even those unskilled in financial management.

4. It can be easily reproduced and widely distributed to interested persons.

5. Often several pages of figures can be effectively depicted in one graph.

6. It allows for a clearer interpretation of the many interrelated factors than figures can provide.

To construct the management by exception graph, the first thing the committee had to do was to establish an allowable deviation. In terms of the sales forecast, *allowable deviation* meant the amount by which actual sales could fall or rise above the sales forecast before management had to determine whether remedial action was needed. In the Acme Company, the team decided that sales could deviate from the forecast by 4 percent in either direction before remedial action would be called for. A deviation of more than 4 percent either below or above the forecast would affect such areas as inventory of raw and finished product, production scheduling, capital and cash positions, labor needs, advertising, and promotion programs, and pricing policy. Each of these programs would have to be reviewed by the management team if control sales deviated from the forecast. This, of course, is the major purpose of a control program: to sound the alarm for further study and action.

Once the allowable deviation was established, all that remained was designing the management by exception graph (see Figure 9-2). At the bottom right is Acme's sales forecast for the year. This is Acme's goal, and when it is transposed to the sample graph on a period-to-period basis, it can be drawn as a straight line, or 100 percent of goals. A graph such as the one in Figure 9-2 could show several different but related factors, such as total sales, last year's sales, bulk sales, and bag sales, through the use of different symbols or lines. For the sake of simplicity in illustrating the principles involved, only total sales and last year's sales are shown. Last year's sales are figured as a deviation from last year's forecast, not from the current forecast. The shaded area is the allowable deviation from our goals. Below the graph an example and formula for determining how the deviations are figured are provided.

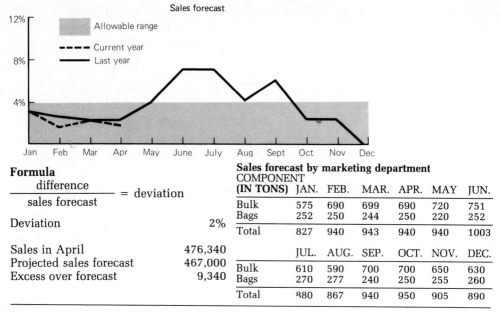

Figure 9-2   Management by exception graph for
Acme Fertilizer Company.

Formula

$$\frac{\text{difference}}{\text{sales forecast}} = \text{deviation}$$

Deviation	2%
Sales in April	476,340
Projected sales forecast	467,000
Excess over forecast	9,340

Sales forecast by marketing department

COMPONENT (IN TONS)	JAN.	FEB.	MAR.	APR.	MAY	JUN.
Bulk	575	690	699	690	720	751
Bags	252	250	244	250	220	252
Total	827	940	943	940	940	1003

	JUL.	AUG.	SEP.	OCT.	NOV.	DEC.
Bulk	610	590	700	700	650	630
Bags	270	277	240	250	255	260
Total	880	867	940	950	905	890

Josephine Drake was aware of the fact that last year several of Acme's competitors had suddenly lowered their prices in April, and that because Acme had not been alert enough, it had taken them several months to meet this challenge. As a result, many thousands of dollars of sales and consequent profits had been lost. Josephine was determined that this would not happen again. Acme had been forced to lower its prices substantially in order to recover lost customers and was now operating on a narrowing gross margin as cost increases, largely due to inflation, became an increasing burden. Josephine knew that other manufacturers were feeling the same pinch, but each had to fight for market share to meet overhead costs.

To illustrate the value of the management by exception approach assume that May sales were up by 6 percent, or 2 percent over allowable deviation. The marketing department would have immediately taken a careful survey of competitors' prices. Perhaps some major competitors were trying to adjust prices to meet increased cost. If this were true, Acme would have several alternatives. It could increase its price, thereby widening its gross margin and profits but maintaining the same relative market share. Or it could increase the volume of sales and market share, thereby causing increased turnover and increased profits. Plant capacity, growth objectives, available funds, and dealer reaction would all play a part in the final decision. Good financial records and proper analysis of them would also be essential to the final decision. Most of the tools that the agribusiness manager would need in order to obtain the information and knowledge so necessary to sound decision making have been provided in earlier chapters, but the final decision will still be subjective in nature. It will be made by a human being and will involve the ability to weave the facts together into a complex whole, using innate knowledge and experience, making the best educated guess, and being willing to take the responsibility for the decision.

In the final analysis, this is always the way it is. That's why management is one of the highest professional callings. Imagine the success rates of two managers, one who uses good financial management skills and systems competing against another who uses rules of thumb or "seat of the pants" decision-making practices. There is no question which manager and which agribusiness firm will succeed in the long run.

CONTROLLING CREDIT

Credit control receives special attention because no other single factor has been responsible for more of agribusiness's serious financial problems. Many firms have even been forced to go out of business because of faulty credit control. New businesses must be particularly wary of their credit control as they fight to establish themselves and attract customers. The extension of credit in most agribusinesses is an important and convenient way for customers to borrow money (because that, in fact, is what it really is). For the agribusiness and its managers, however, credit can create a costly, complex managerial headache.

Credit is Part of Sales

It is important to recognize that the least costly way of doing business is to sell for cash! Many large and successful firms have been built on a cash-only basis.

If cash sales are the least costly method of doing business, then the next principle must state that credit extension can only be justified to the extent that it improves sales volume and profits through turnover. If the extension of credit by a business does not meet this test, it will cause profits to shrink.

In almost every sector of agribusiness, credit is something that the purchaser expects or willingly takes. Buyers often look upon it as a right and are usually unaware of its high cost, a cost that must ultimately be paid for or passed on to the purchaser if the seller is to maintain economic viability.

Two grain and supply elevators in a small Michigan town were in close competition for the farmers' dollars. Other agribusiness firms, basic manufacturers of fertilizer, pesticides, etc., were selecting the largest and most successful farmers and making them direct dealers. Credit terms became looser and looser. Finally, the management of one of the elevators took a long hard look at the cost of credit extension. As a result, they decided to sell on a cash-only basis and reduced prices by the amount of the cost of credit plus the expected increase in volume that they thought a lower price would generate. One of the promotional slogans was, "Why pay more, to subsidize the farmer who never pays?" No one likes to pay for another's debts, and yet, when credit is extended, someone must pay for the cost of bad debts. As a result of their new policy, this elevator ended up with most of the successful farmers as customers. Actually, some farm customers bought from the elevator when they had cash and from its competitors when they needed credit. This is not always the right way for a firm to go, but it is always to be considered a viable alternative to credit extension.

Sales and marketing managers are the leading proponents of credit extension. One of the most successful ways of making salespeople responsible is to make them accountable for credit costs, including bad debts, and putting this cost squarely into the sales profit and budget control system where it belongs. Credit is not an operational cost but a sales cost.

The Costs of Credit

Costs of credit come in many forms, some of which are not so easily recognized by agribusiness managers. Some of the most important of these are:

1. Borrowing money to support accounts receivable

2. Lost earnings opportunities (opportunity cost) for the use of equity funds tied up in accounts receivable

3. Liquidity problems, which can cause a firm's bankers and suppliers to raise interest rates or cut back on credit extension to the firm

4. The costs of losses on bad debts or extremely slow accounts that may have to be discounted

5. The costs of administering the credit program

6. The cost of too free a credit policy, which can actually help some customers get into financial trouble that results in loss of business

7. Too free a credit extension, which can force competitive reaction of lower margins or even freer credit policies

8. The cost of legal and other activities needed to collect accounts receivable

9. The work-time frustration and hard feelings of both managers and customers over disputed accounts

10. The increased risk of accounts receivable to the existence and viability of the firm, and alternative uses of capital

With all these drawbacks it would seem unlikely that credit would be extended at all, yet no other segment of business has a higher percentage of credit usage than agribusiness. The high seasonality and erratic cash flows of marketing crops are undoubtedly the major reason why credit is so prevalent in the agribusiness sector. Competitive forces are such that most agribusiness managers must learn to administer credit programs skillfully.

Some Possibilities for Profit

Since most agribusinesses are in the lending business, one of the options open is to use the extension of credit as a profit center. It is possible to minimize costs or, in some cases, actually make a profit on credit extension. It is becoming common practice to charge interest on accounts payable. Basic competitive conditions, the interest rate the firm itself is paying, and the amount of funds available are the factors determining the rate charged. It is not uncommon for agribusiness firms to charge from 1 to 2 percent per month on unpaid balances.

Caution must be exercised to see that the disclosure of credit terms is made in compliance with the federal Truth in Lending Act.[1] In addition, most states have uniform consumer credit codes that regulate credit terms and interest rates.

Another potential approach is to grant discounts for cash sales. These discounts can be absolute or can be extended for short periods of time, such as 10 days or 30 days from invoicing the customer. A very common discount is 1 percent for 10 days. This means that the purchaser may deduct 1 percent of the invoiced amount if it is paid within 10 days. When such terms are offered by the firm's suppliers, the agribusiness manager should take advantage of them, since the annual savings in rates of interest can be very high. A booklet with descriptions and tables of rates is available from the Federal Reserve System.

A cash discount can be converted to an equivalent annual interest rate. Say that Hilltop Fertilizer wished to reduce its accounts receivable by offering a cash discount to its customers. Say that Hilltop offered a 2 percent discount on items that were paid for in cash within 30 days, whenever an account was due in 120 days (2%/30 net 120 days). Use the following formula:

$$\frac{\text{Equivalent annual}}{\text{interest rate (EAIR)}} = \frac{\text{discount \%}}{100 - \text{discount \%}}$$

$$\times \frac{365 \text{ days}}{\text{account due date} - \text{cash discount period}}$$

$$\text{EAIR} = \frac{2}{100 - 2} \times \frac{365}{120 - 30} = 8.27\%$$

Hilltop has now defined a cost of credit that can be compared with other alternative approaches. It will also help Hilltop to evaluate its own options when paying its bills.

---

[1]*Truth in Lending*, Vol. I, *Regulation 2 Annual Percentage Rate Tables*, Board of Governors, Federal Reserve System, Washington, D.C. 20551.

Retailers also can often avail themselves of such credit card services as Visa and MasterCard. There is a charge for the firm to join and a charge for servicing the firm's accounts. It does, however, insure against bad debts and slow collections and reduce the cost of accounts receivable. Managers must weigh these service charges against their credit-extension costs and select the most profitable alternative.

As in granting extensions of credit, the agribusiness manager should carefully study the use of credit terms available from suppliers and vendors. Strategy in this area, detailed in Chapter 10, can increase the profitability of a firm considerably.

Planning the Credit Program

Careful planning and development of the firm's credit program is the key to success. The first step is to develop goals and objectives for the credit program. These should be clearly stated in terms of increased sales, competitive factors, and profitability.

The second step is a careful analysis of the costs and benefits of a credit program. At this point, it is important that all costs mentioned be considered. Benefits can include earnings through charges levied, increased volume, competitive requirements, and taking early delivery with consequent storage savings.

The third step is to assign responsibilities for the administration and supervision of the firm's credit program. This is a most important function. The person supervising the credit program should operate it within certain defined written policies and constraints developed by top management, such as top limits of credit, credit credentials or worthiness of purchasers, and collection policies.

Determining the credit worth of a purchaser is probably the top priority in avoiding bad-debt loss and slow payment. This requires a careful check of the purchasers against the "3 C's" of credit: character, capacity, and capital.

Character; Capacity; Capital   *Character* refers to the personal habits, conduct, honesty, and attitude of the credit customer. *Capacity* refers to the earnings and cash flow with which the customer can meet personal obligations. *Capital* refers to the solvency or net worth of the credit customer. It is a measure of the collateral or security that can be collected if the customer fails to pay. This is the last resort for collection, and if the manager expects to be forced to liquidate a customer's assets to collect the credit, that sale should not be made in the first place.

This information is available from the applicant, banks, credit references, local and national credit-rating firms, and credit bureaus. A recent survey showed that less than half of the farm supply dealers even went so far as to request a credit application from those who wished credit. No wonder credit loss and accounts receivable problems are so prevalent in agribusiness.

Monitoring the Credit Program

Once the credit program is set up, the manager must know what is happening and how well the program is operating. Several ratios can be helpful in the reporting and analysis of credit programs.[2] Only two of the most critical ones are offered here.

Aging Accounts Receivable   The most important tool in monitoring accounts receivable is the monthly aging of these accounts. Each account from the ledger is summarized and reported on a form similar to the one shown in Figure 9-3.

An increase in the percentage of accounts that are slow paying, or increases in the amounts of receivables, calls for a review of the credit programs and policies before the situation becomes dangerous to the firm's financial health.

To control changes in accounts receivable, a ratio indicating changes in credit sales volume from one period to another is helpful.

$$\frac{\text{Credit sales for current period}}{\text{Credit sales for previous period}} \times 100 = \begin{array}{l} \text{percentage change in} \\ \text{credit sales} \end{array}$$

Bad debts are the agribusiness manager's nightmare. When the agribusiness sells and fails to collect, it is worse than no sales at all. Not only does the business suffer from the loss in gross margin, but it also has to chalk up the loss from the cost of the goods or service sold, plus the aggravation and cost of trying (usually unsuccessfully) to collect the debt. To monitor bad debts, use the formula

$$\frac{\text{Bad debts (\$)}}{\text{Total credit sales}} \times 100 = \text{bad debts as a \% of credit sales}$$

The cost of bad debts is very serious for many agribusinesses. Fig-

Figure 9-3   Summary of Ledger Account.

Period outstanding	Accounts receivable	Percentage this period	Percentage last period	Percentage change
Less than 30 days				
30–60 days				
60–90 days				
Over 90 days				
Total				

[2]A good discussion of credit programs is offered by *Credit Management for Small Business Firms*, North Central Regional Extension Publication 54, Iowa State University, Ames, Iowa 50011 (1978).

ure 9-4 provides a better understanding of just how seriously this cost affects business profits.

The tremendous amount of increase in sales necessary to offset bad debts can be vividly seen in Figure 9-4. For example, a $20,000 bad debt requires an increase in sales of at least $100,000 at a 20 percent margin on sales just to bring profits back equal to sales without the bad debt. Credit sales have to be monitored very carefully or they can quickly eat up all the profits a business is generating.

Because the stakes are so high, a carefully conceived and executed credit program is necessary for any agribusiness and its management team.

SUMMARY

As we have seen, control programs are the means by which an agribusiness manager coordinates the activities of the business, predicts trends and results, amasses data for planning, sets goals, and utilizes the lessons of past experience. Control is achieved by means of basic programs relating to marketing, production, personnel, and financial records, along with more complex programs for larger organizations. The most common control programs are budgets and forecasts, or predictions of business inputs and outputs.

To be effective, control programs must combine both quantitative techniques (linear projection, models, simulation, etc.) and qualitative techniques (consensus, logic, scenarios, etc.). There are sixteen successive steps to developing a control program; of these, the three most central are the review of organizational objectives and goals, analysis of the current situation vis-à-vis those goals, and relation of projected costs (inputs) to projected revenues (outputs). Control programs must be constantly monitored and reevaluated by means of the five SFC (significant factors of control).

An exciting new management technique called management by exception focuses attention on those areas of the agribusiness where problems exist, and makes data easier to produce and understand.

One of the areas in which development of a strong control program is most important is credit control, where upward spiraling costs often cause serious financial problems for agribusinesses. Two possible solutions are to make the extension of credit a profit center or to dis-

Figure 9-4   Sales increases required to offset bad debts.

Bad debt or loss	Margin		
	5%	10%	20%
	(you must increase sales by the amount)		
$ 1,000	$ 20,000	$ 10,000	$ 5,000
$ 5,000	$100,000	$ 50,000	$ 25,000
$20,000	$400,000	$200,000	$100,000

count cash sales. In any event, credit programs should be planned and monitored carefully in order to develop systems for determining a customer's credit worth and for minimizing accounts receivable or outright bad debts.

The agribusiness manager who incorporates these basic tools for control into the daily activities of the business will stand a good chance of developing and maintaining a profitable enterprise.

DISCUSSION QUESTIONS

1. Define control and explain why it is such an important management tool.

2. Explain the purposes of control programs and describe the areas where they are most likely to be found in an agribusiness.

3. What is the basic difference between a forecast and a budget? How are they linked together?

4. Discuss why the budget is so important to the future form that the agribusiness will take.

5. Examine and discuss the use of varied quantitative and qualitative approaches to developing forecasts and budgets.

6. Discuss each of the sixteen steps for developing a control program and the purposes of the steps.

7. List the advantages of using the management by exception management approach to control programs.

8. Using hypothetical figures, add two months to the Acme management by exception graph.

9. Tell why credit is extended and why it is a sales mechanism.

10. Discuss and explain the true cost of credit extension.

11. Under what circumstances can the extension of credit become a profit center?

12. Discuss why creditworthiness is the most important step in extending credit.

13. Examine and discuss the danger credit extension poses to the agribusiness.

14. Tell what control programs you would use to control credit in any agribusiness that you select.

MINICASE

Take a real or hypothetical agribusiness and develop a management by exception control program for that business.

QUESTIONS

1. Write a description of the agribusiness.

2. List all sixteen points of developing a control program and tell how you will handle the program.

3. Develop allowable deviations.

4. Draw a graph and show examples of figures used in its development as per management by exception exhibit.

OBJECTIVES

- Understanding the decision-making process and its role in professional management

- Explain variable and fixed costs and their relationship with the volume of business

- Learn to calculate the break-even point

- Apply volume-cost analysis techniques to important agribusiness decisions

- Describe the critical role of capital-investment decisions to agribusiness

- Develop an appreciation for the time value of money

- Examine and learn to apply basic tools for analyzing capital-investment decisions in agribusiness

Agribusiness managers rely on specialized financial tools for making decisions.
A. Capital budgeting
B. Volume-cost analysis

TO DECIDE NOT TO DECIDE
IS TO DECIDE.

TOOLS FOR MANAGEMENT
DECISIONS IN AGRIBUSINESS

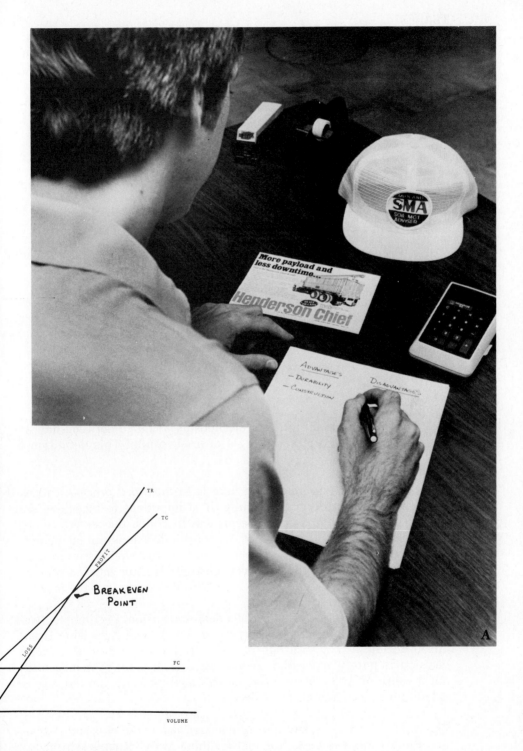

TR

TC

PROFIT

← BREAKEVEN
POINT

LOSS

FC

VOLUME

A

B

Volume Cost Analysis

TEASER

Happy Valley Packing and Shipping Company was rocking along pretty well until new owners took over and began to apply pressure for better performance and a higher return on their investment. But now Brad Johnson, the newly appointed general manager, is struggling with all kinds of questions, alternatives, and ideas for improving profits. Although he has some good accounting information, he is not sure how to use it to answer tough management questions, like:

"How much do I have to sell to cover all my costs?"

"What volume of business is necessary to make 10 percent ROI?"

"If I lower my price 5 percent to sell more, will it pay?"

"Can I afford new electronic sorting equipment?"

"How should I advise the board of directors about which expansion investment is best for the business?"

Professional agribusiness managers view decision making as a process and use analytical tools to help make decisions wherever feasible. Then they complement formal analysis and decision making with their personal experience, judgment, and intuitive feel for the situation.

DECISION MAKING

Definition

"Decision making is the process of choosing a course between alternatives for the purpose of achieving a desired result." This definition is analyzed in the following sections.

Process The first important idea here is in the word *process*. Process implies activity, or doing something. It is important to recognize that good decision making is an active process in which the manager is aggressively and personally involved. Of course, decisions can be made by default; that is, one can do nothing for so long that there is no longer a decision to be made. Putting off decisions until it is too late is a problem most people know something about. But good decision making is active and timely involvement.

Deciding to do nothing is *not* a default decision. Deciding to "wait and see" may be a logical and correct choice. A default decision is failure to decide. It may turn out OK, but any positive result of a default decision is purely accidental. Any success is in spite of management, not because of it; therefore, most professional managers do not rely on default decisions, if at all possible.

Choosing The second key idea in decision making is *choosing*. Choosing implies there is a choice; that is, there are alternatives to choose between. When one has no alternatives, then there is no decision to be made. And, alternatives must be feasible. They must be realistic and reachable. For example, quitting is always an alternative, but it is seldom a realistic one. So it need not even be considered as an alternative in most situations.

Goals Finally, decision making is *purposeful*. Efficient decision making requires that a clear goal be firmly in mind. If one is driving a car without knowing the destination, one is likely to experience considerable difficulty in arriving there. So it is with decision making. If goals are clear, a good decision is much easier.

Goals like alternatives, must be feasible and specific. To say "My goal is to make as much profit as possible" is not much help in operating a fertilizer outlet. It is far too general a goal to be of much use. Maximizing profit is like God, mother, country, and apple pie! Everybody is for it. But a specific goal, such as "To generate a 10 percent return on investment, maintain an annual growth rate of 5 percent, and provide an opportunity for meaningful employment for family members" will be exceedingly helpful in guiding day-to-day decisions.

Decision-Making Process

The decision-making process is simply a logical procedure for identifying a problem, analyzing it, and arriving at a solution. It can be carried out in a formal manner, where many people are involved in its various aspects, work for many months, spend a great deal of money, and publish lengthy reports. Or it can occur informally over coffee in just a few minutes with no written report at all. The more important the issue, the more likely the process is to be formalized. In any case, professional decision making is a systematic process involving several rather specific steps.

The decision-making process involves three necessary elements. First, decision making is built around facts. The less relevant factual information there is available, the more difficult the decision-making process will be. Second, decision making involves analysis of factual information. Analysis may be a highly rigorous statistical treatment utilizing large computers, or it can be simply a logical thinking process, but in either case, it requires careful examination of facts. Finally, the decision-making process requires an element of judgment, a subjective evaluation of the situation based on experience and common "horse sense." Although it is theoretically possible to be completely mechanical in the decision-making process, seldom, if ever, are enough facts available or are there sufficient resources or time to completely analyze it. Human judgment is a necessary part of professional decision making. The steps are as follows.

1. *Problem Identification.* This is often the toughest part. It is easy to confuse symptoms with the real problem. The problem may seem to be low profits, when low profits are simply the result of an inefficient, high-cost distribution system. Once the problem is clearly defined, it can usually be dealt with.

2. *Summary of Facts.* This step brings to the surface and highlights information pertinent to the problem and its solution. It may be critical to note overall company goals, the impact of the problem on the business, environmental factors limiting possible solutions, or technical facts that affect the outcome.

3. *Laying Out Alternatives.* This step identifies and lists feasible alternative solutions, exploring various possibilities. Only feasible solutions should be considered.

4. *Analysis.* This step may require rigorous examination, weighing the costs and benefits of each alternative. It considers both short- and long-term company goals. Although analysis should be objective, the final selection process should include subjective evaluation of alternatives.

5. *Action.* The final step involves carrying out the chosen alternative. Often this requires careful planning prior to the execution. But it is a critical step. Management responsibility goes farther than deciding; it requires execution and results.

DECISION TOOLS

There are numerous tools for analyzing alternatives and making management decisions, and the number is growing rapidly. Some are complex, while others are simple. The decision-making process just described is, in itself, a decision tool. But among the more important decision tools used by agribusiness managers are volume-cost analysis and investment analysis. This is because most agricultural businesses are so seasonal that large investments can be used only for very short periods of time—for example, during planting or harvesting. This high degree of seasonality emphasizes the importance of investment decisions and the uses of fixed assets. The use of volume-cost analysis is explained in this chapter, and it shows how capital budgeting–investment analysis can be used to make investment decisions.

Volume-Cost Analysis

Volume-cost analysis is a tool for examining the relationship between costs and the volume of business done. It analyzes differences in the kinds of costs encountered by every agribusiness and how they are affected by the volume of business done. Volume-cost analysis (or break-even analysis, as it is sometimes called) shows the level of business necessary to break even and to earn a specific amount of profit under various cost and price assumptions.

Volume-cost analysis can show the impact of changes in selling price on the volume of business necessary to reach a certain profit level. It can reveal specifically how anticipated cost changes will affect profit levels. It can be useful in evaluating various marketing strategies, such as advertising and promotion expenditures, individual product pricing, and the amount of usage a new piece of equipment must have to make it pay.

The basis for volume-cost analysis is the separation of costs into two categories, fixed and variable. *Fixed costs* are those costs that do not fluctuate with the volume of business. *Variable costs* are those costs that change directly with the volume of sales. The key question in sorting costs into these two classes is whether the cost is *directly* affected by how much is sold. Said another way, fixed costs are present regardless of the amount of business done. As soon as a business gears up for a particular level of sales, it incurs a certain amount of expense whether or not it makes any sales at all. These are fixed or sunk costs.

On the other hand, some additional expenses are incurred as product is sold. These incremental expenses are not charged to the profit and loss statement if the sale is not completed. These are *variable costs*. Note that the emphasis is on the sale. The actual sale of a product or service is the point of determination. Even in a manufacturing or processing plant, where costs are incurred throughout the production process, the crucial point is the actual sale. Until the sales transaction is completed, no costs are counted as expenses and are therefore included on the profit and loss statement. Instead, they remain in inventory and show only on the balance sheet. If there are no sales during a period, by definition there are no variable costs. Selling something actually causes the variable costs to be incurred.

Some people tend to confuse variable costs with controllable costs, but they are not the same thing. While some variable costs are controllable by management, others are not. For example, gasoline cost associated with delivering products is variable because it is incurred automatically when and only when product is actually sold and delivered. But management usually can do little, if anything, to control it.

On the other hand, advertising costs are generally controllable, but they do not vary directly with sales. Theoretically at least, advertising causes sales, which is the opposite situation from a variable cost. Once the advertising expenditure is committed, whether sales result or not has nothing to do with paying the advertising bill. Thus, advertising is a fixed cost, even though it is controllable.

Perhaps a graphical illustration can further clarify the important fixed- and variable-cost concept. Assume that TCP, Inc. (Texas Citrus Products), has a fixed cost or overhead, as it is sometimes called, of $200,000 per year.

Fixed Costs *Fixed costs* are constant regardless of volume during the period. If TCP, Inc., opens for business but has no sales at all, then its total fixed costs are $200,000. If its sales volume is $200,000, its fixed costs remain at $200,000. If its sales volume is $500,000, its fixed costs are still $200,000. The horizontal line shows that regardless of sales volume, fixed costs will remain at $200,000 (Figure 10-1).

Now, looking at fixed costs as a percentage of sales, if TCP, Inc., sells only $200,000 worth of citrus products during the year, its fixed cost per dollar of sales is 100 percent ($200,000 ÷ $200,000). If sales are

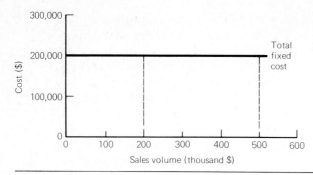

Figure 10-1   Regardless of sales volume, fixed
costs remain the same.

$400,000 of products sold, fixed cost drops to 50 percent. If sales are $500,000, fixed cost drops to 40 percent of sales. At $1 million sales, fixed costs drop to 20 percent of sales. Fixed-cost percentage continues to drop as long as volume is increased in that same physical plant (Figure 10-2). The fact that fixed costs as a percent of sales fall rapidly as sales increase is extremely important to operating efficiency in any agribusiness.

Variable Costs   *Variable costs,* on the other hand, behave quite differently. Assume that the variable cost per ton of sales for TCP, Inc., averages 60 percent of each dollar of sales; that is, every time a dollar's worth of product is sold, a 60-cent cost is incurred (including the cost of goods). At zero sales, TCP, Inc., incurs no variable cost, so the initial total variable cost is zero. If sales are $200,000 and each dollar has 60-cents variable cost, total variable cost would be $120,000 for the period (0.60 × $200,000). At $400,000 sales, total variable cost is $240,000 (0.60 × $400,000) (Figure 10-3).

Now, looking at variable costs per dollar of sales, if TCP, Inc., sells

Figure 10-2   As sales volume increases, fixed
costs as a percentage of sales will decrease.

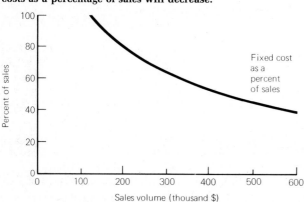

FINANCIAL MANAGEMENT AND CONTROL OF THE AGRIBUSINESS

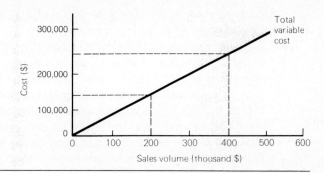

Figure 10-3   **Total variable cost increases with sales volume.**

$200,000, its variable cost per ton is 60 percent. If its sales are $400,000, its variable cost per ton is 60 percent. In fact, no matter what the volume of sales, the variable cost per ton remains essentially at 60 percent, or, in other words, constant (Figure 10-4).

    The key idea can be summarized as follows: (1) *As sales increase, total variable costs increase but variable-cost percentages remain constant,* and (2) *as sales increase, total fixed costs remain constant but fixed-cost percentages fall.*

Special Problems in Allocating Costs

SEMIVARIABLE COST   There is a third type of cost—the semivariable cost. This is a cost that is partly fixed and partly variable, such as the electric bill. There is a fixed charge per month, and then the usage charges increase. These can and should be considered in volume-cost relationships. A simple way of handling semivariable costs is to carefully estimate the fixed portion, the amount that is part of the cost of just being open for business, and then estimate the portion that is incremen-

Figure 10-4   **Regardless of sales volume, variable cost as a percentage of sales remains constant.**

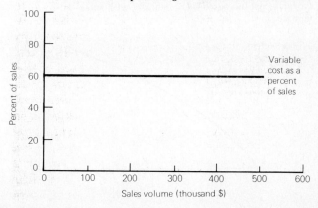

tal with each additional sale. With this allocation of semivariable costs, volume-cost analysis can proceed.

INCREMENTAL COSTS NOT CONSTANT   Another difficulty can be variable costs that increase incrementally with sales, but not along a straight line. That is, as sales increase to higher levels, the additional cost for each unit becomes increasingly smaller, or greater. This situation can be handled nicely, so long as the exact relationships are known. The graphical or mathematical analysis becomes more complicated, but the analysis can be performed and used in the same way (Figure 10-5).

LUMPINESS   Some costs are lumpy, that is, they are fixed within certain sales-volume ranges, but then once a certain point is reached, a whole new set of fixed costs are incurred. For example, when a delivery truck reaches its maximum capacity, sales cannot be increased further unless another truck is purchased. An additional truck suddenly increases fixed costs, such as depreciation, insurance, and licenses for the new truck (Figure 10-6). This lumpiness can also be included in graphical or mathematical volume-cost analysis. It just becomes more complicated.

LENGTH OF TIME PERIOD   The length of the time period under consideration has a great deal to do with whether a cost is classified as fixed or variable. In the very long run, all costs become variable with sales volume. Even depreciation, often considered the classical fixed cost, can vary with the volume of business if the time period is sufficiently long that a new building can be built. For example, over a 5-year period, if the business grows, an entire new set of facilities may be built as a direct result of the increased volume of business. But in the very short run, say 1 day, all but the most direct costs associated with the cost of the product and the actual cost of the sale are fixed and cannot be changed within that period.

Therefore, it is important to define the time period that is under consideration. The time period selected depends entirely on the problems that are of concern and the decisions to be made. Most common

Figure 10-5   Graph of situation when the total variable cost increases incrementally with sales volume.

FINANCIAL MANAGEMENT AND CONTROL OF THE AGRIBUSINESS

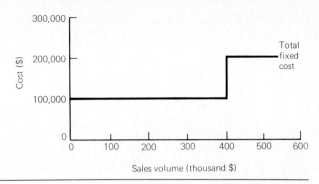

Figure 10-6   Total fixed cost can become lumpy at
a certain sales volume.

time periods considered are reasonably short, such as a season or a quarter, or, most commonly, a year.

Actually, the fine points of separating fixed and variable costs are not critical to making rough approximations of the volume-cost relationships. The analysis, of course, can be no better than the information used in making the analysis. But experience shows that so long as reasonable care is taken in applying the proper definition in allocating costs into fixed and variable categories and a realistic time period is assumed, close approximations of fixed and variable costs may be made without regard to semivariable costs, unequal incremental increases, or lumpiness. Volume-cost analysis can then proceed, providing highly useful insights into important management questions. Of course, if major violations of the simple assumptions are known to exist, caution should be used.

Volume-Cost Analysis Procedure   Take a typical operating statement from Hilltop Fertilizer Co., Inc. (Chapter 6) and analyze the volume-cost relationships. There are four distinct steps in determining the break-even point from the firm's operating statement.

STEP 1: IDENTIFY FIXED AND VARIABLE COSTS   The actual classification of expense items from a firm's profit and loss statement depends on the makeup of each expense item. Thus it is necessary to be familiar with the operation and its accounting system in order to be accurate. For example, rent for one firm may be strictly a fixed monthly amount, while another firm may have a rental contract that ties rent to the level of sales, making it a variable cost.

Take a look at Hilltop Fertilizer Company (Exhibit 10-1) and isolate its fixed and variable costs for the year. Hilltop is an actual retail fertilizer plant in the Midwest; the determination of its fixed and variable costs is based on the actual situation as interpreted by its manager.

Salary and Wages, including Benefits—*mostly fixed;* since Hilltop operates with only full-time labor and pays only minimal overtime, salary and wages are essentially all fixed, with only $3500

213

ITEM	AMOUNT	PERCENT OF SALES
Sales	$1,000,000	100.0
Cost of goods sold	750,000	75.0
Gross margin	$ 250,000	25.0
Operating expenses		
Salary and wages, including benefits	$ 75,000	7.5
Local taxes, licenses	5,000	0.5
Insurance	6,000	0.6
Depreciation	20,000	2.0
Rent and lease	7,000	0.7
Advertising and promotion	5,000	0.5
Office expense	2,000	0.2
Utilities	3,000	0.3
Maintenance and repair	17,000	0.7
Bad-debt loss	2,000	0.2
Supplies	4,000	0.4
Other	4,000	0.4
Total operating expense	$150,000	15.0
Net operating profit	$100,000	10.0
Interest expense	15,000	1.5
Net profit	$ 85,000	8.5

in overtime wages. Once Hilltop gears up for the year, its labor cost is essentially locked in regardless of the volume of business. If Hilltop used part-time seasonal labor during the busy season, as many agribusinesses do, then that portion of the payroll costs would be variable, since it is not incurred until sales volume reaches a certain point, then increases incrementally with additional sales. Overtime pay is regarded as variable, since it is encountered when sales reach higher levels.

Local Taxes and License—*fixed* because it is constant regardless of sales.

Insurance—*fixed* because it does not depend on sales.

Depreciation—*fixed* becuase it does not depend on sales.

Rent and Lease—*fixed* because it does not depend on sales.

Advertising and Promotion—*fixed* in this and most cases. Only items like trading stamps or incentive gifts are tied to sales.

Office Expense—*fixed*, generally, since most costs of running an office are incurred whenever the office is open.

Utilities—*fixed* in this case, since very little of Hilltop's utilities are tied directly to sales. In firms where large electrical motors are run as volume increases, a significant portion of utilities may be variable.

Maintenance and Repair—*split* into one-half fixed and one-half variable in the case of Hilltop. This is because the corrosiveness of fertilizer forces much maintenance and repair regardless of usage. Yet other maintenance and repair is dependent on sales levels.

Bad-Debt Loss—*variable,* since it is usually tied closely to the level of sales. The more sales, the greater the amount of bad debts that are usually encountered.

Supplies—*variable* in this case, although it depends greatly on the type of business and what is included in supplies.

Other—*split* between fixed and variable according to its makeup. The manager of Hilltop indicates that a rough 50–50 split would be his best judgment.

Interest Expense—*fixed* because it varies with the amount of money borrowed, not sales volume. Interest on long-term loans is clearly fixed. The status of interest on short-term, in-season loans is less clear, but borrowing to finance inventory is not caused by the sale. It is to enable an *anticipated* sale. Only when borrowing is done because a sale has been made is interest considered variable.

Cost of Goods Sold—*variable;* in fact, it is the most perfect variable cost (and usually the largest). The accountant does not charge the cost of goods (whether manufactured or purchased for resale) as a cost until the product is sold. Thus it fits the definition of variable cost perfectly.

STEP 2: SUMMARIZE FIXED AND VARIABLE COSTS   Fixed and variable costs should then be summarized. Total dollar fixed costs are summed first. Then variable costs per unit of sales are summed. The unit base can be either in physical units, such as tons, bushels, and gallons, or in dollars. Since most agribusinesses deal in several different physical units, using dollars is usually more meaningful (Exhibit 10-2).

The fixed–variable cost summary shows that Hilltop committed itself to a cost of $145,000 the day it opened its doors for business. Additionally, every time it sold a dollar's worth of product, it incurred, on the average, an incremental or additional cost of 77 cents.

STEP 3: CALCULATE THE CONTRIBUTION TO OVERHEAD   CTO (contribution to overhead) is the heart of volume-cost analysis and many crucial management decisions. It shows the portion of each unit of sales that remains after variable costs are covered and that can be applied toward the fixed or overhead costs. Each time a unit of product is sold, the variable costs must be covered first. Anything that remains makes a contribution to overhead.

In this example, $1 of sales, of course, generates $1 income. Of this, 77 cents must go to cover variable costs. This leaves $1.00 − $0.77 = $0.23 as a contribution to overhead on each $1 of sales.

Hilltop Fertilzier Co., Inc.
Summary of Fixed and Variable Costs
1984

EXPENSE	FIXED COST (DOLLARS)	VARIABLE COST (% OF SALES)
Salary, wages, and benefits	71,500	0.35
Local taxes and licenses	5,000	
Insurance	6,000	
Depreciation	20,000	
Rent and leases	7,000	
Advertising and promotion	5,000	
Office expense	2,000	
Utilities	3,000	
Maintenance and repair	8,500	0.85
Bad-debt loss		0.20
Supplies		0.40
Other	2,000	0.20
Interest expense	15,000	
Cost of goods sold	_____	75.00
	145,000	77.00

Income (sales)	$1.00
Variable Cost	−0.77
Contribution to Overhead	$0.23

STEP 4: CALCULATE THE BREAK-EVEN POINT The question is, "How many units (dollars) of sales must there be, with each unit contributing 23 cents toward the $145,000 overhead, to completely cover all costs?" (e.g., "How much sales does it take to fill the fixed-cost tank?"—see Fig. 10-7). A step-by-step analysis helps clarify this question (Exhibit 10-3).

If Hilltop opens its doors but sells nothing during the period, it incurs its fixed costs of $145,000, but has no income, so the entire $145,000 is a net loss. If they manage to sell one unit ($100) of product, they incur the fixed cost of $145,000 *and* the variable cost of $77 for that

Figure 10-7 Sales needed to fill the overhead tank.

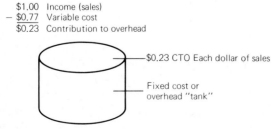

$1.00 Income (sales)
− $0.77 Variable cost
$0.23 Contribution to overhead

$0.23 CTO Each dollar of sales

Fixed cost or overhead "tank"

Volume-Cost Relationship for Hilltop Fertilizer Co., Inc. **EXHIBIT 10-3**

$100 UNITS	INCOME	TOTAL FIXED COST	TOTAL VARIABLE COST	TOTAL COST	PROFIT	TOTAL CTO
0	0	145,000	0	145,000	− 145,000	0
1	100	145,000	77	145,077	− 144,977	23
2	200	145,000	154	145,154	− 144,954	46
3	300	145,000	213	145,231	− 144,931	69
.						
.						
.						
6,304	630,400	145,000	485,408	630,408	− 8	144,992
6,305	630,500	145,000	485,485	630,485	15	145,015
6,306	630,600	145,000	485,562	630,562	38	145,038
.						
.						
.						

unit. The total cost is $145,077 against an income of $100.00. The loss is $144,977. Pretty bad, but this loss is not so great as if they sold nothing. The loss is reduced by $23.

Assume that they sell two $100 units. Then fixed costs and the $77 variable cost for each unit total $145,154, against an income of $200, for a loss of only $144,954. The loss was reduced by another $23. Calculations on a sales volume of three $100 units indicate that losses are $144,931, again reduced by $23.

The obvious and critical question then is, "How many times must this process be repeated before the firm reaches the zero-loss point?" Or, stated differently, "What is the firm's break-even point?" Each time another $100 unit is sold, its income is used first to cover its own variable cost of $77. The remaining $23 ($100 − $77) is used to help cover the fixed cost or "overhead." At this CTO rate, the sales volume necessary to cover all costs (the break-even point) is simply:

$$\frac{\$145,000}{\$0.23} = 6304.35 \text{ units or } \$630,435$$

The CTO is very easy to determine. It is the selling price per unit (SP) minus the variable cost per unit (VC).

$$\text{CTO} = \text{SP} - \text{VC} = \$1.00 - \$0.77 = \$0.23$$

Thus the basic formula for the break-even point can be

$$\text{BE} = \frac{\text{fixed cost}}{\substack{\text{contribution} \\ \text{to overhead}}} = \frac{\text{FC}}{\text{CTO}} = \frac{\$145,000}{\$0.23} = 6304.35 \text{ units or } \$630,435$$

If Hilltop's sales are $630,400 during the season, its profits will be − $8. If sales are $630,435, its profits will be $0. If sales are $630,500, its profits will be + $15. If it sells $630,600, its profit will be $38. It is very important to recognize that Hilltop makes absolutely no profits until it sells $630,435. From then on, every dollar of sales throughout the rest of the period generates a profit of 23 cents.

The profit and loss statement showed an average profit of 8.5 percent of sales for the entire period. But this can be quite misleading, since no profits are made until sales hit $630,435. Then profits occur at the rate of 23 cents per dollar of sales.

Throughout this example we have used dollars as the basis for analysis. It is possible, and sometimes more meaningful, to use physical units, such as tons or gallons, as the basis rather than sales dollars.

Uses of Volume-Cost Analysis PROFIT PLANNING Volume-cost relationships are useful for much more than just calculating the break-even point. They also help determine the volume of business necessary to generate certain levels of profit, which is an essential part of profit planning.

Since income above variable costs is profit once the overhead has been covered, a similar calculation can be used to obtain the additional sales necessary to reach a given profit level. If Hilltop has a net operating profit goal of $85,000, it will take an additional $369,565 sales above their break-even volume of $630,435 to achieve it. In other words, they must plan for $1 million sales to hit their profit goal.

$$\frac{\text{Profit goal}}{\text{CTO}} = \text{additional sales necessary} = \frac{\$85,000}{\$0.23} - \$369,565$$

Management must follow through with a sales program that will generate this volume. (Note that Hilltop's actual sales were, in fact, $1 million, and net operating profit was $85,000.)

CHANGES IN COSTS Volume-cost analysis also helps answer questions about how changes in the cost structure will affect profit levels. Suppose, for example, that Hilltop is considering the purchase of an *additional* truck costing $10,000 that would be depreciated over a 5-year period. The annual fixed costs for this additional truck, including depreciation, are projected to be $2850. Variable operating costs for the new truck should be about the same. A quick calculation shows that $12,391 in additional sales is needed in order to maintain the same profit level.

$$\frac{\text{FC}}{\text{CTO}} = \frac{\$2850}{\$0.23} = \$12,391$$

Management then must decide whether the new vehicle will generate at least $12,391 *additional* sales annually. If it will, then it should be considered. If not, then it would not be worthwhile. (Note that in the example of a new truck, additional fixed costs—another driver, storage space, etc.—might be necessitated. If so, the total increase in fixed costs might be substantially higher than $2850, thereby increasing the additional sales needed by considerably more than $12,391!)

Another use of the analysis is to determine the effect of changes in variable costs. For example, suppose that Hilltop's supplier increased prices to Hilltop, so that the cost of goods sold increased by 1 percentage point, but competition in the area was so keen that Hilltop could not increase retail price. The result is that the CTO is lowered.

Old CTO $= 100 - 77 = 23$ BEP $= \dfrac{\$145,000}{\$0.23} = \$630,435$

New CTO $= 100 - 78 = 22$ BEP $= \dfrac{\$145,000}{\$0.22} = \$659,091$

New BEP $-$ old BEP $=$
$\$659,091 - \$630,435 = \$28,656$

This result shows that if Hilltop absorbs the cost increase rather than increasing their price, their break-even point will increase by $28,656. Or, if their volume remains at $1 million, their profit will drop by $10,000.

Similarly, shrewd purchasing of products or a reduction in manufacturing costs reduces cost of goods sold and variable costs. In Hilltop's case, buying fertilizer at 1 percent less would increase the CTO to 24 cents, and so decrease the break-even point by $26,268 or, at the same $1 million sales volume, increase profits by $10,000.

The impact of any cost change can be anticipated using these techniques. Managers who are skillful in the application of volume-cost analysis find it very useful in projecting probable results of various alternatives before making final decisions.

CHANGES IN PRICE   Volume-cost analysis is also very useful in analyzing the impact of changing prices. Since CTO is selling price per unit less variable cost per unit, then any change in selling price directly impacts the CTO. For example, if Hilltop drops prices by 5 percent, its break-even point jumps from $630,435 to $805,556—a whopping 28 percent.

Old CTO $= 1.00 - 0.77 = 0.23$

Old BEP $= \dfrac{FC}{CTO} = \dfrac{\$145,000}{\$0.23} = \$630,435$

New CTO $= 0.95 - 0.77 = 0.18$

New BEP $= \dfrac{FC}{CTO} = \dfrac{\$145,000}{\$0.18} = \$805,556$

And further, all sales now generate a contribution to overhead and profits of only 18 cents, compared to the previous 23 cents.

One word of caution about price changes, particularly in the fertilizer industry: Lowering the price may increase sales only temporarily. Since total fertilizer usage is reasonably constant in a trading area during a season, and competitors may react with a similar price cut, the net effect may be to lower price and CTO for everyone without any appreciable increase in sales. The obvious result is much lower profits (or higher losses). If more agribusiness managers really understood this particular relationship and bothered to push a pencil, their competitive strategy might be different!

In only the most unusual circumstances can a firm afford to sell any product at a price lower than its variable cost. The variable cost for a product represents, for all practical purposes, the rock bottom price for that product. To sell when variable cost is not being covered means that some of the variable costs are not covered and *none* of the overhead can be covered. Losses will be less when the sale is not made at all because only fixed costs are lost then.

Graphical Analysis *Graphical illustration* of volume-cost relationships is quite useful for many managers as a means of visualizing how changes in price, various costs, or volume impacts profit. Figure 10-8 illustrates Hilltop's break-even point and graphically shows its profit at the current $1 million sales volume. (Note that the profit is the difference between the total revenue and total costs at that volume.) The impact of almost any cost or price change can be shown by simply drawing in the change and observing the resulting effect on profits.

One of the best features of volume-cost analysis is its simplicity and its applicability to real-world situations. Any manager with a profit and loss statement and an understanding of fixed- and variable-cost con-

Figure 10-8   Graph of volume-cost relationships, Hilltop Fertilizer Co., Inc.

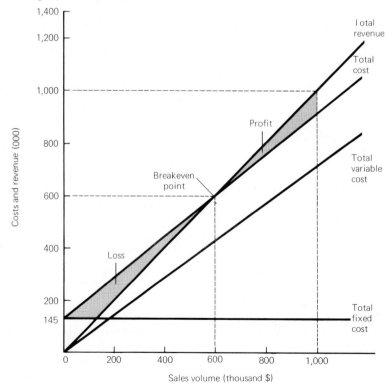

FINANCIAL MANAGEMENT AND CONTROL OF THE AGRIBUSINESS

cepts can estimate the impact of various decision alternatives on profit levels. Although the categorizing of fixed and variable costs may not be perfect, experience has shown that a good approximation can be made relatively easily. And the conclusions are fairly accurate so long as the proper definition of fixed and variable costs is used.

Capital-Investment Analysis

An area of major consequence for agribusiness managers is making capital-investment decisions. Capital investment refers to the purchase of equipment or facilities that usually require relatively large financial outlays and will last over a long period of time. Typical capital investments might include trucks, manufacturing equipment, or storage facilities. Such expenditures tie up funds for long periods and release them slowly as the investment produces income. The impact of these investment decisions may affect the business for years to come.

There are many investment decisions that Hilltop Fertilizer might face in the normal course of business activity. (1) *Expansion projects:* Would it be profitable to enlarge the plant now? (2) *Replacement:* Should their custom application floater be replaced now, or should it be kept for another year? (3) *Choosing Among Alternatives:* Which would be more profitable, stainless steel or iron storage tanks? (4) *Lease or Buy Decisions:* Is it cheaper to lease equipment or buy it outright?

In all such situations there are really two steps in the decision process. First, alternatives must be screened to weed out unprofitable or unrealistic projects. Then alternatives must be preference-ranked according to their profitability.

Risk and Investment When money is tied up in capital investment, management expects to get more back than was invested in the project. The excess of revenue over cost is referred to as the return. The return should be higher than that which could be earned by putting the same money in a "safe" place, such as savings accounts or government bonds. The return should compensate for the risk associated with the investment.

Some people think that if their business borrows the money to purchase a new piece of equipment, they have transferred the risk to the lender. In reality, this is just not true because the bank is sure to be repaid, except in the extreme case of bankruptcy. If the manager makes a bad decision, the total business will suffer the loss because the loan will be repaid from other, more successful ventures.

There are many methods for making capital-investment decisions. Some of them are simple, while others are quite complex, requiring sophisticated mathematical analysis. Four methods will be discussed here. Listed in order of complexity they are: felt need, payback period, simple rate of return, and the present value.

FELT-NEED METHOD The felt-need method is actually not much of a method, since it is nothing more than management response to current pressures. It is more of an impulsive action based on "gut feel," hunches, and guesses than anything else. Capital-investment decisions of this type are often spawned by crises, when management must respond to the urgency of the immediate situation. Consequently, these decisions are often ill-conceived and can easily lead to failure.

This is not to imply that the felt-need method always yields poor results or is an improper method. When the engine on the only delivery truck blows in peak season, the decision to replace the vehicle immediately is so obvious that formal analysis would be unwarranted, and perhaps even detrimental to getting back on the road again quickly. Even in less urgent situations, some managers seem to have an intuitive feeling about investment decisions that proves, over time, to be good judgment. While it is difficult to argue with proven success, good sense says that a more systematic, thoughtful approach to capital-investment decisions is bound to be more productive in the long run, especially when it is buffered by management experience and judgment. The larger or more complex the decision, the less appropriate the felt-need method becomes.

PAYBACK PERIOD   The length of time it will take an investment to generate sufficient additional profit to pay for itself is called the payback period. Payback-period analysis assumes that the annual net-profit estimate includes *all* additional profits to the business, not just what is directly generated by the investment. This simple tool allows the agribusiness manager to compare investment alternatives and determine which will recoup its initial investment in the shortest period of time and so be the most desirable.

For example, suppose that Hilltop Fertilizer is considering the purchase of a truck-mounted power soil probe to take soil samples, and that this outfit costs $8000. The firm plans to charge customers for the full-profit soil samples. Estimated annual net profit to the total business before depreciation is $1500. (Note that since depreciation is in itself a method of offsetting initial cost, it must be omitted in calculation of the payback period.)

A second investment alternative being considered is a new pickup truck costing $6000. Estimated annual net profit before depreciation is $1000.

$$\text{Soil probe} \quad \frac{\text{Payback}}{\text{period}} = \frac{\text{investment}}{\text{average annual net profit}} = \frac{\$8000}{\$1500/\text{year}} = 7.33 \text{ years}$$

$$\text{Pickup truck} \quad \frac{\text{Payback}}{\text{period}} = \frac{\text{investment}}{\text{average annual net profit}} = \frac{\$6000}{\$1000/\text{year}} = 6 \text{ years}$$

Generally, the shorter the payback period, the better the investment. So it would appear from this simple method that the pickup truck is the better alternative because it will pay for itself in 6 years, compared to 7.33 years for the power soil probe.

FINANCIAL MANAGEMENT AND CONTROL OF THE AGRIBUSINESS

The payback-period method is widely used, partly because of its simplicity. But it ignores the length of life of the investment. If the pickup truck wears out in 6 years, while the power soil probe lasts 12 years with regular earnings, this method might change the decision. Although this omission is a serious drawback, when cash flow is critical, the payback method is useful, and it is certainly better than the felt-need method.

SIMPLE RATE OF RETURN   Simple rate of return refers to the profit generated by the investment as a percentage of the investment. The most common variation of this method uses the average return and the average investment to give a more accurate analysis. For example, suppose that Hilltop is considering the purchase of a self-propelled fertilizer applicator with flotation tires that reduces soil compaction and upgrades the services provided farmers. The net returns expected from this $50,000 investment decline over its life because of increasing maintenance and repair costs.

Simple rate of return is perhaps the most commonly used method of capital-investment analysis. It considers net earnings over the entire expected life of the investment. It is easy to understand and is consistent with ROI goals imposed by management. In fact, many firms have estimated ROI standards that serve as a cutoff point for investment projects. Unless an investment proposal exceeds these minimal standards, it will not be seriously considered. A standard of 15 to 25 percent is common for most firms.

When a firm uses the simple rate of return to analyze several investment alternatives, it simply ranks the projects according to the rate of return and selects the project with the highest return.

The chief limitation of the simple-rate-of-return method is that it

Example of Calculation of Simple Rate of Return **EXHIBIT 10-4**

YEAR	NET RETURN BEFORE DEPRECIATION	DEPRECIATION
1	18,000	10,000
2	17,000	10,000
3	16,000	10,000
4	15,000	10,000
5	14,000	10,000
Total	80,000	50,000
Average	16,000	10,000

Average investment = 50,000 ÷ 2 = 25,000

$$\text{Simple rate of return} = \frac{\text{average net income} - \text{average depreciation}}{\text{average investment}}$$

$$= \frac{\$16,000 - \$10,000}{\$25,000} = 24\%$$

fails to consider the timing of the cash flow. When the initial net return is high but falls off quickly, the situation is far different than when the initial net return is low but increases.

A consequence of this problem is that incorrect conclusions may be drawn because the method fails to consider that a dollar returned now is significantly more valuable than a dollar of return received several years later. The meaning of the time-value of money is explained more fully in the next section.

PRESENT VALUE   Present value is the current value of an investment that will yield a specific amount on a given future date. This concept is based on the time-value of money; that is, a dollar now is worth more than a dollar received at some future date, because of the interest that that dollar could earn in the meantime.

One thousand dollars invested today for 1 year at 10 percent will be worth $1100 at the end of the year. So, the present value of $1100 at 10 percent for 1 year is $1000. The $1100 investment has been "discounted" to its present value of $1000.

The formula to calculate the present value is

$$\frac{\text{Present value}}{\text{of investment}} = \frac{\text{expected income}}{(1 + i)^n} \qquad \begin{aligned} i &= \text{interest rate} \\ n &= \text{number of years} \end{aligned}$$

so

$$\text{Present value} = \frac{\$1100}{(1 \mid 0.10)^1} = \frac{\$1100}{1.10} = \$1000$$

Suppose that at high school graduation a relative gives a new graduate a note promising him or her $1000 four years later upon graduation from college. Assuming that the time-value of money is 7 percent (interest rate), what is the present value of that gift? Although the formula is the same as before, this is more difficult to calculate.

$$\text{Present value} = \frac{\$1000}{(1 + 0.07)^4} = \frac{\$1000}{(1.07 \times 1.07 \times 1.07 \times 1.07)} = \frac{\$1000}{1.3108}$$
$$= \$762.90$$

To make things simpler, managers often use tables of present values (Exhibit 10-5) or use financial calculators to quickly calculate the present value of any investment. In this example, the present value of $1 four years from now at 7 percent is given in the present-value table as 0.7629, so the present value of $1000 would be

$$\text{Present value} = \$1000 \times 0.7629 = \$762.90$$

In other words, if the relative invests $762.90 today at 7 percent interest, compounded annually, that investment will be worth $1000 in 4 years.

Compounded annually means that interest earned during the first year ($762.90 × 0.07 = $53.40) will be added to the original investment (principal) ($762.90 + $53.40 = $816.30), so that in year two, the entire investment ($816.30) will earn interest at the 7 percent rate. Each year

FINANCIAL MANAGEMENT AND CONTROL OF THE AGRIBUSINESS

Present Value of $1 (Compounded Annually)*   **EXHIBIT**

YEAR (N)	1%	3%	$(1 + r)^{-n}$ 5%	6%	7%
1	0.9901	0.9709	0.9524	0.9434	0.9346
2	0.9803	0.9426	0.9070	0.8900	0.8734
3	0.9706	0.9152	0.8638	0.8396	0.8163
4	0.9610	0.8885	0.8227	0.7921	0.7629
5	0.9515	0.8626	0.7835	0.7473	0.7130
6	0.9420	0.8375	0.7462	0.7050	0.6663
7	0.9327	0.8131	0.7107	0.6651	0.6228
8	0.9235	0.7894	0.6768	0.6274	0.5820
9	0.9143	0.7664	0.6446	0.5919	0.5439
10	0.9053	0.7441	0.6139	0.5584	0.5083
15	0.8613	0.6419	0.4810	0.4173	0.3624
20	0.8195	0.5537	0.3769	0.3118	0.2584
25	0.7798	0.4776	0.2953	0.2330	0.1842

YEAR (N)	8%	9%	$(1 + r)^{-n}$ 10%	12%	14%
1	0.9259	0.9174	0.9091	0.8929	0.8772
2	0.8573	0.8417	0.8264	0.7972	0.7695
3	0.7938	0.7722	0.7513	0.7118	0.6750
4	0.7350	0.7084	0.6830	0.6355	0.5921
5	0.6806	0.6499	0.6209	0.5674	0.5194
6	0.6302	0.5963	0.5645	0.5066	0.4556
7	0.5835	0.5470	0.5132	0.4523	0.3996
8	0.5403	0.5019	0.4665	0.4039	0.3506
9	0.5002	0.4604	0.4241	0.3606	0.3075
10	0.4632	0.4224	0.3855	0.3220	0.2697
15	0.3152	0.2745	0.2394	0.1827	0.1401
20	0.2145	0.1784	0.1486	0.1037	0.0728
25	0.1460	0.1160	0.0923	0.0588	0.0378

Prepared by R. B. How, Department of Agricultural
Economics, Cornell University.

additional interest earned is added to the investment, and it too earns
interest.

A more realistic example of how present-value analysis might be
used by the agribusiness manager follows. Assume that Hilltop is considering the addition of another self-propelled custom applicator costing
$60,000. Hilltop's owners insist that any additional investment return a
minimum of 14 percent. Based on internal records from operating costs
of current application equipment and the best estimates of customer response to additional service equipment, the following net cash inflows
are expected from the new custom applicator:

YEAR	NET CASH* INFLOW
1	$22,000
2	15,000
3	14,000
4	12,000
5	16,000†

*Net cash inflow is the excess of income over cash expenses attributed directly to the investment. Depreciation and other noncash expenses are not included.
†Includes $3000 from sale of applicator as scrap.

The net cash inflow generally declines each year because of increased maintenance and repair costs as the equipment gets older. As a result, there is a different present value associated with each year. The total present value of the investment is:

YEAR	NET CASH INFLOW	14 PERCENT DISCOUNT FACTOR*		PRESENT VALUE
1	$22,000	0.8772	=	$19,298.40
2	15,000	0.7695	=	11,542.50
3	14,000	0.6750	=	9,450.00
4	12,000	0.5921	=	7,105.20
5	16,000	0.5194	=	8,310.40
				$55,706.50

*See Exhibit 10-5.

The net present value of this investment at 14 percent compounded annually is $55,706.50, which is considerably less than the $60,000 cost of the investment. This means that the investment will not meet the owners' 14 percent criterion. If a purchase price of $55,000 could be negotiated for the custom applicator, then it would meet the 14 percent return criterion.

Capital-investment decisions are among the most important decisions made by management. Their impact is long range and greatly reduces the flexibility of the business. Although simplistic approaches such as intuitive feel or the payback period are widely used methods of making investment decisions, they may lead to incomplete or even wrong conclusions. By recognizing the time-value of money, managers can get a much more realistic picture of investment alternatives.

SUMMARY

Decision making is one of the primary responsibilities of agribusiness managers. Professional managers approach this activity in a systematic way, identifying the problem, summarizing facts, laying out and analyzing alternatives, and taking action. Their analysis often utilizes a wide variety of analytic tools to aid their decision.

Volume-cost analysis is one of the more powerful tools used by agribusiness managers. By separating fixed costs (those not related to volume of business) from variable costs (those directly related to volume), managers can study the impact of a variety of cost and price changes on their profit and determine the amount of business necessary to break even. They can even project the amount of business necessary to reach a certain profit level.

Another widely used tool involves the concept of the time-value of money. Investment decisions must take into consideration the cost of tying up money in investments over periods of time. Discounted cash flow and the net present value of money are methods for evaluating various investment alternatives that are widely used by agribusiness managers.

DISCUSSION QUESTIONS

1. What is meant by "default decisions"? Explain the possible consequence of default decisions to the agribusiness.

2. Suppose the midwinter doldrums and the everyday routine have really gotten to you, when out of the blue a belated Christmas check for $300 from a rich relative arrives by mail. Formally demonstrate the use of the decision-making process to decide your course of action.

3. Explain the difference between variable costs and controllable costs.

4. A particular cost can be variable under some circumstances but fixed in others. In the following expense items, what conditions might make each fixed and what might make each variable? Which do you think each generally is, fixed or variable? Why?

    labor

    sales compensation

    snow-removal costs

    truck rental

    cost of goods sold

5. What are the major assumptions made in determining the break-even point?

6. Why is the felt-need method of investment decisions used so widely, especially in smaller agribusinesses? Why is it often effective? Why does it often fail?

7. Explain the "time value of money" concept.

8. Which method of capital-investment analysis discussed in this chapter is most powerful, and why?

CASE PROBLEM: HAPPY VALLEY PACKING PLANT

Happy Valley Packing Plant packs and ships apples and stores fruit for area growers. Brad Johnson, Happy Valley's new manager, was being pressured by the owners to evaluate several possible changes in the business, including a major upgrading of the packing line. Perhaps you can help Brad by applying some of the decision tools discussed in this chapter.

Volume-Cost Analysis

Cost accountants have recently determined that Happy Valley's annual fixed costs are $100,000, and the variable cost is $1 per bushel. Their annual volume has been about 125,000 bu, which is somewhat under what they believe to be their maximum capacity, 160,000 bu. For the last two seasons Happy Valley has charged growers $2 per bushel for their services.

QUESTIONS

1. Calculate Happy Valley's break-even point.

2. Happy Valley's owners have $300,000 invested in the company. What volume of business is necessary to give them a 15 percent return on the investment?

3. Happy Valley uses itinerant and local part-time labor and so has great flexibility in scheduling labor for the packing line. But recently, there has been much talk about unionizing, which might increase labor costs from 50 cents per bushel to 60 cents per bushel. Analyze the impact of this increase on Happy Valley's operation.

4. What would be the impact of a salary increase to supervisors and the manager amounting to $10,000 annually?

5. One grower, a regular long-time customer of Happy Valley, is considering putting in his own packing shed. This would reduce Happy Valley's volume by 20,000 bushels. What would be the impact on Happy Valley's business?

6. In order to expand its service to growers, Happy Valley is considering enlarging its cold-storage facility, nearly doubling the apple storage area and reducing spoilage losses. It is hoped that such a new service would keep current customers happier and even increase business. Engineers estimate that the expansion will cost $100,000; this can be depreciated over a 10-year period. Variable costs should remain constant. How much additional business will Happy Valley need to make this alternative viable?

7. Another alternative for consideration is changing the price to growers for processing and packing their fruit. What would be the

impact of various prices on Happy Valley's break-even point? What would the price change do to profits if Happy Valley could maintain its volume at 125,000 bu? Completing the following table may be helpful.

Happy Valley Profit and Break-Even Point Response to Price Changes

PRICE $/BU	VARIABLE COST/BU	CONTRIBU- TION TO OVERHEAD	FIXED COST $	BREAK- EVEN POINT— BU	AT 125,000 BU		
					TOTAL REVENUE $	TOTAL COST $	TOTAL PROFIT $
1.70							
1.80							
1.90							
2.00	$1.00/bu	$1.00/bu	$100,000	100,000 bu	$250,000	$225,000	$25,000
2.10							
2.20							
2.30							

8. Using graph paper, carefully plot Happy Valley's fixed costs, variable costs, total costs, and total revenue, showing the break-even point. Draw the chart to scale and carefully label all lines. Then, using a dotted line, demonstrate what happens to the break-even point as prices change.

Capital-Investment Analysis

Happy Valley has the option of significantly upgrading their plant by adding electronic sizing and sorting equipment. The cost of this equipment is $30,000, with an expected life of 5 years. Equipment of this nature is not expected to have an appreciable salvage or scrap value. There will be a significant labor savings involved. Initially, the new equipment will require little maintenance and repair, but as it gets older, the cost of maintenance will go up sharply. Generally, Happy Valley's owners and management feel that a 14 percent return should be expected from any new investment project before it can be undertaken. Expected net returns before depreciation resulting from the investment are as follows:

YEAR	NET PROFIT (SAVINGS) GENERATED	DEPRECIATION
1	$15,000	$6,000
2	12,000	6,000
3	8,000	6,000
4	3,000	6,000
5	2,000	6,000

QUESTIONS

1. Initially, before any calculations, what is your general reaction? Should Happy Valley invest in the new equipment?

2. What is the payback period for this investment?

3. What is the simple rate of return for this investment?

4. What is the present value of this investment, using the 14 percent minimum return required by the owners?

5. What are the limitations of each of these approaches?

6. In the final analysis, do you believe this investment project would be good for Happy Valley? Why or why not?

MARKETING
IN AGRIBUSINESS

OBJECTIVES

• Describe the flow of agricultural products through the market system to the consumer

• Explain the concepts of form, time, place, and possession utility

• Analyze the factors affecting operational and pricing efficiency

• List the various functions in the marketing process

• Measure marketing costs and identify the factors affecting the farmer's share of the consumer's dollar

• Summarize the various government programs that affect the agricultural marketing process

Marketing of agricultural products is a complex process involving many types of agribusiness.
A. Harvesting
B. Marketing
C. Transporting
D. Milling
E. Bread

WHAT GOES UP MUST COME DOWN . . . BUT OFTEN IT DOESN'T UNTIL IT'S TOO LATE.

11

THE AGRICULTURAL MARKETING SYSTEM

THE MARKETING SYSTEM

As a consumer, one may sometimes be intrigued by the vast variety of products offered at the local supermarket, and wonder how all those products traveled from their point of origin to the local store. The process by which products flow through the system from producer to final consumer is called marketing. Specifically, *marketing* may be defined as the study of the physical and economic flow of products from the producer through intermediaries to the consumer. Marketing involves the many different activities that add value to a given product as it moves through the system.

The marketing system in the United States today is extremely productive, very complex, and, in absolute terms, very costly. Like all business activities in the free enterprise system, marketing is guided by the profit motive. Consumers are ultimately responsible for guiding the flow of resources in the marketing system through their dollar "votes" in the marketplace. Marketing is sometimes criticized as being wasteful and inefficient and is often accused of creating high profits for the intermediaries between producer and consumer. However, in the American economic system, consumers benefit from the high degree of competition among firms in the marketplace. With few exceptions, this marketing system offers consumers more variety and higher quality than the systems in other countries.

There are just under 2.4 million farms in the United States. Products may flow through various channels in the food distribution system—processors, manufacturers, brokers, wholesalers, and retailers. Food reaches the final consumers through supermarkets, restaurants, or countless types of specialty shops. In 1984 there were over 500,000 public and institutional food service establishments in the United States. Of this total, 156,000 were grocery stores[1] and more than 350,000 were restaurants.[2] The number of fast food outlets alone have increased from 38,650 in 1963 to over 122,000 in 1982. Food away from home takes an increasing percentage of the consumer's food dollar—37 percent in 1982, compared with 28 percent in 1962. By 1990, food away from home is expected to take 45 percent of the food dollar.

The path that goods take from producer to final consumer is called the *marketing channel*. The type and complexity of the marketing channel varies with different commodities. The roadside market is a very simple marketing channel, from producer directly to consumer. However, most products undergo further processing at different levels of the marketing channel and pass through many firms before they reach the ultimate consumer.

Exactly the same type of marketing system exists in the farm supply industry. In this case, however, the farmer is the consumer and the basic manufacturer of farm supplies is the producer. Farm supplies flow

[1]*Progressive Grocer,* 52nd Annual Report of the Grocery Industry, April 1985.

[2]Van Dress, Michael G., and Judith Jones Putnam, "American Eating Places," NFR-21, Winter 1983, pp. 22–25.

from the manufacturer to the farmer in much the same way and with the same marketing functions performed as in the marketing of agricultural products to consumers.

PROVISION OF UTILITY

Marketing begins with farm supplies moving to the farm, continues with a raw product at the farm level, and culminates with a desired finished product at the consumer level. A hog on a feeding floor in Iowa in January is a far different product from a ham sandwich in Yankee Stadium in July. The changes that transform the live hog into the desired consumer product are referred to as adding *utility*.

There are four types of utility: form, time, place, and possession. All marketing agencies earn their livelihood from contributing utility to products. The farmer adds *form utility* by raising the hog to market weight. But a live hog in Yankee Stadium is of little value to the hungry baseball fan. So meatpackers add form utility by breaking down the carcass into various pork cuts and producing canned hams, and the concessionaire adds still more utility by making up sandwiches.

Inventory holders, such as meat wholesalers, add *time utility* to the product by storing the hams, thereby ensuring that sufficient quantities of product are available when needed. Trucking firms and railroads help to add *place utility* by physically moving the hams from Iowa to New York.

Many firms in the marketing system facilitate movement of commodities by matching buyers with sellers. Commission agents help the farmer to find buyers for livestock. Many wholesalers buy from various packing and processing plants. These individuals add *possession utility* to the final product as the ham moves through the system to the concession vendors in Yankee Stadium.

Price differences between two or more locations reflect place utility. As the price of corn in New Orleans increases relative to the price of corn in Chicago, changes in shipping patterns will occur. In this case, more corn will be shipped to New Orleans. If this continues, a point will be reached where there is a glut in New Orleans and a shortage in Chicago, at which time prices will move in the opposite direction, until theoretically the market comes to equilibrium.[3] Price differentials of this nature tend to reflect the differing costs of transportation between various points.

Price differentials among different grades of products usually reflect differences in form utility. Various grades of milk serve as a good example. Some milk may be utilized for manufacturing purposes, ice cream, cheese, and butter, for example, while a different grade of milk may be utilized for drinking purposes. The higher grade used in fluid milk for table consumption would command a higher price. Manufacturing-grade milk receives a lower price because the quality standards are less strict.

[3]In actuality, the market may never reach equilibrium, given the influence of ever-changing market conditions.

The relationship between product prices and possession utility is less clear. However, in the marketing process any fees, charges, or commissions for connecting buyer to seller are added into the final consumer price. The purpose of selling directly to consumers is to reduce the charges for possession utility. Any time an intermediary is forced to own and hold inventory, it must be financed. These finance charges for possession utility are included in the purchase price of the product.

MARKETING EFFICIENCY

The term *marketing efficiency* is often used in evaluating the performance of the marketing process. It reflects the consensus that outputs of the marketing process should be produced "efficiently." New technologies or procedures should be adopted only if they can increase the efficiency with which the marketing process is performed. *Efficiency* may be defined as increasing the "output-input" ratio, which generally may be accomplished in any one of four ways:

1. Output remains constant while input decreases

2. Output increases while input remains constant

3. Output increases more than input increases

4. Output decreases more slowly than input decreases

Two different dimensions of marketing efficiency are able to increase the output-input ratio. The first is called *operational efficiency* and measures the productivity of performing marketing services within the firm. The second dimension, called *pricing efficiency*, measures how adequately market prices reflect the production and marketing costs throughout the total marketing system.

Operational Efficiency

Operational efficiency consists of the raw ratio of marketing output over marketing input:

$$\frac{\text{Marketing output}}{\text{Marketing input}} = \text{operational efficiency}$$

This measure of efficiency is concerned with the physical activities of marketing. Output per worker hour is one often-quoted productivity ratio that measures operational efficiency. Farm supply stores calculate sales per worker hour to monitor operating efficiency. Fertilizer plants watch "throughput per spreader" (tons of fertilizer sold per distribution unit) to measure operating efficiency.

In marketing, increased operational efficiency is actually synonymous with cost reduction. Typically, a substitution of machinery for labor has been associated with improved efficiency. A seed processor buys new bagging equipment when the equipment is expected to reduce the required amount of labor, thereby improving operational efficiency.

Shifting to 15 dozen plastic totes for distributing eggs to supermarkets reduces delivery costs. Palletization of farm supplies by wholesalers and manufacturers also reduces costs significantly. New molded containers for California plums and nectarines may reduce spoilage or damage and allow for larger shipments. Any improvements in *quality* of output also enhance operational efficiency.

Pricing Efficiency

Pricing efficiency, on the other hand, assumes a physical output-input relationship that remains constant. It is concerned with how effectively prices reflect the costs of moving the outputs through the marketing system. The prices that consumers pay for goods delivered by the marketing system should adequately reflect all marketing and production costs. In a perfectly competitive economic environment, prices will adequately reflect all such costs. Firms in the industry are free to enter and exit the marketing-production process as they desire. The demands of consumers are reflected through the marketing system through price signals, resulting in profits and losses.

Pricing efficiency is often used to evaluate the performance of the market as it compares to the bench mark of a perfectly competitive market. If the market is dominated by a few firms that conspire to maintain high prices, the situation would be interpreted as being less than price efficient. Many things can result in pricing inefficiency: consumers who lack sufficient information about alternatives, or firms that dominate a market because of location or excellent personnel, in which case their prices may not reflect cost adequately.

A Paradox

There is a possible paradox between operational and pricing efficiency. It is possible for the government to impose new market regulations that improve pricing efficiency at the cost of reducing operational efficiency. For example, requiring prices and quantities of all sales of fertilizer to be publicly reported might significantly help farmers to establish the going price, which would improve pricing efficiency. However, these new reporting regulations might increase individual firms' operating costs to the point where operational efficiency was reduced. This conflict between the two efficiency norms must be resolved by careful examination of the trade-off between the two. Governmental agencies and marketing professionals must objectively examine which alternatives provide the maximum net benefits to society.

MARKETING FUNCTIONS

There is no mystery about the way agricultural products gain utility and move from the producer to the consumer. Several specific activities or functions form steps in the successful execution of the marketing process. Marketing functions are not necessarily carried out in a fixed order, but they must be accomplished. In some cases, as with a grower-owned roadside fruit market, all the marketing functions take place in a very short time and in a very direct manner, with only the producer and the final consumer involved. In other cases, such as the case of Texas rice marketed in the form of breakfast cereal, the functions are very complex, involve dozens of different firms and hundreds of people, and require months to complete. But in both cases, the same marketing functions are required. The manner in which marketing functions are carried out varies tremendously from product to product, but is usually an orderly process that evolves over time as conditions change.

There are three major types of marketing functions.

1. The *exchange function* must be performed; that is, the product must be sold and bought at least once during the marketing process.

2. Certain *physical functions* must be performed, such as transporting, storing, and processing the product.

3. Various *facilitating functions* must occur in the marketing process. Somehow there must be at least a minimal amount of market information available; someone must accept the risk of losses that might occur; often the product must be standardized or graded to facilitate the sale of the product; and finally, someone must own the product and provide the financing during the marketing process.

Exchange Functions

Exchange functions involve those activities that are concerned with the transfer of ownership in the marketing system. Certainly, demand-and-supply analysis has direct application to this area (see Chapter 5). Prices are determined, in our competitive economic system, as buyers and sellers meet to exchange commodities. People involved in that process could include brokers and commission agents, whose livelihood comes from matching buyer with seller. These people may or may not take title to the goods they handle; in any event, they are exchanging a service for a fee.

The exchange function receives much attention from economists and managers because price is determined as part of this activity. Much attention is given to the method of price determination. Are there a large number of sellers and buyers, that is, is there competition? Does one group have an economic advantage over the other? What is the competitive nature of markets within this system? These questions and many others are asked by the market researchers who study the performance of the marketplace. Both parties to any transaction seek the most favorable price possible. Market performance studies measure the relationship of price to product value to determine whether consumers are reaping the full benefits of a competitive economic system.

Buying The buying function is present at all levels of the marketing channel. At the primary level, buying involves the interaction of the producer or the producer's agent and the processor, the wholesaler, or, less frequently, the consumer. Typically, the buying activity in one marketing system involves the processor's purchasing raw material from the primary producer, the wholesaler's buying the finished product from the processor-manufacturer, the retailer's buying from the wholesaler, and finally the consumer's buying from the retailer. This final step receives a great deal of attention because it involves the total population; it is also the only phase of the marketing channel in which the consumer is directly involved. Thus the success of the entire marketing process is finally judged by consumers' buying behavior.

Selling Someone can buy something only when someone else sells something, so selling is an integral part of the exchange function. For producers, deciding when to sell is the primary marketing issue. Whenever farmers across America gather, the question "How's the market doing today?" is bound to enter the conversation. With some farm products, particularly grain, farmers have a wide span of time in which to sell, ranging from preharvest forward contracts that promise delivery several months in the future, to postharvest decisions to store grain production and sell it several months after harvest. With other farm products, such as most livestock products and horticultural crops, there is little flexibility in selling time. Once the product is ready for market, there is no possibility of postponing the sale because the product will deteriorate if it is held. Increasingly, however, there is a trend toward contracting production of agricultural products for a specific price and delivery date, particularly with more perishable products. This system helps create a more orderly marketing process.

Most agricultural products are bought and sold several times during the marketing process. Agribusiness usually lends great emphasis to the selling function and exerts extensive efforts to perform this function in an effective manner. For the agribusiness firm, selling involves first a careful consideration of specifically what product will be sold and how it will be positioned in relation to competitive products, that is, how it will differ from other products. Then a *promotional* program must be devised to make potential customers aware of the company's product. This program involves careful consideration of the product's *price* to ensure that it will be competitive, yet generate sufficient income to cover expenses and realize a profit. A *distribution* system must be established to place the product where it can be conveniently purchased when the consumer wants it.

The way in which these variables fit together must be determined by management. Merchandising techniques based upon studies of many consumers and their buying habits are very useful to the successful agribusiness manager. Chapter 12 discusses in detail how the selling-marketing function is carried out within the agribusiness firm.

Physical Functions

Time, place, and form utility are added to the product as it is transported, stored, and processed to meet consumer wants.

Transportation Agricultural products are transported from farms to consumers by nearly every conceivable method, because of the wide variation in types of agricultural products. Cut flowers and some fresh vegetables are highly perishable and must immediately be trucked or flown to selling points so that they can be consumed within hours of harvest. Much agricultural production moves by truck from farms to local or terminal markets. Railroads carry vast quantities of farm products, particularly grain, to processors and to port facilities. Often, grain moves in special 100-car trains called *unit trains* in order to reduce marketing costs. Barge traffic on America's Great Lakes and major rivers is a slower but significantly cheaper means of transportation for much of the grain harvest.

There is increasing concern about the ability of transportation to meet growing demands. In recent years, very serious transportation tie-ups have resulted from an increasingly inadequate rail system. Many of the system's tracks are no longer capable of handling the traffic, and the supply of available rail cars has proved inadequate for moving grain from rural America and, in many cases, for moving farm supplies such as fertilizer to the farm markets. In fact, some rural areas have had rail service restricted or even removed completely, causing great inconvenience and much higher marketing costs. Transportation of agricultural products is cause for great concern for many agribusinesses and rural communities.

Storage Inventory holders in the marketing system handle the storage of products. This function adds time utility to products and is extremely important to many commodities. With the adoption of new technologies it is now possible to hold fresh fruit and vegetables for a longer period than just a few days after harvest. A recent breakthrough in storage technology now allows tomatoes to be stored indefinitely in aseptic holding tanks without any refrigeration. This allows tomato processing plants to operate at an even rate all year, rather than for just a few weeks during harvest. In fact, it also allows raw food products to be transported hundreds of miles to centralized facilities that cost less to operate. This technology is now being transferred to other food crops, and it should significantly reduce marketing costs.

Storage is equally important to the agribusinesses that supply farmers. Most crop production inputs are bought during a few weeks each year. This presents tough problems for manufacturers and suppliers, who must produce supplies throughout the year to utilize their manufacturing facilities efficiently, but then compress distribution into a very short period. Most chemicals, for example, must be stored in costly temperature-controlled environments. Storage is an expensive marketing function. In 1984, 7.6 billion bushels of corn were produced in the United States. Certainly, not all that corn could be consumed directly after harvest. Some was exported and some was fed to livestock, but most went into storage on farms or in local elevators so that consumption could be spread out over the entire marketing year.

Processing The primary producer adds some form utility to the commodity that moves through the marketing channel, changing feeder steers into fat cattle, a single kernel of corn into ears of corn, or an oblong black seed into a big green watermelon. However, this process does not usually include all the form utility that the final consumer demands at the retail level. Cattle on the hoof must somehow be transformed into packages of steak and hamburger, and kernels of corn must become boxes of corn flakes. This is where the processor plays a vital role in meeting the demands of the consumer. Processors take the raw primary product and turn it into a more desirable form. Processing may involve only a single firm in the marketing channel, or it may be accomplished by three or four firms, with each successively adding another kind of form utility.

Facilitating Functions

Facilitating functions are activities that help the market system to operate more smoothly. They enable buyers, sellers, transporters, and processors to make their contributions without great concern about risk or financing, and to plan an orderly marketing plan.

Market Information An efficient marketing system requires that marketing participants be well informed. Buyers need information regarding supply sources, sellers seek information pertinent to prices in different markets, and consumers desire information about quality, price, and sources of product. Inventory holders seek information about current and future prices in an attempt to decide what and how much to store. Wholesalers need information about transportation rates to compare prices of the same commodity in different geographical locations.

Market information can be obtained from many different sources. Private firms publish a multitude of market letters dealing with fundamental and technical factors relevant to marketing decisions. The government is responsible for reporting prices, production, disposition, and utilization statistics in different markets periodically to keep participants more fully informed of what the future might bring.

Market research through private firms and universities is part of this area of market information. Research results may provide valuable information about the ways in which markets may become more efficient, and about the possibilities of opening new markets or modifying existing institutions.

Risk Bearing Throughout the marketing channel, owners of commodities are subject to risks. These risks may be separated into two general categories: physical risks, such as wind, fire, hail, flood, theft, and spoilage; and market risks.

People usually attempt to limit their vulnerability to physical risks through such means as installing a burglar alarm system in a chemical storage warehouse, or using containers that protect and preserve the quality of grapes in transit. For most physical risks there is a known probability of occurrence of loss or damage, so insurance may be purchased to protect against most losses. The purchase of insurance transfers risk to another party—the insurance company. Insurance companies essentially "pool risk" of the insured.

Market risks, on the other hand, are not so easily dealt with. Market risks include the possibility of price declines, changes in consumer preferences, or changes in the nature of competition. All these risks must be accepted by someone in the marketing chain. Generally, insurance companies will not write a policy guarding against market risks, since it is impossible to actually calculate the probability of loss.

Price changes are among the most important market risks to producers and agribusinesses. Producers often hope to improve their marketing efficiency by obtaining a higher price, but this is hard to accomplish. Current surveys of grain growers illustrate that typically only about 30 percent of all grain is sold at above the yearly average price. Lack of information, poor judgment, or cash-flow problems that force the sale of products often cause sellers to "miss the market." Livestock and dairy farmers have little control over the point at which they can take their product to market.

There are basically four techniques that can aid producers and marketers in transferring or reducing their market risks: (1) diversification, (2) vertical integration, (3) forward contracting, and (4) hedging and futures markets.

DIVERSIFICATION *Diversification* is the technique of adding to one line of business some other lines of business that pose different risks, so that the likelihood of a loss in one area will be offset by the possibility of gain in another. Since most agricultural products are subject to significant market swings and variable weather conditions, additional products or enterprises that are not likely to experience the same trends can greatly reduce the impact of wide swings in the business. The "Don't put all your eggs in one basket" concept has been beneficial to many agribusinesses and farmers.

Interestingly enough, however, there is a trend away from diversification toward specialization, especially at the farm level. This is because the efficiency and cost saving that result from larger, more specialized production units are thought to more than offset the disadvantages from lack of diversification. Today's farmers are increasingly specialized producers who offset market risks through contracting, hedging, and vertical integration.

VERTICAL INTEGRATION *Vertical integration* occurs when an organization takes on other marketing functions in addition to its primary ones, thereby becoming less dependent on other organizations. By controlling its own source of supply or guaranteeing an outlet for products, a farm becomes less vulnerable to market swings. Some large food retailers now label or even manufacture their own brands of canned food. Some large farm cooperatives own their own petroleum refineries rather than depend on private oil companies. Other cooperatives not only buy farm dairy products but process, manufacture, and distribute their own brand to supermarkets.

FORWARD CONTRACTING *Forward contracting* is simply the process of making a buyer-seller agreement about a set price for some future delivery date. This agreement completely removes the risk of price fluctuations for both buyer and seller. When producers are sure before the production process even begins what price they will get for their product, only production risks remain to contend with. Processors can be assured of a reliable supply at a known price, which allows for more efficient operation of facilities. Of course, the market price will fluctuate and is likely to be either higher or lower than the contract price on the delivery date. Either party may gain or lose on the contract price in relation to the market price, but since the price was forward-contracted, the gain or loss is only theoretical, based on a lost opportunity.

HEDGING AND THE FUTURES MARKETS *Hedging and the futures markets* are other systems for transferring the risk of price changes from one party to another. Since no one can actually predict the probability of market risks, estimating what may happen to demand and prices becomes mostly a matter of judgment. At best, it is based on someone's studied opinion, and at worst, it is based on a whim or guess about what the market might do. In either case, there are those who are willing to speculate or gamble on future market prices. Futures markets provide a mechanism by which trading can be handled swiftly, in standardized units of products that are to be delivered at some specified future date and location.

Actually, the futures market does not deal in physical products, but in "promises." That is, traders buy or sell promises to deliver a product on a specific future date. If one July wheat contract is sold, it is a promise to deliver one contract of wheat (specified as 5000 bushels of No. 2 grade) in July of next year. But if in the meantime one *purchases* a July contract of wheat, one has purchased a promise to accept delivery of 5000 bushels of No. 2 wheat in July. The second transaction will cancel out the first, and there will be no actual physical transfer of wheat at all. As long as futures traders offset each transaction with an equal and opposite transaction, they never have to physically accept or deliver the product. In fact, many speculators might not even recognize the agricultural commodity they are trading. Their interest lies solely in the profits they might make from favorable changes in price while they hold the contract. If they are smart, or lucky, they may do very well. But it is a highly risky venture, and great losses can occur quickly. A rule of thumb well accepted by professional traders says that seven out of ten public traders lose money.

Future markets are not just a gambling game, however. They serve a highly useful purpose. When an agricultural producer or business combines the futures market with the cash market (the market where commodities physically change hands), market risks are greatly reduced.

For producers or users who actually intend to deliver or accept delivery of a product, the use of the futures market is quite simple and much the same as forward contracting. If a farmer finds the July wheat futures price acceptable, he or she can sell a contract and guarantee that price. A flour miller may also wish to transfer risk by buying a July wheat contract to accept delivery, thereby assuring a known input price for wheat needed in July. Actually, the farmer and miller are not likely to trade with each other directly; speculators may buy and sell the contracts. Since they are simply trading promises, it is not necessary to buy one contract before selling another one. So long as an opposite trade balances out the first transaction before the contract matures, both the producer and the user have locked in a known price and reduced their risk, and speculators have had the opportunity to make a profit or loss.

Agribusinesses that market farm products use the futures market by *hedging* their purchases. Most agricultural marketing firms, especially grain elevators, prefer to make a profit from storing, grading, and handling, rather than from price fluctuations while they own the product. To do this, they must make immediate and offsetting transactions in both the cash or "spot" market and the futures market.

For example, suppose a cotton merchant buys cotton from a ginner, stores it in a warehouse, and later sells it to a spinner for processing. The merchant's business is warehousing, not speculating on price. But there is the fear that prices might fall while the cotton is in the warehouse, thereby causing serious loss. The cotton merchant could hedge the purchase by doing the following (Table 11-1):

TABLE 11-1

	CASH MARKET	FUTURES MARKET
Step 1 Day of original cash purchase	1. Bought 200,000 lbs @ $0.70 per pound	2. Sold 4 contracts (200,000 lbs) @ $0.74 per pound
Step 2 Day of final cash sale	1. Sold 200,000 lbs @ $0.67 per pound	2. Bought 4 contracts (200,000 lbs) @ $0.71 per pound
Net result	loss of $0.03 per pound	gain of $0.03 per pound

In the cash market the merchant lost 3 cents per pound, just as feared. But in the futures market the merchant made a profit of 3 cents per pound, which completely offset the loss in the cash market. Since the futures market and the cash market tend to move up and down together, this hedging process generally allows marketers to offset risk. Sometimes the markets do not move together perfectly, so not all risk can be transferred, but most usually can be.

Futures markets have been established for many agricultural commodities. Trading is always transacted in standardized units or lots so that traders can be confident of what they are trading. Transactions occur in designated markets, such as the Mercantile Exchange and the Board of Trade in Chicago, where hundreds of traders gather daily to buy and sell futures contracts. Their trades are openly cried out as they meet face-to-face in the trading pits. Often the exchanges approach a state of frenzy as traders try to get the attention of other traders to complete a transaction. But what appears to the casual, uninformed observer to be uncontrolled chaos actually is a highly organized free market activity that reflects the broad market expectations of buyers, sellers, and speculators jointly determining price.

Standardization and Grading Grading agricultural products into specific standardized classes or categories greatly facilitates the buying and selling process and helps the marketing system work more efficiently. It is a highly refined system that includes most agricultural commodities. The USDA establishes and grades many agricultural products to ensure standardization. A corn processor from Indiana can buy an entire inventory of corn from elevators around the Midwest via telephone, without seeing the actual commodity. The buyer knows exactly what quality of corn will be received because of the system of grades used by industry; for example, an order of No. 2 yellow corn at 15 percent moisture and a low percentage of FM (foreign material) would be standard throughout the industry. Sellers, in turn, know the quality of their corn and whether it will or will not meet the buyer's specifications.

Financing Someone must own products at all times. Ownership requires the investment of funds into the marketing process for at least a short period of time. The financing is provided by the marketing firm that actually buys and takes title to the product. Of course, some of these funds may be borrowed from a lending institution, so both bankers and investors become involved in financing marketing.

Not all marketing agencies actually take title to the products they market. Agents acting on behalf of another marketing firm, or even the producer in some cases, add their services without owning the product. Brokers and commission agents bring buyers and sellers together, but, of course, they take less risk than those who own the product.

Each of these functions must be performed in the marketing of any product. The title and exact situation of the person performing a specific function may vary from agribusiness to agribusiness, but at some point in the marketing channel each of these activities must be accomplished.

COST OF MARKETING

Over the years, consumers have demanded that more and more services be built into agricultural products. Instead of canned peas, consumers have begun to prefer peas that have been mixed with miniature onions and butter sauce and packaged in a cooking pouch ready for the microwave oven. The extent of built-in service is further reflected by the fact that for the average American nearly one out of three meals is now eaten away from home. These gradual changes over the past 2 decades have dramatically increased the cost of marketing.

Marketing costs are often measured in terms of the *marketing margin*, which simply reflects the share of the consumer's dollar that is required to cover the cost incurred in the marketing process. Table 11-2 illustrates recent trends in marketing costs and in the residual that farmers share for selected food items. As more and more costly services are added, the farmer's share of the consumer's dollar shrinks. Over the longer term, the average farmer's share is about 40 percent, which suggests that both marketing costs and farm prices are rising.

But a shrinking farmer's share does not necessarily mean that demand for agricultural products is falling off. On an absolute basis, demand may actually be increasing, because the marketing process may create more varieties and types of products at the retail level. Potatoes serve as a good example. Twenty years ago only a few types of potato products were offered on the market, mostly potato chips and raw potatoes in various package sizes. Today there is a wide assortment of fresh, dried, frozen, dehydrated, reconstituted, sliced, diced, boiled, and baked potato products, many of which are packaged with all sorts of entrees and are ready for heating and eating. Farmers receive a much smaller percentage of each retail potato dollar, while total demand for potatoes has increased as consumers have reacted favorably to new potato products.

But the farmer's low share of the consumer's dollar is the target of much criticism. The degree of additional processing through which the raw agricultural commodity must go is closely correlated with the farmer's final share (see Table 11-2). Many reasons for these wide variations can be cited. However, basically four major product characteristics lead to these variations in farmers' shares:

1. *Degree of perishability:* If the product is highly perishable, there are substantially increased marketing costs, including spoilage, special handling, and special storage facilities.

2. *Bulkiness of product:* Increased marketing costs may result from the physical size of the raw product in relation to its value. Typically, the bulkier the product, the higher the cost of storage and

Farmer's Share of the Consumer's Dollar for Selected Agricultural Products*

TABLE
11-2

	1975	1980	1981	1982	1983	1984
Meat	60	50.7	49.3	50.2	47.6	48.6
Dairy	49	52.2	52.0	49.6	49.0	47.8
Poultry	59	54.9	52.7	50.7	53.1	56.6
Eggs	66	66.5	68.2	62.8	65.1	64.9
Cereal and bakery	19	15.4	13.8	10.8	11.1	10.8
Fresh fruits	30	27.9	27.2	27.7	22.5	28.3
Fresh vegetables	34	28.5	31.4	28.9	28.6	28.9
Processed fruits and vegetables	21	18.2	19.3	20.4	18.9	20.3
Fats and oils	34	28.8	27.2	27.2	26.5	31.3
Beef	60	61	58	58	57	58
Pork	42	45	46	50	45	48

Agricultural Outlook, selected issues, 1979–1985,
USDA, ERS.

transportation. This is the reason behind the recent movement of many packing plants from the city to locations near the production.

3. *Seasonality:* If a product is harvested over only a short time period, storage and handling costs may be much greater.

4. *Difference between raw and final product form:* Basically, the more processing and other work that must be completed before the product goes to the consumer, the higher the total marketing cost will be.

Specific costs contained in the food-marketing bill are illustrated in Figure 11-1. Wages and salaries comprise roughly one-half the total marketing costs. As labor grows increasingly concerned with the erosion of its purchasing power as a result of inflation, and organized labor gains greater bargaining power in marketing organizations, this percentage can be expected to increase. Also, government regulations and new restrictions on labor practices have added greatly to the labor costs associated with marketing.

Transportation charges amount to about 8 percent of the total marketing bill. Dramatic increases in this area can be expected as fuel costs soar and railroads increase rates to modernize their existing facilities and capabilities. Corporate profits amount to only about 7 percent of the marketing bill, an amount far less than is generally expected by both producers and consumers, who suspect marketing firms or "intermediaries" of raking in large profits. Profitability, of course, fluctuates greatly

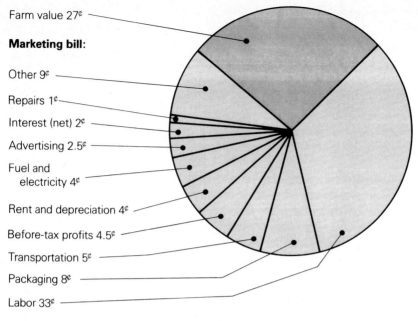

Farm value 27¢

Marketing bill:

Other 9¢

Repairs 1¢

Interest (net) 2¢

Advertising 2.5¢

Fuel and
   electricity 4¢

Rent and depreciation 4¢

Before-tax profits 4.5¢

Transportation 5¢

Packaging 8¢

Labor 33¢

1983 preliminary. Other costs include property taxes and insurance, accounting and
professional services, promotion, bad debts, and miscellaneous items.

**Figure 11-1 What a dollar spent on food paid for
in 1983 [Source: 1984 Handbook of Ag Charts,
U.S.D.A., Agricultural Handbook No. 637,
December 1984.]**

from industry to industry in the food-marketing system. Retail chain grocery stores in 1984 made an average after-tax profit of about 1 cent for
every dollar of sales. Thus the pilfering of a 30-cent package of chewing
gum would mean that the store would lose all its profit on the next $25
worth of sales. In short, most of the increased cost of marketing has come
from the addition of more services to the product, not from excessive
profits for marketing firms.

THE GOVERNMENT AND MARKETING
United States society has chosen to place some restrictions on the free
market system. Some of these are intended to ease the severity of adjustments in the continual reallocation of resources in the economic system.
Others are intended to ensure that the market quickly and accurately
reflects changing consumer wants. But to gain the benefits of legislation
that protects certain segments of society, the market system is subjected
to governmental regulation that significantly affects the marketing process.

Governmental impact on markets is particularly prominent in agriculture because programs affect both production and marketing, and so
are of great concern to agribusinesses that sell to farmers or market farm
products. Farm programs designed to protect the standard of living

among farmers, along with international trade policies that can cause farm prices to jump dramatically, are good examples of government impact on farm production. Consumer protection legislation that regulates labeling and advertising, and pure food and drug laws that control the use of preservatives in food, drastically affect marketing methods and marketing costs. Still other governmental programs are designed to improve the flow of information and decision making in the marketing process. Publicly financed market-information services, periodic crop and livestock reports, and agricultural weather forecasts are good examples of government programs that may improve marketing efficiency.

However, some of these government programs may actually increase the cost of marketing. Limiting the use of food preservatives can raise marketing costs because food shelf-life is reduced. Farm programs that discourage planting will decrease production volume and so cause lowered operational efficiency in marketing. However, the justification for such policies is that the consuming public is protected or in some way obtains valuable benefits that would not otherwise be possible.

Programs Affecting Production

There are so many independent farms, all producing nearly identical products, that it is easy for supply to exceed demand and farm prices to become quite depressed. So long as expected prices exceed estimated out-of-pocket costs, the individual farmer will produce. Even if the full costs of production cannot be covered by the expected price, the farmer usually continues to plant, feed, milk, and harvest in order to minimize losses. In fact, to compensate for the low income, the individual farmer tries to maximize production as a means of increasing personal income. As a result of the individual farmer's response, total agricultural production is increased, which forces prices still lower and makes problems even worse for farmers. Although the market is clearly signaling that production should be cut back, the individual farmer often struggles to increase production and may experience a great deal of economic hardship, particularly the less efficient or marginal farmer.

Because of the traditional agricultural orientation of American society, the importance of food, the necessity for maintaining a strong agricultural sector for national security reasons, and an unwillingness as a nation to allow agriculture to endure the full economic hardships of a completely free market, government regulation has been used over the years to protect the farm sector. Government production programs have varied greatly and have met with varying degrees of success.

The first example of direct government intervention in agriculture was the establishment of the Commodity Credit Corporation (CCC) in 1933. The CCC established the *nonrecourse loan* to farmers. Under this program, farmers could "seal" their grain in storage facilities that were acceptable to the government and obtain a loan that was equal to the number of bushels in storage multiplied by the established support price for the commodity. If the market price increased above the support price, the farmers could sell on the open market and simply pay off the government loan. If the market price failed to rise above the support price, the producer could simply deliver the grain to the government and cancel the loan. Effective support prices were established each marketing year.

Another major government program affecting agriculture was the *set-aside system.* Under provisions of this program, farmers were paid to retire some of their acreage from production each year. Payments were based on established yield figures for each participating farm. Participants in this program were required to sign up for the program in the spring of each year.

Embodied in any plan for protecting farmers is the concept of what is a "fair price." The concept of parity price was established by the Agricultural Adjustment Act of 1933. The *parity price* calculated for each agricultural commodity was supposedly a fair price that would give farmers the same degree of purchasing power in the current period as they had in an established period. The parity ratio, as amended in 1948, may be calculated as follows:

$$\frac{\text{Average price received, most recent 10 years}}{\text{Average index of all prices received, most recent 10 years}} \times \frac{\text{current index}}{\text{of prices paid}} = \frac{\text{current}}{\text{parity price}}$$

Economists and agricultural specialists have long argued over the acceptability of parity. Many feel that the makeup of costs and the technology involved in agriculture have changed so much that the idea of parity is outdated and of no practical use. Yet recently, there has been growth and acceptance of producer organizations that call for a general farm strike until producers are guaranteed parity prices. The final answer to the question of parity will undoubtedly be connected to the degree of government intervention that is acceptable in agriculture and to the extent to which the country wishes the free enterprise system to remain free.

The objective of each of these programs, and many others not discussed here, has been to stabilize agricultural prices and returns to farmers. Ideally, under government programs the harmful effects of short-term price fluctuations would be circumvented and market prices would remain close to long-run equilibrium levels. The government hoped to make the competitive agricultural market even better through these schemes.

Legislation Affecting Agricultural Markets

There is also a myriad of acts, regulations, and agencies that directly affect the marketing of agricultural products. The amount and complexity of this legislation, particularly legislation that relates to protecting consumers, has increased dramatically in recent years. Many agribusiness firms not only find their activities carefully monitored and regulated by government agencies, but must regularly provide extensive and costly reports on various aspects of their business.

As early as 1890 the Sherman Antitrust Act made any restraint of trade illegal. In 1914, the Federal Trade Commission Act established the FTC (Federal Trade Commission), which further detailed the activities that are illegal because they restrict free market activity. The FTC also polices market behavior and continues to be a major factor in monitoring market performance.

In the early 1920s, steps were taken to ensure effective marketplace activities specifically for agricultural commodities. The Packers and Stockyards Act of 1921 is an example of efforts to supervise marketing practices and charges at terminal markets. The Commodity Futures Trading Commission was created to supervise trading in the futures market.

The federal government even enters the market *directly* in some instances. The food stamp program, which enables low-income families to purchase food products at subsidized prices, and school lunch programs, which make some surplus agricultural products available to public schools at a low cost, are examples of federal programs that directly reduce food prices to some groups. In other cases, the government directly buys or sells surplus commodities that it has acquired through various farm programs. Other programs make government-purchased commodities available to selected underdeveloped or disaster-stricken countries at very low prices. These market activities directly affect the domestic market.

Congress has also established many programs to foster educational and research activities that have an impact on the marketplace. The Morrill Land-Grant College Act of 1862 enabled the creation of a nationwide agricultural-college system, which has been responsible for many of the technological breakthroughs that have greatly increased agricultural productivity. As part of this structure, agricultural experiment stations were established by the Hatch Act of 1887 to carry out research programs on all types of agricultural production and marketing problems. And the Cooperative Extension Service was established by the Smith-Lever Act of 1914 to carry out agricultural education programs. This total system is a vital part of today's agricultural structure.

Over the years, there has also been considerable legislative activity designed to inform and protect the consumer. The Meat Inspection Act, passed in 1906 and expanded several times since, established a complex inspection system that ensures food quality for many food products. The Pure Food and Drug Act (1906) has played a very important role in shaping marketing and processing practices. Today, there is greater emphasis than ever before on consumer protection. Concern about healthful foods, cancer-causing food additives, and the impact of pesticides on the environment, among other dangers, are widely expressed. Trends toward greater consumer protection have greatly affected the costs of marketing. For example, the costs associated with meeting government requirements for bringing a new pesticide on the market have increased several times in the past few years. Ultimately, these increased costs must be transmitted through the marketing system and reflected in consumer prices.

SUMMARY
The movement of farm supplies and services to farmers and the flow of agricultural products from farms to the final consumer occur within the agricultural marketing system. It is a complex system, involving literally hundreds of thousands of businesses that perform the basic marketing functions of buying, selling, transporting, storing, processing, informing, risk bearing, financing, and standardizing agricultural products. Each of these market functions contributes in some way to the final value or utility of the product; that is, it adds form, time, place or possession utility.

Marketing is a costly activity. Its cost is measured by the marketing margin, that is, the share of the consumer's dollar required to cover marketing costs. Consumers are increasingly demanding more services built into what they buy; therefore, the farmer's share of the consumer's dollar has been falling.

American society has placed restrictions on the free market system in order to ease the severity of adjustment and to ensure that the market reflects consumer wants. Government regulations and programs are designed to control or affect farm production through production quotas and market price support programs. Other legislation creates agencies to continually monitor business activity to ensure fair trading and to provide market information to producers and consumers.

Agricultural marketing is a complex but efficient system for reflecting consumer wants to producers.

DISCUSSION QUESTIONS
1. Why is marketing agricultural products so expensive? Is it likely to become more or less expensive in the future? Why?

2. A Christmas tree growing in northern Wisconsin in October has considerably less value than a flocked tree in a service club's sales lot on December 15. Explain how utility is added to this product as it passes through the marketing system.

3. Explain the difference between operational efficiency and pricing efficiency.

4. How is marketing efficiency most likely to be affected by a weekly news report that publishes the prices of fifty popular food items at all supermarkets in the community?

5. Select an agricultural product with which you are familiar and trace its most likely movement through the marketing process, ending with the consumer. Identify each marketing function as it is accomplished in the process.

6. Of what value are the agricultural commodities futures markets?

7.   Which product is likely to have a larger marketing margin: 2 percent homogenized white milk or a gallon of fancy-grade French vanilla ice cream? Why?

8.   What would be the market impact of a new government program that reduced the allowable weight of trucks on interstate highways?

9.   What is the concept of parity?

OBJECTIVES

- Outline the marketing concept

- Discuss the elements of the marketing mix

- Review product adoption and life cycles in agribusiness markets

- Delineate the features of agribusiness pricing methods

- Summarize various methods of product promotion

- Examine channels of distribution in agribusiness

Marketing within the agribusiness involves developing a marketing mix that focuses on the consumer's needs.
A. Advertising
B. Distribution
C. Pricing agribusiness products

MARKETING IS SO BASIC THAT IT CANNOT BE CONSIDERED A SEPARATE FUNCTION. . . . IT IS THE WHOLE OF BUSINESS SEEN FROM THE POINT OF VIEW OF ITS FINAL RESULT—THAT IS, FROM THE CUSTOMER'S POINT OF VIEW.———Peter Drucker, *Contributions to Business Enterprise,* Tony H. Bonaparte and John E. Flaherty, eds., New York University Press, 1970, p. 148.

12

MARKETING MANAGEMENT IN THE AGRIBUSINESS FIRM

A

C

THE MARKETING CONCEPT

One popular misconception of marketing within the agribusiness firm is that it is limited to the function of selling; in reality, in-firm marketing includes a wide spectrum of decisions and activities that are intended to satisfy customer needs and wants profitably. The full marketing process identifies customer needs, develops products and services to meet these needs, establishes promotional programs and pricing policies, and implements a system of distribution to customers. *Marketing management* is concerned with managing this total process.

Traditionally, marketing has been viewed as "selling what you have"; today's marketing, on the other hand, focuses on "having what you can sell." Thus the starting point for any marketing program must be the identification of customer needs. Marketing must be customer oriented, not product oriented, and companies that lose this perspective usually find themselves in serious difficulty.

Agribusinesses that have achieved early success usually do so because they have successfully identified and filled a customer need. But it is not uncommon for an organization to become so entrenched in producing its product or service that it becomes insensitive to changes in farmer or consumer needs. Such organizations may come to view the customer merely as a link in their production-distribution-consumption chain, rather than as their primary purpose for being. As a result, they become highly vulnerable to any competitors who happen to be more in tune with the changing market.

Because customers' needs are continually changing, successful marketing programs must also be changing. An agribusiness producing fine leather harnesses in the early 1900s may have been fulfilling a need that ceased to exist by the 1940s. The railroad industry, which refused to acknowledge a growing trend toward truck and air transportation in the 1940s and 1950s, has become a classic example of an industry that suffered severe financial difficulty because it failed to adapt.

COMPONENTS OF A STRATEGIC MARKETING PLAN

The *strategic marketing plan* integrates all business activities and resources logically to meet customers' needs and to generate a profit. It includes five types of marketing decisions that must complement one another. These decision areas are often referred to as the *marketing mix* (see Figure 12-1).

Total Market Decisions

Total market decisions revolve around a thorough analysis of (1) which customers will be targeted and what their needs will be, and (2) the competitive environment. Several sophisticated tools aid the modern agribusiness in its market decisions, including market research, market segmentation, and market penetration.

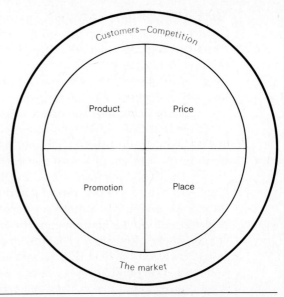

Customers—Competition

| Product | Price |
| Promotion | Place |

The market

Figure 12-1   Marketing mix.

Market Research   *Market research* is particularly useful for understanding customers' needs and potential. Many larger agribusinesses employ professional marketing researchers or outside consultants to study their customers, their competition, and trends in the marketplace. Even many smaller firms develop their plans only after they have conducted special studies of their customers and their product's image.

Marketing research can be based on complex statistical techniques, or it can simply result from informal interviews and observations. But, in any case, it should provide objective, analytical information on which to base marketing decisions.

Market Segmentation   *Market segmentation* classifies customers into segments or categories according to applicable characteristics. By recognizing the common characteristics, needs, or buying motives of each unique segment in the total market, an agribusiness can design specialized marketing strategies that may appeal to the particular segments it wants to serve.

Thus, a feed manufacturer may recognize dairy, beef, hogs, and poultry as clearly different market segments with different needs; further, dairy farmers' operations may be classified as small, medium, or large, according to herd size. Then special promotional programs and pricing schemes can be developed to appeal to well-defined segments, for example, large dairy operations. Marketing programs for targeted agribusiness market segments are thought to be far more productive than mass marketing techniques aimed at the total market.

Market Penetration *Market penetration* relates to strength in a given market segment. Every firm must decide on its optimal level of concentration in a given segment, since limited resources must be directed to the area where they will be most productive. Decisions about the best segments for concentrated penetration rest on data about the type of product, competitive behavior, size of the company, and other factors.

Some firms may choose a single area of concentration, using the rationale that concentrating all their efforts on a single class of customers allows them to do a better job and may effectively block out new competition. A farm supply store that caters only to larger commercial farmers would be one example. Another farm supply store might develop a "dual segment" concentration by building a special display area for lawn and garden equipment and seasonal nursery stock, so that it appeals to surburban homeowners in addition to commercial farmers. Of course, there are a host of factors involved in market-penetration decisions, including size, location, experience, and competition. But once the market segment or segments have been targeted, the agribusiness must concentrate on products that will succeed there.

Product Decisions

Because they are at the heart of the marketing program, product decisions are among the most visible decisions an agribusiness can make. Unless a firm has a strong marketing orientation, its product decisions may rest on tradition, emotion, or internal politics. Decisions that must be made include the mix of different products, the extent of the line of each product, and specific characteristics of each product sold. Products selected for the mix should complement each other technically, in the distribution channels and with consumers, to take full advantage of marketing efficiencies.

Product Adoption and Diffusion The manner in which customers adopt a new technology, a product, or a service is important to a firm's marketing strategy. The adoption process is tied closely to a product's life cycle and suggests how new products should be introduced into the market. The adoption-diffusion of new products was researched by E. M. Rogers, using hybrid seed corn as an example. Rogers suggested that ideas are diffused through the market in systematic stages.

1. *Awareness:* At this stage, people have heard about the product but lack sufficient information to make a purchasing decision.

2. *Interest:* A potential customer becomes interested enough to find out about the product.

3. *Evaluation:* The customer decides whether to try the product.

4. *Trial:* The customer samples the product.

5. *Adoption:* The customer integrates the product into a regular-use pattern.

Some individuals who adopt products more quickly than others tend to be *opinion leaders*. These people are watched carefully and followed by other customers in the market. Their favorable opinions are extremely important to marketers. Many agribusinesses spend considerable time and money identifying opinion leaders and working closely with them in an attempt to build favorable relationships. Some opinion leaders actively attempt to influence others within their sphere. Successful agribusiness marketers and salespeople also work to influence people's decisions. People capable of influencing others' decisions are sometimes referred to as *change agents*. As a new idea or technology is introduced into the market, Rogers found, it will be adopted in a systematic way as more and more users adopt the idea. He classified users into five distinct categories according to how soon they adopt a new idea.

Rogers's research (see Figure 12-2) suggests that the total number of innovators is very small, perhaps about 2.5 percent of a given market. *Innovators* are venturesome people who like to try new ideas. They are not necessarily opinion leaders; since they try so many new things, they may be regarded as a bit strange.

Early adopters (about 13.5 percent of a market) are respected citizens who adopt new ideas quickly but with caution, usually after observing the experience of the innovators. They are usually key opinion leaders in the community and are therefore highly important to the agribusiness.

The *early majority* (about 34 percent of a market) are deliberate people who see themselves as progressive but not generally as leaders. They form a large and important market.

The *late majority* (another 34 percent) tend to be skeptical in their view of new ideas, and adopt them only after considerable evidence has been shown. They follow the majority opinion.

Finally, *laggards* (16 percent) are tradition-bound people who take

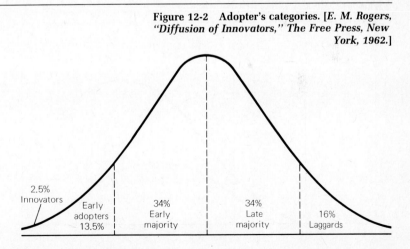

Figure 12-2   Adopter's categories. [*E. M. Rogers, "Diffusion of Innovators," The Free Press, New York, 1962.*]

2.5% Innovators

Early adopters 13.5%

34% Early majority

34% Late majority

16% Laggards

so long to adopt new ideas that by the time the ideas are adopted, they are no longer new.

The manner of new technology adoption suggested by Rogers holds for most new ideas, both within agriculture and outside. "Agrimarketers" who introduce new products can initially gear their total marketing program toward the innovators and early adopters, gradually changing their marketing strategy as the product is accepted by other adopter categories over time.

Product Life Cycles   *Product life cycles* relate to the sales and profits of a product or service over a period of time. There are several distinct phases in the life of a product, from its development and initial introduction to its eventual removal from the market (see Figure 12-3).

The *development* stage is that period in which the market is analyzed, and both the product and the market strategy are developed. During this time there is no income, but there is significant expenditure for product and market development. For example, this is the period when a new rabbit feed is researched, formulated, and tested, while plans are laid for its introduction into the market.

The *introductory* stage is that period in which the new product first appears on the market. Usually, there are high costs associated with introducing a product. The new rabbit feed may require a heavy promotional effort and special offers to dealers to stock the product, all of which reduce the probability of early profits. At some time during the introduction period, the product should begin to show a profit, depending on the degree of its success. The firm might choose to make heavy introductory expenditures to reduce the time for consumer acceptance. Or it might introduce the product without fanfare, simply adding it to the line at perhaps a low initial price, in the hope of minimizing introductory costs. Many strategies are possible.

Figure 12-3   Phases in the life of a product.

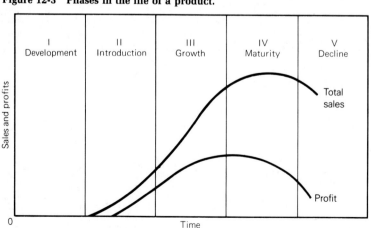

The *growth* stage is a period of rapid expansion, during which sales gain momentum and prices tend to hold steady or increase slightly, as firms usually try to develop customer loyalty. The distribution system is expanded, which makes the product available to a larger market. Profits expand rapidly because fixed costs are spread over a larger sales base. But as the firm reaches for increasingly difficult new markets, costs begin to increase. The visibility of increasing profits often attracts new competitors to the market. As the firm attempts to reach increasingly difficult new markets and the effects of competition begin to be felt, growth slows, and profits, while still increasing, begin to increase at a decreasing rate.

The *maturity* stage is characterized by slow growth of sales or even some decline as the market becomes saturated. Sales lag because most of the potential customers have been tapped and because competitors have entered the market, leaving only slow adopters and replacement sales with established customers. This stage usually lasts longer, so most products in the market are in this stage.

Much marketing activity is designed to prolong the maturity stage by propping up sales and protecting profits. Competition often becomes intense in the maturity stage as competitors battle for market share, often using price as a weapon. Firms struggle to refine their product by changing design, adding features, making new advertising claims, and developing promotional campaigns and incentives to protect or enhance market share. Strategically, firms hope to differentiate their product sufficiently to push it back into the growth stage. But all this additional marketing activity pushes costs up, and profits begin to decline. How rapidly profits fall off in the maturity stage, of course, depends on a host of factors, but this decline is always of major concern to management.

The *decline* stage finds sales declining more rapidly. Changes in consumer preferences or new substitute products may hasten the death of the product. As the product dies, profits slip to zero or worse, and some firms withdraw from the market. The remaining firms may reduce marketing expenditures, until eventually the product may disappear totally from the market.

Many firms find the decline stage very difficult to handle. Executives who have built their professional careers around the growth of a product are sometimes emotionally involved with the product and are thus reluctant to admit its decline. The firm may be embarrassed by a declining product. Marketing managers may legitimately expect sales growth to resume as economic conditions change. In any case, to drop a product and to decide on the best timing for the action pose extreme difficulties. Yet, to prolong the life of a product may sap the firm financially and preclude the market development of new products.

THE BENT ARROW[1] The evolution of a product through its life cycle presents the essence of product decisions for the marketing manager in

[1]Robert T. Davis, "A Marketing Strategy Note," Stanford University Graduate School of Business, Paper No. S-M-163/A, 1975.

the agribusiness firm. Although each product has a life cycle, the life cycle can look very different from one product to another. Some products have very short life cycles lasting only a year or two, while others may have life cycles that spread over dozens of years. One of the marketing manager's jobs is to use marketing tools to prolong the profitable life stages.

Initially, a product or service is often unique in the marketplace. It is a *specialty* early in its life, with little price competition and a relatively good profit position. But over a period of time, as competition discovers the opportunity and enters the market with "me too" products, the product becomes a *commodity,* as respresented by the arrow in Figure 12-4a. Commodity markets are usually highly competitive, low-profit markets.

The marketing manager is faced with the task of turning this arrow back in order to somehow regain the distinctive edge in the marketplace (as represented by Figure 12-4b). By refining their product, changing the design, adding features, expanding the product line, or packaging the product innovatively to facilitate use, marketing managers try to bend the arrow back and help the product regain its specialty status.

A good example of the bent-arrow concept is some widely used agricultural chemicals that originally were sold in 1-gallon (3.8-liter) containers. As competition increased, manufacturers developed bulk distribution to dealers as a means of maintaining a temporary competitive edge and capitalizing on additional distribution efficiencies.

Price Decisions

Pricing is a critical marketing decision because it so greatly influences the dollar revenue generated. It does this in two ways.

1. Price impacts revenue as a component of the revenue equation (Revenue = price × quantity sold).

2. The price level itself greatly affects the quantity sold, through its effect on demand relationships for the product or service.

Complications arise because these two price effects work in opposite directions. Lower prices produce less income per unit sold, but

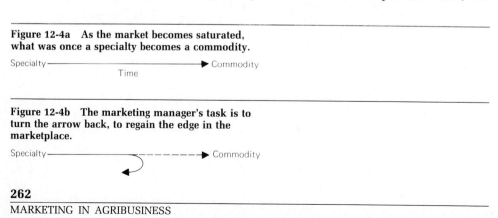

Figure 12-4a   As the market becomes saturated, what was once a specialty becomes a commodity.

Specialty ——————————————▶ Commodity
                        Time

Figure 12-4b   The marketing manager's task is to turn the arrow back, to regain the edge in the marketplace.

Specialty ————————— – – – – – ▶ Commodity

usually generate an increase in quantity sold, while the opposite is true when price is increased. Of course, increased sales mean that fixed costs are spread over more units; therefore, per unit costs may be reduced, at least to a point. The net result is that pricing decisions become a real challenge to managers.

Some price decisions involve highly complex mathematical methods, while others depend on simple rules of thumb or intuitive judgments. The type of product, customer demand, competitive environment, product life-cycle stage, and product mix are some of the factors considered in price determination. Several commonly used pricing methods will be discussed here.

Cost Pricing *Cost-based pricing*, or *cost-plus pricing*, is a simple matter of adding a constant margin to the basic cost of the individual product or service. This margin is intended to cover overhead and handling costs, and leave a profit. In retail businesses, such as farm supply or hardware stores, it is a simple matter to "mark up" merchandise by some percentage.

Cost ($1.00) $\times$ 1.30 (markup of 30%) = $1.30 (selling price)

Farm construction firms sometimes operate on the basis of the cost of materials plus a percentage.

The markup theoretically represents the cost of handling the product or performing the service; it therefore varies with different product lines and among different industries. Actually, the markups seldom reflect costs accurately; they are based more on tradition than on logic.

A major problem with cost-plus pricing is the difficulty of allocating fixed or overhead costs to a specific product or service. Accounting systems simply are not adequate to determine how much of the delivery truck's costs should be allocated to delivering each product. And, even if a method for this kind of determination existed, the cost of keeping track of time spent and related expenditures, would be prohibitive.

Yet, because of its simplicity, the cost-based pricing method is popular, especially for the retailing of large numbers of products. And when a particular markup percentage is widely accepted, competitors find their prices so similar that market stability is improved.

ROI Pricing *ROI (return on investment) pricing* is similar to cost-plus pricing; it, too, begins with the cost of the product, but rather than adding fixed or overhead costs, it adds an amount sufficient to earn a specified ROI. For example, a firm calculates how much profit will be needed to earn 15 percent ROI. Then, assuming a reasonable sales volume, it estimates costs and calculates the total revenue that must be generated. Finally, the total revenue is divided by estimated sales to suggest the necessary percentage that the product must be marked up.

The major drawback of ROI pricing is that the price calculation assumes a certain level of sales volume, when, in fact, the sales will be at least partly determined by price. In fact, the price selected may not generate the sales volume assumed, in which case the system breaks down. Yet the concept of pricing to achieve an acceptable ROI has considerable appeal.

Competitive Pricing   Competitive pricing lies at the other end of the spectrum. While cost-based and ROI pricing methods tend to ignore market conditions, *competitive-pricing* methods essentially base price on competitors' prices. This method simply sets price at the "going rate," according to some general average, or follows the lead of a competitor.

Competitive pricing does not always involve matching the competitors' price; a price may strategically be held above or below that of competitors. A local lawn and garden shop might choose to hold its price consistently above that of a large chain discount store. Or a small, low-cost independent grain elevator may regularly offer 2 cents per bushel more than a large cooperative competitor who dominates the local market.

Because competitive pricing is common in commodity-based markets, it is widespread in agribusiness, particularly in smaller firms whose markets are dominated by larger firms. It works well as long as the smaller firm has a favorable cost structure relative to other firms or is small enough not to be a major threat to the larger firm. Stable markets can sometimes succumb to a price war when the price leader decides to fight it out, and the winner is often the firm that can withstand the financial blows the longest.

When one firm's product mix is quite similar to another firm's, price usually becomes a major factor in the buying decision. While firms struggle to differentiate their products and services, it is difficult to remain much above the market price for long periods. Consequently, most agribusinesses keep a close eye on the market price and vary from it only in subtle ways.

Of course, this phenomenon causes major problems for any agribusiness that does not happen to enjoy a favorable cost structure. Less efficient businesses are forced into financial difficulty because of the necessity of keeping prices competitive. And it is not uncommon for agribusinesses that are in a low-cost position to intentionally exert pressure on their higher-cost competition in order to gain an increase in market share. While there is nothing clandestine or illegal about this, the effects can be devastating for the less efficient agribusiness and beneficial for farmer-customers. This phenomenon is a good example of the free enterprise system at work and is a primary reason for the efficiency of the American economy.

CTO Pricing   CTO (contribution-to-overhead) *pricing* is a method of encouraging extra sales by selling additional product above and beyond the sales projection, at some price slightly greater than the additional out-of-pocket costs of handling the product. In other words, CTO pricing, which is also called marginal-cost pricing, ignores the fair share of the overhead cost that could be borne by the additional product. It assumes the overhead costs will be covered by normal sales as projected, so that if additional products are sold at any price whatsoever that is above their variable cost, they will make a contribution to overhead and profit that would not otherwise exist. (See Chapter 10 for a detailed description of volume-cost pricing.)

The logic of this pricing method is quite compelling when viewed in terms of the marginal or extra sales opportunity. Since many agribusiness supplies are sold on a negotiated basis, there is ample opportunity for using CTO pricing methods to increase sales. Whenever fixed costs are a major component of total costs, as they are in the fertilizer and chemical industries, there is great temptation to utilize this method of increasing sales, making additional contributions to overhead, and increasing profits.

But the big problem is limiting CTO pricing to only marginal or extra sales. In reality, there is a great tendency for competitors to react to the lower "spot" price, which causes the total market price to tumble, leaving the market unstable at best or in shambles at worst. The key is holding CTO pricing to marginal sales.

Penetration Pricing *Penetration-pricing* strategies consist of offering a product at a low price in order to get a great deal of exposure to gain wide acceptance quickly. These strategies are used primarily to introduce new products into a market, particularly price-responsive products that must sell in large volume to reduce costs. Penetration pricing can quickly cut into the sales of established competitors, even in cases where brand loyalty may be a factor. After a new product has gained consumer acceptance, the price may be gradually raised to a more profitable level.

Skimming the Market Skimming the market is almost the opposite of penetration pricing. *Skimming* involves introducing a product at a high price for more affluent customers. Then, as this relatively limited market becomes saturated, the price is gradually lowered, bringing the product into range for less affluent customers. The appeal of this method is the opportunity it affords to maximize profits on new products as quickly as possible. "Skimming the market and sliding down the demand curve," as it is sometimes referred to, works best on products that are new, unique, fairly expensive, hard to duplicate quickly, and sold by firms that are well known and respected in the industry. Mobile communication equipment for farm use seems to have come into the agribusiness market in this manner. New, superior varieties of hybrid seed are often introduced this way, with prices falling as the variety gains wide acceptance.

What the Market Will Bear *What the market will bear* is another method of pricing highly unique products and services; it involves experimenting with various prices, with the objective of finding out and charging the maximum that consumers are willing to pay. This method is used frequently in pricing highly specialized services that vary with each job. It works well where each job is separately negotiated, and where communication among customers is not well developed. This system is most successful when the benefits of the product or service far exceed its price, which makes the price a less important factor. Personalized technical services to farmers and agribusinesses fall into this category.

Discount Pricing *Discount pricing* offers customers a reduction from the published or list price for some specified reason. Volume discounts are common among agribusinesses. Their purpose is to encourage larger purchases, which reduce per unit costs and promote more sales. Volume discounts can be on a per order basis, but they more commonly accumulate throughout the season, and may take the form of a rebate at the end of the season. This is particularly common in the fertilizer industry.

Discounts can also be applied to purchases from certain types of buyers who qualify as dealers or represent some other position in the marketing channel. The seed corn industry in the Midwest makes extensive use of dealer and volume discounts.

Cash discounts are designed to encourage prompt payment for products and services. There are an infinite variety of cash discount programs. Many use terminology such as "5/10, net 30," which means that the customer will receive a 5 percent discount if the bill is paid within 10 days, but the full amount is due in 30 days, regardless. Because of the tremendous problems of seasonality faced by most agribusinesses, cash discount programs are widely used.

Early-order discounts are often given by manufacturers of agribusiness products as an incentive to order and/or take possession of products in the off-season. Because of storage and shipping problems in peak season, many manufacturers aggressively promote early shipment with very significant price reductions. The pesticide market makes wide use of early-order programs, sometimes offering a host of non-price incentives to accompany price discounts, such as "One free with each case ordered." Sometimes price protection programs are included to protect the early buyer against late-season price reductions by guaranteeing customers that if the price falls later, during the heavy-use season, they will receive a rebate, effectively giving them the lower price.

Loss-Leader Pricing *Loss-leader pricing* involves offering one or more products in a product mix at a specially reduced price for a limited time. The idea is to encourage long-term adoption of that particular product. In a retail store setting, the featured item is also expected to draw customers to the store and increase sales in all other product lines. Featured items are sometimes even sold below cost in order to boost store traffic. Loss leaders are common in consumer retail settings, such as farm-home stores and nurseries, but they seldom are productive in selling farm inputs, except in the case of some general farm supplies. Major production supplies, such as feed, chemicals, and petroleum products, do not generally lend themselves well to loss-leader pricing, since they are needed in specific quantities and each major supply item tends to be purchased separately.

Psychological Pricing *Psychological pricing* involves establishing prices that are emotionally more satisfying because they sound better. Odd prices, such as 99 cents, sound a great deal less than $1. "Two for $1.99," instead of "$1 each," gives the illusion of a special deal, and appeals to the customer's instinctive attraction to a bargain.

Prestige Pricing *Prestige pricing,* on the other hand, appeals to a quality, elite image. Many people have a strong belief that "You get what you pay for" and tend to equate price and quality on an emotional basis. Prestige pricing is widely used in agribusiness. Some feed companies offer personalized on-farm sales and technical service, and sell their product at a premium price as their basic market strategy.

A Word of Caution   Pricing is a delicate issue, from both marketing and legal standpoints. There is a great deal of federal legislation that clearly prohibits any form of collusion among firms in establishing prices or discrimination against particular customers. The Robinson-Patman Act (1936) strongly forbids any act that "substantially lessens competition." Any product of like kind and quality that crosses state lines must be offered to all purchasers at the same price, unless it can be clearly demonstrated that the price differences are based on differences in the cost of serving various customers. Similarly, any discounts or allowances made to one customer must be available to all customers. Local businesses that are not involved in interstate commerce and that are the final seller may sell at any price they choose to any customer, so long as they are not in collusion with other sellers.

Pricing can also be a very touchy issue. It is bad practice for any agribusiness employee to discuss prices with a competitor. If a customer brings a price offer made by a competitor, it is permissible to call the competitor for the sole purpose of confirming that offer. But discussion of prices with competitors should be strictly avoided, even among local agribusinesses and their employees.

Promotional Decisions

Promotional activities in the agribusiness are designed to do one thing: sell more of the product or service. The marketing strategy incorporates various methods for informing customers and convincing them to buy. It is basically a communication process intended to modify customer behavior toward a positive buying decision.

The promotion mix chosen by the agribusiness firm is usually a combination of advertising, personal selling efforts, general publicity, and a sales support program. The mix must consider the life-cycle stage of the product, the stage of product adoption in the marketplace, competitors' actions, and available budget. The promotion mix is designed to support and complement the total marketing mix.

Advertising *Advertising* is mass communication with potential customers, usually through public communications media. Some advertising is *institutional,* or intended not to promote a particular product but rather to build goodwill for the total company or industry. Most advertising is *product* advertising, designed to promote a specific product, service, or idea.

Advertising performs several important functions. First, it creates awareness about the product, which facilitates personal selling efforts. In some cases, public exposure through communications media lends a degree of credibility to the product. Psychologically, a potential customer comes to feel that a nationally advertised product must be worth looking at. An advertisement can motivate a customer to seek out the product, or can at least serve as a reminder of the product's existence. Advertising also performs an educational function, helping customers to learn more about the product and its use. Finally, ads can reinforce the value of a purchase that has already been made. Research suggests that recent purchasers of a product are among those most likely to read an ad for that product.

Much advertising is initiated and sponsored by manufacturers of agribusiness products. Some of this advertising is oriented toward the dealer or distributor to influence ordering and selling decisions. But much manufacturer-sponsored advertising is aimed toward the final consumer; in this case, the farmer. The idea is to encourage ultimate demand to "pull the product through the pipeline." Geographically broad-based advertising is usually the sole responsibility of the manufacturer. But local advertising, cooperatively sponsored by the manufacturer and the local dealer or distributor and called *cooperative advertising,* is also very common in agribusiness. Local ads are usually prepared by the manufacturer, with the name of the local agribusiness inserted and the cost jointly shared. The manufacturer may also supply the local agribusiness with flyers, posters, or product brochures, and may even send direct-mail advertisements, with the local business name imprinted, to local customers.

There is a wide variety of communications media ready to carry the agribusiness's message. Television is expensive and not widely used to communicate with farmers, except in predominantly rural areas for frequently purchased products with broad usage. Radio is used more commonly by local agribusinesses, since it is less expensive and can target its farm audience by tying into agricultural programs, such as market news and farm broadcasts. Many aggressive local radio stations in rural areas employ professional farm broadcasters who do such a good job of covering agricultural news that they attract a strong following for the products they advertise.

Other media forms include handbills and flyers sent directly to high-potential customers. Several organizations specialize in providing mailing lists of farmers in special categories. For example, it is a relatively simple matter to mail promotional materials exclusively to hog farmers in Iowa and Illinois.

Ads in rural newspapers are relatively inexpensive, but their actual value is very difficult to measure. Coupons can give some agribusinesses a clue to the ad's effectiveness, but coupons do not lend themselves well to most general farm supplies.

Local, regional, and national farm magazines are an important method of communication with the farm consumer. Trade magazines geared to specific types of agribusinesses are also widely used to communicate with dealers and distributors.

Advertising budgets are a problem for most agribusinesses, since it is difficult to determine the actual effect of advertising on sales. Large manufacturers of agribusiness products and their advertising agencies spend a great deal of money attempting to measure the effectiveness of different ads. As one executive put it, "I know half of my advertising is wasted—and if I could determine which half, we'd cut it out!" This is a big problem for smaller agribusinesses because one person is generally not able to devote exclusive attention to advertising. Many local agribusinesses believe advertising to be an unnecessary cost, and limit their advertising to high school yearbooks, which is purely a public service or public relations tactic. They argue that their best advertising in the local market is "word of mouth," and choose to allocate their promotional dollars to customer meetings and personal contacts, or simply to sell at a lower cost. Advertising budgets for local farm-oriented businesses are generally limited to 1 to 2 percent of total sales or less.

Sales Promotion *Sales promotions* are programs and special offerings designed to nudge interested customers into making a positive buying decision. There is an almost infinite variety of such tools, and many are used extensively by agribusinesses to support personal selling activities. These tools are often expensive, but are felt by many to strongly influence customer decisions.

Some of these programs are aimed directly at the final consumer, the farmer. Giving potential customers hats, ski caps, jackets, belt buckles, pens, note pads, and a myriad of other "freebies," all imprinted with the company logo, has become so common that farmers and ranchers have come to expect it. And more and more often, larger producers are being "entertained" over dinner by marketing people as a means of getting their undivided attention.

Such sales-promotion programs are an integral part of agribusiness marketing strategies. Many suppliers and retailers feel trapped by these kinds of promotions, but because of competitive pressures, are afraid to cut back on them. Thus expensive promotions and incentives should be entered into carefully.

Other promotional programs include educational-sales meetings sponsored by suppliers and retailers for farmers, ranchers, and growers. Evening meetings and day-long seminars, often including a complimentary meal, provide much important technical information to producers, while subtly promoting the use of chemicals, hybrids, feeds, livestock breeds, and the like. Field days where farmers see products and services demonstrated in the field are highly popular and effective. Regional trade shows where large numbers of suppliers attract hundreds of thousands of farmers are also common. Farmer meetings and shows have become an important communication and educational link between suppliers and producers.

The variety of sales promotions used in selling to dealers and distributors is even more elaborate. Sales contests and incentive vacation trips are so common that some especially productive agribusiness managers may "earn" trips to several exotic resorts for themselves and their spouses in the slack season, at the expense of their supplier. Dealer and distributor meetings during the winter months are usually well planned, educational, and often elaborate and entertaining. Some suppliers develop educational and technical training programs for their customers' employees.

Not all agribusinesses become extensively involved in well-developed promotional programs. Some choose instead to concentrate on service and price. But promotional programs are particularly common among suppliers of farm inputs.

Personal Selling At some point in the marketing process, a sale must be made and ownership of the product must be transferred. This requires human effort of some sort. In most agribusinesses, the salesperson intentionally plays an important part in the promotion process. Promoting a product through personal-selling efforts provides the most flexible and highest impact possible, since the salesperson can tailor the promotion to individual needs, assuming that the salesperson is effective.

Most of agribusiness is highly dependent on personal selling. Even small local agribusinesses that do not formally designate anyone as a salesperson rely heavily on personal contact and interpersonal communications to promote their product. Often the managers spend much of their time promoting products and services through personal contact. In larger agribusinesses, the personal-selling process is far more formalized and highly structured. Management of the sales force and its organization take on great significance. Selecting, training, compensation plan, and territory allocation all become critically important in the management of personal selling activities in the larger agribusiness (see Chapters 14 and 15).

Place Decisions

Every agribusiness must decide how to move products to its consumers. Marketing channels are systematic ways of transferring both the physical product and the ownership as efficiently as possible. In many ways, the channel is a communication system linking the producer to the consumer. Consumer demand signals flow through the system to manufacturers, while supply and availability signals in the form of prices and costs flow to consumers. In many cases, independent agribusinesses known as middlemen facilitate the transfer of ownership and physical product. In other cases, manufacturers find it more efficient to sell directly to the consumer.

Physical Distribution Physical distribution decisions are particularly important to much of agribusiness, since so many farm supplies are bulky and highly seasonal in demand. Literally millions of tons of phosphate must be moved from Florida mines, and millions of tons of potash must be shipped from western Canada to farms and ranches all over the United States and Canada. At the same time, literally millions of tons of grain must be moved from local storage to the coast for shipment to overseas markets.

In season, rail car and truck shortages can cause spot supply shortages, bottlenecking agribusiness products in the distribution system. This slowdown becomes a problem for many agribusinesses, since quite a few agricultural producers supply world markets from a single plant. Consequently, marketing strategy increasingly incorporates plans for assuring an adequate physical distribution system. Policies encouraging larger storage facilities at local levels, company ownership of rail cars, company-operated truck fleets, unit trains with 100-car shipments of the same commodity, and transcontinental barges and pipelines are becoming common as a means of ensuring timeliness and reducing costs.

Even at the local level, agribusinesses are highly concerned about physical-distribution problems. Bulky products must be broken down into prescription quantities to meet the needs of individual farmers quickly during intense high-use periods. Bulk feed delivery, on-farm storage, custom application of chemicals and fertilizer, on-farm breeding services, and a myriad of other products and services must be delivered effectively. Much of this physical distribution requires a great deal of highly specialized equipment and labor. Indeed, physical distribution at all levels incurs a high marketing cost and is critical to the agribusiness.

Market Distribution Market-distribution decisions are concerned with who owns and controls the product on its journey to the customer. This has important implications for how the marketing functions will be carried out. The market channel selected is closely tied to the physical-distribution problem. But the question of who owns the product and who performs the various market functions required to transfer a product from the manufacturer to the consumer is much broader.

There are three basic systems used by most agribusinesses (see Figure 12-5). Each system differs in the extent and type of involvement of the middleman. In each system, all marketing functions are per-

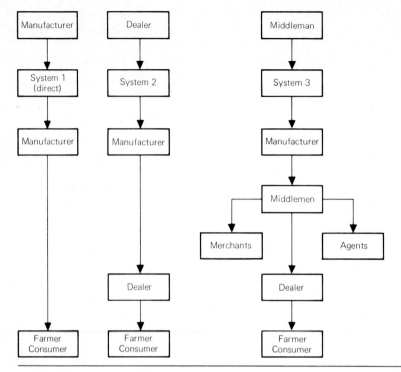

Figure 12-5   Major agribusiness distribution channels.

formed. That is, products are owned, transported, financed, and stored. But in each system these functions are performed by different parties.

In a *manufacturer–direct-distribution system,* the manufacturer sells directly to the farmer. All marketing functions are performed by the original producer, who owns and controls the product until it is purchased by the final user. This system has the advantage of ensuring that the product will be priced, promoted, and sold in ways that are acceptable to the manufacturer. Some firms believe it allows them to be more aggressive in the marketplace, because they can create and control their image with customers. This method is used widely by smaller local or regional manufacturers, who can develop their own sales force as they grow. It also works better where customers are concentrated. As the business grows and customers are distributed more widely, with increasingly different characteristics and needs, it becomes increasingly difficult to manage the direct-selling system. Marketing to widely different customers often requires at least regionalized marketing policies, which become increasingly difficult to administer effectively. However, when organizations give their sales force considerable autonomy, the system can be effective even on a regional or national scale. A good example is the Moorman Feed Manufacturing Company, which sells directly to farmers.

Note that many companies that sell directly do so by establishing their own wholesale and retail systems. The product must be physically transported and distributed as in any other system, but in the direct system company-owned warehouses and/or retail stores will be used, which allows manufacturers to ship and store products whenever and wherever they choose. This freedom provides some real economic advantages.

In a *dealer-distribution system,* manufacturers sell their products to dealers, who, in turn, sell products in their own local market. The big advantage is that the local dealer is more in touch with the needs of local customers and can maintain the flexibility to serve both manufacturers' and customers' needs quickly and efficiently. This eliminates the tendency for an executive 1000 miles away to fill local storage space with a product simply to gain more room in a full warehouse, even though local farmers may not need the product in large quantities that season. And some feel that independent dealers are more highly motivated to serve the local customer than are company employees.

Some manufacturers give their dealers (who may be called distributors, even though they sell directly to farmers) the right to sell their products. Although the manufacturer cannot control the sales areas of dealers, giving dealers this right can strategically limit the number of dealerships. To maintain the right to sell the products, dealers agree to maintain certain levels of service to customers and promote the products in special ways. There may even be a contractual agreement, sometimes called a *franchise,* spelling out the responsibilities of both the dealer and the distributor. The A O Smith Harvestore Company uses a limited dealer organization, choosing to sell through a few large independent dealers to distribute their silo feed storage systems.

Other manufacturers encourage distribution through as many dealers as possible. Products that are frequently purchased and less expensive generally tend to be mass-marketed in order to maximize convenience to the buyer and saturate the market. Animal health products and many hard lines of farm supplies are marketed in this way. Products are sold to the dealer almost as they would be to a farmer-consumer. As farms and ranches grow bigger, many manufacturers are beginning to recognize them as "dealers," especially if the farmer resells at least some product to a neighbor. In effect, the traditional manufacturer-dealer-farmer system seems to be breaking down in some product lines.

The *middleman,* or *distributor system,* uses both middleman-distributors, or wholesalers, and dealers to market products to farmers. This more complex marketing system usually evolves for economic reasons. Larger organizations can more easily afford to develop their own marketing system. Independent middlemen may already have a well-developed network of transportation, salespeople, and customers, and their size allows them to operate quite efficiently. They can often add a new product line much more cheaply than the manufacturer can establish a whole system. This allows manufacturers to concentrate on what they do best—manufacturing product—and allows middlemen to do what they do best.

Merchant-middlemen, who actually take title to the manufacturer's product, are called distributors, jobbers, wholesalers, or cooperative buying groups. They physically order, receive, and distribute products. As totally independent businesses, they make their own decisions, relying on manufacturers only for technical assistance and information. Agricultural chemicals are sold largely through regional wholesalers whose sales force sells to dealers, who in turn sell to farmers.

Agent-middlemen perform the function of helping products move through the system, but they do not take title to the product and usually do not physically handle the product. Agent-middlemen are known as brokers, sales agents, and manufacturer's representatives. They are independent businesses that simply locate customers, negotiate a deal, and receive a commission for the transaction. Agents and brokers often specialize in certain product lines and types of customers. Their primary tool is communication. In markets in which shortages are occurring, brokers are usually able to locate extra product for a special price. They perform the important function of bringing buyers and sellers together.

The total distribution system can be far more complex than is described here. Many manufacturers may use several different systems simultaneously. For example, the Agrico Company, a large fertilizer manufacturer based in Oklahoma, markets fertilizer through its own retail outlets, through independent fertilizer dealers, and through large regional wholesalers. The distribution system gradually evolved out of changing products, customers, and the competitive environment.

SUMMARY

Marketing management is concerned with marketing decisions *within* the agribusiness firm. Its object is to develop, execute, and control a strategic marketing plan that will satisfy customers' needs while generating a profit for the firm.

The strategic marketing plan must integrate all facets of business activity. First, the corporate mission is defined, objectives and goals are established, and a step-by-step strategy for accomplishing those goals is laid out; then the plan is executed through daily activities or tactics.

Market managers must first carefully analyze the market, identifying various segments or classes of customers who have unique characteristics so that marketing programs can be adapted to major segments.

The marketing plan has four major decision areas called the marketing mix. Product decisions determine what products or services to offer. Each product has a life cycle, with distinct phases from its introduction to its demise. As products are introduced they move through a systematic adoption and diffusion process that offers the marketing manager important opportunities to market the product.

Pricing decisions are critical to marketing success. Pricing strategies are based on competitive actions, consumer responses, and internal cost considerations. Promotional decisions determine the proper mix of advertising, publicity, selling, and sales support programs needed to reach sales objectives. Finally, place decisions concentrate on the methods and channels of distribution that will optimize sales and profits.

All elements of the marketing mix are critical decision areas for the marketing manager.

DISCUSSION QUESTIONS

1. Explain the difference between a product- or sales-oriented marketing plan and a consumer-oriented marketing plan. Why is this difference important to an agribusiness?

2. What is meant by a market segment? U-pick fruit and vegetable farms probably appeal more to some market segments than to others. Identify and characterize two market segments that you believe might be important to this agribusiness.

3. Most agribusinesses that retail fertilizer to farmers also sell pesticides. Why do you suppose this is so? What marketing decision does this illustrate? What other products or services would you think might be included and why?

4. Draw a product life-cycle curve for large, four-wheel-drive farm tractors. Where would you estimate this product's life cycle is currently at? Why? What might manufacturers do to prolong its life?

5. If you were introducing a new electronic dairy feeding system that would reduce feeding costs by 20 to 25 percent, what pricing policy would you suggest? Why? Would you stay with this policy indefinitely? Why?

6. What products might be good loss leaders in retail farm and home stores? Why?

7. What advertising media alternatives would most local farm suppliers have? Which ones do you think might be effective for a local farm supply cooperative?

8. Why do you suppose manufacturer-sponsored incentive trips to resorts for meeting sales goals are so widely used? Give a reason why some agribusiness managers might not like them.

9. What are the advantages of a manufacturer's selling directly to a farmer rather than to a middleman? Why can a dealer sometimes do a better job marketing to farmers than a manufacturer can?

S & S COMPUTER COMPANY

Over the course of three years, while they were both working and pursuing college degrees, Scott and Sam became very interested in computers. Scott had the skills necessary to write very sophisticated computer programs. Sam, on the other hand, was very outgoing and liked to deal with people. Sam had majored in agricultural sales and marketing, while

Scott's major was in agribusiness management with a minor in computer science.

Sam and Scott wanted to start their own computer software company upon graduation. They had saved about $20,000, and they had tentative backing from a bank in the local area. They decided that they would like to start their business in the agricultural area with programs dealing with feed rations and herd management, and maybe some marketing programs.

QUESTIONS

1. What market segments would S & S serve best in the near future?

2. Suggest a product-service-mix strategy that might be effective with these segments.

3. What promotional strategy would you suggest for this company? Should this change a few months down the road if the firm is successful?

4. How should the firm price its product to be effective with the market segments you have identified?

- Outline the procedure for a marketing audit

- Analyze how sales forecasts are made and how they are used in the agribusiness firm

- Develop methods for analyzing competition

- Review techniques for studying customer attitudes and opinions

Agribusiness managers use a variety of marketing tools to analyze their markets and develop a strategic plan.

A. Collecting field information

B. Market analysis

THE MATERIALS ARE INDIFFERENT, BUT THE USE WE MAKE OF THEM IS NOT A MATTER OF INDIFFERENCE.———Epictetus

13

TOOLS FOR MARKETING DECISIONS

MARKET PLANNING TOOLS

Managing a marketing program in an agribusiness can be a complex task, particularly in larger firms with many products. Nearly all agribusinesses face highly seasonal demand that creates the possibility of critical bottlenecks in servicing customers. Unpredictable weather patterns further complicate market planning, and volatile agricultural commodity prices often cause the demand for farm supplies and services to fluctuate. Because of their complexity, agrimarketing programs require a great deal of planning. Successful managers spend much time analyzing their market and mapping their strategic plan.

Agrimarketing managers not only build a marketing program from the marketing mix, as discussed in the last chapter, but they also utilize a wide assortment of analytical tools and concepts to assist them in the planning process. Some of these tools are highly sophisticated and involve complex mathematical models and elaborate marketing information systems. Other tools are simply logical approaches or even subjective "gut feelings" for the market.

Marketing Audits

Nearly every agribusiness and certainly all publicly owned companies have financial audits performed regularly by outside auditors to ensure that there are no discrepancies or malpractices that could cause serious problems for the business. Similarly, a marketing audit is an objective examination of a company's entire marketing program. The marketing audit studies the firm's marketing objectives and its plan for accomplishing these objectives in light of its resources, its distinctive strengths and weaknesses, and market conditions (see Figure 13-1).

The first step in a marketing audit is to carefully analyze how the agribusiness is doing with each product or service it markets. This step involves estimating total market potential, determining the firm's share of the market, and attempting to identify what factors are responsible for the firm's market position with each product or service.

Second, the marketing audit identifies the firm's distinctive competencies, that is, areas where the firm is particularly strong in relation to the competition. Distinctive competencies include financial, human, product, production, and distribution advantages. These distinctive competencies often form the basis for the total marketing strategy. For example, consider an artificial-breeding company that is fortunate enough to have an extremely good line of bulls with exceptionally high performance records. This measurable product quality distinction can form the basis for a quality-oriented promotion program with consistently high prices, a relatively small field sales force, and considerable emphasis on progeny testing.

The third step reviews market and environmental conditions in the marketplace. Marketing factors external to the firm are evaluated, and sometimes probabilities are attached to expected trends. This information helps agribusiness managers to shape their marketing policies.

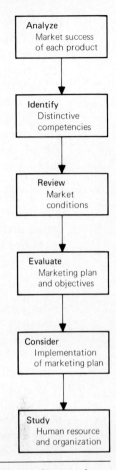

```
┌─────────────────┐
│ Analyze         │
│   Market success│
│   of each product│
└─────────────────┘
         │
         ▼
┌─────────────────┐
│ Identify        │
│   Distinctive   │
│   competencies  │
└─────────────────┘
         │
         ▼
┌─────────────────┐
│ Review          │
│   Market        │
│   conditions    │
└─────────────────┘
         │
         ▼
┌─────────────────┐
│ Evaluate        │
│   Marketing plan│
│   and objectives│
└─────────────────┘
         │
         ▼
┌─────────────────┐
│ Consider        │
│   Implementation│
│   of marketing plan│
└─────────────────┘
         │
         ▼
┌─────────────────┐
│ Study           │
│   Human resource│
│   and organization│
└─────────────────┘
```

Figure 13-1   Marketing-audit procedures.

The fourth step is to objectively evaluate the agribusiness's overall marketing plan and objectives as they are being practiced. If there is no written plan or if the objectives are not measurable, it is extremely difficult to determine how effective the marketing performance actually is. In rapidly changing markets, marketing objectives can become out of date. Through this analysis, the marketing plan can be made more realistic in terms of the current market conditions. For example, a feed manufacturing company that has an objective of a 10 percent annual increase in poultry-feed sales at a time when the poultry industry is declining might do well instead to hold poultry-feed sales constant and devote more resources to expanding hog-supplement sales.

Fifth, the marketing audit should consider how the marketing plan is to be implemented. A good plan remains ineffective if it is poorly executed. Continuing to use the same channels of distribution because "That's the way we always do it" may be a poor choice and could lead to the demise of the business. Do incentive travel packages offer the best type of sales promotion for dealers, or would it be best to return dollars as a rebate—or perhaps just sell at lower prices in the first place? The implementation analysis considers how effectively the marketing strategy complements the marketing objectives.

Finally, the marketing audit objectively studies the human resources and their organization. Are salespeople adequately trained to advise growers on technical matters? Should technical specialists in the field report to the area sales manager, or should they report to the home office? Do field salespeople have the right amount of price authority to fulfill the marketing objectives? Evaluating human and organizational factors is one of the most critical facets of the marketing audit.

The marketing audit should be performed as objectively as possible. It is difficult for managers to evaluate their own program objectively because they created it, so managers should consider hiring an outsider to periodically review the program. A qualified consultant can objectively evaluate a marketing program and raise important questions about the allocation of time, effort, and financial resources.

Sales Forecasting

Although agribusiness markets are well known for their volatility, agribusiness managers cannot escape the responsibility of forecasting sales volume. Nearly every management decision includes a critical assumption about sales volume. All production schedules are built around projected demand. Raw-material purchases are based on expected sales. The personnel function of hiring and firing is greatly influenced by anticipated sales. Cash needs are based on sales forecasts. Capital investments in new facilities are determined by sales projections. The fact is that a great majority of management decisions and the entire planning process rest squarely on forecasted sales.

Sales forecasting involves simply estimating sales in dollars and physical units as accurately as possible for a specific period of time. It involves forecasting sales for the total market, and determining what share of the market can be captured (see Figure 13-2).

Both short- and long-term sales forecasts are useful for agribusiness. Short-term forecasts, usually one season or shorter for agribusiness

---

Figure 13-2   Sales forecasting model.

General economic forecast

Total market forecast

Specific product forecast

firms, are useful in formulating current operating plans. Longer-range sales forecasts are important to plant-size adjustments. The longer the time period forecasted, the less accurate the forecast is likely to be.

Difficulty and complexity notwithstanding, agribusiness managers must make general market forecasts. Their forecast may be explicit and prepared in a formal manner by economic and marketing analysis, or it may be composed of implicit, informal assumptions based on a variety of observations. Often it is based on historic trends adjusted to accommodate current economic conditions.

General Economic Forecasts *Economic forecasts* consider broad factors that affect the total economy. Government programs, inflation, the money supply, international affairs, interest rates, and a host of other factors are included. A great many government and private economists spend much time tracking economic trends and making projections. These opinions are watched carefully by agribusiness managers as they formulate market plans.

Market Forecasts Forecasts for specific industries or products are based on general economic forecasts and a great deal of information about each specific industry. Agricultural economists continually monitor changing economic indicators that measure agricultural trends. Some use complex mathematical methods (econometric models) to predict demand for various products and commodities.

But the task is so complex that it is impossible to make accurate projections consistently. In fact, if it were possible to predict market conditions accurately, the prediction itself would be likely to change the market, thereby making the prediction inaccurate. If buyers and sellers knew what was going to happen, they would probably behave differently, thus changing the outcome. Instead, there is such a variety of "guesstimates" that agribusiness managers usually collect several opinions and then formulate their own ideas.

Forecasting market demand has been researched extensively. For example, agricultural economists have discovered various cycles in livestock production. Hog production seems to cycle every 4 years, while the cattle cycle is about 9 years. During these cycles, prices fall as the number of animals on feed increases, and profits decline. As a result, some less efficient producers exit from the market, livestock numbers drop, and prices gradually increase. The cattle cycle is longer because of the length of the gestation period for cattle, and it takes more time to increase production. Obviously, these cycles are extremely important to feed companies, milling equipment companies, livestock marketing firms, and meat processing companies.

The demand for most farm supplies is a *derived demand*. This means that the demand for a specific type of product or service depends greatly on the demand for another product or service for which it is used. The demand for fertilizer, for example, is a function of the demand for the crops it helps produce. When the manager of a fertilizer plant in the Midwest is projecting the demand for nitrogen, the corn market is carefully considered. The manager knows that the price farmers anticipate for corn in the next season will greatly affect the amount of fertilizer they will want to buy. Consequently, agribusiness managers are careful students of the market for whatever products their supplies help to produce.

Not surprisingly, there is a great interest in current information on nearly every product produced by farmers. Summaries and analyses of market conditions for nearly every agricultural product are distributed widely each day. Important grain and livestock market information is instantly flashed to analysts and agribusinesses as transactions occur throughout the day, through a network of Teletype communications. Government reports estimating current and projected acreages and livestock numbers are released frequently throughout the year to help agribusinesses monitor trends and adjust their plans.

Sales Forecast   The actual sales forecast for a specific product within the firm is, of course, based on the general economic forecast and the market forecast. *Sales forecasting* methods include projecting objectively from past trends and adjusting these projections subjectively to take into account the expected economic and market pressures. This simple method is probably the most widely used.

Information sometimes filters in from the sales force itself. Salespeople in some agribusinesses are asked to detail sales forecasts for each of their major accounts. Accumulated sales estimates from all field salespeople offer grass-roots information about sales expectations. This method is particularly valuable where competition is intense, as in the case of agricultural chemicals. Of course, these estimates seldom give much thought to changing economic conditions, and cannot reflect the impact of next year's market mix.

Consumer surveys and test panels offer a great deal of information about buying intentions. Several regional and national organizations, such as Doane's, Inc., and the *Farm Journal*, continually monitor farmers' attitudes and plans for the coming season. A panel of farmers may be paid a nominal fee to give detailed reports about their intended farm plans on a regular basis, then report actual decisions. Results of these private research studies are made available to subscribers on a fee basis. Farmers' planting intentions are also monitored by the USDA and released periodically throughout the year.

Analyzing Competition

Knowledge of the competition is an important part of marketing strategy. Although it is usually unwise to simply *react* to competition, it is equally unwise to ignore competitors, unless, of course, the firm is so large that it completely dominates the market. In fact, dominant firms are often vulnerable to competitive encroachment. Some marketing experts even theorize that the larger and more successful a firm is, the more likely it is to fail. This is because large, successful firms often become "fat and lazy," and perpetuate the way of doing business that helped them become successful. As markets and consumers change, the old ways become increasingly outdated, and smaller, more aggressive firms may begin to take over. Clearly, successful firms must continually monitor competition.

One simple but effective method for analyzing competition is completing a formal strength-and-weakness analysis for each competitor. This format simply lists the key strengths and weaknesses of a competitor, then logically develops a strategy that capitalizes on the competitor's weaknesses. In this example (Exhibit 13-1), a local farm-machinery company has noted several key facts about Red Dot Tractor and Implement Company that can become critical in the local firm's marketing plan. The locally owned company has developed a strategy that emphasizes its local ownership and flexibility in servicing farmers.

Such information may seem so obvious to field marketing people that this exercise seems unnecessary, but formalizing it in this manner,

Competitor Strength and Weakness Analysis Compiled by Prairie Equipment Company	EXHIBIT 13-1

COMPETITOR: Red Dot Tractor and Implement Company
DATE: January 15, 1986

STRENGTHS	WEAKNESSES
1. New store	1. High overhead cost
2. Good location	2. No outside salespeople
3. Large parts inventory	3. Poor on farm repair service
4. Quality "short lines"	4. Major equipment line not well accepted in local market
5. Favorable credit terms	5. Manufacturer-owned store less flexible to meet local needs
6. Manufacturer-owned store has sound financial backing	6. New manager not well known in the area

Strategy for competing against Red Dot
- Emphasize importance of dealing with a local business, keeping money in community
- Upgrade emergency farm repair vehicle and promote this service
- Hold open house to familiarize customers with our location
- Promote local owner's long-term interest in community and understanding of local needs

discussing it thoroughly, and developing a competitive strategy often improves communication, even in small firms, and results in a more uniform approach. When all significant competitors are analyzed periodically, there is a far greater likelihood that a logical marketing plan will be developed and executed.

Analyzing Market Penetration

Agrimarketers are often so involved in selling and servicing that they "can't see the forest for the trees." This is particularly true in smaller or local agribusinesses, where marketing people "wear many hats" and have limited time to devote to market analysis. It is common, for example, for much of the sales volume to be concentrated in limited geographical areas, while other areas have little market penetration, and marketing people can get so involved that they may fail to notice the imbalance in their market coverage.

There may be physical reasons for an imbalanced market penetration. An interstate highway may make access to some areas difficult. Certain types of farms may be concentrated in some parts of the market area. More often, friends, relatives, or just well-established customers seem to predominate in one local area. Salespeople tend to spend less time in areas with which they are less familiar. In short, many agribusinesses have undiscovered market potential near them, if they were just able to discover and cultivate it. One way of discovering these areas of untapped potential is through a market-mapping technique. All current customers are pinpointed on a large wall map of the local market area (see Figure 13-3). It is a good idea to color-code customers by volume of business, type of products purchased, or other informative characteristics.

Once this mapping has been completed, visual observation provides a great deal of information about weak and strong areas. When this technique is first used, it is often a real revelation for marketing and management people. The customer map suggests areas in which sales efforts should be targeted. When effort is concentrated in a new area and new customers are obtained, that market usually grows rapidly.

One of the best ways to learn what customers think about a product or service is to ask the customers themselves. Agribusinesses can gain much valuable information, which can help in formulating market plans, by communicating directly with customers through surveys, interviews, and informal conversations. Although there may be some reluctance among some customers who do not want to be bothered or who distrust intruders, experience shows that the majority of agribusiness customers are cooperative and willing to share their opinions. When this information is used properly, it is invaluable in making marketing decisions.

Market research relies heavily on surveys of various types to track customer attitudes. Elaborate customer interviews lasting an hour or more may provide a great deal of information about purchasing deci-

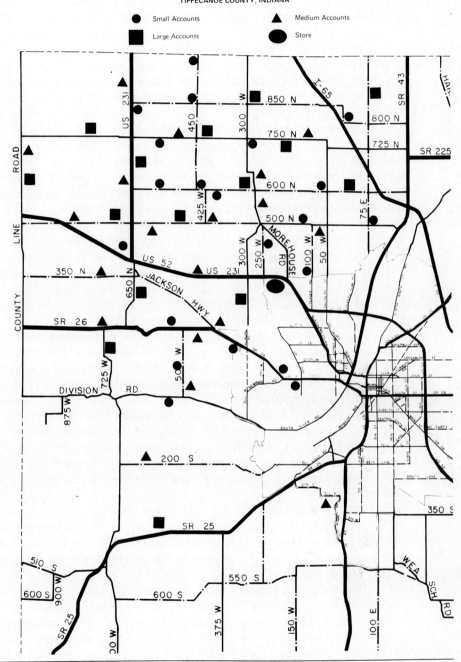

PRAIRIE EQUIPMENT COMPANY
CUSTOMER MAP
TIPPECANOE COUNTY, INDIANA

● Small Accounts   ▲ Medium Accounts

■ Large Accounts   ⬤ Store

Figure 13-3   Customer map for Prairie Equipment
Company.

sions, attitudes, and how the product is used. Such in-depth interviews must be developed and performed by trained interviewers; they are therefore quite expensive, often averaging $100 or more per interview.

Telephone interviews are gaining in popularity because of their lower cost. But it is impossible to collect as much information by telephone because telephone interviews seldom last more than 15 minutes, and it is difficult to explore very extensively in such a short period of time. Phone interviews by professional market researchers may cost from $15 to $20 per interview.

Mail surveys are probably the most widely used method of studying customer opinions and attitudes. Mail questionnaires can be short or long, but longer ones usually get a much lower response rate. Even a brief mail survey is considered successful when 15 percent of the questionnaires are completed and returned. It is also difficult to collect much detail or in-depth reasoning behind purchases from the mail survey. Yet because they are relatively inexpensive, mail surveys are considered a good way of collecting some kinds of market information.

In any case, mail surveys must be very carefully tested, since improperly worded questions can cause the results to be virtually meaningless. The meaning of a question may be clear to the author of the survey, but totally confusing to the respondent—or worse, it may be misunderstood, with the result that it elicits incorrect information.

FGIs (focus-group interviews) are another method of learning more about customer attitudes, a method that is growing rapidly in popularity. The focus group, or "snowball interviews" as it is sometimes called, is a quick and inexpensive way of obtaining a reading on customers. It is simply a recorded discussion among six to ten customers, guided by a skilled moderator. It is not a formal interview so much as it is an informal discussion where people get to know each other well enough to talk freely. As barriers break down, participants begin to react to each other and the conversation "snowballs," hopefully yielding much valuable information about how customers feel about important marketing issues.

The key to success in a focus-group interview is the synergistic effect of the informal discussion. The moderator plays a very important but extremely subtle role, making sure the right subjects are covered and that no one dominates the discussion. The moderator is also careful not to bias responses.

Focus-group interviews can provide many new ideas and perceptions from the customer's viewpoint about advertising programs, packaging, quality of products, performance, and relative comparisons of competitors. Group interviews also add a great deal of support and help to clarify more quantitative surveys because they can suggest how strongly impressions are held. Tape-recording the interviews for more detailed analysis can be useful.

However, focus-group interviews can also be misused. They can generate very few factual data. Results are very difficult to tabulate or quantify. Some group members may tend to dominate and to influence the thinking of others, perhaps creating a "bandwagon" effect. Thus it is critical not to extend the results of focus-group interviews beyond their intended use.

Still, focus-group interviews offer a highly productive and relatively inexpensive method for gaining insights into customer attitudes and for generating marketing ideas.

SUMMARY

Planning a marketing strategy requires a variety of techniques and tools to analyze markets and make decisions. Some tools are simple applications of logic, while others are highly sophisticated analytical models.

A marketing audit is a thorough and objective examination of a firm's marketing program. With it market performance and potential for each product are analyzed; distinctive competencies (i.e., areas of unique strength relative to competition) can be recognized; current and future market conditions are reviewed; current marketing programs are evaluated; execution of the marketing program is considered; and finally, the human resources available and their organization are studied.

Sales forecasting is another highly useful marketing tool that is especially valuable in agribusiness because of the volatility of agricultural markets. It usually begins with general economic forecasts and becomes more and more specific as the forecaster moves toward forecasting sales for an individual product or service.

Marketing managers must also analyze competition and monitor their marketing programs. Formal competitor strength-and-weakness analysis is a useful tool that suggests strategic marketing approaches for competing with each competitor.

Various marketing-research methods provide invaluable information for developing marketing plans. Simple tools, such as pinpointing customers by type or size on a map, provide much information. Customer surveys and personal and group interviews are also popular methods. Marketing managers must synthesize information from a variety of sources to assist them in developing a successful marketing program.

DISCUSSION QUESTIONS

1. What is the purpose of a marketing audit? Why is it important to have outsiders involved in marketing audits?

2. Why are sales forecasts particularly difficult to make in agribusiness firms?

3. What is meant by derived demand? Explain why the demand for animal health products is a derived demand.

4. Give some of the reasons why customer maps often show customers clustered in particular areas. What can be done about it?

5. What are the benefits of preparing strengths-and-weaknesses analysis sheets on competitors?

6. What are focus-group interviews? Are they of much use to small local firms? What are some important limitations of the focus-group interview?

A BIG ASSIGNMENT

"Yes sir, I have had an agribusiness course," Steve Turner said as he looked across the large desk. His new boss was sitting on the other side of that desk, and, frankly, Steve wondered what was coming next. He had just accepted a summer internship that would begin in a few weeks, but he had no idea of what his assignment would be at Valley Co-op Producers.

"Do you know anything about marketing, Steve?" asked the manager.

"A little, sir," answered Steve nervously, still not sure what he was in for.

"Well, we'd like you to prepare an analysis of our farm supply marketing program this summer, Steve. As you know, we have three divisions: feed, fertilizer, and general farm supplies—all sold out of our store here. Although we want you to spend some working time in each division this summer, we'd like you to spend 2 days each week talking to people, looking at our records, or whatever you want to give us a good idea of where we stand in the feed market. Our feed sales have been dropping off lately, and I think it's because our equipment is getting old and our service is bad.

"The board of directors is considering expanding our feed business with a new feed mill, but we aren't sure. There are a lot of cost factors that I'm working on, but I'd like you to take a look at the market side. Then we'd like you to make a report on what you find at our August board meeting. It's a big job, but we'd like to know what you can come up with."

Steve swallowed hard. He wanted to make a good impression—and it did seem like a great opportunity to learn a lot about the business. Yet he wasn't sure he was up to it. He wasn't even sure how to begin.

QUESTIONS

1. What market analysis tools should Steve consider using in this case?

2. What kinds of information would you think Steve needs to find before he can complete his assignment successfully? How might he get this information?

3. Outline a procedure that Steve might use to make his analysis and report.

OBJECTIVES

• Describe the role of sales and selling in generating agribusiness profits

• Explain the interrelationships of agribusiness salespeople, their customers, and the agribusiness itself

• List the rewards of successful selling in agribusiness

• Identify the different types of selling common to agribusiness

• Explain the salesperson's relationship with and support from agribusiness staff

• Describe the characteristics that most agribusiness salespeople have in common

• Explore the activities that prepare professional agribusiness salespeople

This poster describes the role of selling in agribusinesses.

SELLING IS THE FUEL OF FREE ENTERPRISE.

14

THE SELLING PROFESSION IN AGRICULTURE

IF NOBODY SELLS, A TERRIBLE THING HAPPENS:

nothing.

A message to and for marketing people from
Philip Office Associates, Inc., Dayton, Ohio,
513/461-1300.

SALES AND SELLING

This poster on the office wall of an Indiana feed manufacturer aptly describes the importance of selling in the free enterprise system. The entire economic structure of the United States is based on consumers' reactions to the alternatives placed before them by hundreds of thousands of businesses. In fact, businesses cannot survive unless they satisfy customers. Although customers' choices are limited by the alternatives presented to them, these alternatives are broad and change as rapidly as technology, economics, and consumer tastes permit. Selling helps consumers to choose among alternatives.

Sales-Profit Relationship

In its simplest form, *selling* is the act of transferring ownership of goods and services. Because money is the recognized medium of exchange, selling involves the trading of goods and services for money or business income. The profit and loss statement emphasizes the importance of sales in business. It begins with sales, then subtracts all costs associated with those sales, and finally identifies how much profit resulted (see Chapter 6).

Other factors intervene, of course, so the sales force does not shoulder all the responsibility for sales. Product availability and distribution, and the way in which the legal environment requires the business to function both have their effect. But many of the expenses of running a business are incurred just by the very existence of the business. These overhead expenses occur regardless of how much revenue is generated. If the selling effort does not generate enough sales to cover overhead as well as the expenses associated directly with sales, the business will go bankrupt. Profit, which begins with sales, becomes the primary (though not necessarily the only) motivation for the existence of the business.

In many agribusinesses, the salesperson bears direct responsibility for profits. Particularly in smaller firms, those who are selling are often authorized to conduct price negotiations with customers; therefore, they have direct responsibility for generating a gross margin that is sufficient to cover expenses and leave a profit. In larger organizations, it is more common for salespeople to wield little or no price authority. In these cases, higher-level management assumes pricing authority, leaving salespeople responsible only for sales. In firms where responsibility for sales and profit become separated, or where those responsible for sales become enamored with simply generating more volume, significant profit problems often arise.

What Is Selling?

Profits may begin with sales, but sales begin with selling. *To sell* is an active verb, which is to say that it involves *doing* something. Sometimes selling activity simply "enables" the sale to occur, because the customer was already aware of, needed, and recognized the value of a particular product or service.

On other occasions, potential customers may be unaware of the product or service's existence or unaware of their own needs, in which case the selling will begin at the fundamental point of first identifying the customer's need and then convincing the customer of that need. A cattle feeder may fail to recognize that the daily rate of gain of his or her stock could be increased by 15 percent by changing the feed ration slightly and incorporating a particular feed additive.

And in still other cases, a potential customer may recognize the basic need but may not understand how the value of a particular product or service can far exceed its cost. One state of Washington wheat producer feared that a new $110,000 combine would "cost too much" and so had not seriously considered trading harvesters. But an aggressive implement dealer, focusing attention on the individual circumstances, showed the producer how the combine would save money by reducing labor costs and grain losses, and saving precious harvest time.

It is important to recognize that selling does not *create* needs among customers. Rather it fosters customers' awareness of existing needs and then shows how the needs can be met. Selling must also arouse "wants"; that is, the customer must want the product or service in order for the sale to be made. The issue of whether customers can be made to want something they do not really need is an interesting one and is the subject of much debate.

Some people think of selling as being beneficial primarily to the seller, whose profits from the sale are obvious. Yet in a very real sense, both the seller *and* the buyer profit from the transaction. The buyer trades dollars for a good or service that is believed to be of greater value to the buyer than the money paid out.

Of course, customers do not always benefit as greatly from a purchase as they had anticipated. When customers are disappointed, businesses often agree to make refunds or adjustments because they realize that the benefit to the customer must be greater than the dollars given up; otherwise, the business is likely to lose the customer.

The benefit to the customer is often measurable in dollars and cents, just as it is for the seller. A Wisconsin dairy farmer who spent $50,000 to purchase and install new milk-handling facilities expected to recoup her expenditure in cost reductions. Her calculations showed an expected reduction of 40 worker-hours per week and a significant reduction in disease problems. These reductions would allow her to recoup the initial outlay within 4 years and show a return on investment of 10 percent over the life of the equipment.

Sometimes the profit to the final user cannot be expressed only in dollars. Consumer satisfaction or pleasure may be a less tangible form of profit, but it is no less important, especially where the customer is the final consumer. Even when the customer intends to use the product as input for business purposes, the sale often hinges on an important element of anticipated satisfaction that is highly intangible.

Selling as a Process

Professional salespeople are keenly aware that selling is a highly individualized endeavor. They will concede that there is no one way to sell. Instead, each sale is affected by three variable factors: (1) the salesperson, who has a unique personality, experiences, and skills; (2) the customer, who has a unique personality, needs, and beliefs; and (3) the situation itself, which involves its own unique background and circumstances. Any attempt to apply one rigid set of rules to every salesperson, customer, and situation vastly oversimplifies the process, can be misleading, and is often insulting to professional salespeople. The professional salesperson must be skilled and flexible enough to evaluate the diverse factors affecting each sale. The individual must use a highly developed sense of judgment in adapting to the changing situation throughout the sale.

Yet selling is a *process*, and though each sale is different, there are general procedures and techniques that have been tried, tested, and proved by thousands of successful professional salespeople over the years. Knowledge of these procedures forms the basis of selling ability. It is only after mastering the basic techniques that the professional salesperson can learn how to choose the most productive selling approach and adapt it to each unique selling situation in a creative, highly individualized way.

As the foregoing implies, selling skills can be learned. While some people seem to have a greater affinity for selling than others, nearly everyone can learn the basic steps and skills involved in successful professional selling. Agribusiness professionals have found these skills helpful not only for the actual selling of goods and services, but for a wide variety of responsibilities. Such responsibilities include the motivation and supervision of other employees through the process of "selling" them on ideas. Consequently, basic selling skills are a necessary tool to help the agribusiness manager perform more effectively.

Selling in Agribusiness: A Unique Challenge

Selling in agribusiness offers its own unique characteristics, which make it a distinctly rewarding kind of challenge. First of all, many agribusiness salespeople sell to farmers and ranchers, either directly or through sales to third parties who then work with the agricultural producers themselves. In either case the customer is likely to have a strong rural or agricultural orientation and value structure, and this is particularly true at the production-agriculture level. Although it is difficult to pinpoint the precise nature of this "agricultural ethic," its existence is crucial to the selling process in agribusiness. This ethic is often communicated as a "camaraderie of the soil" that shares concern about farming as a way of life. It tends to value practical farm-life experience, sweat of the brow, and a facility with the language of farming. As a result, there is a tendency for agriculturalists to exclude outsiders until they have proved their understanding of the agricultural ethic, after which there is a tendency toward embracing such people in the camaraderie. Although it is possible for those without production-agriculture experience to gain acceptance the challenge is formidable, especially for those who must work directly with production-level agriculture.

Secondly, agribusiness selling typically revolves around long-term repeat business that has its basis in service. Most market areas can boast only limited numbers of customers, most of whom are members of a close community. This is true whether the area is a local farming district or a larger dealer market that covers several hundred miles. Under these conditions, customer-salesperson relationships commonly span several years of steady service, and tend to change only when serious problems arise. (This is not to imply a low level of competition. Quite the opposite is true: agribusiness salespeople must work extremely hard to attract new customers.) It is not uncommon for a strong personal relationship to develop between the salesperson and the customer, once the customer experiences a sense of "being taken care of." This special relationship is most common in the fields that work directly with production agriculture, such as farm supply and marketing firms.

Thirdly, selling in agribusiness generally demands a high degree of technical skill and a knowledge of agriculture. The agribusiness salesperson often plays an integral part in customers' business decisions. The dairy marketing field technician, for example, provides farmers with crucial information about disease-control and milk-quality problems on the farm. The very selling strategy of countless agribusinesses centers on this all-important aspect, the provision of knowledgeable technical information and service by well-trained field personnel.

Fourthly, most agribusiness sales jobs are extremely varied and seasonal. Each new season in the crop or livestock year brings a completely different set of responsibilities in serving the customer. For example, at various times the agricultural chemical salesperson may actively solicit new business, make early-order sales presentations, check out distribution problems, handle in-season technical product-use problems, work with end-customer complaints, collect payments on accounts, make market projections for next year, check inventory levels, and hold farmer-dealer information meetings.

Despite some unique characteristics, however, selling in agribusiness involves many of the same procedures and techniques that are common to the selling process in all fields (see Chapter 15).

REWARDS AND DISADVANTAGES OF SELLING
In the past, selling has suffered from an unfortunate stereotype, that of the fast-talking, pushy, unethical salesperson who goes from door to door "selling farmers milking machines and then taking their cows as down payment." But today's professional agrisalespersons are a different

breed. They are well trained, technically competent, and highly concerned about long-term relationships with their customers. As a result, they can look forward to a number of rewards.

Financial Rewards

Because of the importance of sales to any organization, professional salespeople, especially productive ones, generally earn good incomes. Young people who graduate from a university, college, or technical agricultural program with a school and work record that indicates skills in leadership, dealing with people, and agribusiness are usually considered to have selling potential. Opportunities and salary potential for these people are often considerably above average starting rates. Technical training and work experience with agribusiness is especially valuable in agribusiness selling. For more experienced salespeople, performance records are the primary factor in determining income.

Many agribusiness selling jobs feature some type of direct financial incentive, either a commission on each sale or a year-end bonus based on sales. Incentive programs appeal to many professional salespeople, because they feel such programs are a direct reward for their successful efforts. For some type of selling jobs, however, direct incentive programs are difficult to set up.

For example, when the salesperson's job is primarily to assist and work with dealers who actually buy through a distributor, as is the case with most agricultural chemical companies, salespeople are generally paid a straight salary. In such cases, salespeople's salary increases are usually based on their supervisor's evaluation of their performance. They may also share in the company's profits at the end of the year. In nearly every case, salespeople find their financial rewards tied very closely to performance.

Advancement

Closely associated with the financial rewards of sales is the opportunity for advancement. Salespeople who are aggressive and productive are usually offered opportunities for increasingly more responsible sales positions (see Figure 14-1). Initially, this may mean a larger territory or a greater number of important customers, but it may eventually mean moving into sales management and supervising less experienced salespeople. Commensurate pay increases usually accompany such advancement. In larger organizations, advancement of this type is usually well defined and measurable, and requires several geographical relocations by salespeople as they move up through the sales organization. In smaller, more localized companies, advancement is often not so formal in terms of title and peer prestige. The opportunity for professional growth in the smaller, local organizations comes in the form of broader market penetration, community respect, development of close working relationships with customers, and added responsibility in the company.

Successful experience in professional agribusiness selling can also lead to opportunities for advancement into general management or other

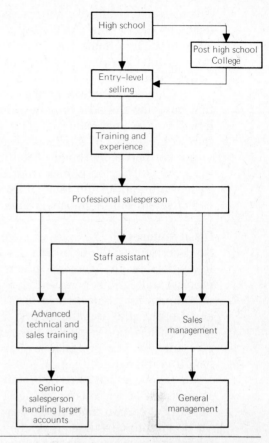

Figure 14-1   Professional selling career path.

areas of the business. Most firms value field selling experience highly. Some, particularly marketing firms, require at least some field selling experience as a prerequisite for any important management position, except for positions in highly technical areas. Consequently, field selling is often a good stepping-stone into many areas of staff and line management. In fact, some marketing-oriented agribusinesses insist on sales experience before promotion into administrative positions.

The tendency (especially among young people) to view sales as only a stepping-stone to something else is becoming less common. Many companies even build several different levels or designations into their field-force sales structure to ensure that successful, experienced career salespeople carry titles that give them appropriate status and allow them to reap the financial rewards they deserve.

Personal Rewards

Many salespeople argue that the greatest rewards from selling are personal. They place a high value on the lifestyle associated with their jobs, and derive great satisfaction from the challenges of making a sale and closing the deal. The number of satisfied customers and the dollars generated by their efforts are viewed as tangible evidence of a job well done. They feel comfortable with the flexibility of their schedules, their freedom to organize their own time as they believe is best, and their essentially autonomous operation as business managers.

They often speak of the close customer-salesperson friendships that have developed over time. Helping customers to solve their problems in areas that relate directly or indirectly to their company gives them a great deal of satisfaction, and being regarded as an expert in an important part of agribusiness builds their self-esteem. But to many, the ultimate satisfaction comes from the opportunity to work closely with agriculture and all the intangibles embodied therein, an advantage that can offset all but the most extreme disadvantages.

Disadvantages

No description and discussion of a career can be complete without some indication of the career's potentially disadvantageous aspects, and professional agribusiness selling is no exception. It is, for example, not uncommon for a salesperson to invest a great deal of time and effort on a proposal or the preparation of a sales presentation, only to have it flatly rejected. Rejection is part of the job, and though no one asserts that it is pleasant, the true professional has developed skills and techniques for handling it graciously.

Likewise, customer complaints are completely avoidable only if a salesperson never sells anything. The hours, too, can be very long, particularly at certain times of the year. Because most agribusiness salespeople do not punch a time clock, they often have to rely on self-motivation, which is far easier to muster when the outlook is rosy. Though salespeople work closely with many others, in many cases they are geographically isolated from their peers, other salespeople in their own company, and even from their supervisors.

In short, some aspects of the job can be considered serious drawbacks, depending on the individual's needs and lifestyle. Those who find selling rewarding tend to place the majority of their emphasis on the many rewarding aspects, and recognize that all jobs present some disadvantages.

TYPES OF SELLING IN AGRIBUSINESS

Agribusiness selling can be categorized either by the type of product or service being sold, or by the level of the marketing system at which the sale occurs. The latter method of classification is particularly significant, since the level at which a sale occurs (manufacturing and processing, distribution and wholesaling, retailing, farmer and rancher, or final consumer) exerts a tremendous influence on the type of selling involved.

Selling to Manufacturing and Processing Firms

Agricultural manufacturing and processing firms generally take raw materials and manufactured inputs and combine them into products to be used by farmers, ranchers, growers, producers, and in some cases, the final consumer of food and fiber products. Large numbers of industrial and manufacturing companies produce industrial inputs for the manufacture of agricultural products. Our study of agricultural selling at this level will concentrate only on firms where the unique facets introduced by the firm's basis in agriculture are important and are reflected in the operation. Feed-manufacturing firms, seed-processing companies, and meatpackers are good examples of this special category. Such firms, though industrial in nature, require a unique understanding of agricultural practices, technology, and trends to be effective. A specialty-equipment manufacturing company producing citrus processing equipment for packing houses, for example, uses salespeople who demonstrate a keen understanding of engineering mechanics, fresh fruit physiology, and general agriculture.

Salespeople who sell to these firms usually deal with purchasing agents, engineers, and other highly specialized personnel. Four or more years of college in a technical area is common among professional salespeople in this specialty. Very often the manufacturer or processor will maintain very close agricultural ties and will continually relate business decisions to their impact on the farmer-customer; for this reason, an agricultural background helps the salesperson to be more effective with manufacturing and processing firms.

Salespeople who call on agricultural manufacturing and processing firms usually cover a wide geographical area, perhaps several states. They often travel by plane because of the broad dispersion of potential customers, and they may often be on the road for several days at a time. Sales are large but infrequent. Manufacturing and processing firms agree to contract sales for a lengthy period of time, to guarantee regular shipments. The salesperson calls as frequently as possible to service the account; solve any shipping, billing, or technical problems; encourage the use of the product; and maintain the relationship. Salespeople often get to know several people at the plant, especially those who actually use their product.

Selling to Distributors and Wholesalers
The manufacturer may sell to distributors or wholesalers, who in turn move the product to retailers or directly to farmers. Agricultural chemicals, for example, are generally sold to a distributor. Greenhouse and nursery supplies are usually sold to a wholesale distributor who carries a wide variety of products for use by nurseries and greenhouses.

Salespeople who sell to distributors usually work with the buying agents who actually place the orders, but often spend considerable time with dealers and even the final users. They assume the responsibility of *pulling it through the pipelines*, which means that they funnel field orders through an appropriate distributor. In some firms, the salesperson never actually takes an order; instead, all orders go directly from the buyer to the manufacturing plant. A common feature of the salesperson's job at this level is building and staffing exhibits and displays at trade

301

shows or conventions. In some product lines the salesperson may sponsor, arrange, and conduct final-user and dealer informational-promotional meetings in the off-season.

Salespeople who work with distributors and wholesalers usually have offices in their homes. They travel a great deal, but because their geographical area is rather limited, they are seldom gone for more than one or two nights in a row.

Selling to Retailers

Generally, the distributor or wholesaler sells to retailers, who in turn sell to the farmer. Agricultural-pesticide distributors, who usually have their own sales force, are a good example of this.

In other cases, the manufacturer sells directly to the retailer. A good example of this exists in the fertilizer industry. Farm-equipment manufacturing representatives also generally sell directly to the local retailer. In each of these examples, salespeople visit retailers in their territories on a fairly regular basis, and usually work closely with dealers to service the farmer-customer. They will often help the dealer by sponsoring local promotional programs, perhaps developing advertising materials, helping to train dealer-salespeople in technical matters, troubleshooting product complaints with farmers, and generally providing service.

Salespeople who call on retailers usually do not travel large geographical areas, depending, of course, on the concentration of agriculture. Generally, they are home every night (at least at some hour). They have offices in their homes and report to supervisors who may be as much as 300 miles away.

Similar sales jobs exist in larger manufacturing companies that own their own retail outlets. Company-owned stores are usually serviced or supervised by an area representative of the parent company, who serves much the same function as the salesperson calling on independent dealers. In some cases, area representatives may also have line-management authority over several company stores, but their main responsibility is to assist sales through the retail outlet.

Regional agricultural-supply cooperatives commonly have area field staff to assist local cooperatives. Though technically they are not salespeople, they function in much the same capacity and use many of the same tools in motivating local co-op personnel.

Selling to Farmers and Ranchers

No matter what channel the agribusiness has chosen to distribute its products or services, it must eventually interact with its ultimate customer; in many cases, this means the farmer, rancher, grower, or producer. To many people, this is the most exciting level of selling. It usually involves a great deal of close contact with farmers in a local area, and it generally entails on-the-farm calls and visits, which keep the salesperson very close to farming itself.

At this level of selling, a strong farm background is thought by many to be essential to successful selling, though there are notable exceptions. Many companies selling at this level can point to highly successful salespeople who have not had the benefit of direct agricultural experience. In any case, sensitivity to specific farm problems that are relevant to the product or service is critical.

It is common for the salesperson to develop close business and social ties to both farm and ranch customers, ties that often extend over an entire professional career. Large national companies and locally owned independent dealers offer essentially the same set of sales responsibilities at this point.

The salesperson can expect to only rarely spend nights away from home. A company vehicle may or may not be assigned, but if it is, it is likely to be a pickup truck. The work is usually very seasonal, which means that peak agricultural seasons require very long hours.

Selling to Final Consumers

In some agribusinesses, a significant part of the business is conducted with nonfarm consumers; that is, in lawn and garden shops, nurseries, greenhouses, "pick-your-own" produce farms, and the like. These firms are an increasingly important part of agribusiness, and they offer a variety of opportunities for those who are interested in agriculturally oriented selling. In most cases, consumers come to the business as they would to any other retail store.

Successful selling generally requires a thorough technical but practical knowledge of the product line. The hours are normally quite regular, though they must conform to customer convenience. Although customers often present problem situations, they also represent a challenge to the salesperson who likes developing solutions, and they enable such salespeople to reap the personal and financial rewards of accomplishment.

THE SALESPERSON

The agribusiness salesperson is directly responsible not only for generating revenue through sales, but for providing service that is the mainstay of a successful ongoing relationship with customers, and for representing the company in the market area. The different facets of the selling responsibility are generally divided according to whether they require direct or indirect selling skills. Figure 14-2 presents a job description for a typical entry-level feed-salesperson position at a local cooperative.

Direct Selling Responsibility

Direct selling is the traditional and most basic function of the salesperson. The direct selling process involves prospecting for new customers, precall planning, getting the customer's attention and interest, making presentations, handling objections, and closing the sale. These steps may be carried out in formal or very informal ways.

Even for those salespeople whose primary function is to assist while others handle the direct selling, the direct selling function is crit-

Job Title: Feed Salesperson
Purpose: Responsible for feed sales in entire county.
Supervision: Works under direct supervision of county manager and is held responsible for sales results

Major areas of responsibility:

1. Responsible for feed sales to livestock farmers in entire county.
2. Helps farmers increase their profits by advising them of proper livestock production.
3. Promotes Co-op products and Co-op image to improve customer relations.
4. Sells and supervises livestock contacts.
5. Responsible for feed sales at a profit for County Co-op.

Duties:

1. Sells complete supplements, premixes, and animal health products to livestock farmers in entire county.
2. Works with elevator manager on sales territory.
3. Sells Co-op benefits, services, and feeding programs to customers.
4. Follows up on sales to make sure farmer is satisfied.
5. Helps farmer maintain proper records.
6. Plans promotions to increase feed business.
7. Consults with customer in sanitation, medication, and special problems.
8. Develops, promotes, and supervises all contacts.
9. Makes sales calls daily and reports results to manager.
10. Prepares and maintains an up-to-date prospect list.
11. Handles feed complaints.
12. Checks competition for prices and sales practices and reports results to manager.
13. Reviews monthly sales and tonnage figures with manager.
14. Helps develop annual sales budget.
15. Follows pricing and credit policy established by manager.
16. Knows and interprets county policies.
17. Assists other departments by referring leads immediately.
18. Plans and schedules use of time.
19. Promotes and develops good customer relations.
20. Controls company car expense.
21. Attends sales and product meetings as directed by manager.
22. Studies and recommends ideas to improve operations and profits.
23. May do other duties as directed by immediate supervisor.

Goals:

1. Increase sales over last year by 20 percent.
2. Increase feed profits by $10,000 over last year.
3. Make five sales calls per day.
4. Hold four feeder meetings during year.
5. Develop new sales and promotion ideas by January 15.
6. Keep manager informed of results.
7. Pick up 100 new feed customers this year.

Figure 14-2   Typical job description for feed salesperson.

ical. A machinery manufacturer's sales representatives must often directly sell their clientele on specific programs or policies offered by the manufacturer. They may well become involved in training dealer-salespeople in direct selling techniques. Of course, if direct selling does not occur in their area, their services may no longer be needed. The direct selling process is described in detail in Chapter 15.

Indirect Selling Responsibility

Interestingly enough, indirect selling usually takes up far more of the agribusiness salesperson's time than direct selling. Indirect selling includes the service functions and follow-up provided by the salesperson. A long list of activities fall in this category, as shown in Figure 14-2.

Market Intelligence   Market intelligence is a common responsibility of the salesperson. It may be a formally stated responsibility or an informal expectation, but in either case the company recognizes that the salesperson is in a position to know what is going on in the field. The salesperson is expected to keep the company informed about competitors' actions, prices, product performance, how customers are feeling, weather and crop conditions, and inventory levels. Many companies even require a brief weekly report to the supervisor. This information is extremely valuable for supervisors and managers when they are making company-wide decisions.

Technical and Product Information   Technical and product information is an important part of a salesperson's job. Customers expect professional salespeople to be fully knowledgeable about the agribusiness's products and services. Therefore, most companies provide much detailed information about the products and services sold. The salesperson must become an expert, especially when a limited number of products is involved. Many companies provide intensive product-information training for new salespeople during the first few months on the job. Often detailed product-information notebooks serve as a continual reference.

All this is not nearly so complicated as it may seem. Though the technical product information may seem quite complex and baffling to an outsider or to a new employee just starting out, most salespeople who have been on the job for even a few weeks become quite competent in the technical aspects. Education beyond the high school level, particularly in technical areas, makes this job much easier and makes the salesperson more adept at working with customers. Some companies even require college training for sales jobs.

Handling Complaints   Handling complaints is usually the salesperson's responsibility. Though this function is rarely a favorite part of the job, it is usually not a major problem. Only occasionally does a salesperson encounter a really difficult customer. Most customers are quite reasonable, even when they have a complaint, and most companies have well-developed procedures for handling complaints. A well-handled complaint often turns into a real "plus" for the salesperson because it establishes new credibility and rapport with the customer.

Collecting   Collecting may be part of the salesperson's responsibilities. An old agribusiness saying warns that "The sale is not complete until the money is collected." A salesperson who sells indiscriminately without concern for when and how payment will be made can create real problems for the company. One account that cannot be collected can wipe out all the profits for an entire region. Even when customers pay late, the cost to the parent company is usually significant. It is not uncommon for firms to make sales representatives responsible for collecting payments from customers who are late in mailing their remittances. Again, the vast majority of customers pay on time and so create no difficulty for the salesperson.

Public Agency Contacts Public agency contacts are frequently part of the salesperson's job. It is usually considered important to maintain a positive relationship and good communication with county agents, university researchers, or other public agency representatives, who may well be opinion leaders in the market area. These people are often an excellent source of current information and can be very influential with at least some customers. The salesperson may call regularly on selected officials.

Trade and Public Relations Trade and public relations are an important part of the job. How the general public and potential customers perceive the company is often very much a function of how the salesperson represents the company. The salesperson may work to build the company image through involvement in some community activities, and frequently takes part in trade shows, exhibits, field days, tests, and educational programs.

To most people, the salesperson is the company, because he or she is their only direct contact with it. Everything the salesperson does or does not do is part of this overall impression or image. The more local the company, the greater the significance of this impression. Even the salesperson's conduct in personal and business affairs has an important reflection on her or his effectiveness as a salesperson. Whether or not this is "fair," professional salespeople must realize the situation for what it is, and adapt to it.

Paperwork Paperwork, budgeting, and administrative duties are a part of most professional salespeople's job requirements. Most salespeople submit weekly reports on their activities, the number of calls they made, and market conditions. Usually, they must fill out order forms, take occasional inventory, and collect special information for company surveys. Most salespeople are asked to prepare annual sales forecasts for their area and to develop their expense-budget requests. Salespeople must keep accurate expense records and fill out expense statements for reimbursement. All this is probably not as time-consuming as it sounds, and when handled properly it can clear the way for more immediately productive duties.

Support for Salespeople

Most agribusinesses do not expect their salespeople to "go it alone"; there is usually a team of specialists to support the sales effort in a variety of critical areas. The team's primary purpose is to assist the salesperson in the field and to ensure an effective total marketing program. The actual number of specialists supporting the sales force varies, of course, with the size and nature of the company. Some large multinational agribusiness manufacturing companies have literally hundreds of marketing people involved in highly specific functions. Smaller, local, independent agribusinesses may have only a few support persons, whose duties tend to be less specific.

The salesperson's relationship with the support team (see Figure 14-3) is not all one-way; the salesperson is constantly feeding information to the support staff as part of a regular working relationship. This information is an important input for increasing the support staff's ability to carry out its own servicing responsibilities.

The Supervisor   The supervisor is the most common and probably the most valuable support person available to the agribusiness salesperson. Supervisors often carry such titles as "district manager" or "sales manager" and are ultimately accountable for all sales in their geographical area. Consequently, they typically exhibit a great deal of interest in the success of their salespeople and work closely with them to enhance their chances of success. Salespeople usually maintain contact with their supervisors at least weekly, and even more often if the need arises.

The supervisor generally passes along a great deal of information to new salespeople, especially in the first few months on the job. Detailed procedures and product information are spelled out through much close contact. It is not uncommon for a sales supervisor to spend several days in the field, calling on customers and introducing the new salesperson to them, as well as providing the new salesperson with helpful information about selling skills and methods.

A Training Program   A training program is another common support service for salespeople. It is becoming increasingly common to give salespeople considerable formal training in selling skills, product information, and general company orientation. Sometimes training is accomplished through self-study materials. At other times, it requires a few days to several weeks at headquarters. However, all companies still rely very heavily on on-the-job training.

Figure 14-3   Relationship of salesperson to key support staff.

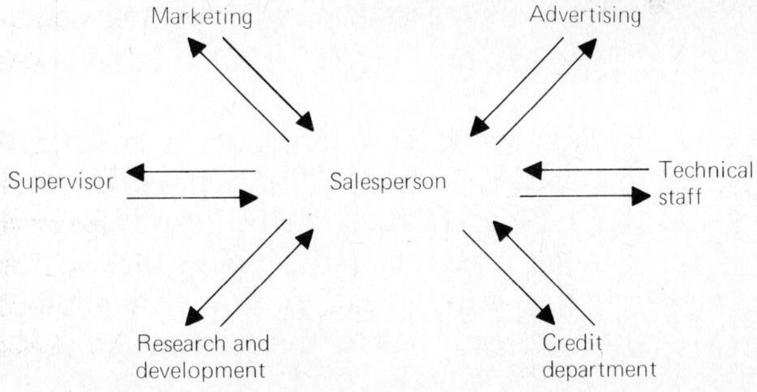

Increasingly, business firms, especially larger ones, are incorporating programs of regular periodic training, even for experienced salespeople. These sessions are often conducted by professional company trainers or outside consultants, and they usually provide very useful brushups for the professional salesperson.

Technical Support Technical support is frequently available in the form of special technologists who are on call at regional or home office locations to troubleshoot for the sales force. Most farm-equipment companies assign agricultural engineers especially to help their field representatives solve special customer problems. Agricultural-chemical companies usually have entomologists and agronomists on call to help with customer complaints or special-use product questions. Cattle feeders who are highly concerned about a slow rate of gain in feeder cattle and suspect a nutritional problem might contact the feed salesperson, who after an initial check might call in the company feed nutritionist to help analyze the problem and suggest a solution.

Advertising and Promotion The advertising and promotion department supports the salesperson by creating customer awareness of products or services. National and local advertising programs often open the door for salespeople and make their jobs easier. In some industries—animal health products, for instance—the advertising department even develops special advertisements that can be personalized to fit a particular dealer and be placed in local newspapers, or on radio or television. It is not uncommon for the parent company to split the cost of local advertising with the dealer. Advertising can become an important sales tool for the salesperson.

Marketing Department The marketing department often develops special incentives that salespeople can use as aids to selling. Horticultural-supply manufacturing firms frequently develop "early order programs" and special price incentives to increase business. "Bonus point" incentive programs to earn free trips to exotic resorts are common in the agricultural-chemical industry, and can give the sales representative an important edge. When manufacturers offer incentive trips to Hawaii, Europe, or South America, it is not uncommon for salespeople to accompany their customers, which often becomes an incentive for the sales force.

Research and Development Research and development, especially in larger manufacturing firms, provides an important indirect support for the selling effort. It is the responsibility of the R&D staff to find and develop products and services that will meet customer needs. Their efforts provide the salesperson with the basic product; and the better the product is, the easier the salesperson's job. The research department that makes a breakthrough in the development of a new variety of forage grass can make a seed salesperson's job very exciting and productive.

Credit Department   The credit department is often viewed by salespeople as more of a hindrance than a support group, primarily because a salesperson who did not have to be concerned about credit approval for the customer could probably sell more. Yet, because collecting the money for a sale is an essential part of selling, the credit department often saves the salesperson a great many headaches. The guidelines established by the credit department are usually valuable in keeping the salesperson on solid ground financially.

What It Takes to Be a Professional Salesperson
Many studies have attempted to determine what it takes to be a good professional salesperson, but none is really conclusive. For every characteristic that good salespeople appear to have in common, there are many exceptions. The personal qualities needed seem to be highly individualized, depending on how each person uses personality characteristics in selling situations. For example, contrary to popular assumption, some excellent salespeople tend to be rather introverted, that is, not particularly talkative, extremely careful, and conservative, which is far from the stereotype of a salesperson.

There are, however, some general characteristics that successful salespeople tend to find helpful, including determination and desire, self-motivation, and enthusiasm.

Determination and Desire   Determination and desire, which represent an internalized commitment to accomplish an objective, seem to be common traits among successful salespeople. Desire, along with hard work, often accomplishes wonders in overcoming deficiencies in technique.

Self-motivation   Self-motivation, or the ability to actually pursue an objective through self-discipline, is critical to successful salespeople, and greatly complements determination and desire. Most sales jobs allow the salesperson a great deal of freedom without close supervision. Much depends on the individual salesperson. Seldom is there a time clock to punch or a routine to follow, or someone to tell the salesperson specifically what to do and when to do it. A good salesperson must decide what to do and then aggressively pursue the fully internalized goal.

Enthusiasm   Enthusiasm is an important element in successful selling. Probably nothing is so contagious as enthusiasm (except apathy). Salespeople who are excited about their product or service and what it can do for the customer have a real advantage. Enthusiasm does not necessarily mean extreme behavior; even quiet people can display sincere belief in what they are doing. Customers are quick to perceive how the salesperson really feels about the product or service.

Ability to Work with People   The ability to enjoy working with people is another characteristic common to successful salespeople. Selling is a people-oriented business, and a salesperson must work with a wide range of personality types and value systems. While it may be natural to like some people better than others, it is also necessary for the salesperson to feel comfortable with many kinds of people.

Self-improvement   Constant self-improvement is necessary for successful salespeople. The job frequently changes and requires new and different approaches. Technological changes can quickly outdate the information of the salesperson who is unwilling to spend time keeping up. Effective salespeople must stay ahead of their customers, and must continually search for ways to perform more professionally and skillfully.

Sensitivity to People   Sensitivity to people is critical to success. A good salesperson is able to hear what people feel as well as what they say, that is, to pick up on the small clues that are silent but clear messages, to empathize with the customers, and to identify with their needs. A good salesperson has a genuine interest in and cares for others as individuals, not just as prospective buyers.

Intelligence   Intelligence of the common sense variety is vital. There is no type of selling that does not require problem solving, that is, analyzing, synthesizing ideas, and making logical decisions.

Honesty   Honesty and a sense of ethics that is in tune with that of the clientele are essential to survival as a salesperson. Nothing can undermine a salesperson's success as quickly as questionable integrity. Not only is it important to *be* honest and ethical, but the salesperson must strive to *appear* honest and ethical as well. Reliability is another part of this characteristic: whether or not the salesperson who makes a promise can be trusted to follow through.

Ability to Communicate   The ability to communicate ideas clearly to others is invaluable. Salespeople do not need to be speech contest winners or public speakers; in fact, some very successful salespeople have speech impediments. The crux of the matter is being able to convey ideas clearly so that others can understand them, and to listen to and understand what others are saying.

Neat Appearance   A neat appearance also carries some importance. Fairly or unfairly, many customers seem to judge a person or the person's product or service on the basis of his or her appearance. Maintaining a neat appearance does not require buying expensive clothes or following the dictates of high fashion; rather, it means making a consistent effort to dress to fit the occasion and to be clean and well groomed. The important thing is not how the salesperson perceives himself or herself but how he or she is perceived by others.

Preparing for a Sales Career

Although many different types of training and experience can be useful in preparing for an agribusiness sales career, there are some special experiences that are especially helpful. For a young person in a 2- or 4-year college or university program, these experiences can add significantly to the probability of success.

Technical Background in Agriculture   A technical background in agriculture is highly valuable. Coursework that is related to specific areas of primary interest in agriculture can be very useful. Only in rare circumstances can college courses provide students with adequate knowledge in a specific product area. However, taking such courses does prepare students to absorb more specific information once they are on the job. Students studying horticulture, for instance, learn a great deal of general and technical information in classes, but invariably must learn much more about the responses, characteristics, and diseases that relate specifically to an individual job. The function of classwork is to place the future salesperson in an excellent position to learn the detail needed for specific jobs later on.

Communications and Social Sciences   Communications and social science coursework is helpful, since selling is first and foremost a people-oriented job. An understanding of people and the full development of skills in dealing with them are extremely valuable. After a few years on the job, salespeople invariably indicate that they wish they had taken more courses in these areas.

Agricultural Business Management Support   Agricultural business management, accounting, and law should be selected as support courses. These subjects are considered mandatory by the many professional agribusiness salespeople who must deal with increasingly sophisticated agricultural business managers (farmers and ranchers, dealers and wholesalers) about business issues. Opportunities for advancement into management are significantly enhanced by this background.

Extracurricular Activities   Extracurricular activities form an integral part of the total education experience. Employers are quick to search out evidence of the ability to relate well with others and a willingness to seek or accept leadership responsibility. Students who can demonstrate these kinds of experiences, through school clubs and other organizations, are usually considered excellent candidates for top sales positions. Experiences that relate to the student's own professional area provide a particularly good preparation for selling, and pay off handsomely on the job.

Work Experience   There is no substitute for real-world experience. For those who have not been raised on a farm or ranch, field experience is invaluable. Many people argue that the only way to learn to communicate with farmers and ranchers is by performing their job at some time or other. For this reason, on-farm experience is highly valued by most employers.

Even for students who have been raised on a farm or ranch, it is important to gain additional experience in an agribusiness during college. Though such work may mostly involve physical labor, like hauling fertilizer or mixing feed, it provides an excellent insight into how agribusiness really works. A professional feed field technician can be far more effective after having mixed feed personally and knowing what it entails.

Many schools, especially 2-year colleges, offer work-study or cooperative-education programs, wherein students can integrate college courses with on-the-job experience. Some schools even offer academic credit for these work experiences. Graduates of these programs are usually in great demand by agribusinesses, and for good reason. They have demonstrated both academic and real-world preparation, and they are highly likely to succeed on the job.

SUMMARY

Selling is an integral and fundamental part of America's free enterprise economy. All businesses depend on the sales process to generate income. Without adequate sales, a business cannot survive.

Selling is the process of helping people buy. It links the customer to the business. It has an important educational dimension because it helps customers become aware of alternatives that can benefit them. Whenever an exchange takes place, both the seller and the buyer expect to benefit.

Professional selling in agriculture seldom means door-to-door superficial contacts. It is often an ongoing long-term personal relationship that is based on a high level of technical ability. It is a highly individual job in which each person is responsible for his or her own performance.

There are many rewards associated with agriselling. Financially, the selling profession can be especially rewarding. It is also an excellent route for advancement and personal satisfaction. But it is hard work, and it can be discouraging when things do not go well.

There are many levels of agriselling. Some people sell only to distributors and dealers, while others call on farmers. Still others deal directly with the general public. Each level has its own unique lifestyle, but all utilize professional selling skills that involve close working relationships with customers.

The salesperson has a variety of responsibilities in addition to actual selling. Salespeople must monitor the market for information necessary to company decisions, provide technical support for their customers, handle complaints, collect accounts, maintain good relationships with public institutions in their area, and do a great deal of paperwork. But they have a lot of support. Most salespeople receive special training, have technical specialists to call on for help, can utilize company advertising and promotional programs as selling aids, and can count on their supervisor to assist them when problems arise.

There are a great many different personal attributes that are important to successful selling, but there is no one set of characteristics that are necessary for success. Some people seem to be naturally inclined toward sales, but nearly everyone can develop the skills necessary to sell successfully.

DISCUSSION QUESTIONS

1. (a) List ten adjectives that describe what you believe is the stereotype most people have about salespeople. What is the general nature of these adjectives?

(b) List ten adjectives that describe agribusiness salespeople as portrayed in this chapter. What is the general nature of these adjectives?

(c) Compare and contrast your lists. Why do you think differences and similarities between the two lists exist?

2. Develop a table or chart showing how the five types of selling discussed in this chapter compare with each other in the following areas:

(a) knowledge of the technology

(b) probable travel involved

(c) direct contact with farmers and agricultural producers
Which of these types of selling would be most appealing to you, and why?

3. Review and list the major areas of responsibility of agribusiness people. Identify which of these areas primarily involve:

(a) information transfer

(b) communications

(c) money

(d) applied psychology
(Note that some areas of responsibility might require more than one of these skills.)

4. Using the personal characteristics of successful professional agribusiness salespeople as listed in this chapter, evaluate a salesperson you know or have heard about. How may each of these characteristics affect the individual's chances for success?

AN OPPORTUNITY FOR BRAD
Brad Johnson had just returned to school after working as a summer intern for a farm supply business near his hometown. It had been Brad's

first real exposure to agribusiness, except as a customer, picking up supplies for his father's farm. He had spent most of the summer filling in for people on vacation, which had given him the opportunity to take a good look at the total business. Of course, it had been hard work and long hours, especially early in the season, when the bulk of the work had been fertilizer delivery and application. He had not been particularly interested in fertilizer before, but the overtime hours had allowed him to save the money he had needed for the fall term. In fact, the money had been his primary reason for taking the job.

The internship had made a real impact on Brad's career plans. He had always thought he wanted to farm. His father had said he could come back to the family farm, but Brad knew that that would require more land. He felt his father wanted him to come back, but his father would never really say so. Brad's little brother also liked farming. But Brad had enjoyed the summer experience so much that he was pretty confused.

Then, at the end of the summer, the general manager had given Brad some real encouragement. He had made it clear that they were pleased with Brad's performance and were interested in talking further about developing a full-time field-technician position for Brad in fertilizer and chemicals. If it worked out, Brad would be responsible for sales to farmers, making recommendations about crops and fertilizing, taking soil samples, organizing and holding grower meetings, and helping with custom fertilizer application during the busy season.

But Brad was uncertain. Although he had had several general agriculture courses and some agronomy, he did not feel he was ready to tell a farmer who owned a large tract what his fertilizer-chemical program should be. Another concern was selling. Brad had always had a poor impression of "peddlers." Even if he did take the job, he was not sure he had the skill to communicate with experienced farmers, especially since he had not turned twenty-one yet. He became apprehensive when he thought about standing in front of a meeting. Still, it might be exciting, and the salary the manager had mentioned sounded good.

Brad was keenly aware that he had only one more year of school, and that some of his courses were locked in. But he had some flexibility, especially in his last term, when there were several electives he could take. It was a big decision, determining the best course of action.

QUESTIONS

1. What are the pros and cons of Brad's possible agribusiness opportunity?

2. What things could Brad do during his final year to prepare him more fully for the job opportunity? (Consider both academic and nonacademic possibilities.)

3. What suggestions could you make to help Brad keep his options open?

OBJECTIVES

- Develop methods of locating and qualifying prospective agricultural customers

- Develop specific objectives and strategies for sales-call interviews

- Approach customers on a sales call, build rapport, learn what a customer's needs are, and generate interest in the product or service

- Deliver a sales presentation that will convince the customer of the product's benefits, handle any objections or concerns, and close the sale

- Explain how follow-up service prepares for continuing sales

Professional agriselling requires communication and technical skills in a variety of circumstances.
A. On the farm
B. In the store
C. In the nursery
D. In the field

EVERY PERSON IS A
SALESPERSON . . . SELLING
THEMSELVES AND THEIR IDEAS
CONTINUALLY.

THE SELLING PROCESS

A

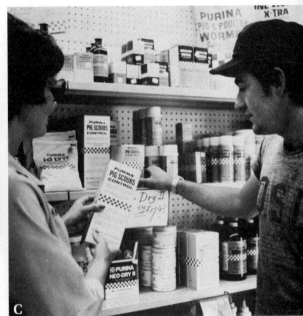

C

B

D

GETTING STARTED

Dan Cooper and his father, Bill, agreed that they would have to expand feed sales significantly to generate enough income to support two families. Expanding sales would be Dan's primary responsibility when he returned to the family business after completing his college work in agriculture. But frankly, he was a bit concerned about the whole thing. Although he had worked in the business before, he was not sure about selling. He just did not like the idea of pushing things on people. On the other hand, he knew farmers needed feed, and he was sure that Cooper Feed Service had both a quality product and good service.

Bill Cooper had started the business 23 years ago and was a well-respected feed man in the community. Competition with a co-op and two independents was tough in their 10-mile market area, but the amount of livestock and poultry made it a good market. Bill had reinvested much of his profit in the business over the years and had continually upgraded facilities. The latest addition was a minicomputer used to formulate feeds to customer specifications.

Until now, Cooper Feed Service had relied mostly on word of mouth and repeat business. They had the facilities to expand business. But Dan just was not sure how to begin to increase sales. . . . .

THE DIRECT SELLING PROCESS

It is a common misconception that the selling process involves nothing more than talking to customers and getting an order signed. The fact of the matter is that the selling process includes thorough, painstaking preparation before a customer call is ever made. In addition, agribusiness salespeople devote a substantial portion of their time to servicing their accounts. There are some agricultural industries in which salespeople never actually take an order; and it is not uncommon for some salespeople to dedicate precious selling time to making formal sales presentations to the customer. However a salesperson's time is divided, he or she must never lose sight of the primary objective: to generate sales and increase revenue for the firm. This means that every contact with the customer is designed to maintain or expand business with that customer in some direct or indirect way. Not surprisingly, the ultimate objective of all selling activity is to sell.

The selling process embraces the various elements involved in preparation for the sales call, the sales-call interview itself, and the follow-up activity after the sales call. Figure 15-1 shows the major steps in the sales process. Although these steps are not always followed in the exact order shown in Figure 15-1, the process shown is logical and is commonly followed.

Preparation

Many different kinds of preparation precede the salesperson's first contact with a customer. The salesperson prepares by becoming quite knowledgeable about the product or service, about the market, and about

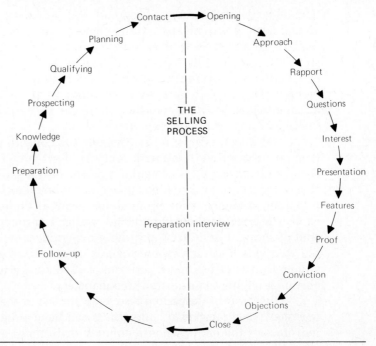

Figure 15-1 The selling process.

the customers being served. Without a thorough understanding of these important areas, the salesperson usually evidences a lack of confidence that hampers effective selling. This is why many agribusinesses budget considerable time and money to train new salespeople. Even the new salesperson who has just completed a successful academic program in an appropriate technical area of agriculture still has to absorb some practical and highly specific information about the individual company and its products. Many firms prefer to begin with only a brief orientation, after which they send the new salesperson to the field under close supervision. After a few months, when the new salesperson has had enough experience to put additional training into perspective, the firm follows up with more detailed formal instruction. There is nothing like a few complex technical questions from a hard-nosed customer to bring home the importance of product or market knowledge.

Knowledge is only part of the salesperson's preparation for selling. Hours of the salesperson's time are frequently devoted to prospecting for customers, qualifying the prospects as they develop, and then making the initial contact that may result in a sale.

Knowledge Knowledge implies more than simply knowing about the product. It involves a keen awareness of the ways in which the market works, the ins and outs of competitive strategies, the strengths and weaknesses of competitors, the many customer needs and problems to be anticipated, the business and agricultural practices that are common among customers, and the unique characteristics of key regular and potential customers. Some of this knowledge can be gained through formal study of company literature, but most of it has to be gained through experience. Consequently, most firms structure the first few weeks or months of work to include frequent contact with senior sales personnel or supervisors, so that new salespeople can be helped to learn the maximum amount from their experience.

But knowledge is not exclusively the concern of new salespeople. It is an appropriate continual concern of all professional salespeople. Changing technology is a regular element of the selling challenge. Constant efforts to improve personal, social, and business skills offer another important dimension for professional growth. Professional salespeople expect to upgrade their knowledge regularly through independent self-study, company seminars, and daily experiences in the field. Salespeople who ignore the importance of this continual upgrading process usually end up with mediocre performance records because they are incapable of servicing their customers adequately.

Successful salespeople also keep abreast of their rapidly changing markets. The strategies of competitors can have a drastic impact on selling success; therefore, when a competitor initiates a new credit policy, alert salespeople quickly adjust their own selling strategies to counteract any negative effects. Similarly, salespeople keep informed about changes among their own customers, where the changes are occurring, and how much variables may alter customer needs. This is not quite so easy as it sounds initially, since many salespeople may have up to 200 accounts or more.

One especially useful technique for staying current with the market is to locate all the salesperson's customers on a map, perhaps a wall map, with different color map pins for different sizes of customers in the total market area. This technique often reveals previously unnoticed "holes," where penetration of the market is poor and customers are few and far between. An analysis of such poorly penetrated areas frequently leads to successful modifications in marketing strategies; this technique is particularly valuable for local retail farm supply and marketing firms, where distance effectively limits the potential market area.

Another effective technique for keeping abreast of the market involves a detailed written analysis of market strengths and weaknesses, both for the firm and for key competitors. This written statement focuses attention on numerous areas of comparative advantage and disadvantage, and so has important implications for sales presentations. Agribusiness salespeople should not overreact to the competition or allow the competition to determine their market behavior. Yet all salespeople need to be keenly aware of the relative strengths and weaknesses of their products, so that strengths can be emphasized and the effects of weaknesses minimized.

Prospecting *Prospecting* is the process of identifying and locating potential customers. Many ingenious ways of prospecting have been devised, and their effectiveness depends largely upon the type of agribusiness and upon the skills of the salesperson involved. These methods generally fall into three broad categories: (1) cold calls, (2) cool calls, and (3) leads.

COLD CALLS   Some highly successful companies rely exclusively upon *cold calls,* which involve simply stopping by every farm or agribusiness in the market area. This method of prospecting can be quite productive even for companies that do not rely on it exclusively, since the law of percentages suggests that cold calls will turn up at least some prospects. Cold calls are known to be productive for one local certified soybean-seed dealer in the Mississippi Delta, for example, and they are equally productive for a grain-bin representative in central Iowa, suggesting that the method is particularly effective where there is widespread demand for the product or service. Although some professional salespeople describe this kind of prospecting as "distasteful," and although it can be less productive than more concentrated methods of prospecting, many agribusinesses deem it effective. These firms often require their sales personnel to devote a portion of their time to cold calls.

COOL CALLS   *Cool calls,* which involve calling on those you believe to be likely prospects, generally succeed more often than cold calls. A feed salesperson who sells pig starter once reported that canvassing her market area for farms with farrowing operations yielded more impressive results for her aggressive sales program than even the most ambitious number of cold calls.

This method places the responsibility for identifying potential customers squarely on the salesperson's shoulders. One method for identifying potential customers relies upon visual observation. Machinery salespeople are alerted to observe the condition of certain types of equipment as they drive past farms and ranches in their market area. A marketing field technician makes a mental note of what acreages different growers have planted.

Sometimes commercial organizations sell lists of addresses for all the subscribers to certain magazines. These subscriber lists then yield names of potential users of specific products or services. Noting attendance at local or regional education meetings that are sponsored by the Cooperative Extension Service, universities, or trade associations frequently helps to identify prospects to follow up.

LEADS   *Leads,* or prospects that have been taken from knowledgeable sources, form one of the single most productive methods of prospecting. *Cool leads* are those potential customers whose need for a product or service may or may not be current. *Hot leads* are those potential customers whose need is believed to be current. Such customers may be definitely planning to buy, or they may simply have a current need that they can be convinced to fill with the salesperson's product or service. Because hot leads are by far the most productive method of prospecting, most salespeople choose to follow up such leads before they spend time on cool or cold canvassing methods.

Good leads develop from a variety of sources. Successful company advertising usually results in numerous requests for information from potential customers. Trade shows and exhibits, which are common in many areas of agribusiness, often generate leads by drawing interested customers. In some agribusinesses, salespeople from one product division may learn that their customers are in the market for other company products, and may alert the other product divisions to the lead. A farm supply firm that already sells feed to a farmer should recognize the potential for acquiring that farmer's fertilizer business as well.

But current customers remain one of the very best sources for leads. Satisfied customers often are willing, and even anxious, to share news of their wise decisions and good fortune with their peers. Many customers feel that the wisdom of their own purchase decision is reinforced when the very same decision is reached by their friends. The sharp agribusiness salesperson can capitalize on this tendency by querying current customers about others who might be able to benefit from the company's products and services. The salesperson then uses this lead as an opener when contacting the new potential customer.

Qualifying Prospects   Common sense dictates that salespeople should make sure their prospects are qualified to buy before exerting tremendous selling effort on them. Agribusinesses with a purchasing agent or with one owner-manager may have one clear-cut decision maker, although this is not necessarily so. For years, farming and ranching were thought to be male-oriented businesses, in which the decision was made by one person, but salespeople are beginning to recognize that the decision to buy rests in the hands of husband-and-wife partnerships.

Other stipulations that determine whether a prospect is qualified include the prospect's ability to pay. A prospect who wants and needs the product may not necessarily be able to afford it. Any customer whose financial condition may jeopardize collection of the account should be considered unqualified.

It is also the salesperson's responsibility to determine whether the potential customer's need is well suited to the company's product or service. If not, then it is bad policy to sell to that customer because the resulting dissatisfaction may create bad publicity among more qualified customers.

Planning the Sales Call   The *planning step*, or *preapproach*, involves the salesperson's preparation prior to actually making the sales call. It is a step that is critical to the success of the sales call. The preapproach includes collecting information about the customer, developing a sales-call objective and strategy, and preparing for specific aspects of the sales call. The extent and formality with which the planning should be carried out varies widely with the situation. Where the customer-salesperson relationship is well established and the salesperson is highly experienced, the planning may be minimal. Underestimating the importance of the planning step can, however, create very embarrassing situations, even for the seasoned salesperson. Some veterans relate stories about calling on customers and asking them what brand they are using, only to discover that it was their own.

INFORMATION Much information about a potential customer goes into building a sales presentation. The exact nature of the information depends upon the circumstance, but almost invariably it includes the following.

1. **About the agribusiness**

   name

   general size of the business or farm

   brand of product or service now in use

   relationship with current supplies

   problems or dissatisfactions with current suppliers

   past experiences and relationships with the firm

   name of buying authority (the buyer)

   ownership structure of the firm

   power structure of the organization

   image that the business promotes among its customers

   company philosophy, objectives, and strategy

   credit rating and ability to pay

   operating strengths and weaknesses

   company policies that may affect purchase decisions

   physical facilities that may affect purchase decisions

2. **About the buyer for the agribusiness**

   hobbies and interests

   age, education, and background

   social and professional interests

   personality type

   personal peculiarities and obvious value structure

This information is essential for developing a personalized sales-call strategy to be utilized with each customer. It can be used to tailor the opening, the interest-building, and the type of presentation that is most likely to be productive. For example, one salesperson found that a large agribusiness had a buyer who was extroverted, saw herself as a community and industry leader, had never tried the salesperson's firm before, and had recently had shipment problems with her present supplier. At the same time, the salesperson handled a small account with an introverted husband, wife, and two sons who ran their own business, were slow to adopt new techniques, had been doing business with the same supplier for the last 7 years, and saw no reason to change. Needless to say, that salesperson did not approach both potential customers in the same way.

Obtaining information about the customer can sometimes be a problem. Most people are somewhat averse to salespeople who "nose around" and ask too many questions. Agriculturally oriented people have been known to become quite uncomfortable when a salesperson seems to know a great deal about them, especially before a definite relationship has been established. So even obtaining the necessary information can be hazardous to the development of a potential relationship.

As with prospecting, much information can be obtained by visual observation. As the salesperson passes the place of business, he or she should simply note such things as the extent of storage space, the available equipment, and the brands and programs that are being advertised.

Current customers with whom the salesperson has a good relationship are good sources of information about potential customers. Different impressions should be gleaned from different people, and a composite of the potential customer built from different sources. Other, noncompetitive professional salespeople who call on the customer may also be good sources. Still other sources include published advertisements; trade association directories, which often provide limited information about members; county agents; and sales supervisors.

Finally, the customers themselves should not be neglected as a source of information. Since so much of agribusiness selling revolves around technical problem solving, the most natural thing in the world is to go directly to the customer for the information necessary to make a sound proposal. Although the term preapproach refers mostly to preparation before the call, the ongoing nature of agribusiness selling suggests that calling on the potential customer for some technical information to help in the preparation of a major presentation may be quite appropriate.

SALES-CALL OBJECTIVE Before the salesperson can prepare a sales presentation, a sales-call objective must be developed. The *sales-call objective* is a tangible, measurable objective of what the salesperson expects to accomplish during the sales call. The salesperson who does not have a specific objective clearly in mind will find the planning process frustrating, and is likely to appear disorganized and unconfident to the customer. It is a good idea to actually write down the sales-call objective.

This technique may bring to mind ideas that the salesperson might overlook with less formal methods. And after the call has been completed, the written objective facilitates evaluating the success of the call. Many find that listing the call objectives along with the daily itinerary of sales calls is an efficient way to do business.

The sales-call objective need not to be so straightforward as getting the customer to sign an order. Although the ultimate objective of all professional salespeople is to generate sales, a particular call may represent only one small part of that total process. The salesperson who visits a veterinary supply distributor to check current inventory levels for a new chicken wormer is demonstrating a perfectly acceptable sales-call objective. Convincing a prospective dealer to attend a special dealer-management seminar where he or she will be exposed to many satisfied regular customers is a tangible objective. Occasionally, the sales-call objective is simply to create goodwill. Although goodwill calls are acceptable, failure to develop sales-call objectives for such calls sometimes results in a majority of calls that are little more than social in nature. Written sales-call objectives help to increase the productivity of professional salespeople.

SALES-CALL STRATEGY Once information about the customer has been gathered, it should be used to develop a specific plan of action. This plan of action is designed to maximize the potential for success with that customer. The sales call should emphasize those aspects of the product or service that provide answers to the customer's needs or problems, and aspects that are more advantageous than those of competitors. The strategy should include such things as the timing, location, and circumstances of the call, all of which should maximize the call's effectiveness. Is it best to set up an appointment or just to stop by? Should the call be at the customer's place of business or in "neutral" territory? What time of year would be best for the call? The successful salesperson asks and answers many such questions.

The strategy should incorporate a degree of subtlety, so as not to antagonize the customer. Sometimes there is a fine line between knowing enough about the customer to zero in on key issues, and exhibiting so much knowledge about the customer's problem that he or she feels the whole area is "none of your business." The sales-call strategy should capitalize on available information by orienting the sales call toward the most productive areas rather than simply trying to impress customers with the depth of information that the salesperson has acquired about their businesses. During the sales call, the discovery process should be allowed to flow naturally and smoothly, and the information that has been gathered should be used to guide that process.

PREPARING THE SALES CALL The process of actually developing specific aspects of the call, including any materials that may be needed, is known as preparing the sales call. The more experienced the salesperson is, the less time is required to plan the details of the call. Yet this can be a very productive process, even for seasoned salespeople. It is a matter of selecting the proper approach and opening, planning transitions from rapport building to the presentation, selecting the most important benefits, anticipating objections and deciding the best way to handle them, and finally choosing a probable close. It is a matter of thinking ahead and planning.

The suggestion about formally sketching a sales-call objective and strategy may seem like an academic exercise, but thousands of dollars may be riding on the effectiveness of the sales call. The tendency for inexperienced salespeople is to discount the value of planning. Conversely, even highly experienced salespeople spend considerable time planning for important calls. To ignore the potential value of proper preparation is foolhardy.

Making Contact   All the planning in the world may go for naught unless the salesperson calls on a prospective customer at precisely the right time and under the right conditions. Making contact can be very difficult. Many agribusiness salespeople encounter strong prejudices against sales personnel; others find that prospective customers are just plain busy. Customers sometimes protect their privacy by surrounding themselves with such barriers as secretaries, receptionists, junior executives, assistants, hired workers, and spouses. Selling these "buffer" people on the importance of taking up the buyer's time can be half the battle. These intermediaries should be treated with respect and courtesy, since their importance is difficult to overestimate.

Delay is an unavoidable part of any sales job, since buyers and important executives frequently make salespeople wait. Yet waiting too often or for too long can become a habitual game. A salesperson's time must also be valued highly, particularly when there are other calls to make. Alerting the customer to this fact by rescheduling an appointment after a brief wait may partially solve the problem. Incidentally, waiting time can be used effectively rather than wasted. Productive salespeople spend their spare moments reviewing preparation for either the upcoming call or later calls.

Appointments are standard in many areas of agribusiness selling, and increasingly so in many agricultural industries, including farms. By making appointments, the salesperson shows that he or she recognizes the value of customers' time. Appointments also help salespeople to employ their limited time more productively. Many agribusiness salespeople who work out of their own homes set aside the first hour of the morning for making or confirming appointments before they begin their actual travels.

The telephone has become a great time-saver. This sales tool is probably underused by most salespeople. If used properly, it can add greatly to the effectiveness of agribusiness salespeople. In fact, it is increasingly common in highly concentrated areas of agriculture, such as the San Joaquin Valley of California, for agribusiness salespeople to have mobile telephones installed in their cars or trucks. This allows them to maintain constant contact with their customers as problems arise, as well as to confirm appointments.

Receptionists and secretaries are vital to any salesperson's success. Experienced salespeople have learned how to respect the position of such intermediaries, and to work through them rather than trying to get around them. A sincerely friendly attitude is often the key. Most need to know why the salesperson wants to see their bosses. If the salesperson has done the necessary homework, the simplest thing is to refer to some specific plans that must be discussed. If the call is in any way a follow-up call, that fact can be pointed out. Relationships with receptionists, as with the customers themselves, are often long-term and repetitive, and so require continued maintenance.

Once contact with the customer has been achieved, the salesperson moves out of the preparation stage and into the heart of the selling process, the sales-call interview.

The Sales-Call Interview

The *sales-call interview* is the act of establishing customer contact, developing or renewing a positive relationship, discovering the customer's needs, convincing the customer that the salesperson can meet those needs, and securing the customer's commitment. The sales-call stage is the image that everyone calls to mind when selling is mentioned. It relies heavily on interpersonal skills, and is best described as being primarily a communication process. To an untrained observer, a sales call by an effective agribusiness salesperson may appear to be a casual conversation among business friends, during which pleasantries, industry gossip, and even occasional barbs are exchanged. Yet seemingly innocent conversations can have important undertones for the alert salesperson who skillfully seeks information about the customer's concerns and needs, about the current market conditions, and about competitive activity. The fertilizer dealer who kiddingly asks a chemical sales representative whether "This year's incentive trip to Acapulco will be any good" may be transmitting important messages that the representative can use to advantage in a later visit. On the other hand, the sales interview may adopt a decidedly formal air, where each of the basic steps from rapport building to the close is distinct. In agribusiness selling, the more formal and complete sales call may occur only when major new products or programs are introduced, as is common with agricultural chemicals; or the complete process could occur in almost every sales call, as is more common when selling agricultural equipment. The point is that the sales interview, whether formal or informal, is a systematic communication process that can be productive both for the salesperson and for the customer. It involves several time-honored stages of activity, such as the approach, rapport building, asking questions, generating interest, the presentation itself, the trial close, handling objections, and, finally, the close.

Approaching Customers The method of approaching a customer is absolutely critical to the success of the sales call. This brief greeting sets the stage and tone for the entire interview. Both the customer and the salesperson create impressions and draw conclusions about each other. Each consciously and unconsciously perceives and makes judgments about the other. Spoken and nonverbal messages from both parties bear upon the outcome of the interview. Salespeople can gain or lose control of the sales call simply on the basis of how they handle themselves during the initial contact. And it is during that contact that an awkwardness in the relationship can surface, especially when the salesperson has minimal experience.

Five basic points to consider when approaching customers are as follows.

1. *Dress in good taste* Cleanliness and neatness are basic to professional selling. Personal grooming, including hairstyle, must fit within the tolerance limits of customers' tastes. It is understandably frustrating to realize that a customer's personal tastes may influence a sales relationship, but the simple fact is that they do. A salesperson must either remain within the boundaries of his or her customers' normal values or risk alienating them. This phenomenon is particularly important among agricultural buyers, whose prevailing value structure tends to be rather conservative. Whether or not this is fair is not the relevant point. The fact is that a value structure does exist and must be dealt with by the professional agribusiness salesperson.

2. *Be mindful of car manners* For many agribusiness salespeople, their cars and the way they are driven constitute the first chance to make visual impressions on the customer, particularly for those salespeople who are concentrating on rural-area customers. The industry abounds with stories about unfortunate salespeople who have parked in the general manager's "personal spot," driven into the farmer's driveway in a manner that the farmer thought reckless, or backed over the customer's son's tricycle and lost a potential sale.

3. *Greet customers with friendly confidence* The consensus among professionals is that it is best not to be overly aggressive or assuming until definite rapport has been established. Although a warm smile and a firm handshake make for a good beginning, some customers have expressed discomfort with the handshake, and have viewed an outstretched hand as a sign of aggression, so care should be taken. This problem is reported particularly by saleswomen who call on male customers, though attitudes are slowly changing. Where appropriate, however, nothing surpasses the personal warmth of a sincere handshake for beginning the sales call on a productive note.

4. *Introduction* The salesperson should introduce himself or herself clearly by stating his or her name and company. This idea has merit even in situations where the salesperson has called on the customer before, unless both have come to know each other very well. The introduction generally places customers more at ease. Many salespeople wear some type of identification where it can be easily seen to reinforce their name with the customer and to spare the customer the embarrassment of not remembering a salesperson's name. An alternative would be to reinforce the introduction by handing the customer an accompanying business card.

The salesperson must be sure to state the customer's name exactly during the introduction. Many salespeople are reluctant to clarify matters by asking a customer to repeat the name, especially in cases where the two parties have previously met. Yet it is perfectly acceptable to re-ask the name at every appropriate opportunity until it is fixed clearly in the mind. However, the salesperson should be on guard against overusing the customer's name, since the customer may become suspicious of a too-friendly salesperson who appears to have overstepped the bounds of the relationship.

5. *Have an icebreaker in mind*   Getting the conversation started is the hardest part, especially for new salespeople. Once the ice is broken, however, things usually go more smoothly. Knowing something about the customer and about the situation can help. Some salespeople say that it is useful to have an opening statement firmly in mind, as long as one is ready to adapt to shifting circumstances.

Possible openers include:

1.   Asking a question about an area of mutual interest

2.   Commenting about some known customer interest or hobby

3.   Referring to an issue covered in the last meeting

4.   Complimenting the customer genuinely

5.   Giving a small gift that is somehow related to the sales call

6.   Providing a copy of technical material that may be of interest

7.   Indicating that a mutual acquaintance suggested the visit (if that is indeed the case)

8.   Offering to help the customer with some task

9.   Simply stating the sales purpose

Building Rapport   The first few minutes of the sales call are usually devoted to building rapport with the customer, which helps both the customer and the salesperson feel comfortable with the situation and develops mutual trust. This period also gives the salesperson an opportunity to learn more about the customer's temperament and personality, to size up the situation, and to adapt the predeveloped sales call strategy to the particular situation. Building rapport demands that the social skills of the salesperson be highly developed.

Another important benefit of the rapport-building process is the discovery of interest areas and of inferences that can be drawn about the customer's needs and values. The alert salesperson makes a mental note of a farmer's obvious pride in having finished planting early, and prepares to highlight any timeliness benefits of the company product during the latter part of the call.

Although socializing can be enjoyable, salespeople must remember that busy customers may react negatively to interruptions that are lengthy. Excessive use of time for socializing also subtracts from the salesperson's precious selling time. As with so many other delicate questions in establishing customer-salesperson relationships, proper balance must be achieved and maintained.

One of the main objectives of rapport building is to encourage the customer to talk. This is accomplished by asking questions and striving for customer response. Many salespeople mistakenly believe that their job is to keep talking themselves. A successful call, however, usually finds the salesperson interacting and directing the interview, while the customer does the majority of the conversing. As the interview progresses, the salesperson looks for "bridges" or transitions from general socializing to the true purpose of the call.

Questions   Throughout the interview, one of the salesperson's most indispensable tools is the question. The salesperson who tactfully asks questions is able to focus attention on the customer and learn about the customer's needs and interests. It is amazing how often carefully designed questions can lead customers to their own conclusions, which is far more persuasive than being "told" outright by a salesperson. Customers often sell to themselves, and the skillful salesperson simply facilitates the process.

The effective use of questions in a sales interview is a skill that can be learned. The manner in which a question is asked may make all the difference. Tact demands that the salesperson avoid appearing nosy or controlling while asking questions. When questions flow appropriately within the conversation and are asked with genuine interest, they are usually more successful. Care should be taken to phrase questions nonthreateningly so that they can be answered in a positive way. It is of little value to embarrass a customer or to force the customer to admit ignorance. Try not to make the inquiry in such a way that it forces the customer to adopt a polarized position, particularly when that position is counterproductive to the sales-call objective. Open-ended questions that are designed to get the customer talking are usually better than questions that can be answered with "yes" or "no."

Salesperson: Looks like you had a good season! Any bottlenecks?
Customer: No—things went pretty well—except for some days we fell behind. My people just couldn't keep up—then they'd hurry, and that's when we'd make some mistakes.
Salesperson: Things kind of got cramped sometimes, huh?
Customer: No more than every year I guess, but we did lose some business a couple of times.

Salesperson: John, it sounds like your biggest limitation on business is your workforce at peak season. Is that right?

Customer: Yes—just can't get enough people we can trust on the equipment, nowadays.

Salesperson: How many days are you short in most years?

Customer: Usually 3 to 4 weeks, I guess.

Salesperson: About a month? If I could show you a way to handle the same amount of business with two less people—and end up with better service, would you be interested?

Notice that this salesperson has successfully probed into an area of concern to the customer and then moved the conversation to the product. The questions were designed to encourage customer response and to identify a need that the salesperson could meet.

Generating Interest   As the interview progresses, the salesperson must move gradually from introductory, socially oriented conversation to the main subject of the sales call. To accomplish the sales call objective, the salesperson must generate the prospect's interest in the item that the seller has to offer.

Interest in a product or service is generated when the customer recognizes a need that the product or service can meet. When the customer is keenly aware of a need, the interest is correspondingly high. The customer may even request a sales call to discuss the need. This happens, for example, when a grain farmer who plans to expand a grain storage and handling system seeks to actively explore alternatives with a knowledgeable salesperson.

In other cases, the customer may lack awareness of a particular need. Here the interest step is much more complex and may involve an educational process. One nursery manager was unaware that the nursery's current pruning equipment and practices made their trees more susceptible to disease, and that new pruning equipment could reduce the incidence of the disease enough so that yields and profits would be increased.

Methods of generating interest include:

1.   Making reference to cost savings or to potential increase in profit

2.   Telling a story or anecdote about the product

3.   Sharing an experience that relates to the product or to the need

4.   Making a startling statement about the product's benefits

5.   Showing or demonstrating a beneficial feature of the product

6.   Stating openly what one believes the problem to be and why the customer may be interested in exploring possible solutions

The interest step is designed to direct the prospect's attention to a genuine need for the product, and to prepare that prospect for learning about the product itself. Interest building is a bridge to the main part of the sales call, the presentation.

The Presentation   The presentation is the very heart of the sales call. Its primary objective is to present the product or service so effectively that the customer will see it as satisfying a particular need. In many respects, the sales presentation can be likened to relating an interesting and convincing story, with the purpose of motivating the customer to a positive buying decision. Through it, the salesperson systematically presents important selling points or reasons for buying in such a way that they can be understood and accepted easily. Its proper use also encourages customer questions, and answers them in a manner that strengthens the message. The presentation may be highly technical and may require that the salesperson have a thorough understanding of the product and of all its features. In some cases, it may include helping customers to identify and understand their need more clearly as a prerequisite to accomplishing the sales-call objective. In any case, the presentation should be designed to help the customer respond favorably to the proposal.

The length and manner of the presentation depend greatly on a host of factors that relate to the customer, to the salesperson, and to the situation. The most effective presentations are tailored to the specific needs of the particular customer. In most areas of agribusiness selling the salesperson knows far more about the technical aspects of the product and its use than the customer wants or needs to know. Care should be taken not to give customers more information than they need to make their buying decision. Nor should the product be "oversold" through implications that it will perform better than it actually may. Customer discontent is related to expectation level. False expectations can lead to serious problems in the future.

As a general rule, the salesperson should strive for customer agreement on each selling point as the interview proceeds. That is, the salesperson should work toward getting the customer to believe and accept each piece of factual information as it is presented. This systematic acceptance of selling points leads logically to a positive buying decision on the part of the customer.

Although the presentation tends to be dominated by the salesperson, it should be far from a monologue. The more dialogue, the more successful the call is likely to be. The salesperson should use questions freely, and check to see whether there is customer agreement. He or she should also encourage customer questions because they reveal how far along in the buying process a customer is.

Throughout the sales interview, but particularly during the presentation, alert salespeople will heed customer clues when specific points spark keen interest. Areas of particular customer interest are known as *hot buttons*. Clues, such as a series of questions about some specific area or careful examination of some aspect of the product, may indicate areas of important concern to the customer.

When customers lean forward, move their eyes rapidly, or look interested, they are providing nonverbal clues that may pinpoint high interest areas. The effective salesperson capitalizes on these clues by adding detail at crucial points and by reemphasizing interest areas at summary points in the interview.

Features, Advantages, and Benefits The technique called *features, advantages, and benefits* is a systematic presentation of factual information about a product, given in such a way that customers can clearly recognize the potential gain from purchasing the product. This technique concentrates on the benefits that the customer will derive rather than on the physical characteristics of the product.

A *feature* is a descriptive, measurable fact about the product. Often features are technical, such as weight, density, shipping schedule, and billing procedures. An *advantage* is the direct physical or operating result of the feature. Advantages are the direct consequence of a feature, and are usually reflected in their impact on the operation. A *benefit* is an interpretation of what the advantage is likely to mean to a particular customer. It is often stated in terms of personal gains, and always in terms of value received by the customer.

Customers buy to get benefits; that is, they buy what the product can do for them. When a product is sold in terms of the value that the buyer may derive, the buyer's motivation for purchasing may be enhanced. A farmer does not simply buy seed corn. Farmers buy hybrid XP400, which will give them enough additional yield to finance a vacation trip with their families. It is foolhardy to assume that the customer is aware of the benefits, even though they may seem perfectly obvious to the salesperson. Each benefit should be carefully pointed out, or at least clearly implied, in terms that are crystal clear to the customer. It is no accident that most commercial advertisements show the customer happily enjoying the benefits gained from the purchase. An ad is likely to show a dealer proudly operating the new piece of equipment in one scene, and enjoying more leisure time with the family in the next.

The features, advantages, and benefits method of scoring selling points works best when it is integrated into the conversational tone of the presentation. Initially it may be helpful to use the following lead-in phrases: "Because of . . . (feature) you will be able to . . . (advantage), which means that . . . (benefit)." This general pattern can be expanded and adapted extensively to fit the circumstances, but basically it serves as a logical way of helping customers to understand what benefits they may expect (see Figure 15-2).

It is generally useful to make sure that the customer has accepted each benefit as it is explained. This conducts the customer to a logical buying conclusion. A salesperson will sometimes use a brief rhetorical question, such as "And that's important, isn't it?" The seller will then watch for some sign that the customer has accepted and internalized the point before moving ahead to other points. If any one point seems to

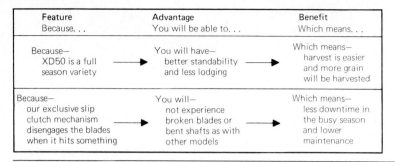

Feature Because. . .	Advantage You will be able to. . .	Benefit Which means. . .
Because— XD50 is a full season variety →	You will have— better standability and less lodging →	Which means— harvest is easier and more grain will be harvested
Because— our exclusive slip clutch mechanism disengages the blades → when it hits something	You will— not experience broken blades or → bent shafts as with other models	Which means— less downtime in the busy season and lower maintenance

Figure 15-2   The relationships among features, advantages, and benefits.

spark a particular interest or raise a question, the salesperson will reinforce or clarify the point before proceeding. Otherwise, confusion and/or resistance may creep in, which will make successive points more difficult to sell.

Skillful salespeople often refer back to an earlier moment in the sales interview when the importance of a particular point was established and agreed upon. Perhaps the customer had indicated a need or concern whose resolution is an obvious strong point of this product. This becomes a golden opportunity on which to capitalize tactfully. For example, early in the interview the alert salesperson may have extracted a customer comment about safety concerns resulting from the frequent use of inexperienced operators at harvest time. When the exclusive slip-clutch system is brought up, the salesperson can suggest, "Now this feature is a particularly important safety device for your operation, isn't it, Pete?"

Proof   Professional salespeople must be ready and willing to prove everything they say, even though that proof is usually not requested. If the salesperson's claims are questioned and cannot be supported, the salesperson quickly loses credibility. Subsequent points, which may be quite accurate, will be regarded as suspect by the customer.

Features can usually be proved easily because they are highly technical and measurable. Company manuals and brochures as well as invitations for personal inspection serve as proof of a feature's existence. Advantages may be supported by technical information, by personal observation, or simply by logical deductions. Benefits may be obvious and measurable, but they are usually not completely tangible. No matter how obvious the proof may seem, the customer may need to have it spelled out.

Proof is not only a means of supporting selling points as they occur in the presentation, it is also a highly valuable selling tool in itself. It provides a convincing way of driving home important sales points in dramatic ways that make lasting impressions on customers.

Demonstration is one of the most powerful forms of proof. There is nothing quite so convincing as seeing, feeling, tasting, hearing, and sensing the product or service in action. Experiencing is the most forceful kind of demonstration. It not only proves selling points but often just about sells a product. Getting the farmer into the driver's seat to operate the equipment on his or her own farm is a costly, but powerful, form of selling. Calculating the specific costs and benefits of owning and operating an on-farm feed mill is highly productive. A detailed proposal showing the profitability of changing bulk shipments can be very convincing. Of course, there is nothing more damaging as a demonstration that fails; therefore, demonstrations must be planned very carefully.

Illustrations are another form of convincing proof as well as being a useful selling tool. General models developed by the company support staff can vividly illustrate how a proposal can work.

Comparisons that are well documented and practical are also useful tools. The comparisons must be closely related to the customer's situation or they will lose impact.

Testimonials are used widely in agribusiness selling, particularly when the salesperson is selling directly to producers. Farm magazines are full of advertisements that draw heavily on the testimony of other producers. These ads simply relate other customers' experiences, and they are often effective and convincing.

Test results supplied by independent researchers or even by the company itself are useful forms of proof. Although manufacturer-sponsored tests are considered suspect by many customers, they can still be used to illustrate many points. Public and private performance tests of chemicals, seed varieties, and livestock breeding stock are widely used.

Company-supplied literature can be useful. This literature is particularly valuable for documenting a product's features. Engineering performance information can be detailed in a way that is usually quite acceptable to most customers.

Logical analysis is an effective form of proof that appeals to the minds of many customers. The method involves nothing more than a logical thought process derived from accepted facts to support the salesperson's claims.

Conviction *Conviction* is the customer's belief and decision that a product will be of benefit. It is the stage at which the customer has inwardly accepted the proposal as offered, and begins to think in terms of actually using the product. This belief may occur even though the customer has not yet verbalized a definite intention or made a commitment.

One effective technique for achieving conviction involves helping customers to see themselves actually using the product or service and gaining the benefits from that use. Gradually, as the customer comes to accept and internalize the ideas presented by the salesperson, the sale nears completion. Skillfully and subtly, the professional salesperson guides the customer through the conviction stage by wording questions carefully, clarifying ideas, and helping the customer to visualize reaping the benefits of the product:

> And that's what our full-service policy is about, Ms. Valdez. We know how many things you have to do in April, and we feel we can help you be more effective by custom-applying your fertilizer and chemicals, professionally and expertly. This would leave you free to concentrate on ground preparation, logistics, and careful planting. In a year like last year, that'd be a big help, wouldn't it?

It is important not to push too hard or too fast. The customer must come along at an individualized speed. Even when the benefits may seem perfectly obvious to the salesperson, pushing too aggressively can easily cause the customer to rebel. Once customers begin to feel pushed, resistance builds rapidly. If this occurs, the best tactic is usually to back off quickly before the customer's mind is made up. Then take a fresh approach, perhaps by getting the customer talking again.

Trial Close The trial close is a technique designed to find out whether the customer is ready to buy. It is a "trial balloon" to see at exactly what stage in the buying process the customer is. If the customer indicates that a decision to buy has been or is about to be reached, the salesperson will attempt to close the sale. If not, then the salesperson should continue the presentation. Essentially, the trial close sends out "feelers" that determine the next course of action.

Trial closes often appear in the form of questions. These questions fit neatly into the normal flow of conversation, but they yield important information about the customer's thinking processes. For example, salespeople will ask, "Well, what do you think of that plan?" "When could you stop by to see the demonstration?" "How much credit would you need?" "Which model would work best in your operation?" A positive response to any of these or similar questions would indicate that the customer has accepted the basic proposal and is well on the way to a positive buying decision. The next obvious step is to clarify final details and close the sale.

A trial close should be made whenever the customer gives a buying signal. *Buying signals* are verbal or visual clues that the customer has decided to buy the product. When a customer asks, "And what about the guarantee?" it is usually an indication of serious interest. When the customer leans forward and examines the label with obvious interest, attempt a trial close.

Another good time to try a trial close is immediately following the strong points of the presentation. If there have been several points, summarize them very briefly and make a trial close. Similarly, after a detailed plan or illustration has been presented, the salesperson should attempt a trial close. Whenever a question or objection has been raised and proof successfully supplied, the salesperson should use a trial close.

If the customer has been satisfied, the trial close may show readiness to complete the sale. If not, the salesperson will undoubtedly find himself or herself handling objections.

Objections An *objection* is the customer's negative reaction or expressed concern about the product or about any selling point that has been made. It constitutes a reason for not buying. If the customer's concern is legitimate, the salesperson must deal with it constructively in order to complete the sale. Because of their negative character, objections can upset the balance of inexperienced salespeople. But objections offer valuable insights into the customer's thought processes, and present crucial issues for completing the sale. Rather than meeting objections with fear and trembling, salespeople should view them as a challenge. Sometimes objections result from a simple misunderstanding, and the barrier can be broken down easily. At other times, the objection is really an excuse or "smoke screen" that is designed to hide the real reason for not buying. Most of the time, however, it is a legitimate concern that, if dispelled, may well result in a sale.

Experienced salespeople seldom hear new objections; most concerns have already been handled numerous times. This factor results in preparedness to deal with objections from a position of strength. Less experienced salespeople can counter by anticipating probable objections and preparing responses for each anticipated concern. Preparation and practice hold the key for most salespeople.

Objections may arise at any point in the sales interview, even at the very beginning. Generally, they should be dealt with immediately to prevent them from becoming barriers to accepting subsequent ideas. Only when the objection involves highly technical information that will be developed later in the interview should the discussion be postponed. Even in those cases, the objection should be acknowledged, and deferred until later in the presentation only with the customer's approval.

The objection that is suspected of being an excuse or smoke screen should be dealt with differently. Some customers may be reluctant to admit that money is a problem for them; thus they may ask to "think it over for a while." The first step is to check out excuses thoroughly to ensure their validity. Asking questions to clarify the objection is usually helpful. Sometimes the most appropriate course of action is to ignore the excuse as if it had never been heard. This approach may be particularly useful when the customer is simply delaying the decision for the third time, and a critical date is approaching. Another suggestion is simply to confront the customer with, "Mary, if we find a solution to that problem, can we complete this transaction?"

Handling Objections There are countless ways of handling objections, and no one method is best for all situations. However, there are several commonly used techniques that can be adapted to varying circumstances and people.

ASK QUESTIONS Customers' explanations of their objections may well disclose key issues in meeting the objections. Questioning creates extra time for the salesperson to decide how to deal with the objection. Even more importantly, questions start the customer talking, explaining more about individual needs and concerns, and providing more essential information. It is not uncommon for a customer to actually develop a solution to her or his own objection as the conversation proceeds. Frequently, customers convey additional information about the specifics of their situation as they answer the salesperson's questions. This information could be highly useful in the later stages of the selling process.

"Brian, why do you feel that our prices for your produce are not as high as those offered by other firms?"

"How many deliveries each week will you need to keep our product on your shelves, then?"

RESTATE AND CLARIFY One of the most effective techniques for handling objections is to simply reword the objection and feed it back to the customer. This ensures that the salesperson understands the objection correctly. It is surprising how often salespeople think they understand the nature of the objection when, in fact, they do not. Restating and clarifying removes the obstacle and embarrassment of dealing with the wrong objection. Additionally, this technique reassures the customer that he or she has communicated successfully with the salesperson. The customer is usually flattered to know that a pressing objection is being taken seriously. Like the method of asking questions, this technique often uncovers important information that is essential to the sale.

The professional agribusiness salesperson rewords an objection very carefully to capture the customer's true feeling because this may be the crucial dimension. Sometimes a judicious choice of words softens the objection slightly, thereby making it easier for the salesperson to handle.

And finally, restating and clarifying gives the agribusiness salesperson more time to determine exactly how the objection should be handled. This is particularly important for less experienced salespeople.

"You feel that hydraulic system isn't powerful enough to handle your situation. Is that right, Pat?"

"From the questions you raise, you seem to have concerns about how this variety withstands windstorms, right?"

BOOMERANG The boomerang technique cleverly "turns the tables" on a customer's objection. This reversal is accomplished when a salesperson first agrees with the objection, then alters the customer's point of view so that the objection becomes a positive selling point. The boomerang method is often used when the customer has misunderstood or misinterpreted the significance of some product feature. It does not involve disagreeing with the customer's conclusion, but agreeing with the customer's original statement and then showing how this seeming disadvantage actually works to the customer's benefit.

"Yes, John, that dual-switch system does take more time to disengage—and that's exactly why we designed it that way. The extra effort required helps prevent engaging the auger accidently. Will your son ever be helping you after school, John?"

"YES, BUT . . ." The "yes, but . . ." technique concedes that the customer has a valid point, but then goes on to reduce the significance of the negative factor in relation to other information. Psychologically, this technique has the advantage of not contradicting the customer directly, but at the same time placing the idea in its proper perspective. This method is very commonly used in conjunction with other techniques.

"Yes, it does come in only 1-gallon containers; however, this can become a real savings when it comes to returning unused and unopened product at the end of the season."
"You're right, our price is higher. But remember, our price includes delivery and no payment until June."

DENY Occasionally, it is necessary to directly deny an objection that a customer has raised. When a customer has based an objection on misinformation, the best approach may be to politely and tactfully, but firmly, declare that the information is incorrect. The salesperson must be ready to back up an opposing position, but the risk involved in frankly contradicting the customer may have a high payoff. When using this approach, it is imperative for the salesperson to help the customer save face by offering a possible reason for the misinformation or by suggesting that it is a common misconception.

"Tony, a lot of people seem to be under the impression that parts are hard to get, but that just isn't so. Our centrally located parts depot, coupled with our unique express handling system, means *any* part can be in your hands in less than 12 hours."

ACCEPT Occasionally, a customer will raise an objection that is quite valid and cannot be countered in any reasonable way. In this case, simply agree that the customer has a valid point, leave it to the customer to evaluate, and move on to the next point. The best way to regain momentum is to make sure that the customer has enough information to put the objection into proper perspective. Do not dwell too long on the issue, lest the extra attention lend the issue undue importance.

"Yes, that's right, Jim. But as with anything, you must weigh the pluses and minuses to see what is best for you."

IGNORE Simply pretend that the objection was never voiced. This technique should be used *only* when the objection was clearly not intended seriously. When objections are made in jest, they can be either laughed off or ignored. But needless to say, any serious objection should never be ignored.

If a customer cannot afford or does not need the product after having been given a reasonable opportunity to buy it, these objections must be accepted. A salesperson only wastes valuable time by concentrating too long on a single customer.

The Close If objections have been handled successfully, the salesperson is ready to close the sale. The *close* is the act of securing a commitment from the customer. A successful close accomplishes the sales-call objective. In many cases, this means a signed order or a verbal commitment to buy, but it may be simply a customer agreement to do something specific. In any case, a successful close provides tangible evidence of accomplishment.

Closing is very difficult for a great many salespeople. Basically, it involves nothing more than asking for the order or for some form of commitment. Yet many professional salespeople find this step quite uncomfortable and are often less than effective in executing it. For some, the fear of being refused invokes reluctance. Others fail to recognize the importance of a formal effort to close, assuming that closing will somehow take care of itself. Still others lack skills in closing techniques. But among the most important reasons for agribusiness salespeople is a cultural value system that makes it very difficult to ask anyone for anything, and especially to ask anyone to buy something. This common taboo against asking for money may seem illogical, but for many agribusiness salespeople it is a difficult personal barrier to overcome.

A confident attitude is critical to closing successfully. The salesperson who sounds apologetic or unconvinced often conveys negative signals that destroy much of what has been built up in the presentation. The close should not be treated as a joke but as serious business. The salesperson should act positively to convey the impression that completing the sale is the only logical next step.

WHEN TO CLOSE There is no one time at which a close should be attempted. The alert salesperson is *always* ready to close. It is not necessary to wait until all the sales points have been covered thoroughly. The professional salesperson always maintains sufficient flexibility to close whenever the customer is ready, even though all the prepared material may not have been covered.

Certainly, an appropriate time to attempt to close is immediately following an obvious buying signal from the customer, or after a positive response to a closing feeler. Good judgment is required to ascertain the right time to attempt a close. And good judgment comes from experience.

CLOSING METHODS   There are five well-known techniques for closing.

1.   *Direct close*   The direct close is the most straightforward and obvious method. Simply ask for the order.

"OK, may I go ahead and send in the order?" This close is commonly used by agribusiness salespeople when the sales call has been very candid and positive throughout. It is also appropriate when there is a clearly defined relationship in which it is presumed that the salesperson will continue to service that account. This closing method simply verifies the continuation of that assumption, but wisely does not take the account for granted.

2.   *Summary close*   The summary close is also popular among agribusiness salespeople. Used most often when the presentation has been long or complicated, it summarizes the major selling points and then asks for the order or for some other commitment. The summary close concentrates mostly on the anticipated benefits. It subtly takes advantage of the agreement that has been reached on each major selling point, and suggests that completion of the sale as the logical consequence of all the selling points. Often these selling points are summarized in sequence so that the customer can also visualize them as the close progresses.

"OK, Elsa, now let's take stock of what we've said.

"First, we showed how the early-order program locks in lower prices.

"Then we calculated an interest savings of . . . .

"Now, it seems clear that this is a program designed to fill your needs. Can we get it started today?"

3.   *Choice close*   The choice close offers the customer a choice between something and something, not something and nothing. It assumes that the customer is buying, and offers no obvious alternative. The choice close is a powerful close, particularly when some sales resistance has been dealt with satisfactorily.

"Would you like to begin with 500 or 1000 pounds?"

"Should I have them ship the full inventory line, or should we begin with only the limited line?"

The less experienced salesperson may initially feel that the choice close is manipulative or too aggressive, and so may be reluctant to use it. Yet when the customer has responded favorably to the presentation and to the salesperson's handling of objections, the choice close fits smoothly into the flow of conversation and is often quite effective.

4. *Assume close*   The assume close never asks for the order, but assumes that the customer has already made a positive buying decision and propels the customer toward enacting that decision. It is used primarily when little sales resistance has been encountered and the salesperson believes that the customer has responded favorably to the proposal. Although there are many forms of the assume close, each features a statement implying the positive buying decision, then initiates the process of finalizing the purchase.

The aggressiveness of the assume close is awkward for some agribusiness salespeople, who feel that it pushes the customer too fast. Its success depends on its application to appropriate circumstances. Most professional salespeople can easily tell whether the customer has found solid agreement at each step. When the relationship is good, the assume close is a natural extension of the presentation.

The routine assumption: "OK, then you'll stop by Monday to sign the papers."

The command assumption: "Then you need special starter 33A. I'll get that out tomorrow."

The dramatized assumption: "Bob, you'll be pleased with this new sprayer. The time you'll save in flushing the tank alone will make it well worth the money."

Each of these assumptions would normally accompany, or be immediately followed by, the next formal step in finalizing the sale, perhaps completing the order sheet. If no resistance is encountered, complete the step. If resistance or discomfort becomes apparent, then deal with it as a type of objection.

5.   *Special-feature close*   The special feature close describes some special feature of the product that has not been previously described. It is appropriate only when not all the selling points have been covered in the presentation. Some points may have been reserved to be used as a special incentive at this point. This technique is often used when there have been many objections and something more is needed at the end to help the customer finalize the decision.

The *inducement* is a special feature that is available to everyone who purchases now. It offers an extra incentive for immediate purchase.

"And the reason I'm calling on you now is that August is a special bonus month. You get one free with five when you order in August."

The *concession* is something extra for a specific customer. Care should be taken in using concessions, since legally the same "deal" must be available to all customers. It is not necessary to publicize the deal, but the deal must be available to other customers should they request it. Often, the concession takes the form of a special service by the salesperson.

"And if you decide today, I can just drop the merchandise by here tomorrow on my way home."

The *last chance* emphasizes the fact that the opportunity will not be available if it is not accepted within a certain time period. This may sound like a threat if it is not handled properly. Yet, factually stating the terms of a sale is a useful closing technique.

"Myron, this price list is effective only through Friday. We already have word that a 7 percent increase is coming. I'd sure like to get your fall order in today."

When the Objective Is Accomplished   After the sales-call objective has been accomplished, finish any necessary mechanics, compliment the customer on the buying decision, thank the customer for his or her business, make sure that the customer knows what to expect next and when to expect it, and leave quickly. There is usually little good to be accomplished from remaining for any length of time: lingering too long presents an opportunity for the customer to change the decision.

When the Answer Is "No"   Sometimes, perhaps often, the customer may refuse to become committed to the proposal, even after a good sales presentation. When this occurs, try not to push so hard that the customer refuses to reconsider the proposal at a later time. If possible, get an invitation to call again sometime. In agribusiness selling, it often takes many calls for a sale to be completed. Even when the sales presentation has not been effective, be sure to thank the customer for taking time with you; then leave graciously.

The Follow-up
In almost every type of agribusiness selling, the follow-up after the formal sale makes the big difference in long-term successful selling. The *follow*-up includes all the customer's experiences with the company or product after the sale has been made. It embraces delivery, billing, collecting, using, servicing, and maintaining the product. Since most agribusiness selling occurs in a tightly knit community or market area, and since it concentrates heavily on repeat business, servicing the account is critical to successful selling. In most areas of agribusiness selling, considerably more time and effort is expended in servicing the account than in the formal sales presentation.

In most companies, the majority of the postselling functions, such as delivery, billing, and maintenance, are the direct responsibility of someone other than the salesperson. Yet to the customer, the salesperson is the person responsible because the salesperson is the one who is most visible. If anything goes wrong, it will be the salesperson who will ultimately suffer the greatest penalty in terms of difficult or impossible future sales. Although this may not seem fair, it is a fact of life that the salesperson must accept working responsibility for the way in which the company services a customer. The professional salesperson recognizes and accepts this responsibility by acting as a liaison between the customer and the company. It is of great importance to long-term success for the customer to feel taken care of.

The servicing of the customer actually begins with the sales call itself. Customers should understand completely what will happen next and when it will occur. The old adage that all discontent is relative to expectation is certainly true for the relationship of the customer and salesperson after the sale is completed. The salesperson should make absolutely sure that the customer knows when to expect delivery and billing, and what the terms of payment will be. It is also a good idea to reassure the customer that the salesperson is willing and anxious to handle any questions or problems that might arise.

One effective technique for promoting customer satisfaction is to recheck the situation directly after the projected delivery date by revisiting the customer. This is often a critical time period. The salesperson is in a position to deal with the problem of late shipments. Confusion about merchandise and its use can be clarified at this time. Generally, an indication of concern gets things off to a good start. This call-back is most critical for newer customers, for sales of highly technical products, or for unusually large sales.

Billing and collections procedures often present critical difficulties. In a great many agribusinesses, the total billing process is the responsibility of a central office. The salesperson does not become involved in the situation unless a problem surfaces. When a problem with collection does occur, it usually places the salesperson in an uncomfortable position. Yet there is a great deal of truth to the statement that "A sale isn't complete until the money is collected." Many companies make the salesperson who made the sale responsible for initial collection efforts on problem accounts. Only a very small percentage of accounts become problems, but those few accounts can develop into uncomfortable situations. Most collection problems can be avoided by fostering the customer's understanding of the credit policy at the time of the sale, and by working closely with the company credit manager in the initial extension of credit. Those problem situations that do arise require the utmost in tact on the part of the salesperson. The objective is to make the collection without alienating or losing the customer.

Servicing the account can mean a great many things, depending on the nature of the product or service involved. However, it is usually valuable to make a brief call on larger accounts during or just after the peak use period, to confirm the customer's satisfaction with the product. If there is any dissatisfaction, it is imperative for the salesperson to know it. Often dissatisfaction results from some misunderstanding that can be corrected easily if caught at this time. If customers are unhappy, it is far better for them to complain to the salesperson than to other customers.

This call makes a very good impression on the customer by establishing that the salesperson really cares how the customer is doing. It sets the stage for continued sales.

CONCLUSION

The challenge of the sales process depends both on the endless variety of products or services and on the unique characteristics of the customer, the salesperson, and the situation. Yet the basic principles of selling can be applied to agribusiness selling in a way that capitalizes on the unique characteristics of the agricultural environment. Professional agribusiness selling offers a strong base for those entering the agribusiness management profession. Those who choose to pursue a career as a professional agribusiness salesperson will also find it a rewarding challenge.

SUMMARY

Professional selling is a highly individual process. Each salesperson, each customer, and each situation is unique. Yet selling is a process that can be learned by applying certain principles. Professionals then use these special selling skills in a variety of circumstances to improve the probability of sales.

Preparation is the first technique or step. Agrisalespeople must be knowledgeable about their product, the prospect, and the market. They therefore spend time prospecting for and qualifying new customers and planning a sales-call strategy that will improve their chances for success.

The first few minutes of the sales call are often the most critical because they set the tone for the entire interview. During this period the salesperson must build rapport, ask questions to learn more about the customer, and arouse interest in the product. There are various techniques that can be utilized, each of which can be productive, depending on the circumstances.

Making the presentation itself is often thought to be the core of the sales call, but it can be done well only if the planning and opening have been well executed. In the presentation, the salesperson describes the features, advantages, and benefits of the product, makes demonstrations, and offers proof where necessary. This is a conversational period during which the salesperson attempts to instill conviction in the customer. Sometimes the customer may raise objections (reasons for not buying) that must be dealt with. When the customer is satisfied, the sale will be closed.

The days, weeks, or months following the sale are also a critical part of the sales process. In this follow-up period, the customer should be serviced to ensure satisfaction, thereby hopefully creating the possibility of future sales.

The sales process is a logical approach to discovering customer needs and convincing customers that the product or service offered can meet those needs. Each salesperson approaches the problem differently, but the same principles are helpful to every professional salesperson.

DISCUSSION QUESTIONS

1. Why is it a good idea to write out the sales-call objective and sales-call strategy as part of the preparation for important sales calls?

2. List the various methods of prospecting. Which is likely to be most effective in selling nursery supplies to landscapers, nursery owners, greenhouses, and orchards? Why?

3. Describe both a positive and a negative experience you or someone in your family has had with the service provided after a purchase. What are the implications of each of these situations, and what is the potential for future sales?

4. Select an agricultural product, preferably a supply product that you are familiar with.

(a) Spell out at least three features and corresponding advantages and benefits.

(b) Suggest what type of proof might be used appropriately in a sales call for this product.

(c) List at least three objections that you might anticipate from a customer, and suggest how each could be handled.

(d) What types of closes would be appropriate and would make you feel comfortable in a sales call with this product? Why do you feel that these approaches might work?

CASE PROBLEM

Frank Bradley was just bringing the last of his herd into the holding shed for the evening milking as Dianne Cooper drove past on her way home. "Boy, I sure would like to have Frank's business," she thought. "Selling Frank feed for his 60-cow herd would really help us get the sales increase we need."

The next day she asked her father about Frank's dairy operation. Her father knew Frank, but had never dealt with him, except for some occasional animal health product business. Dianne had learned that Frank had used G & H Feeds for the last several years.

"Old Frank is really quite a guy, and one of the best dairymen in this area, some say," her father told her. "I understand he's an officer in the DHIA and still works with the 4-H club. I think his daughter showed the champion 2-year-old at the fair last year."

According to Dianne's father, Mrs. Bradley was the most outgoing member of the family and was fairly assertive. He also thought she had a strong voice in many of the farm decisions.

Dianne knew Frank's son, Jim, slightly. They had gone to different high schools, but had gone to many of the same parties. Jim was still living at home and helped out on the farm, but was working full-time at the PCA (Product Credit Association).

"Oh, by the way, Dianne," her father said, "I just heard that Bud Peters over at G & H Feeds is retiring before long. Bud has always worked closely with Frank. Maybe this is a good time to talk to Frank about doing some business with us."

Dianne agreed. She knew it was an important opportunity and she should at least plan it carefully. But she was not quite sure how to start.

QUESTIONS

1. Develop a sales-call objective for Dianne's first call on Frank Bradley. (Be realistic; it is not likely that Dianne can land his business in one call.)

2. Map out a strategic plan for Dianne's first sales call.
   (a) Suggest how she should make contact with Frank.
   (b) Lay out an approach that she could use on her first contact.
   (c) Suggest how she might develop rapport on the first call.
   (d) What questions should she use to learn more about Frank's needs?
   (e) How can she get Frank interested in doing business with her?

3. What additional information would be helpful for her in preparing her initial sales call?

IV

OPERATING
THE AGRIBUSINESS

OBJECTIVES

• Evolve a sense of production management; give its background and definition

• Describe the features of analysis, synthesis, extraction, and fabrication

• Differentiate between intermittent and continuous production

• Discuss the special problems encountered by handlers of agricultural products

• Envision production as a total system

• Summarize the components involved in a plant-location decision

• Identify the factors that are considerations in determining the size of a plant

• Differentiate between process and product layouts

• Describe common methods of dealing with materials-handling problems

• Risk management in the agribusiness

Purchasing in the agribusiness is an important factor affecting profits.
A. Ordering supplies
B. Purchasing raw materials

EVERYTHING IS WORTH WHAT ITS
PURCHASER WILL PAY.

16

PRODUCTION PLANNING IN THE AGRIBUSINESS

A

B

BACKGROUND

The industrial revolution that originated in the England of the 1750s is known throughout Western civilization as the means by which the production of goods was stepped up to a feverish pitch. What is less well known is the fact that it took a century, and a man an ocean away, to tame and manage that feverish production through systematic study of its processes. His name was Frederick W. Taylor, and he is often viewed as "the father of scientific management."

Taylor and His Followers

Born in Pennsylvania in 1856, Frederick Taylor understood the pitfalls of production well; he had been a laborer, an engineer, and an individualist whose habit of excelling at his work set him apart from his co-workers. In the haphazard factory environment of his time, workers often dictated their own production procedures and were entitled to keep their methods secret. None of this made for efficiency of production.

Taylor attacked the chaos head on with his "scientific," or analytical, approach. Among other things, he favored:

1. A standardized set of procedures for the same job each time it is performed

2. Determination of the most efficient procedures for each job through scientific comparison tests

3. Careful screening, hiring, and training of workers to match them with the most appropriate jobs

4. A functional division of labor that would allow each person to perform the most suitable task in the production process, with management and workers jointly devising the best system for division of labor

Taylor's followers applied his approach to an even wider field. Henry L. Gantt was best known for devising and implementing scientific wage-incentive plans, and for introducing bar-chart analysis as a means of controlling manufacturing and scheduling work. Frank B. and Lillian M. Gilbreth pioneered the field of time and motion study by breaking down activities into smaller, manageable parts and by analyzing the components of fatigue. In one way or another, all of these people were engaged in the scientific study of work processes, and all made a contribution to what is now known as production management.

DEFINITION

Production can be described as the set of procedures and activities that result in the creation of a product or service. If this is so, then it is not too difficult to envision *production management* in a general way as the complex network of decisions that support the production process. In the early days of production-management studies, factories were the main beneficiaries of advancements in knowledge and techniques. Today, we have begun to recognize that all agencies producing a product or service, including supermarkets, warehouses, and offices, can benefit from careful production planning and management. The upshot is that in a wide variety of businesses, the principles of production management have been incorporated into the interactions of labor, materials, and machines; cost and quality controls; and the design and location of facilities. In agribusinesses, production-management principles have proved useful in improving methods of collecting, sorting and grading, processing and manufacturing, and packaging and shipping agricultural products. All these activities take place within the framework of one of four production processes (see Figure 16-1).

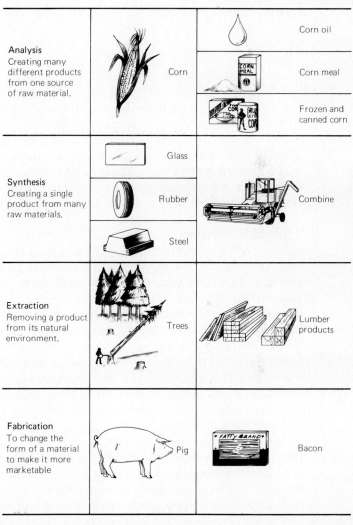

Figure 16-1   Processes of analysis, synthesis, extraction, and fabrication.

Analysis
Creating many different products from one source of raw material.

Corn — Corn oil, Corn meal, Frozen and canned corn

Synthesis
Creating a single product from many raw materials.

Glass, Rubber, Steel — Combine

Extraction
Removing a product from its natural environment.

Trees — Lumber products

Fabrication
To change the form of a material to make it more marketable

Pig — Bacon

Production Processes

The process of *analysis* involves creating many different products from one source of raw material. Depending on how it is processed and packaged, corn can appear on the consumer's table fresh, frozen, in a can, as oil, or in cereal. Agribusinesses that depend on one raw material for the making of many products may find it practical to locate their facilities nearer to the source of raw material than to the ultimate market. As shall be seen, the factors involved in such a decision include not only cost but the perishability and bulkiness of the raw material.

Synthesis is the exact opposite of analysis; by its use a single product is constituted from a variety of raw materials. Since these raw materials may come from an assortment of different locations, sometimes at great distances from each other, firms engaged in synthetic processes often locate near their ultimate market site for the sake of convenience. In this way, when the raw materials are assembled, processed, and packaged as one product, they can be shipped to market at minimal cost.

Two other kinds of production processes deserve mention in passing; one relates to natural resources, the other to a change in form. *Extraction* occurs when a product is extracted from a natural setting, as when trees are felled for lumber or food flavorings are derived from the leaves, fruits, nuts, or flowers of wild plants.

Fabrication, on the other hand, deals not with natural forms but with the change in form of some basic material to make it more marketable. Hogs and cattle are butchered, cut up, processed, and packaged to appeal to the consumer as various cuts of meat.

Sometimes two production processes occur simultaneously; thus, as hogs are transformed into hot dogs, pork chops, sausages, etc., they are simultaneously undergoing both analytic and fabricating processes.

Types of Production

All production processes form part of a total production network. That total network may be one of two types, continuous or intermittent, depending upon the continuity of the production.

Continuous In *continuous* production, inputs flow in an uninterrupted way through a standardized system to produce outputs that are basically the same. Continuous-flow agricultural-chemical companies, canning plants that use assembly-line techniques, and agribusiness office workers who process standard forms are engaged in continuous production. Since variations in the process are minimal and creativity is not a major factor, continuous production is usually felt to be a relatively simple and undemanding operation.

Intermittent *Intermittent* production can best be described as a process that involves variable outputs, variable procedures, and often variable inputs as well. A dairy-processor producing cheese, butter, ice cream, and various other dairy products will be engaged in many different sequences and activities to provide such a variety of products. Flexibility will be required in the use of machinery, placement of workers, and transportation links, both from agricultural producers and to wholesalers. There is no one flow of inputs through a streamlined funneling system with a single purpose; instead, the diversity of the operation makes for intricate problems in location, transportation, storage, and scheduling.

Agricultural Production: Special Problems

Some of the problems inherent in the production of agricultural products have already been hinted at: perishability and bulkiness, for example. Both these factors have widespread implications in the choice of plant location, method of transportation, and scheduling. Other factors are involved too, such as the seasonality of products and variations in quality, quantity, or value.

The farm supply industries are engaged in highly seasonal production processes. During the peak season, facilities are often strained to the utmost to produce the services and products farmers need to consume within a very short time. While the manufacture of farm supplies is scheduled as evenly as possible throughout the year to maximize efficiency, lack of sufficient storage to accommodate peak season needs places tremendous pressure on production facilities as they struggle to keep up.

In some cases, seasonality is related to problems of perishability. It is no secret that fruits and vegetables are highly perishable and must be processed quickly to prevent spoilage. At the same time, some of these products are so highly seasonal that processors, canners, freezers, and packers are left with virtually idle facilities after a peak season in which they rush to handle the perishable items. Some industries have evolved ingenious and successful ways of counteracting this dual problem; the tomato industry is one. It has been found that storing tomatoes in aseptic, nonrefrigerated, stainless steel vats effectively eliminates problems of deterioration. Operations that produce tomato products are now able to run consistently for 12 months without fear of spoilage, thus reducing costs during the peak season and increasing productivity in the off-season. Fresh tomatoes can now be shipped across the country in aseptic railroad cars, which produces a significant savings in transportation costs.

Variability in quality and quantity is another plague of the agricultural industry. Processors, canners, and freezers of lobster and shrimp, for example, must weigh and differentiate among fish of unequal quality. Eggs and milk must be graded, as are many other products. In some cases, product weights must be standardized to fit certain-size packages or selling weights; this can sometimes produce waste.

Yet another problem typical of agricultural products is bulkiness; the costs for shipping bulky bags of oranges from Florida to the Pacific Northwest can be astronomical. Such costs are reflected in the final price to the consumer, which, if it is too high, may reduce demand for the product and, therefore, sales. Handlers must also wrestle with the physical problems of storing bulky products as they await processing or shipping; as with most problems, this difficulty, too, is reflected in costs.

A final difficulty experienced in the production of agricultural products is variation in value. Price efficiency demands that production managers manufacture outputs with the highest possible value consistent with the costs of production. A dairy-processor may find that cheese has a higher market value than milk for table consumption; but if its value is only one-third more than that of milk, and it requires twice the production cost, then price efficiency tends to favor producing the milk. Because there is such a wide variety of value in agricultural products (in different cuts of beef, for example), this is an important area for agribusinesses to explore.

PLANNING PRODUCTION

As in other management areas, production management requires careful planning. Among the issues involved are the location of facilities, plant size, layout, purchasing, inventory, and production control. All these issues are part of a total systems overview.

Production as a Total System

No area of management is immune to the *systems* concept, whereby the manager is compelled to view the area under control (in this case production) as a total, interrelated, and interacting system. Every decision related to a production issue has a kind of domino effect on the remaining factors of production. When John Rubin, manager of production for the A & J Soup Company, decided to increase production by one-third, he found that labor costs, plant operating costs, and inventory were all affected. An agribusiness manager who is able to predict all the possible effects on production variables from changing one variable is successfully employing the systems outlook. The three parts of this system, location, size, and layout of facilities, will be covered in the remainder of this chapter. Purchasing, inventory, and controls for schedules and quality will be dealt with in Chapter 17.

Location When agribusiness managers choose a site for their facilities, they generally consider four interrelated issues: (1) their source of raw materials or supplies; (2) labor availability; (3) location of markets; and (4) special incentives offered in different areas.

SOURCE OF MATERIALS As has already been indicated, agribusinesses may wish to locate close to their source of raw materials if the business basically requires only one raw-material input and that material is costly to ship in its raw state. Since cattle would be bulky and costly to ship from Iowa to New York, they are usually slaughtered near their source and shipped long-distance in the more manageable form of boxed beef. In other cases, agribusinesses require so many different raw materials from locations at such great distances from one another that it is not practical to locate near the source of any one material.

LABOR AVAILABILITY   Different sections of the country offer different kinds of labor. A white-collar suburb is not a good place to locate an assembly-line canning factory, nor is an urban ghetto the best place for an agribusiness's executive offices. In addition, some areas require higher wages and benefit incentives for workers because they are expensive areas in which to live; the entire textile industry located in the South to lower its labor costs. In other areas employers may expect high rates of productivity and little absenteeism or turnover. Unions are stronger in some parts of the country than in others; locating in these areas may result in costly strikes and wage increases. Finally, agricultural companies that require a great deal of research may find it advantageous to locate near a large land-grant university. All these factors must be taken into consideration in choosing a location.

LOCATION OF MARKETS   In cases in which the necessary raw materials are numerous or easy to ship in their raw state, locating near a market may give an agribusiness an advantage. Proximity to markets is especially important to retailers, since customers will not travel long distances to buy from a retailer.

SPECIAL INCENTIVES   Agricultural industries that require large amounts of water or power must locate in areas where such supplies are plentiful. Certain areas will even offer special tax, zoning, and water-power incentives to businesses locating there. Community taxes on sewer, garbage, and utility uses; state and local income taxes; real estate taxes; and other kinds of taxes must all be considered. A locality that is anxious to attract agribusinesses will have to offer a number of lucrative incentives.

Size of Plant   No matter what the location, optimal plant size becomes an important dimension of the agribusiness. In many ways, larger units are easier to operate, but too large a plant can be a costly "white elephant" for an agribusiness due to a combination of factors.

ECONOMICS OF SIZE   According to the economies-of-scale principle, larger plants usually result in a lower cost per output unit. However, several smaller plants might offer more flexibility in terms of proximity to sources of raw materials or to market destination, which in turn would result in lower transportation costs. Other factors help to determine the true economic value of a large plant operation.

SEASONALITY AND PATTERNS OF PRODUCTION   As already noted, a highly seasonal agricultural product can produce some special headaches for a production manager. A plant that is large enough to handle peak productivity levels becomes a costly operation when output levels are significantly reduced. In such cases, it may actually be more economical to run several smaller plants and to close down operations that are not needed during the off-season. This does not reduce the drain of costs associated with an unused facility, but it does limit expenditures for the day-to-day running of a totally unnecessary part of the operation.

IMPACT OF INFLATION Agribusinesses committing themselves to large, expensive operations must consider the spiraling rate of inflation in the past several years and the likelihood that costs will increase significantly over the next few years. In addition, the amount of capital available today will decrease in buying power fairly quickly. This prediction is not intended to discourage expansion and growth, but rather to encourage in-depth, realistic financial assessment.

QUANTITY OF OUTPUT NEEDED One of the most important determinants of plant size is the quantity of output required. An agribusiness that is able to sell millions of units of output on a steady basis is not likely to invest in small plant facilities. At the same time, managers must consider long-range factors and be able to predict continued demand at that high level to justify the long-term investment of funds in a mammoth facility.

MULTIPLE VS. SINGLE SHIFTS An alternative to the maximum-capacity facility, if the labor is available, is the multiple shift. Theoretically, it is possible to produce twice as much in a plant with double shifts, while limiting the need for space by spreading out the working hours. However, agribusiness managers must consider all the factors before jumping to this conclusion. Research indicates that night-shift workers tend to be less productive and less alert than day-shift workers, for the simple reason that the human body does not operate at peak efficiency at night. Some agricultural-chemical companies by their very nature may be involved in ongoing operations that require multiple shifts; but in plants where this is not the issue, managers must evaluate carefully the costs of a larger facility versus the costs of increased, less productive, and possibly more accident-prone labor.

Layout When planning the physical layout of a plant, consideration must be given to all the processes and procedures that the plant is engaged in, their quantity and quality requirements, and any future changes in product kind, quality, or demand. All this must be accounted for within the framework of the most cost-efficient design. There are two basic categories of layout.

PROCESS LAYOUT A *process* layout arranges activities by function. Thus, in a process layout, regardless of the product being created or assembled, all like functions are grouped in the same place—that is, canning equipment with canning equipment, inspectors with inspectors, etc. Process layout is related to intermittent production, since each function is capable of handling different facets of a variety of products (see Figure 16-2).

PRODUCT LAYOUT *Product* layout is geared specifically to the continuous production process because it produces one product at a time, step by step, with one function following another in sequence as the product

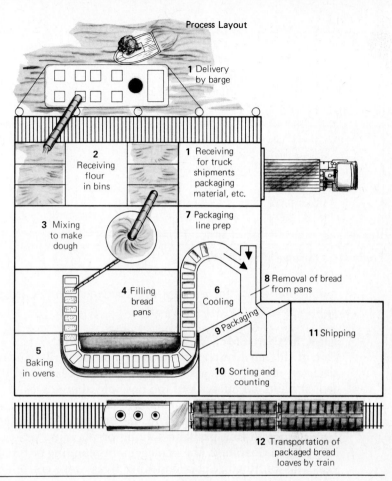

1 Delivery by barge

2 Receiving flour in bins

1 Receiving for truck shipments packaging material, etc.

3 Mixing to make dough

7 Packaging line prep

4 Filling bread pans

6 Cooling

8 Removal of bread from pans

5 Baking in ovens

9 Packaging

11 Shipping

10 Sorting and counting

12 Transportation of packaged bread loaves by train

Figure 16-2   Example of a process layout.

is assembled, and with few variations in product (see Figure 16-3). Workers grading and packing peaches on a conveyor belt, for example, are operating within the framework of a product layout. One person may remove debris, the next may be responsible for sorting, while another oversees packing into crates, and so forth.

MATERIALS-HANDLING PROBLEMS The materials-handling problems experienced by a plant vary according to whether the layout is process or product oriented. The main idea with process layouts is to allow for flexibility, since products will not follow any one unvarying sequence. This requirement is generally met by means of cranes, mobile trucks, and tractor trains for heavy loads. Skids, pallets, and forklift trucks are used for rapid movement of less weighty loads.

With product layouts, communication and transportation between points on the production line must be direct and effective. Conveyor belts are often felt to accomplish this objective, though other arrange-

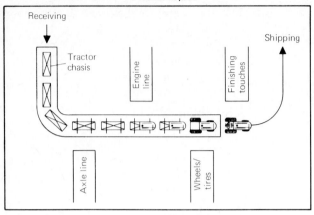

Product Layout

Receiving

Shipping

Tractor chasis

Engine line

Finishing touches

Axle line

Wheels/ tires

Figure 16-3   Example of a product layout.

ments that allow for a direct flow between points are possible. Gravity chutes are yet another possibility.

RISK MANAGEMENT IN THE AGRIBUSINESS

One of the most important functions of the agribusiness manager in the decision-making process is the careful delineation of the specific problem at hand, an analysis of the possible alternatives, a listing of the criteria involved in selecting a specific course of action, and then selection of the best possible solution to the problem. In various sections of the text, guides to this problem-solving or planning process have been developed. In Chapter 2, the management planning or problem-solving process was outlined. Goals and objectives were considered important to proper agribusiness decision making.

More specific analytical techniques for management decision making were presented in Chapter 5. Here the marginal analysis techniques for problem solving were presented. It was noted that managers first need to consider what question they are trying to answer: how much to produce, how much variable input to use, or what enterprises the firm should enter into. If the correct question is asked and data are available, the solution to the problem is fairly straightforward.

Additional quantitative problem-solving techniques were presented in Chapter 10. Volume-cost or breakeven analysis is one of the most useful management tools available today. It is critical that managers know the cost structure under which they must operate. Utilizing this management tool allows the decision maker to determine the level of sales necessary to cover all costs or to reach a specific profit goal. However, the most important use of breakeven analysis is in the solution of "what if" questions. In other words, how much more must the firm sell if variable costs increase 2 percent? Or, alternatively, what is the impact on breakeven if the firm cuts its selling price for a particular product?

These problem-solving tools make the assumption of operation under certainty. This means that under any problem circumstances, the manager is able to specifically delineate all possible actions and the outcomes of all of these individual actions. Today this is rarely the case. Actually managers must make important agribusiness decisions under conditions of risk or uncertainty. Let us develop an example and compare and contrast decision making under certainty, risk, and uncertainty.

Suppose that your firm has outlined three possible plant expansions, called actions A1, A2, and A3. In the planning process the production and marketing teams within the firm have established profit goals for each action in each of three different "economic environments." These economic environments are defined as E1, expansion; E2, stable growth; and E3, recession. You then develop a matrix, as outlined below, that fits the pieces of the decision-making process together. On the left side of this matrix are the three specific actions that management could take, and on the top of the matrix the specific environments are listed.

ECONOMIC ENVIRONMENT

		E1	E2	E3
A	A1	12	6	1
C				
T				
I	A2	8	10	−1
O				
N				
S	A3	4	3	7

The figures within the matrix represent profits from each of the courses of action under each economic environment. If the firm is operating under certainty and is a profit-maximizing firm, the course of action is easy to select. Under certainty the firm is able to "look down the road" and identify the economic environment that will prevail at the time the action must be selected. Thus, if a period of expansion E1 will occur in the future, action A1 would be selected. This results in the highest payoff (profit) under the given economic environment, 12. Alternatively, if stable or recessionary times will be present in the future, actions A2 and A3, respectively, would be selected since they provide the highest payoff.

The example presented is oversimplified but gets to the point of decision making. Very rarely do managers know exactly the state of the environment for the future. Only in the very short run can conditions closely resembling certainty prevail. Decision making under certainty is basically a problem of allocating resources to their highest return.

Risk and Uncertainty

A more typical case for the agribusiness manager would involve the same matrix as above, but with the manager only able to establish some reasonable probabilities regarding each economic environment. Now the manager is operating under conditions of risk. This assumption is much more relevant to much of the decision making that managers perform today. Decision making under conditions of risk assumes that each action leads to a set of specific outcomes (the payoffs) and that the probability of each outcome is known.

Now the manager must attach probabilities to each economic environment to calculate an "expected payoff" for each course of action. A profit-maximizing manager will then select the highest expected payoff.

Probabilities of each economic environment occurring may be developed from historical data, from "expert" opinion, or from a combination of the two. Assume that the following probabilities have been developed for the payoff matrix presented previously:

ECONOMIC ENVIRONMENT	PROBABILITY
E1	.40
E2	.25
E3	.35

Note that there must be a 100 percent probability that one of the three economic environments will occur. Once the probabilities have been established, the manager must calculate the expected values for each of the possible courses of action.

Thus, the expected value for action A1 would be calculated as follows:

$$E(A1) = .40(12) + .25(6) + .35(1) = 6.65$$

Likewise,

$$E(A2) = .40(8) + .25(10) + .35(-1) = 5.35$$

and

$$E(A3) = .40(4) + .25(3) + .35(7) = 4.80$$

Given the payoffs developed in the matrix for certainty and the probabilities developed for the different economic environments, the manager would select course of action A1. This is the strategy that would maximize the expected payoff. Further analysis may be necessary if two expected payoffs are very close in value. Then the manager may want to look at the variation of the individual payoffs and attempt to select the course of action that minimizes the variation of the payoff.

Decision making under uncertainty involves one further complication. Here one or more of the possible courses of action results in outcomes whose probability is not known. Obviously decision making under uncertainty is extremely subjective, but some decision-making plans may help the manager select the best possible action.

Four basic alternatives have been developed to guide managers in planning under uncertainty. These alternatives are:

1. Wald—the maximin strategy
2. Hurwicz—the alpha strategy
3. Savage—the minimax regret strategy
4. LaPlace or Bayesian—equal probability strategy

Which strategy one should select depends on how optimistic or pessimistic the management outlook is and how conservative or liberal the management philosophy may be within the particular agribusiness firm. Each of these strategies is outlined below.

Wald The Wald strategy is often called the most pessimistic of the strategies that deal with uncertainty. It is a very conservative decision-making strategy that tends to allow the firm to maximize security while assuming that the worst possible scenario will always happen.

The decision-making rule in calculating expected payoffs for the Wald strategy is simple. First, determine the worst outcome of each of the individual courses of action, then pick the action which yields the best possible worst outcome. Thus, the Wald strategy is called the maximin strategy because it selects the maximum of the minimum payoffs from each individual course of action.

In reviewing the matrix we have developed previously, the Wald strategy would select as follows:

	E1	E2	E3	WORST POSSIBLE
A1	12	6	1	1
A2	8	10	−1	−1
A3	4	3	7	3

Course of action A3 would be selected because it provides the highest payoff if the worst possible result happens. As one can imagine, this is a very conservative strategy and tends to select the action that may best be suited for firms that cannot afford to take chances.

Hurwicz The Hurwicz or alpha criterion strategy takes a different view of the decision-making process under uncertainty. The decision maker is asked to select a *coefficient of optimism* that applies to the maximum payoff for each course of action and a *coefficient of pessimism* that is tied to the minimum payoff for each action. Again, decision making utilizing this strategy is very subjective. Obviously, managers who are very optimistic will select courses of action that vary dramatically from those chosen by managers who are more fiscally conservative.

A weighted average of the high and low payoffs for each action is calculated, and the selection is based upon the highest weighted average. Imposing the Hurwicz criterion on our payoff matrix would result in the following:

Assume that the coefficient of optimism is .6
Thus, the coefficient of pessimism is .4

A1 = .6(12) + .4(1) = 7.6
A2 = .6(10) + .4(−1) = 5.4
A3 = .6(7) + .4(3) = 5.4

Action A1 would be selected because it has the highest weighted average payoff.

Savage The Savage criterion establishes a "regret" criterion which encompasses the idea of opportunity costs. A regret is defined as the absolute difference between a specific action's payoff and the highest payoff available given the particular economic environment. After calculating the maximum regret for each course of action, the manager should select the course of action that produces the smallest maximum regret.

Again returning to our payoff matrix, we would perform the following calculations:

	E1	E2	E3	REGRET MATRIX E1	E2	E3	MAXIMUM REGRET
A1	12	6	1	0	4	6	6
A2	8	10	−1	4	0	8	8
A3	4	3	7	8	7	0	8

The regret matrix is calculated from each column of the payoff matrix. Thus, given economic environment E1, action A1 is the highest payoff course of action. Actions A2 and A3 must be evaluated relative to the best possible action. The differences between the payoffs for A2 and A1 and those for A3 and A1 within the same economic environment E1 represent opportunity costs. If, given E1, A1 is selected, there is no opportunity cost. The best action has been selected. However, if A2 is selected given E1, then an opportunity cost of 4 is borne by the firm. The regret matrix is calculated in this fashion.

Given the payoff and regret matrix of opportunity costs as outlined above, the Savage criterion would select action A1 in an attempt to minimize risk for the firm. This strategy may work best in long-run decision making or project evaluation, where the economic environment under which the firm operates can be expected to change dramatically.

Bayesian or LaPlace The final strategy for dealing with uncertainty actually shifts the problem to one of dealing with risk. The Bayesian strategy assumes that the probabilities of each economic environment are equal. Like the Savage criterion, this strategy is probably more useful for long-run economic decisions and less likely to give the best strategic decisions in the short run. For example, suppose that there are five assumed economic possibilities: depression, recession, stable growth, moderate growth, and substantial inflation. Under the Bayesian strategy, each of these states of the economy would be given an equal probability. In the short run, if the economy is in a moderate recession, there is in all likelihood very little probability that it will change to a high-inflation economy. Thus, in the short run it is not logical to assume equal probabilities for all economic environments.

Once the Bayesian strategy has been selected as the most likely for the problem at hand, the calculation and selection of the optimal action is rather straightforward. If we return to our example one more time:

$$E(A1) = .33(12) + .33(6) + .33(1) = 6.33$$
$$E(A2) = .33(8) + .33(10) + .33(-1) = 5.67$$
$$E(A3) = .33(4) + .33(3) + .33(7) = 4.67$$

Each of the economic environments is assigned a probability of .33. The expected payoff for each of the actions is calculated using a method similar to that used to calculate payoffs under risk. In our case, action A1 would be selected, since it results in the highest expected payoff.

Decision Making Utilizing Risk and Uncertainty

These quantitative decision criteria are presented to illustrate the methods that have been developed for dealing head-on with the problems of risk and uncertainty. Historical data regarding outcomes are relatively crucial to decision making under risk. Based on these data, the manager is able to develop some forecast for the probability of occurrence and tie these probabilities to the expected payoff results.

Under uncertainty, the manager is faced with a much more complicated task. Basically, the manager must disregard any probabilities and realize that data that will allow computation of these probabilities are not available. An alternative approach, which in some cases is acceptable, is to simply assume that all probabilities are equal.

The primary purpose of including this section is to note for the student that decision making in the real world is, in most cases, a relatively complicated task when done properly. On the other hand, the new employee who sees the boss consider a complex problem and make a decision immediately must consider that experience is often a good guide in the decision-making process. The experienced manager may not go through the rigors of calculating payoff matrices for various actions, but does in some implicit fashion attach probabilities to some subjective judgment regarding the level of risk the firm is willing to take or give some implicit value to the degree of optimism concerning the future.

Decision making is a very dynamic process. The more tools you have to help guide you in making important management decisions, the better off you, and your firm, will be.

SUMMARY

Production management involves a complex network of decisions that affect the production process. Four kinds of production processes (analysis, synthesis, extraction, and fabrication) relate to the number and kind of raw materials, or number and kind of end products. Production may be either intermittent or continuous, depending on whether it is handled by function to produce variable outputs or handled as a continuous, step-by-step process to produce very similar outputs. Production of agricultural products is hampered by severe problems of seasonality, perishability, bulkiness, and variations in quantity, quality, or value. Production involves planning, and must be viewed as a total system involving location, size, and layout of plant; purchasing; inventory control; and production controls. There are several categories that affect each of these decisions, and agribusiness managers are urged to consider all factors and their effect on the total system before making a decision.

Risk management is an important consideration in many agribusiness decisions today. In making many capital expenditure decisions, managers must consider the many different economic climates possible in the long run. Four alternatives for dealing with risk and uncertainty were presented: Wald, Hurwicz, Savage, and LaPlace or Bayesian. The strategy one selects depends upon how optimistic or pessimistic the management team must be in making the decision.

DISCUSSION QUESTIONS
1. How do you view the agribusiness production manager's role? How does this role relate to the systems approach?

2. Why is Frederick Taylor called "the father of scientific management"?

3. Give examples of agricultural products that undergo the processes of analysis, synthesis, extraction, and fabrication.

4. What is the difference between intermittent and continuous production? How does this difference affect choice of layout?

5. In your view, what are the most serious problems posed by the special nature of agricultural products? Can you think of ways in which agricultural products may actually present advantages to the production manager?

6. What factors are involved in choice of plant location? Name some agribusiness companies whose locations reflect consideration of these factors.

7. How is the optimal size for an agribusiness plant determined?

8. How would you solve materials-handling problems in a process layout? In a product layout?

9. How would you select one of the criteria available to evaluate risk and uncertainty in the agribusiness? Explain.

OBJECTIVES

- Describe the bases for efficient purchasing decisions

- Explain the importance of inventory control

- Identify the different kinds of inventory, and pinpoint their relationship to the order-point concept

- Summarize the features of the two main inventory tracking systems

- Differentiate between PERT and CPM scheduling methods

- Explain the importance of quality control

Efficient operations require constant monitoring of production schedules, costs, and product quality.

A. Meat inspection
B. Cotton processing efficiency
C. Feed-mill production scheduling

PRODUCTION IS NOT THE APPLICATION OF TOOLS TO MATERIALS, BUT LOGIC TO WORK.————Peter Drucker, *Drucker: The Man Who Invented the Corporate Society*, John J. Tarrant, Warner Books, Inc., New York, 1977.

17

CONTROLLING PRODUCTION PROCESSES IN THE AGRIBUSINESS

A

B

C

PLANNING GIVES WAY TO CONTROL

As has been seen, the total agribusiness production system involves planning such factors as plant location, size of plant, and layout. Once the (hopefully) ideal plans have been made a reality and facilities are in operation, production managers are faced with a different task: controlling the processes that are underway. Controls must be set on purchasing, inventory, scheduling, and quality.

Purchasing

An agribusiness's purchasing is of three kinds: products for further processing, products to be resold, or products to be used directly in the products. If net profits in the agribusiness are 5 percent of sales, then a 1 percent reduction in purchasing costs will fall through to the bottom line, increasing profits by 20 percent over their previous level. This astounding figure illustrates the relationship between costs of production and the firm's ultimate profits. "Cost efficiency" is more than a banner to wave; it is a factor directly involved in the profits for which the business exists.

Efficient Purchasing Cost-efficient purchasing involves five interrelated factors: quantity, quality, price, time, and service.

QUANTITY Purchasing agents are under an obligation to consider a variety of bids and negotiate for large pruchases. The most lucrative of these bids or negotiations will undoubtedly offer the agribusiness substantial savings for buying in quantity. However, the situation is not that simple; if shipments are not delivered on schedule or cannot be stored adequately, for example, the net result may not be savings but an increase in cost.

QUALITY Quality is another factor that purchasers must consider. If a canned-fruit factory requires a particular kind of vat to retard spoilage, substitution of a similar product that is cheaper but less effective will not result in an ultimate cost savings. Errors in the quality of materials purchased can be avoided through the use of detailed *specifications* that will enable the purchaser to compare product quality in a competitive-bid situation.

PRICE Price is a significant factor in purchasing decisions, and, as we have seen, it is closely related to such considerations as quantity of order and quality of material. Both these considerations must be examined before the purchaser can decide which offer is the lowest price for acceptable goods, particularly since minor differences in specifications may not make much difference in effectiveness, but may have a great effect on cost.

TIME While buying in quantity may offer agribusinesses significant savings, usually those savings are not free. The manager must not forget that large quantities of goods are seldom used immediately, and that there are costs associated with storing them. Carrying costs, including storage space, recordkeeping expenses, taxes, insurance, and interest lost on capital tied up in inventory, can eat up as much as 35 percent of the inventory's purchase value. If this is the case, whatever savings are gained through buying in quantity may be lost, and it may even turn out to be more costly to buy in bulk. Agribusinesses must be certain that whatever goods they purchase will be used in a reasonable period of time. At the same time, enough must be purchased so that agribusinesses will not miss sales opportunities for lack of finished goods.

SERVICE Another factor in the choice of supplier is the kind of service that each provides. A supplier who underbids all competitors but delivers materials so late that the production process is held up may wind up costing the agribusiness more than the saving would warrant. One alternative is to purchase one-half the necessary materials from one supplier and one-half from another, so that a delay on the part of one of the suppliers would only affect delivery of one-half the goods needed.

A Word about Purchasing Departments As is implied in the foregoing section, efficient purchasing requires people who are knowledgeable in dealing with suppliers, accepting bids, and handling purchase negotiations. A purchasing department or agent with experience will get to know which suppliers offer dependable service, quality goods, and decent quantity discounts. It is the purchasing department that measures the savings of a particular bulk-buying deal against the carrying costs of inventory and stock, rate of turnover, and availability of facilities. These complex and delicate issues are best handled by specialists; therefore, an agribusiness that has attained even moderate size should consider hiring specialists to handle the purchasing function. Just as cost savings can be tremendous in the hands of an expert, so loss of savings opportunity can be at least as great in the hands of a novice.

Ethics of Purchasing The purchasing agent for an agribusiness has an obligation to exert his or her best efforts to secure the highest quality materials at the lowest possible cost. At the same time, it must be recognized that the purchasing agent is placed in a potentially difficult situation. Suppliers who wish to secure an agribusiness's account may not rely exclusively on fair and ethical methods of competition. It is a sad fact of human nature that in some competitive circumstances, suppliers will attempt to bribe individuals who perform the purchasing function. Purchasing agents may be offered payola in return for information on competitors' bids or a granting of contract. Purchasing agents who encounter this situation should remember that their firms have placed them in a position of trust. To the extent that the individual's future is tied to the success of the agribusiness, it is to an employee's advantage to make the best possible deal for the agribusiness and to always deal fairly and honestly in handling purchasing functions.

Relationship between Financing and Purchasing The relationship between financing and purchasing can be summed up in two words: cash flow. The amount of capital invested in the agribusiness's inventory must be enough to purchase and store all necessary materials (to handle sales demand comfortably) and still have a steady cash flow. It is not unknown for an agribusiness to tie up as much as 25 percent of its capital in inventory, which can result in cash-flow problems if it is not carefully budgeted and planned for.

Controlling Inventory

Purchasing and inventory control are closely related. As was indicated in the previous section, huge stores of purchased materials can tie up much-needed capital in storage and carrying costs. Agribusiness production managers attempt to keep their inventory counts current and accurate, so that they can alert the purchasing department when more stores are needed and so that they can decipher trends in turnover. Several kinds of inventory control enable them to do this.

The Order-Point Concept Rita Macready is vice president in charge of production for a farm supply manufacturing company located in Indiana. Though the firm manufactures several farm supply products, one of its most profitable items is garden tillers. Rita's company sells garden tillers at an average rate of twenty-five per week. When the warehouse stock of garden tillers reaches a certain, agreed-upon level of depletion, called the *order point*, Mike Torres, the warehouse manager, sends Rita an order for more. The total process takes 2 weeks (3 days for Mike to handle the appropriate paperwork and have it delivered to the factory, and 1.5 weeks for the order to be filled, sent, and received at the warehouse). The amount of stock that Mike has on hand when he reaches that critical order point depends on the kind of inventory being used.

PIPELINE INVENTORIES *Pipeline inventories* are the minimum amount of inventory needed to cover the period of time between the warehouse's reordering and its receipt of the additional stock, or *lead time*. Since the average demand for garden tillers is twenty-five per week, and it takes Mike 2 weeks to receive the order, he will need at least fifty garden tillers in stock to avoid depletion and lost sales during the lead time.

CYCLE OR LOT-SIZE INVENTORIES Despite the fact that Mike and Rita's lead time is 2 weeks, it is not necessary for Mike to issue an order every 2 weeks. For example, suppose that each truck were capable of loading and delivering 100 garden tillers. In the pipeline inventory system, this would mean that a truck delivering every 2 weeks would go from factory to warehouse half-empty. Rather than use this costly method of operation, and go through twice as much paperwork, Mike would probably order 100 garden tillers every 4 weeks. Since cycle inventories may be considerably larger than pipeline inventories, it goes without saying that employment of this method is subject to constraints of space.

BUFFER INVENTORIES We have been assuming that Mike and Rita are dealing with rock-steady weekly demands, invariable lead times, and

OPERATING THE AGRIBUSINESS

standard truck capacities. In the real world of agribusiness enterprise, this is never the case. Demand varies from week to week, as does the length of time it takes to get an order filled. These differences are taken into account by *buffer* inventories, which provide additional stock to offset potential variations.

SEASONAL INVENTORIES   As explained in Chapter 16, agribusiness products are often highly seasonal. Mike and Rita might sell as many as 200 garden tillers a week in peak season, or as few as two during the off-season. Rita has the choice of planning for much higher labor costs at peak season or for costly storage of extra garden-tillers in off-season. Both these risks can be avoided by seasonal inventories. Under this system, storage space is provided for products whose demand is not constant so that more are available during peak seasons.

Forecasting and Trends   All the foregoing discussions of inventory have presupposed one vital factor: knowledge of demand. The *demand forecast* is the hinge on which everything revolves: what raw materials and equipment to buy, the size of storage facilities, scheduling of labor and materials, and even the basic design of the plant. Forecasts are generally made within the framework of three time spans: immediate, medium-range, and long-range. To be effective, they should take into account not only trends of past performance in the agribusiness but also general economic and consumer-preference trends.

Tracking Inventory   Keeping track of inventory is usually accomplished by means of one of two methods, perpetual or periodic. Though periodic inventories are far more common in agribusiness, they are often used in combination with perpetual systems.

PERPETUAL   *Perpetual* inventory is exactly what its name indicates, a running account of stock on hand. Whenever sales are made or inventories are replenished, the total amount is subtracted from or added to the previous inventory total. Usually, a count of inventories to be received is also kept, to eliminate the dangers of overordering. The advantage of this system is that the inventory count is always current. The disadvantage is that it requires a cumbersome amount of recordkeeping, and it is not completely reliable if employees forget to add to or subtract from the total.

PERIODIC   *Periodic* inventory is an actual physical count of stock on hand, conducted at regular intervals of, say, 6 months. Often the agribusiness is closed for a day or more to enable employees to conduct this count. This kind of inventory has the disadvantage that, taken by itself, it leaves the day-to-day status of the inventory in doubt. It may also require the periodic closing of the business. However, recordkeeping is minimized. Also, once taken, the periodic inventory tends to be more reliable than a perpetual accounting. Many agribusinesses use the periodic inventory for scrupulous accuracy, but keep an informal count of the inventory supply on a day-to-day basis to prevent potentially disastrous out-of-stock conditions.

Controlling Production

Control of production flow and quality are two of the most important daily functions of the production manager.

Scheduling Methods   The scheduling methods that an agribusiness uses depend upon its size and complexity of operation. A small firm will have a relatively straightforward method of scheduling. Among the larger operations, however, some of the so-called "network models" have caught on. Two of the most famous of these are PERT and CPM.

PERT   The PERT (program evaluation review technique) model was developed by the U.S. Navy to schedule operations on the massive Polaris missile project. It is estimated that PERT saved the Navy 2 years of work on that project, and production managers for large companies have been using this sophisticated technique ever since.

PERT involves a diagrammatic representation of the network of activities in which an operation is engaged (see Figure 17-1). The circled letters represent way stations where activities have reached some kind of completion or culmination point. The heavy lines in between represent the activities themselves, which are of a certain estimated duration. Broken lines represent what has come to be called *slack time*, or places where the schedule can give a little without endangering performance of the next activity. The paths from the beginning to the end of the sequence that are set in heavy lines are called *critical paths*, or paths that have absolutely no slack time. With all this information in hand, agribusiness managers can determine the least amount of time it will take to complete a project, the greatest amount of time needed (the critical path), and the slack-time options that are available. PERT is a way of

Figure 17-1   Diagram of the PERT scheduling method. Heavy lines represent critical paths; broken lines are slack times.

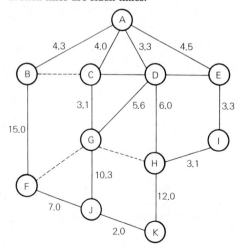

schematizing the relationships among interdependent scheduling variables, and determining which steps in the process must be given preference in order to complete the project.

CPM   E. I. du Pont de Nemours & Co. developed the CPM (critical path method) of scheduling at about the same time that the U.S. Navy developed PERT. As the name indicates, CPM networks bear similarities to those of PERT. The main differences are in diagraming: activities occur in the circles, with arrows pointing from activity to activity.

PROBABILISTIC NETWORKS   Both PERT and CPM are basically *probabilistic networks*, which is to say that the estimated duration of each activity is not standard from network to network, but determined in each case by probability. The probable activity time is determined by averaging the most optimistic, most pessimistic, and most likely durations for the activity. Thus, if Rita Macready thinks that it is most likely to take 1.5 weeks to deliver garden tillers to the warehouse, but 2 weeks at the outside, with a possibility of 1 week if all goes well, she is going to estimate 1.5 weeks, the average of the three figures, as the most probable time for delivery.

Quality Control   Quality controls are of two kinds: control of inputs and control of outputs. Control of inputs has already been discussed under the topic of purchasing. Just a word here about quality control for outputs: it does the production manager absolutely no good to be cost efficient and profit conscious all along the line, only to lose money when it is discovered that an entire line of goods is defective in some way. The key here is to inspect at least periodic samples to ensure quality, adherence to customer needs, and a low rate of return on merchandise. This kind of spot-checking can also catch major errors before they are repeated throughout a series of goods.

SUMMARY

Agribusiness production managers who wish to maintain control of their operations will have to forecast trends; order purchases that are in line with these trends; control the amount of inventory on hand to see that it is neither too much, which is costly, nor too little, which can result in lost sales opportunities; and employ sophisticated scheduling methods and quality controls. Purchasing is an operation that requires skill, knowledge, and honesty in dealing with bids and negotiations from suppliers. Such factors as quantity, quality, price, time, and service are elements of efficient purchasing. The amount of inventory and kind of inventory systems used depend upon an agribusiness's size, complexity, and management sophistication; PERT and CPM are two highly sophisticated network scheduling models. Managers must periodically inspect outputs to ensure quality and adherence to specifications.

The manager who is able to exercise control over these facets of production will have a tightly run operation that stands a good chance of maximizing profits.

DISCUSSION QUESTIONS

1. What are the components of efficient purchasing, and how do they interface with one another?

2. Why is inventory control important?

3. Explain the order-point concept and the different inventory systems that support it.

4. What are the advantages and disadvantages of perpetual inventory? Periodic inventory? In your opinion, which is better for a large, nationally owned agribusiness?

5. Describe the difference between the PERT and CPM methods. Do you feel they can be applied to small, locally owned agribusinesses? Why or why not?

6. What are the advantages of quality control for an agribusiness's outputs?

V

HUMAN RESOURCE
MANAGEMENT IN AGRIBUSINESS

OBJECTIVES

• Explain the interrelationship between managing personnel functions and managing employee motivation in agribusiness

• List the nine functions of personnel management in agribusiness

• Differentiate between job specification and job description sheets

• Describe methods of recruitment and of selecting an employee in agribusiness

• Follow the major steps of job orientation in an agribusiness

• Identify the factors that determine compensation and fringe benefits

• Summarize the purposes, pitfalls, and benefits of performance appraisal in agribusiness

• Describe the purpose and kinds of training programs in agribusiness

• Select valid criteria for promotion in agribusiness

• Explain the purpose and format for an exit interview

• Develop a brief history of labor unions, and identify the basic conflict between unions and management in agribusiness

Agribusiness managers must determine the proper organizational structure and control, motivate, and guide employees.
A. Directing and motivating personnel
B. Organizational chart

THE TASK IS NOT TO MAKE THE POOR WEALTHY, BUT PRODUCTIVE———Peter Drucker, Quoted in John J. Tarrant, *Drucker: The Man Who Invented the Corporate Society.* New York, Warner Books, Inc., 1977.

18

PERSONNEL MANAGEMENT

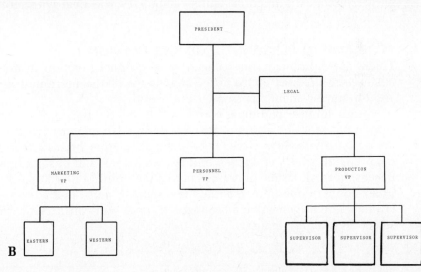

B

THE FORGOTTEN ASSET

If agribusiness managers were to be asked to name their firm's assets, most would list their land, equipment, trucks, cash, and the like. Too often the forgotten element is the most important asset any business has—its people. No matter what the physical and financial assets of a firm, it is the way people use those assets that determines the firm's success or failure. Because some managers fail to view employees as an asset, they are unwilling to invest time and money in the personnel function; to such managers, personnel management is simply a routine matter of filling positions and keeping them filled. Firms that embody this attitude never reach their full potential, no matter how much managers spend to develop their firm's talents and resources and refine the tools and methods for producing a product or service. In the final analysis, most agribusinesses offer services and products that do not differ significantly from those offered by other companies. The telling difference between any two firms is the people who staff them.

In many ways, paperwork and physical work are easier than "people work." People cannot be run through a computer or lined neatly on a piece of paper. Each one is a unique human being with individual needs, feelings, and emotions. This makes the personnel-management function complex and difficult, but mastering it can yield a high dividend in productivity and financial success. Careful planning and attention to personnel matters are essential to achieving a high level of productivity.

The Scope of Personnel Management

Basically, personnel management can be divided into two separate but closely related areas: (1) managing the functions, and (2) managing employee motivation. In other words, the mechanics of personnel and the fine points of motivating people to contribute up to their maximum potential are interdependent. If the person and the job are not matched, motivation is not likely to occur. The emphasis in this chapter will be on personnel as a function, while Chapter 19 will deal with motivating employees.

PROBLEMS IN PERSONNEL ADMINISTRATION

Three major problem areas plague the personnel function in most agribusinesses: the size of the firm, knowledge of the personnel function, and top management's personnel philosophy.

Sometimes, particularly in small firms, the personnel function is carried out more by accident than by design. No matter what the size of the agribusiness, jobs have to be defined, people hired, governmental requirements met, employees trained, wages set, and customers served. Because a small agribusiness usually cannot afford to hire qualified full-time people to handle personnel management, personnel administration is often left to general management to deal with on a crisis basis or, sometimes, totally ignore.

There is no absolute size of firm, in terms of numbers of employees or sales volume, that dictates when a full-time person should be designated to handle personnel management. The kind of agribusiness, its complexity, the diversity of its jobs, and its degree of seasonality are all factors. A rough rule of thumb is that once an agribusiness has reached 75 to 100 full-time employees, management should examine its need for a full-time qualified personnel administrator. Another helpful guide is that a full-time personnel department can be profitable when 1 percent or less of total wages will support that department's budget.

One might examine a relatively small agribusiness to determine its options in handling the personnel function. For example, the Calhoun County Farmers' Elevator is rather typical. Ralph and Betty Ames own the facility as partners. They purchased the business from their parents, who recently retired and moved to Florida. They sell and spread fertilizer and agricultural chemicals; handle feed, some tools, seeds, and veterinary supplies; have grinding and mixing facilities; and store, buy, and sell grain. Counting themselves, they have nineteen full-time employees, and they employ six to eight part-time employees during the busy season. In addition, the bookkeeper comes in every day for 4 hours. While the business has grown somewhat, the number of employees has remained relatively constant because of some new equipment that has been added.

Until recently, the labor force had been stable, and the Ameses felt that they had no personnel problems. Yet in the last year, the following events have occurred: an employee lost an arm in an accident; the workers' compensation insurance rate increased; the firm has been cited for over a dozen violations of safety laws; and both partners have been forced to spend several days driving trucks, running the mill, and the like. Because of the accident in which an employee lost an arm, Ralph had to cancel a trip to Europe that he and his wife had planned for 3 years. While five employees have been with the organization for over 10 years, the records show that last year twenty-four new people were hired. The elevator employees have no fringe benefits other than those required by law. Ralph and Betty agree that only the less desirable have applied for jobs lately.

Calhoun County Farmers' Elevator has no program or written personnel policy. A rudimentary form is used as a job application. Applicants are interviewed and hired by whichever partner is there. There are no definite, set qualifications, and job functions are not described on paper. Training and orientation often consist of "You go out and help Ralph in the mill." Because expenses are high, the wage policy consists of "pay as little as you can." Except for a token raise each year for everybody, raises are generally given only when a person wants to resign, and at that point it is often too late.

Larger firms are often guilty of having personnel programs nearly as haphazard as those of the Calhoun County Farmers' Elevator. Sheer size forces a more fully developed program, but such a program can be almost as ineffective when poorly run. One well-known, relatively large agribusiness with over 2000 employees provides a good example. The personnel director was promoted to his job some 15 years ago, primarily because he had been a troublesome labor union steward. He has had no formal personnel training, and, more importantly, has never tried to learn more about his job in any organized way. Top management is responsible for the situation because its philosophy and attitude rank the personnel function as relatively unimportant. "Find the bodies" and "pay them as little as possible" are the two primary personnel objectives. In this firm, the personnel director is not regarded as top management, and is not included in the important planning and policy-making processes. In fact, the warehouse superintendent and maintenance supervisor have far more influence than the personnel director. Labor productivity is down, turnover and absenteeism are high, grievances increase, strikes are anticipated, and top management wonders why.

Things must change in both these firms, or they will lose business to competitors. Personnel problems have a way of affecting productivity, costs, and, ultimately, profits. Both these firms evidence the major problems (size, managerial philosophy and attitude, and skill and knowledgeability of the personnel staff) found in managing human resources. In this chapter the personnel function is traced and ways to help the agribusiness manager maximize the returns from the human resource investment are suggested.

THE FUNCTIONS OF PERSONNEL MANAGEMENT

The steps by which personnel management finds the right people for the right jobs and provides for their continued productivity and development are:

1. Determining the firm's personnel needs

2. Finding and recruiting people

3. Hiring or selecting people

4. Orienting people to their jobs

5. Setting terms of compensation and fringe benefits

6. Evaluating performance

7. Overseeing training and development

8. Providing for promotions

9. Handling termination or transfer

Literally thousands of people enter the job market each month. Some of them have never worked before, while others have had long years of experience and training. Each of these prospective employees has the potential for performing a lifetime's service as a loyal, stable, productive employee, and the same potential for being a dissatisfied, unhappy, unproductive employee. The agribusiness manager's challenge is to tap the hidden resources of each new employee, a process that begins with the evaluation of the firm's personnel needs.

Defining the Jobs to Be Done

This first step in personnel management is the one most often missed by those courageous enough to accept the perilous responsibility of managing people. The reason why this step is neglected is that, practically speaking, it does not seem absolutely necessary. One can hire people without knowing specifically what job they are supposed to do, or why or how they are supposed to do it. Some managers tend to "shoot first" and then "hang up the target." The challenge of defining the job rests on a sound, well-developed organizational plan (see Chapter 19). Every position should have job goals that contribute to the firm's success.

The job should be defined by means of two approaches: (1) job specifications, and (2) job descriptions.

Job Specifications   A *job specification* sheet spells out the qualifications needed to perform a job satisfactorily. One such sheet should be developed for each job, regardless of the size or kind of agribusiness. In the Calhoun County Farmers' Elevator, one of the partners or some other person, perhaps the office manager, should be put in charge of the personnel function. Delegation of this responsibility to one person will help free top management from crises that occur because of inadequate personnel programs. The person to whom the personnel responsibility is delegated can develop a job specification sheet that uses the following format:

1. The purpose of the job—its goals, and the activities necessary to their accomplishment

2. The kind of job—its supervision, training, responsibilities; whether it is a dead-end job, or one offering growth and promotion

3. The requirements of the job—educational level, experience, special skills, physical strength or condition, emotional or personality factors, and so forth

4. Any special ways to determine the applicant's ability to do the job—testing, past work history, and the like

Every manager may want someone who is simultaneously as creative as Edison, as intelligent as Einstein, and as wise as Solomon, but such perfect people just do not exist. Qualifications that are set too high can be just as bad as those that are set too low. For this reason, job specifications should reflect the actual needs of the job. Generally speaking, a series of concise statements will suffice for a job specification. The person who supervises the job in question can often provide a wealth of information and help to the personnel administrator. If the agribusiness manager cannot inventory the requirements of a job, it may be wiser to leave it unfilled, since the manager will never know whether or not it is being done well. Exhibit 18-1 can be a helpful guide to agribusiness managers as they develop the job specifications or inventory the job.

Job Descriptions   At the same time that job specifications are being developed, a job description should also be formulated. A *job description* stresses a job's activities and duties, and, as with a job specification, the immediate supervisor of the job in question is the best source of information about what activities are important to the job.

The format of a job description is simple (see Exhibit 18-2):

1.   A brief summary paragraph of the job and the goals it is intended to accomplish

2.   A list of the duties, responsibilities, and attendant authority

3.   A statement defining lines of authority

4.   An indication of how and when job performance and standards will be evaluated

EXHIBIT Example of Job Specification
18-1

CALHOUN COUNTY FARMERS' ELEVATOR: Job Specification

JOB: MILLHAND

---

1.   Purpose of job: *To service customers' needs in unloading grain, mixing and loading feed, and filling customers' orders.*

2.   Responsibilities: *To direct and assist farmers in unloading grain rapidly and efficiently, to operate feed-mixing equipment, to load mixed and bag feed; to maintain clean and safe conditions at all times; and to service customers promptly and courteously.*

3.   Requirements:
     Education   —*High school diploma*
     Experience   —*Farm background or 1 year elevator experience*
     Physical   —*Good health and free from dust allergies*
     Personality   —*Must be friendly and outgoing*

4.   Opportunities: *This position provides necessary experience to move into management as mill supervisor and eventually into sales or general management.*

5.   Special Considerations: *Any applicant must be willing to work in dirty conditions and to work as many as 4 to 6 hours overtime in harvest season.*

CALHOUN COUNTY FARMERS' ELEVATOR: Job Description
JOB: Millhand

BRIEF DESCRIPTION
The primary responsibility of the millhand is to assist customers in unloading
grain, grinding and mixing feed to customer specifications, bagging or loading
feed onto trucks, and filling customer orders for premixed feeds and animal
health products. The job will require overtime hours during harvest season. The
millhand has a great deal of customer contact and is responsible for providing
friendly, efficient service to farmers.
DUTIES AND RESPONSIBILITIES

1. Unload grain

2. Grind and mix feed to customer specifications as per work order

3. Load feed

4. Fill customer orders as per work order

5. Maintain clean and orderly conditions in stock room at all times

6. Sweep and clean all work areas daily

7. Maintain and enforce all safety regulations at all times

8. Take inventory of products weekly

9. Perform routine maintenance of mixing equipment as scheduled

10. Maintain helpful, friendly attitude with customers at all times

SUPERVISION
Millhands report to and receive instruction from the mill supervisor. The
supervisor will have authority and responsibility for all activities in the
elevator. Suggestions or complaints should be made through the supervisor.
EVALUATION
Performance of millhands will be evaluated semiannually on the anniversary
date of their employment. This evaluation will be completed by the immediate
supervisor, initialed by the general manager, and discussed with the millhand.
This evaluation will establish strengths and areas of needed improvement by
the millhand. It will serve as the basis for wage increases and promotions.

While the specifications of the job description should be exact
enough to provide guidance for the employee and the supervisor, they
should also be flexible enough to allow for special situations, emergencies, or changes.

It seems almost unnecessary to say that finding the right person
for the job requires a careful appraisal of the qualities needed by the
person filling the job, and of the duties to be performed and responsibilities to be assumed. Yet the management of many agribusiness firms,
large and small, pays little if any attention to these two important aspects of the personnel process.

Finding or Recruiting Employees

Prospective employees can be secured from many sources. The qualifications for the job, its wage or salary, the kind and size of organization, and the location of the agribusiness will play an important part in finding employees.

One of the best sources of prospective employees is recommendations made by good employees already in the organization. There is no better recommendation for the personnel program of a firm than to have present employees tell their friends, "This is a good place to work." Many well-managed firms have long lists of people who want to work for them because of present employees' satisfaction with their jobs.

If some present employees see the available position as a promotion, those employees may be good prospects for the job, assuming that they are qualified. If the job requires special training or education, school placement services or counselors can provide help in finding recruits. Private employment agencies and government employment services can often help turn up the applicant needed. The wise manager is always alert to the existence of top-notch people in competitors' firms or others who may be interested in a change of jobs. Advertising in newspapers, trade journals, and the like can also provide applicants.

Selecting the Right Person

Each of the available applicants should be screened against both the job specifications and the job description for that particular job (Exhibit 18-2). First, the job applicant should be compared to the job specifications. A good job application form should elicit information on personal history, education and special skills, experience, personal references, and previous employment.

Care must be taken in designing the application so that it does not violate the civil rights acts, which make it illegal to discriminate against any person on the basis of race, color, religion, sex, age, or national origin. A firm that is audited for civil rights violations will be glad it has designed a job specification sheet for each job. If these are carefully drawn to represent those factors needed to perform the job successfully, and if the person interviewing the applicants has filled them out honestly, the firm will be better able to defend its hiring practices.

The job application need not be fancy, but it should provide the applicant with a chance to present qualifications in an organized and fair manner. The task of finding and screening applicants should fall to the person(s) responsible for the personnel function. There are several reasons for this: (1) the person doing the screening interview develops a great deal of skill through experience; hence, that person is the most qualified for the task; (2) there is a consistency in interviewing when one person handles all interviews; and (3) when a personnel specialist handles this function, others are not interrupted in their tasks.

Attempts to learn whatever needs to be known bring the skills of the interviewer into play. Matching the job specification and job description against the application blank can provide good solid facts, but the interviewer's subjective judgments must be depended upon to determine the applicant's attitudes, personality, and ability to get along with and communicate to others.

For best results, the interview should be planned in advance. The interview should be held in a private, quiet place where the applicant recognizes that the manager's interest is real and that the job is important to the organization. When the interview begins, the manager should help the applicant relax. Hobbies or outside interests, the last job and how it went, previous supervisors, and the applicant's aspirations might be asked about. After the preliminaries are over, the manager should ask leading questions and be a good listener, that is, not monopolize the conversation. The applicant should be given an accurate description of the background of the firm and the job in question. The position should not be either under- or oversold. When interviewing, it is useful for the manager to give applicants a copy of the job specifications and job description sheets, so that they will have this information to refer to. Some applicants may eliminate themselves from consideration at this point, thereby saving much time, money, and heartache for both the firm and the applicant at a later date.

References can be helpful *if* they are checked out. The manager should check to see whether the information given by the applicant is correct as well as whether the reference is a positive one. Checking by phone has an advantage over checking by letter. People may tell more than they will write on paper, and the tone of voice, along with the things that are not said, can be significant. Judgment must be used in interpreting references, and good references from former employers are the manager's best criteria.

Testing can also be helpful in screening applicants for some jobs, but the manager must make sure that the tests really measure what it is necessary to measure. In any event, tests should not be the only criteria for hiring. Testing is most often done in five general areas: intelligence, aptitude, personality, manual dexterity, and physical condition. Some testing programs are more accurate than others. For example, manual dexterity and physical fitness tests are usually quite accurate in predicting a person's performance capabilities, while attitude or personality tests have a lesser degree of accuracy. If the test is valid in meeting job requirements, the manager's success in matching jobs with people can be improved significantly.

Once the personnel director has reduced the list of candidates to two or three qualified persons, the immediate supervisor should interview them and make the final selection. This important step builds the relationship between the supervisor and the new employee in two ways: (1) new employees tend to have a positive feeling toward supervisors who have personally selected them, and (2) the supervisor who has taken part in the selection process tends to have a special feeling of responsibility for helping the new person succeed on the job.

Job Orientation

When the manager has done his or her best to find and select the best potential employees, the successful applicants must be introduced to their new jobs. Every time someone is hired, the organization is betting heavily on that person's success. The right start, quick adjustment, and future productivity depend on job orientation. At the start, the new employee is more receptive than at any other time to the attitudes necessary to produce a long-lasting and successful career.

Job orientation involves four major steps:

1. Introducing the company to the employee

2. Establishing job relationships and encouraging familiarity with the facilities

3. Helping the employee to begin the job

4. Following up and evaluating the employee's adjustment

The first step in orientation is making the new employee aware of information about the company and the job. The history, nature, and scope of the organization, and information relative to hours of work, pay, fringe benefits, rules or restrictions, company policies, regulations, overtime, special programs, and facilities should be reviewed. A tour of the entire facility will help to foster an overview of the organization and an understanding of where the employee fits in. Of course, the new employee will not be able to remember all this information, so it is helpful for it to be written down for future reference. In a small organization, this may involve a couple of mimeographed sheets; in a large organization, it may take the form of an employee handbook.

The second step is establishing job relationships. Here supervisory responsibility should be outlined. The new employee should be introduced to his or her new supervisor and fellow workers, and to the union steward if there is one. The physical layout, parking, washrooms, lunchroom, etc., should be pointed out. The immediate supervisor should review work-related matters, such as safety regulations, coffee breaks, and job expectations. It is often helpful to assign a new employee a "buddy" who will help him or her to get acquainted and feel at home in the new job.

The next step is helping the employee to actually begin the job. Supplies, safety devices, equipment operation, work accessories, and the like should be pointed out, even if the new employee has previous experience. After these explanations, the supervisor should allow the new employee to try the job. The speed of this phase will vary according to the level and complexity of the job; the supervisor should not try to push too much at the new employee at once, but should let learning occur step by step. The supervisor should be sure to stress the required work habits and the norms and expectations of job performance. Again, a fellow worker assigned as a buddy can be helpful in giving the new person proper orientation. Managers must recognize that, like it or not, much of what the new employee learns about how to do the job and about work habits and attitudes will come from fellow workers.

The final step in orientation is follow-up. Good personnel managers do not assume that things are going well; they make sure that they are. This routine follow-up is usually best handled in an informal, on-the-job situation. The manager should determine how the new employee is getting along on the job and with fellow workers and supervisors. The manager should learn what problems exist, if any, and help solve them. Follow-up is not only useful in making sure that things are going as they should, and allowing for corrective action, it also affords an opportunity to encourage new employees and assure them of management's continuing interest.

In large companies, orientation may be handled by several persons, while in the smaller firm the manager may do it alone. Some larger firms have orientation schools or sessions. These may be several days in length, particularly for management or administrative jobs. The more that fellow employees and immediate supervisors are involved, the more they will feel responsible for the new employee's success as a team member. Fellow employees and immediate supervisors should be trained to perform this function. Even the smallest firm should have a planned job orientation program to ensure that new employees get off to a good start.

Compensation and Fringe Benefits
Many agribusiness firms do not have firm policies regarding compensation and fringe benefits; the philosophy is to give as little as possible. While costs of wages and fringe benefits are very important and must be controlled, the real measure of their cost is in terms of productivity. The agribusiness firm must consider both its ability to pay and competing compensation rates for similar jobs in the area. Often the local chambers of commerce or trade associations can provide guidelines for wage and salary levels.

Securing motivated employees and keeping them satisfied requires good wages and fringe benefits. Fringe benefits, which are becoming increasingly more important in finding and keeping good employees, range from those required by law to health benefits, vacations, sick pay, life insurance, and retirement benefits. The management of larger firms will devote considerable time to the development of fringe benefit policies. Their counterparts in smaller agribusiness firms can consult insurance companies and other firms in the area for guidance in determining the kinds and costs of fringe benefits for their employees.

Compensation in wages and fringe benefits requires careful study by management. The job, competitive factors, employees' need for recognition and self-esteem, and the skills and knowledge required all play a part. Compensation satisfies employees' need for security and provides concrete feedback on how valuable their contribution to the organization actually is. The compensation program of the agribusiness firm must consider the true cost of compensation in terms of the jobs that need doing. The firm's ability to pay must be measured against the person's productivity. The entire system of private enterprise is based on rewarding people according to their productivity or the risk they are willing to take.

Evaluating Performance

Performance evaluation is here to stay. It surfaces in all agribusinesses, even in those in which there is no planned program for appraisal. Managers and employees both need a carefully conceived and developed evaluation program to:

1. Improve future performance

2. Identify employees with untapped potential, in order to increase their challenge

3. Provide employees with a bench mark of their achievements

4. Provide information relating to decisions about promotions and pay

5. Provide the manager with guides for helping employees in the future

The modern approach to performance appraisal not only evaluates the workers and makes them aware of their contribution, but focuses on goals and the results of the workers' efforts. Good evaluation programs concentrate not only on past performance but on future opportunities as well.

Evaluation is often viewed with apprehension by both the manager and the subordinate. The manager should remember that evaluation is a tool and not a weapon, crutch, or cure-all. Its major purpose is to improve performance, not to punish employees. The successes as well as the failures of both the manager and the managed are recorded when evaluation is used.

As with any tool, the effective use of performance appraisal depends on the skill of the operator as well as the quality of the tool. The evaluation instrument itself should be as objective and clear as possible. Letting the subordinate use the document for self-evaluation prior to the session is helpful. A comparison of the management and employee ratings opens the way for a good communication flow. Managers must understand that they are not in the position of "playing God," but rather are seeking an honest two-way discussion aimed at positive reinforcement of morale and improved productivity. The evaluation should be conducted in a private, quiet place where it will be uninterrupted. The manager should be informal and willing to listen and should put the employee at ease as quickly as possible. Discussion of personality factors should be avoided if possible, but if the subordinate is in the mood for such a discussion, then the manager may make the most of the opportunity.

Follow-up procedures after the evaluation give the manager a chance to encourage improvement if and when it occurs, and also keep the manager current on changes in performance. Follow-up (particularly when a subordinate's rating was substandard) allows the manager the opportunity to offer commendations and suggestions, and, if necessary, to exercise disciplinary practices to improve performance.

New employees should be evaluated formally with great frequency. Established employees should be evaluated at least semiannually to ensure that work performance is progressing satisfactorily. An annual checkup is just not sufficient to catch and change work habits or productivity factors that need improvement.

Formal evaluation does not replace the need for the day-to-day evaluation that is a constant part of the manager's job. Employees want and need on-the-spot feedback if they are to enjoy satisfaction from their jobs.

Evaluation must measure two things, work habits and personal traits, as well as success at reaching job goals. Many agribusiness firms are using a relatively new concept of management called management by objective (see Chapter 19). Exhibit 18-3 is an example of a simple traditional employer appraisal form.

Training and Development
Training needs vary according to the circumstances. The kind of agribusiness, the level of complexity of the job, and the experience and educational level of the employee all determine the kind of training needed. Training programs are devised to meet one or more of the following objectives: reduce mistakes and accidents; increase motivation and productivity; and prepare the employee for promotion, growth, and development. Managers seek to increase each employee's value to the firm through training.

All training programs should be based upon specific objectives and meet the test of the following formula:

What should be known − what is known = what must be learned

The employee's present abilities and future capabilities should be analyzed by the person responsible for this function, with the help of the employee. Unless employees wish to develop their skills and add to their knowledge, training efforts will be wasted.

Training and development programs fall into the following major categories:

1. On-the-job

2. Formal in-house

3. Outside formal

CALHOUN COUNTY FARMERS' ELEVATOR
Employee Evaluation

Employee _____ Date _____
Job _____
Work Habits
  Areas of Strength:
    1.
    2.
    3.
  Areas for Improvement:
    1.
    2.
    3.
Personal Characteristics
  Areas of Strength:
    1.
    2.
    3.
  Areas for Improvement:
    1.
    2.
    3.
Employee Growth Plan for Next Period

_____

_____

_____   _____   _____
Supervisor   Manager   Employee

On-the-Job Training Most training in small agribusiness firms, or at lower job levels in large firms, is handled on the job. Here the objective is very simple: to teach the skills or procedures for accomplishing a specific task or job. Even at this level, what needs to be taught should be committed to paper. A simple outline of the major points will usually suffice.

Next, the manager must decide who is to do the training, and be sure that that person understands the job operations, safety rules, etc. Regardless of the job, the actual process will be one of show—do—judge. The supervisor should show them step by step how to do the job—let them do it—then evaluate and offer suggestions and encouragement, until a sufficient level of skill has been developed. When explaining something, it often helps to ask the employee to repeat it in his or her own words to ensure understanding. The training period will vary with the complexity of the job, the experience level of the employee, the skill of the teacher, and the ability of the employee to learn. The benefits of training are quality work, efficient work, and safe work, all of which are vital to the business and to the employee.

The *apprenticeship*, a method whereby a new employee works with and helps a more experienced person, and learns under the experienced person's direction over a period of time, can be of great help in jobs requiring greater skills. Many agribusiness firms are training salespeople, skilled operators, and managers by means of this system.

Formal In-House Training Managers of smaller agribusiness firms do not have as many options for formal internal training and development as do those of larger firms, where people devote full time to the training function. Many more training opportunities are available to all sizes of firms today, if managers will just take the time to seek them out. For example, groups or individuals can be trained by representatives of suppliers, trade associations, consultants, manufacturers, and school or university teachers. Films, videotapes, slidetapes, audio tapes, correspondence courses, and programmed learning kits are but a few of the options available to all agribusiness managers for enriching their training programs. Every conceivable topic, from management to trimming a head of lettuce, is available in some form. Suppliers, trade associations, and extension-service personnel can help the trainer locate the latest and best training aides. Committee meetings can provide a convenient and fertile ground for training and development if the agendas are carefully controlled and directed toward this end. Sharing of information in this setting can satisfy the need for employee recognition and participation, and can help make employees feel a part of the organization.

Formal External Training and Development Agribusiness abounds in conventions, conferences, lectures, workshops, seminars, and the like, on every known subject. In addition, there are trade schools, extension courses, high school and university courses, and business and trade courses. Almost every community has most of these alternatives available. Most agribusinesses will be affiliated with an association or group that sponsors educational experiences. The trick is to use sufficient self-discipline to determine what specifically must be learned. The managers of many businesses, because training is so necessary and so popular, are not discriminating enough in their choices of educational experiences to improve their employees' productivity. Employee participation in selecting the best training options is often beneficial. In today's fierce competition, a firm's people, from top to bottom, should be challenged by learning. This is recommended not only to improve basic skills (the best way of doing anything has not been discovered yet), but to encourage the good psychological effect on people of working for a progressive, aggressive firm interested in developing its employees. Training and development involve some cost, but the returns in the form of a more dynamic, effective human resource far offset this expenditure; training of employees should be regarded as an investment in the future of the firm.

Promotion and Advancement

An agribusiness firm's promotion program and policies are related to the aspects previously discussed. Finding and hiring promotable people, determining their compensation, and overseeing the training and development programs, all lead to the question of promotion, since promotion is an extra form of compensation. To many, promotions mean, "I've done a good job—the firm appreciates me!" One of the prevailing controversies is whether promotion should occur from within, or whether outside talent should be sought instead. The real question is what the job requires in skills, knowledge, and communication ability, and who is best qualified to fill it. A strong recommendation can be made for promotion from within, provided that the right people are available. Such a program encourages employees to do their best in developing and growing. In other words, promotion can be a strong motivational factor. At the same time, management must be careful that the firm does not become too inbred to allow new ideas, approaches, and methods to be introduced from time to time. Often the challenge of change is offered when someone is brought in from the outside.

The criteria for promotion then become the critical factor. Several criteria must be considered, the most important of which is the qualifications that are needed to fill the job. This is an absolute. Failure to meet this demand will cause the firm to become a victim of the Peter principle, which states that employees tend to be promoted to their level of incompetence.

Once the needs of the job have been ascertained, seniority or length of service must be considered. In a unionized operation, this can become the primary consideration. Other factors to evaluate are the merit or contribution of the employee in the past, and the employee's attitude and personality (in particular, the ability to function with whatever the new team will be). A careful evaluation program will prove its value here. The employee's potential for growth must also be considered. Finally, the individual employee must want the promotion and feel able to handle the new assignment. Too often managers assume that everyone wants to be promoted, when, in fact, some employees may lack the confidence needed to handle this step. Perhaps there are other ways of recognizing and rewarding a particular employee besides promotion. Offering added responsibility and pay, without increased stature in the organizational hierarchy, may be the better way in some cases.

Agribusiness managers must continually guard against the greatest error made in promotion. Simply because a person excels at one job is no guarantee that the same person will excel at a job higher up the ladder. For example, a good millhand may not be a good truck driver, nor will a good salesperson necessarily make a good sales manager. To reiterate: the job and the person must be matched.

Termination and Dismissal

It is inevitable that each employee will eventually leave the firm. Some will quit, some will be fired, some will retire. In every case, the loss to the firm and the pain for the employee should be held to a minimum by the good agribusiness manager. The leaving of any employee can be seen as a learning experience, if the manager takes the time to conduct an exit interview. An *exit interview* simply gives the person who is responsible for the personnel function the opportunity to do two things: make sure the employee leaves as a friend (if possible), and find out what caused the termination and what changes could be made to prevent such occurrences in the future.

Even if the employee has been fired or has quit in anger, a well-conducted exit interview that allows the person to express dissatisfaction will often at least calm the troubled emotional waters. A friend or even a neutral is better than an enemy. Every termination has a reason, and the firm must accept responsibility for a failure. At the very least, the wrong person was hired.

Turnover is one of the most expensive of all business costs. Estimates of the cost of replacing an unskilled worker have been placed at $300 to $400. Filling high-level positions often runs into thousands of dollars. There is the direct cost of finding, hiring, orienting, and training a new employee. There is also the indirect cost from a job unfilled, from the time needed for the new employee to develop skills, from poor production once the old employee has decided to leave, and very likely from poor morale among other employees if turnover is high.

The exit interview should be based on the following questions.

1. Was the selection process adequate? Were enough candidates interviewed? Did applicants understand the job, wages, and working conditions? Were job descriptions and job specifications used? Were references contacted?

2. Were the person and the job matched carefully during placement? Were job specifications and job descriptions used?

3. Was orientation to the job adequate, and did the new employee feel at home and a part of the team?

4. Were wages, fringe benefits, and working conditions reasonable, fair, and competitive?

5. Was the problem a personality conflict with supervision or with fellow workers? Were discipline and work rules fair? Was favoritism or erratic or unusual discipline used?

6. Was the employee given a chance to grow and develop? Was training given in a meaningful way? Were promotion policies understood and fair?

There is a real loss to all concerned when termination and turn-over occur for any reason. The answers to the above questions in an exit interview are quite likely to be biased, especially if the person is quitting or being fired. However, the need for reasons is very real, since it is one good way of getting feedback on potential or existing weaknesses in the agribusiness's personnel program. Such an interview can provide a means of securing greater productivity from the firm's human resources.

THE LABOR UNION

Many of the larger agribusiness firms deal with *unions*, or organized labor, which are organized essentially to protect and promote the interests of their members. Since the majority of agribusinesses tend to be small and located in rural, more conservative areas of the country, they do not have labor unions. As conditions change, however, more and more agribusiness firms face the potential of becoming organized by unions. Some believe that large federated and regional cooperatives offer organized labor easier access to local-member or affiliate workers. During the past decade, national labor unions have shown a great deal more interest in organizing agricultural workers. No agribusiness firm can really consider itself immune from this thrust.

As managers and workers view the business world, both believe that productivity and profits are essential to the great success of the economy in the United States. The question on which management and labor are divided is what share of these profits and productivity each should receive. What the student must remember is that workers need strong, profitable enterprises to compensate them well, and management needs productive workers to make reasonable profits.

Unions have become a potent force only since the 1930s, when the Norris-LaGuardia Act (1932) and the Wagner-Connery Act (1935) gave workers the right to organize and bargain collectively with their employers. Many states also passed legislation called *closed shop laws,* which, in essence, required everyone working for a company that has voted in a union to belong to that union. Some labor unions are small or local in nature, and are usually referred to as *shop unions.* They may encompass as little as one firm or even just certain workers within a firm. Most of the more than 20 million union workers in the United States belong to the nearly 200 national or international unions, such as the Teamsters (the largest), United Auto Workers, and United Steel Workers.

A union is organized within a firm when employees petition the National Labor Relations Board (a governmental agency) to conduct an election. Laws and regulations require that certain conditions be met, and if everything is in order, the vote is conducted. If over 50 percent of the firm's designated workers vote for a specific union to represent them, the firm must deal with that union and develop a labor contract. These labor contracts can and usually do deal with wages, fringe benefits, other forms of compensation, seniority, promotion, hours of work, layoffs,

HUMAN RESOURCE MANAGEMENT IN AGRIBUSINESS

grievance procedures, and mediation. Most of the areas discussed in personnel management are referred to in the contract. It is essential that the agribusiness firm consult competent legal advice if it is confronted by an attempt to organize its workers, or if a union already exists and management is forced into collective bargaining and contractual relations with its workers.

When an agribusiness is organized, it is not a case of management dealing with labor; rather, it is a case of business managers dealing and negotiating with labor union managers. Labor union managers are usually highly skilled and well-paid representatives of the unionized workers. The process called *collective bargaining* is, broadly speaking, one in which employers and representatives of employees attempt to arrive at agreements governing the conditions under which the employees are willing to work for the employer. If the collective bargaining process fails and no contractual agreement is reached, workers then have the right to withhold their services, or *strike*. A strike is used by both parties to apply economic pressures to the other until an agreement is reached.

The labor union and organized labor are a well-established part of the American scene. Their continued success and growth seems likely, since managers' and workers' ideas of the ideal split of power and of profits from business activities will always be different. Collective bargaining offers a process whereby these divisions are determined while the free enterprise system is maintained.

SUMMARY
Human resources are the most important asset of any agribusiness. The personnel function of management is concerned with administering the mechanics of employment. The larger the agribusiness, the more formal and complex the process; but the personnel function must be accomplished in any agribusiness.

Personnel management begins with determining employment needs. This usually requires defining the job and developing job descriptions so that the right type of person can be recruited. Recruiting involves searching for qualified candidates, interviewing, and assisting in the selection of the best person. And, once a new person is on the job, it is a personnel function to see that he or she gets off to a good start with proper orientation and training.

Another personnel function is the development and administration of employee benefit programs; insurance, retirement, health care, safety, continuing education, and related programs are all designed to increase the welfare and productivity of employees, and all require a great deal of effort on the part of management. The personnel manager is also responsible for ensuring that the firm meets complex government and labor union regulations concerning employees and working conditions.

In most agribusinesses, the personnel function also includes regular evaluation of employee performance and ensuring continual professional growth through ongoing training and development programs.

Training may consist of informal, on-the-job training or formal seminars, but in either case it should lead to greater productivity.

The personnel manager must also become involved in the termination of some employees; that is, the manager must ensure that employees' rights are not violated and that there is just cause for dismissal.

Personnel managers are often designated to coordinate the agribusiness's relationship with labor unions. Negotiating union contracts and carrying out contract specifications are difficult but important personnel functions.

DISCUSSION QUESTIONS

1. Why are employees sometimes called the forgotten asset?

2. At what point should an agribusiness consider hiring a full-time personnel administrator?

3. What are the main functions of personnel management?

4. Draw up job specification and job description sheets for an agribusiness job with which you are familiar. Contrast and compare them. What are the main differences? Are there any similarities?

5. What elements are contained in a good job application form?

6. What are the most effective ways to screen applicants? What are the strengths and weaknesses of each?

7. Explain the steps involved in job orientation.

8. What part do compensation and fringe benefits play in turnover rate? How is the real measure of their cost taken? What is the purpose of a formal performance evaluation program? What should the program contain?

9. Evaluate the effectiveness of each of the three major types of training and development programs for agribusinesses of varying sizes. What does each program contain?

10. What criteria determine promotions?

11. Formulate the purpose and format of an exit interview.

12. What effect have the Norris-LaGuardia Act and the Wagner-Connery Act had on business?

13. How is a union organized? What do its labor contracts usually deal with?

CALHOUN COUNTY FARMERS' ELEVATOR: REVISITED
Review the description of Calhoun County Farmers' Elevator at the beginning of the chapter. Imagine that Ralph and Betty Ames were to call you in as a consultant to clear up their personnel problems.

QUESTIONS

1. What would be your first recommendation?

2. How would you rearrange Ralph and Betty's current job priorities?

3. What should a training program consist of?

4. What can be done to decrease employee turnover?

5. What can be done to attract qualified personnel?

6. How would you go about modifying current wage and benefits policy?

7. Describe the process of defining each job function and qualification.

OBJECTIVES

• Differentiate between responsibility, authority, and accountability relationships in agribusiness

• Describe the formal organizational structures in agribusiness

• Apply organizational principles to formal business organization

• Explain the impact of informal organization and relationships on the success of the organization

• Identify various leadership styles among agribusiness managers

• Review widely used theories of managing and motivating employees

• Use the transactional analysis model for basic human behavior concepts

Managing personnel includes developing various programs to benefit individuals and groups of employees.
A. Working with organized labor
B. Planning employee benefits

WORKING WITH PEOPLE IS DIFFICULT, BUT NOT IMPOSSIBLE ———Peter Drucker, Quoted in John J. Tarrant, *Drucker: The Man Who Invented the Corporate Society*. New York, Warner Books, Inc., 1977.

19

MANAGING HUMAN RESOURCES IN AGRIBUSINESS

A

B

PEOPLE MANAGEMENT: STRUCTURE, LEADERSHIP, AND MOTIVATION

Agribusinesses are made up of people working together toward a common purpose. As soon as the agribusiness involves more than one person, a variety of organizational, personnel, leadership, and motivational issues inevitably arises. The larger the organization, the more complex and critical the issues become. Since one of the fundamental responsibilities of management is to acquire, organize, motivate, and control its human resources to accomplish its business objective as effectively as possible, management must address whatever complex issues may challenge that responsibility.

Managing the human resources in an agribusiness has many dimensions. First, it involves the total personnel function, that is, recruiting, hiring, training, evaluating, promoting, administering compensation and benefits, firing, and, in some agribusinesses, working with organized labor (see Chapter 18). But in addition to handling the formal personnel function, management must develop an organizational structure whereby the responsibility, authority, and accountability of individuals are clearly defined. Then management must concentrate on directing and supervising day-to-day activities. Leadership becomes critical to business success as managers seek to motivate and control human resources to maximize productivity. Although much remains to be learned, a great deal is known about leadership styles and the conditions that motivate people. Managing people successfully requires more than a charismatic personality; it requires an understanding of the basic concepts of supervision and leadership. In short, managing the agribusiness is concerned with handling people.

Greenthumb, Inc.: Handling People in a Growing Business

Greenthumb, Inc., was founded 6 years ago by Marie and Bob Jordan. Capitalizing on Marie's experience in managing a retail lawn and garden center, Bob's experience in a commercial greenhouse, and a tidy inheritance, Marie and Bob made their dreams a reality. Beginning modestly with a small greenhouse and an attached lawn and garden shop, they quickly established their business in the community. Marie's creative ads in the local paper and her outgoing personality helped the business to prosper. Bob's natural talent for growing things and his previous experience as a field supervisor for a large corporate greenhouse provided a steady supply of quality bedding plants and flowers for sale in the store.

It was simple at first. During the first 2 years, Marie and Bob did just about everything themselves, with the part-time help of one older man and several high school students. Things were going so well that in the third year they decided to purchase six adjoining acres and begin growing some of their own nursery stock. The business was growing so rapidly that Marie and Bob had to begin adding some full-time help; they just could not take the long hours required to handle all the work.

During the third year, they also hired three managers: one each for the nursery, the greenhouse, and the retail store. Several workers reported to each of these managers, the exact number depending on the season. Marie assumed the role of assistant general manager. She handled everything when Bob was away on buying trips and kept the books and records.

Adjusting to the larger business was a genuine struggle. It became harder and harder to stay in touch with customers, and it seemed as if Marie and Bob no longer got to do some of the things that had been so much fun at first. Yet they were successful and the profits were good, so they continued to expand and grow.

Then, in the fifth year, things began to go wrong. By this time there were thirty-five people working at Greenthumb during the peak season. Actually, there was no one predominant problem; instead, there was a succession of little things, such as inventory damage in the cramped warehouse, high turnover in part-time help, and costs that began to get out of hand, with no one seeming to know where or why. Most serious of all was the costly increase in insect and disease problems in the nursery and greenhouse.

Both Marie and Bob felt they had lost touch. Bob simply could not be on top of the technical production problems because he was tied up with management problems. Besides, many of the disease problems were beyond his experience. Similarly, Marie had had no real training in accounting, but she did realize that Greenthumb needed better financial information to make good management decisions.

They therefore interviewed and hired an aggressive young woman who had a degree in horticulture from the land-grant university and had co-oped for a large grower. They also hired an accountant who had graduated from a local business college 5 years before and had worked as office manager at a farm supply store. Both Marie and Bob felt that these two new staff members, although relatively costly additions to the payroll, would pay off in increased effectiveness.

This system worked well for Greenthumb for several months. But then, early in March of her second year, the horticulturist walked into Bob's office and quit. She said she was fed up with "pushing on a string," as she put it. After a rather emotional discussion, it became clear that her frustrations resulted from a series of incidents where she had strongly recommended several cultural practices to the nursery manager, only to be ignored. Finally, after she discovered that some new stock had been planted too deep and was likely to die, she had taken matters into her own hands. The nursery manager had been away for the morning, and she felt it necessary to handle the problem immediately, so she told two part-timers to spend the morning resetting the stock. When the nursery manager returned and found that the horticulturist had pulled the workers off the job he had assigned them to, he was livid and confronted her. There had been quite a scene in the field, and several workers seemed to enjoy the fracas.

Greenthumb has reached a point where it is almost controlled by its people problems. The business has been profitable and has potential for considerably more growth. What is not clear is how the business can best be structured.

ORGANIZATIONAL STRUCTURE

Organizations depend on two kinds of structure for smoothness of operation: the formal structure that serves as the foundation for all activities, and the undercurrent of informal interpersonal relationships that also affects activities.

Formal Organization

Cultural tradition and thought in the United States accords individuals the right to own and control property. Because of this, the fundamental responsibility for the business and for its assets belongs to its owners. Society itself holds owners accountable for the resources and assets at their disposal, just as a pet owner is liable for any damages caused by the pet.

Owners, either directly or through duly elected representatives (the board of directors), share this responsibility with professional agribusiness managers, and delegate to them the authority to make decisions on their behalf. In turn, management is held accountable for the success of the business. Management then develops an organizational structure specifying the various responsibilities, authority, and accountability of employees, whose task it is to help develop and execute plans for accomplishing business objectives.

Responsibility, Authority, and Accountability   *Responsibility* is the obligation to see a task through to completion. It may be a contractual obligation or it may be voluntarily assumed, but it cannot be given away. Responsibility can be shared with another person or group, but it can never be passed downward with no further obligation. The obligation remains undiluted with its originator.

Authority is the right to command or force an action by another. Authority allows instructions to be given to another with the expectation that they will be carried out explicitly. Authority is a derivative of responsibility, since it must come from the ultimate source of responsibility.

Accountability involves being answerable to another for performance. Associated with accountability is the notion of a reward for acceptable behavior or a penalty for unacceptable results. It, too, is derived from responsibility.

The formal organizational structure of an agribusiness defines areas of responsibility and authority, and delineates who is accountable to whom and for what (see Figure 19-1). The larger the agribusiness, the more formalized and structured its organization is likely to be. In fact, in very large businesses it is not uncommon for specialists in organiza-

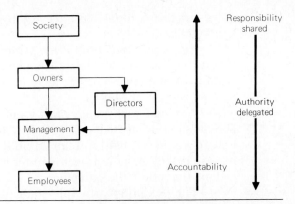

Figure 19-1 Responsibility, authority, accountability relationships. Responsibility originates with society itself and is shared downward through the business. Authority is delegated accordingly, with each level being held accountable for areas of responsibility.

tional development to constantly review the organizational structure, with an eye toward changes that may facilitate the total management process.

Principles of Organization Much has been learned about what makes an organizational structure successful. Many factors can be cited, but the most far-reaching is the human element: personalities, value systems, and feelings. Although organizations are always in a fluid state, because they are continually changing, there are several key principles that are useful in determining a proper organizational structure.

The *span-of-control* principle states that the number of people who can be supervised effectively by one individual is limited. The maximum number depends on many factors, including the frequency of contacts that must be made, the type of work, the level of subordinates, and the skill of the supervisor. In military organizations, the number of individuals directly supervised is seldom more than four to seven, while on assembly lines where work is routine, a supervisor may oversee thirty to forty people.

The *minimal layer* principle states that the number of levels of management should be kept as low as possible, which is consistent with the goal of maintaining an effective span of control. As organizations grow, there is a tendency for the levels of management to proliferate, but each additional level increases the complexity of communications and the opportunities for breakdowns.

The *delegation downward* principle states that authority should be delegated downward to the lowest level at which the decision can be made competently. This allows upper management to concentrate on more important decisions. At the same time, delegation of authority never relieves the delegator of the original responsibility. The boss always remains responsible for everything that happens under his or her supervision.

The *single-accountability* principle states that no person should report to more than one boss. The obvious confusion and frustration that would result from reporting to more than one supervisor makes this a common sense principle.

The *parity of responsibility* and *authority* principle states that a person should have enough authority to carry out assigned responsibilities. It would be totally unfair to hold employees accountable for areas in which they have not been granted enough authority to make the decisions that affect the outcome.

The *flexibility* principle states that an organization should maintain its structural flexibility so that it can adjust to its changing internal and external environments. Organizations are always changing. Since the organizational structure involves human personalities, changing the power structure can be a very touchy business; people often feel threatened by change and tend to resist it. Periodic reviews and a mechanism for changing structure are necessary for healthy organizations.

Types of Organizational Structures   The foregoing organizational principles give rise to three primary types of organizational structure: line, line and staff, and functional. There are actually many variations on these basic types, and a pure organizational type seldom occurs. Generally speaking, the larger the business, the more complex the structure.

LINE ORGANIZATION   *Line organization* is a structure in which there is one simple, clear line of authority extending downward from top management to each person in the organization. Each subordinate reports to only one person, and everyone in the organization is directly involved in performing functions that are primary to the existence of the business (see Figure 19-2).

The line organization is ideal for smaller agribusinesses, such as Greenthumb, in their first few years. In such cases, lines of authority and accountability are simple and cannot be easily confused; communication channels are clear and rapid, with few people involved. Top management are often the owners of the business, who find it easy to stay informed and can call the shots with little problem. Marie and Bob Jordan, as the managers of Greenthumb, Inc., could react quickly and personally to a shoplifting problem in the retail store or a disease problem in the nursery, because of their proximity to the problem area.

But as a business grows, it becomes more complex. The more people there are and the more levels of management that are added, the less effective the pure line organization becomes. Lengthening the chain of command reduces the speed of important decisions and increases the probability of communication breakdowns. If an assistant nursery manager is hired and nursery workers are specialized into field hands, delivery persons, and mechanics, the owner/manager may not learn of a feud

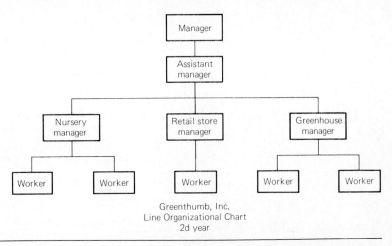

Greenthumb, Inc.
Line Organizational Chart
2d year

Figure 19-2 Example of line organization. Each person is directly involved in a primary function, has only one boss, and is in the direct line of authority.

between two delivery people until one of them quits, unless the lines of communication are working exceptionally well.

Furthermore, there is really no place in a line organization for specialists. It is only as a business grows that it requires a more diversified structure. As Greenthumb grew, it became obvious that an office-manager–accountant would be needed, as well as a professional horticulturist to advise on matters of disease control, propagation, and field practices. In a line organization such specialists should be in a position to offer advice, but should not be directly involved in the line of authority over activities in the nursery or greenhouses.

LINE AND STAFF ORGANIZATION   The *line and staff organization* is a variation on the line organization; the difference is that it includes a place for the specialists (see Figure 19-3). In this system, staff personnel have direct accountability to key line managers and are responsible for offering advice on problems or providing services in their area of specialization. Typically, these specialists have no authority of their own, except perhaps over assistants who may be assigned to them. Their advice can be accepted or rejected by line managers, who retain responsibility for all decisions.

Greenthumb management is likely to find the advice of a staff horticulturist and accountant invaluable in making technical decisions and analyzing operating costs. The highly trained horticulturist can work with and advise about disease problems in the nursery or propagation problems in the greenhouse, or can assist with customer problems in the retail store. Under this system, no one is required to accept all the specialists' suggestions, but professional advice and services can be extremely beneficial to the business.

MANAGING HUMAN RESOURCES IN AGRIBUSINESS

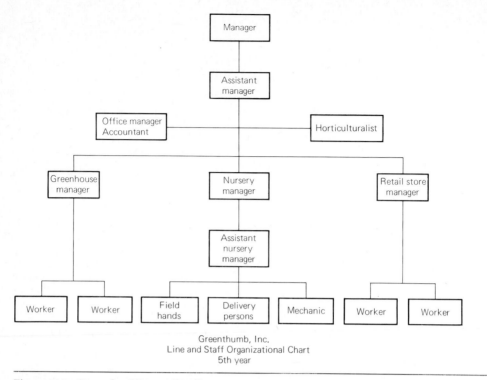

Greenthumb, Inc.
Line and Staff Organizational Chart
5th year

Figure 19-3 Example of line and staff organization. Staff positions have responsibility to give advice, but have no authority.

Staff specialists can be advisory, they can handle service problems, or they can serve control functions, as do quality inspectors in a processing plant. In any case, they do not have line authority over others in their organization, and this is one major drawback of the line and staff organization.

Staff specialists must be positioned so as to avoid undermining the authority of line management. This is difficult, since their position and special knowledge often give them considerable status and prestige that can easily be misapplied to others down the line. Changes or policies that these staff specialists may legitimately suggest may not be welcomed by line managers or workers. Specialists may feel so strongly about a particular issue that they may apply pressure or go directly to the worker, rather than working through the chain of command. If Greenthumb's horticulturist tells nursery workers to begin treating growing beds with insecticide, it may be in direct conflict with the nursery manager's established work schedule and will create much confusion among employees and ill feelings with management.

FUNCTIONAL ORGANIZATION Functional organizational structure meets the problem of staff specialists' authority head on by granting them authority in the areas of their specialty (see Figure 19-4). The hor-

HUMAN RESOURCE MANAGEMENT IN AGRIBUSINESS

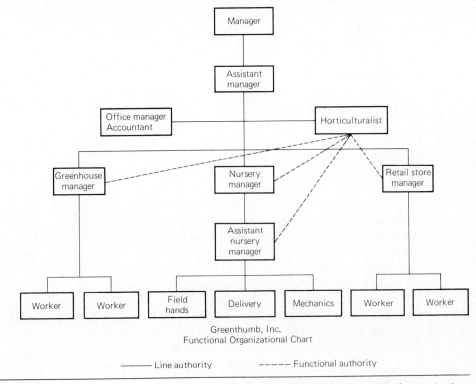

Greenthumb, Inc.
Functional Organizational Chart

——— Line authority   ————— Functional authority

**Figure 19-4   Examples of functional organization.
Staff positions have authority in functional areas.**

ticulturist who sees the need for an immediate insecticide treatment of
bedding plants has the responsibility and the authority to command
workers to make the application.

Of course, functional organization offers an almost unlimited potential for conflict and confusion. Who has the highest authority? From
whom do workers really take orders? The key to making the functional
structure work is coordination of staff and line management efforts. A
cooperative attitude and good communication are essential. Although it
violates the single-accountability principle, this system appeals to many
agribusinesses, especially larger ones. Such businesses have found that
the advantages of functional organization outweigh the disadvantages.

Communication: The Key to Success   No matter how well thought out
the organizational structure is, there will be times when it breaks down.
Agribusinesses, large and small, are complex operations that do not always work the way they are laid out on paper. No organizational structure is better than the people of whom it is composed. Their understanding of the structure and their willingness to work within it are essential
to its effectiveness. Yet even when people are trying to make it work,
problems arise. People have emotions, misunderstandings, and ego

needs that sometimes get in the way, especially during seasonal peaks of hectic activity, when they get physically and emotionally tired.

Effective organizations recognize the need for interpreting the formal structure in terms of the human element, by adjusting and working through misunderstandings when they occur. No organizational structure can be successful without a constant concern about honest but tactful communication at all levels.

Informal Organization

The formal organization is concerned primarily with the activities of people as they perform their job functions.[1] But the formal organizational structure cannot possibly control all the personal relationships that exist in any agribusiness. Whenever people come together, informal relationships develop that can greatly affect the effectiveness of the formal organization. The informal organization is primarily concerned with interpersonal relationships among people, that is, their emotions, feelings, communications, and values.

The informal organization is crucial to the success of any organization, since it contributes greatly to the fulfillment of individuals' personal needs. A great many (if not most) professional people and workers spend as many or more hours on the job than they do at home or with their families. And for some who may have less than satisfying home lives, the hours spent on the job may be a primary source of ego fulfillment and social relationships. Their role on the job, their status among peers, and their personal feelings about their job are critical to their well-being; therefore, all these factors directly affect how well the formal organization works.

Managers who cultivate a positive informal organization (often called *lubricating* the organization) will discover a desirable fringe benefit: the formal organizational structure will be much more productive. Any gaps caused by unexpected situations can be handled far more easily. Communications will be facilitated through informal channels. The span of control can be lengthened because people will work together more effectively. The end result is that more work gets done better.

On the other hand, where the informal organization is ignored, results are less predictable, people are less flexible, and they may spend considerably more time in activities that are counterproductive to company goals. Managers who ignore the power of the informal organization, who dictate without regard to sensitive interpersonal factors, may even experience "malicious obedience" among employees, that is, a situation where an employee spitefully carries out a superior's command to the nth degree, even when the employee knows that such literalism is not called for in the situation and will produce a negative result.

Informal organization begins with the primary group, or the peo-

---

[1] An excellent, in-depth discussion of informal organization can be found in E. B. Flippo and G. M. Munsinger, *Management*, 4th ed., Boston, Allyn and Bacon, 1978, chaps. 10–12.

HUMAN RESOURCE MANAGEMENT IN AGRIBUSINESS

ple with whom an employee works most closely. Within this group, as in the larger organization, relationships develop as the result of status, power, and politics.

Status is the social rank or position of a person in a group. Status and symbols of status exist in every group. Symbols include title, age, experience, physical characteristics, knowledge, physical possessions, authority, location, privileges, acquaintances, and a host of other factors, depending on the situation.

At Greenthumb, Inc., the issues of who gets to drive the newest pickup truck and who has the first locker in the clean-up room have become status symbols among workers. Insensitivity in assigning trucks to work crews could create problems in the organization. Status is not necessarily bad, however, because it helps people fill ego needs and can serve as a method by which managers can motivate workers.

Power is the ability to control another person's behavior. Power may come from the formal authority issued through the chain of command, or its source may be less formal, arising out of respect, knowledge, status, proximity to a source of power, or control of a resource.

Effective agribusiness managers recognize the importance of power, both their own and that of others in the organization. They can use power productively to accomplish corporate objectives, or they can abuse their power to emphasize their own importance. Managers must recognize that by withholding full cooperation, employees can exert a great deal of unofficial power themselves.

Marie and Bob Jordan must recognize the power plays currently operating between the nursery manager and their staff horticulturist. Both are struggling for power they believe is rightfully theirs. The nursery manager may feel threatened by the horticulturist's higher position and knowledge, or he may undervalue her because of her sex. The Jordans must deal with the informal aspects of the power struggle as well as the formal organizational questions.

Politics is the manner in which power and status are used. It is the manipulation of people and situations to accomplish a particular goal. Everyone is at least superficially familiar with the formal political process of give-and-take, individual and group coalitions, and wheeling and dealing. The formal political process in the state or national sense is a complex but systematic application of power and persuasion. Within the agribusiness, however, politics is an intricate part of the informal organization. Although it is likely to be more obvious in larger organizations, politics is necessary for getting things done when one lacks total authority to dictate an action, and can be useful even when authority is present.

The greenhouse manager at Greenthumb, Inc., understands the role of politics, so he will plan his request for an automatic overhead sprinkler very carefully. He knows that investment funds are limited and that he will be in direct competition for them with the retail manager and the nursery manager. If the office political situation is such that the accountant can and does influence the Jordans' investment decisions, the greenhouse manager may well cultivate a good relationship with the accountant and subtly look for ways of gaining his support.

Politics has positive value: it encourages compromise and offers a way of solving problems without direct, explosive confrontation. In larger organizations, it offers a method for accomplishing things that would be cumbersome to handle through purely formal channels.

While politics may seem manipulative or even unethical to some, it is a fact of life and part of the rules of the game to some degree in all organizations. Effective managers recognize its existence and deal with it realistically.

LEADERSHIP

Managers are designated leaders, formally appointed by the chain of command that originates with ownership. But leadership is much more than issuing authoritarian commands. It requires working with the human element in a relationship with followers, and motivating them to accomplish objectives. Leadership combines personal and organizational goals harmoniously.

There has been much study of leadership and leadership styles.[2] Obviously, business could profit greatly from a consistent way of identifying good leaders, or of teaching selected individuals how to be effective leaders. Although a great deal is known about leadership, there are no consistent or simple answers. There are no stereotypes. What makes a good leader in one situation does not necessarily work in another situation.

Some research suggests that strong will, extroversion, power need, and achievement are the keys. Other work identifies intelligence, social maturity, breadth of development, inner motivation, and a positive human-relations attitude as necessary ingredients. All these items are subjective and difficult to measure. The upshot is that leadership is not clear-cut but fluid, and must adapt to the circumstances.

Styles of Leadership

Although there are no clear-cut dictates of effective leadership, many helpful leadership theories or models have been identified. One of the most popular of these classifies leadership styles as authoritarian, democratic, or free rein.

Authoritarian *Authoritarian,* also called *autocratic,* is a leader-centered style, in which the thoughts, ideas, and wishes of the leader are expected to be obeyed completely, without question. Authoritarian leaders seldom consult followers before making up their minds, and may

[2]E. B. Flippo and G. M. Munsinger, "Leadership Styles," ibid.

change their minds whenever the mood strikes. The hard-nosed autocrat is coercive in relationships with subordinates, and often threatens them if they do not live up to a preordained level of expectations.

Yet there are other styles of authoritarian leadership. *Benevolent autocrats* convince followers to do what they want by being so well liked that no one would consider being disloyal or "letting the chief down." The benevolent autocrat gives so much praise that employees are shamed into obedience.

Another form of autocratic style is that of the *manipulative autocrat,* who creates the illusion that employees are participating in the decision making. This leader's motto is, "Make them think they thought of it."

Note that in each case, all decisions originate with the autocrat, and the autocrat maintains firm control. The only difference among the three is the manner in which the control is exercised.

Some argue that the autocratic style of leadership is always bad and leads to poor performance and ill feeling; this is not so. Although the authoritarian style would seldom be the only method of operation for any given leader, those who are primarily autocratic can show excellent results, particularly when the leader has a good feel for the situation and is very bright. Over a period of time, autocratic leaders tend to surround themselves with followers who enjoy not having responsibility, just doing what they are told. This combination of leadership and following is often quite productive, at least temporarily; but it is limited completely by the individual autocrat's ability and can result in utter chaos if that leader becomes incapacitated. The autocratic style is not uncommon and is perhaps found most frequently in owner-managed businesses.

Democratic   The *democratic* or participative leadership style favors a shared decision-making process, with the leader maintaining the ultimate responsibility for decisions while actively seeking significant input from followers. Research shows that, while this style may require a considerable amount of skill, it stimulates employees' involvement and enhances favorable attitudes toward their jobs. The only real disadvantage is that a democratic leadership style requires management skills and time that may not always be available, so this leadership style may not be appropriate for all situations.

Free Rein   *Free-rein* or laissez faire leadership is essentially no leadership because it relinquishes all decision making to followers. The leader essentially abdicates his or her responsibility to the group and simply joins the group as an equal; thus, the group decides what to do.

Although free-rein leadership may work with some decisions, such as the brand of coffee to purchase for the coffee machine, it seldom leads to timely or consistently good decisions, and often results in a poor outcome and frustration among employees.

Leadership Continuum   The *leadership continuum* developed by W. R. Lassey[3] suggests that the three basic styles of leadership are actually on a continuum. Autocratic leadership, with little or no employee input, lies at one end, while the free-rein style, with management totally abdicating leadership to employees, rests at the other end.

The leader's primary method of interacting with employees may range from telling, to selling, to talking with, to consulting with, to joining as the style of leadership changes (see Figure 19-5). Actually, even leadership styles between points on the continuum are possible, and a leader may wisely select different styles for different situations.

Managerial Grid

One of the most popular and widely used frameworks for the study of leadership is Robert Blake and Jane Mouton's managerial grid concept.[4] These management specialists developed a 9 × 9 checkerboard grid that classifies two important dimensions of leader effectiveness: (1) concern for people and relationships, and (2) concern for production or output. Leaders are classified along these two continua by means of grid coordinates that serve to identify leadership style (see Figure 19-6). The style used in most situations is referred to as the *dominant style*, with other styles identified as *backup styles*. Although a great many combinations can be discovered by a testing procedure, five major classifications of behavioral styles can be readily identified: "impoverished," "country club," "task management," "middle-of-the-road," and "team approach."

1,1: IMPOVERISHED   The impoverished manager evidences little con-

---

Figure 19-5   The leadership continuum. [*W. R. Lassey, "Dimensions of Leadership," in W. R. Lassey (ed.), Leadership and Social Change, University Associates, La Jolla, Calif., 1971.*]

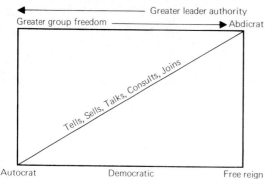

[3]W. R. Lassey, "Dimensions of Leadership," in W. R. Lassey (ed.), *Leadership and Social Change*, La Jolla, Calif., University Associates, 1971.

[4]Robert T. Blake and Jane S. Mouton, *The Managerial Grid*, Houston, Tex., Gulf Publishing, 1964.

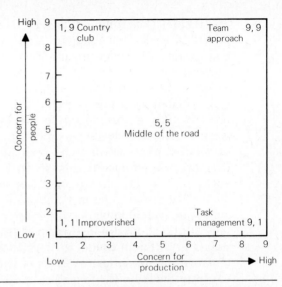

Figure 19-6   The managerial grid. [*Robert T. Blake and Jane S. Mouton, The Managerial Grid, Houston, Tex., Gulf Publishing, 1964, p. 10.*]

cern for people or production; this is a poor manager by anyone's standards. The leader does just enough to get by.

1,9: COUNTRY CLUB   The country club leader has a high concern for people and relatively little for getting the job done. Those who favor this style concentrate on being good persons and being liked. Country club managers are friendly and respect employees, but they frequently have to deal with low productivity.

9,1: TASK MANAGEMENT   The task-management manager has great concern for getting the job done, even if it means sacrificing relationships. Those who follow this style see people primarily as a means of accomplishing tasks; they tend to stress efficiency and controls.

5,5: MIDDLE-OF-THE-ROAD   The middle-of-the-road leader tries to be all things to all people but does not become overly concerned with anything. The manager who favors this style tries to keep things in balance by compromising and is willing to sacrifice some productivity for morale and vice versa.

9,9: TEAM APPROACH   The team-approach manager has a great deal of drive to accomplish tasks, but does not want to sacrifice people to do it. In fact, 9,9 leaders try to involve people to accomplish the tasks, reward people appropriately, and seek a mutual understanding and trust.

Beyond this basic approach there are a host of refinements and behavioral patterns that can, when studied in detail, contribute greatly to leadership effectiveness.

The Fiedler Contingency Theory

Fred Fiedler has developed a slightly different approach to leadership that is related to the managerial grid concept.[5] He suggests that the proper style of leadership is one that varies with the situation. In a situation in which workers are lax and undisciplined, a highly directive, task-oriented approach is likely to be the most productive, at least temporarily. But if this approach is implemented for too long a period, workers may eventually become so discontented with the lack of people orientation that productivity will fall as grumbling takes precedence over accomplishing. At this point, Fiedler suggests, a relationship-oriented approach to management can significantly improve the situation.

The essential point is that both relationship and task-management styles are valuable under different circumstances. This helps explain why different kinds of high-level leadership are required by agribusinesses at different points in their life cycles. A young, rapidly growing organization may require a style of leadership that is significantly different from the style of the mature, well-established agribusiness.

Theory X, Theory Y

Douglas McGregor has suggested a dual theory about human behavior in business that has important implications for management style and methods of motivation.[6] McGregor based his theory on what has come to be known as the "dual nature of humankind." For centuries, philosophers have noted that people have the capacity for love, warmth, kindness, and sympathy, but at the same time can exhibit hate, harshness, and cruelty.

This dichotomy led McGregor to an explanation of management style that is based on assumptions managers make about the people they supervise. McGregor referred to his dual theories as *Theory X* and *Theory Y*.

Theory X McGregor believed that traditional management practices and methods are based on the following set of assumptions about employees:

1. Most employees have an inherent dislike for work and will avoid it if at all possible.

2. People will work only when they are coerced, threatened, or at least controlled in all their activities.

3. Most people actually prefer to be closely controlled because they dislike responsibility and have little ambition.

4. Most people are basically self-centered and selfish.

---

[5]Fred E. Fiedler, *A Theory of Leadership Effectiveness*, New York, McGraw-Hill, 1967.
[6]Douglas McGregor, *The Professional Manager*, New York, McGraw-Hill, 1967.

HUMAN RESOURCE MANAGEMENT IN AGRIBUSINESS

5. Security is very important to most employees, and they are threatened by change.

6. Most employees are gullible, will believe anything, and are not very bright.

McGregor believed that for centuries these assumptions had served as the basis for most management styles: strong control with little concern for employee needs. Most of the supervisory practices resulting from Theory X assumptions have failed to tap the human resource potential in the employees being supervised.

Theory Y At the other end of the continuum is another set of assumptions derived from a belief in the natural goodness and creativity of human beings. Theory Y assumptions include the following:

1. Work, both physical and mental, is as natural as play or rest.

2. People can and will exercise self-control and evidence motivation to achieve goals to which they are personally committed.

3. The level of commitment is dependent on the rewards received for reaching the goals.

4. People basically like responsibility and will seek it.

5. People are naturally creative and have far more capability than is generally utilized.

Theory Y assumptions lead to a very different management style. Theory Y managers focus attention on employees themselves, attempt to draw out their creativity, and appeal to their willingness to accept responsibility. These managers do not abdicate their responsibility and authority to their employees. They are quick to enter into a dialogue that will help the manager and employee arrive at mutually acceptable goals, and to establish a reward system that is fulfilling to the employee. Theory Y management is not an easy style. It requires patience and a great deal of people skill on the part of managers.

Obviously, there is much appeal to the Theory Y management approach, and McGregor was a strong proponent of it, especially early in his career. If one fully accepted these appealing assumptions, there would be little need for time clocks, fixed working schedules, production quotas, and the like. However, the business community has not totally accepted the Theory Y approach; far from it. If the Theory X, Theory Y concept were considered on a continuum, the majority of managers today would probably be on the Theory X side. Even benevolent autocrats are basically Theory X thinkers, though they may not be unpleasant to work with.

It should not be assumed automatically that Theory X management is bad and Theory Y management is good. It is said that McGregor used the Theory X, Theory Y terminology intensively so as not to imply superiority of one style, even though he preferred the Theory Y approach. In fact, McGregor himself softened his strong support of the Theory Y position later in his career when he became a university administrator and personally experienced some of the frustrations associated with applying strong Theory Y management assumptions. Some employees hold Theory X assumptions about themselves and so perhaps prefer to be treated in the appropriate manner. But clearly there is great merit in the Theory Y approach, and agribusinesses have generally moved in this direction.

Management by Objectives

MBO (management by objectives) is a system of management whereby the supervisor and the subordinate jointly (1) set objectives that both agree are reasonable and in line with corporate goals, and (2) determine how performance will be measured in each area of major responsibility. The concentration is on results rather than on the process by which they are achieved.

First introduced by Peter Drucker in 1954,[7] the MBO process usually begins with a very broad set of objectives and sense of direction as established by the board of directors. Top management then develops its own objectives, consistent with the board's framework, and submits them to the board for reaction. Top management then asks middle management to develop and submit goals that are consistent with overall corporate goals as interpreted and applied to the middle managers' respective departments. Then top management and middle management coordinate these goals through a negotiating process until an acceptable set of goals and yardsticks to measure progress have been established. Next middle management works with lower management, until the process has been repeated throughout the organization.

There are obvious advantages to such a system. First, since it accords individuals a certain amount of input into their own goals, employees tend to become emotionally committed to accomplishing whatever they have targeted for themselves. Second, with MBO, the criteria for evaluation become crystal clear and are agreed on by all concerned, which eliminates many problems later on.

The process is also quite time-consuming, however. Often, proposed objectives are submitted, negotiated, and resubmitted repeatedly before agreement is reached. Although the MBO system is intended to enhance communication, its success is built on assumptions of preexisting communication and mutual trust. If subordinates intentionally establish goals that are unrealistically low, so that they can exceed their goals easily and look good, the entire system breaks down. Additionally, there must be commitment to the system from the top down. Whenever top management resorts to dictating all the objectives, others learn quickly what the game is and play accordingly.

[7]Peter Drucker, *The Practice of Management*, New York, Harper & Row, 1954.

Yet the appeal of an effective MBO system is strong; if done properly, it can be highly successful.

MOTIVATION

Motivation is the stimulus that produces action, and action, directed action, is the primary function of management. This is why managers are so concerned with the concept of motivation.

There have been many arguments about whether it is possible for a manager to actually motivate employees. Some say that a good manager is skillful in stimulating others to accomplish target objectives. But others argue that all motivation is really self-motivation, that it comes from within each individual. They say that managers affect the environment and provide the stimulus, but that it is ultimately up to the employee to decide to act. No matter which point of view seems more logical, management is responsible for results and must somehow stimulate, encourage, or coerce the employee behavior necessary to accomplish organizational goals and objectives, or else it must create an environment that will produce the same effect.

Motivation has many dimensions. It can be negative, as when an employee's attitude results in activity that undermines company goals, or it can be so positive that the employee becomes emotionally and personally involved in completing assignments well. Employees can be stimulated by positive rewards or by fear of losing privileges or by undesirable treatment.

Motivation is a topic of much research from which many theories have evolved, but most researchers agree that in some way motivation comes down to a matter of rewards and punishments. By controlling rewards and punishments, management can significantly affect employee performance.

The basic problem comes in trying to determine what rewards and punishments work in which circumstances. The situation is further complicated by the wide variation in people. A pat on the back may be motivating to one person, while a new title may be of paramount importance to another. Employees are motivated by whatever it is they want. Though perhaps a bit simplistic, this approach demonstrates the scope of the problem.

A brief overview of some widely used theories of motivation will provide useful ideas for managing and motivating people in agribusinesses.

Maslow's Need Hierarchy

Motivation focuses attention on the personal needs of human beings, so some understanding of human needs is necessary for effective supervision. One of the most useful and widely used models for human needs was developed by Abraham H. Maslow.[8]

Maslow's need hierarchy is based on the idea that different kinds

[8]Abraham H. Maslow, *Motivation and Personality*, 2d ed., New York, Harper & Row, 1970.

of needs have different levels of importance to individuals, according to the individuals' current level of satisfaction (see Figure 19-7). Needs basic to human survival take priority over other needs, but only until survival has been assured. After that point, other needs form the basis for the individual's behavior.

SURVIVAL   Maslow suggested that every human's most basic concern is for physical survival: food, water, air, warmth, shelter, and so forth. Obviously, humans cannot live unless these needs are at least minimally filled. These most basic needs are immediate and current. It takes only moments for a person gasping for breath to be more concerned about survival than about anything else in the world. Survival here and now is even more critical than survival over the days or weeks ahead.

SAFETY   Once immediate survival has been assured, humans become concerned about the security of their future physical survival. Today, this concern often takes the form of income guarantees, insurance, retirement programs, and the like.

BELONGINGNESS   After they have achieved a reasonable degree of confidence in their safety, people become concerned with their social acceptance and belonging. Social approval and acceptance into a peer group can cause a great deal of self-applied pressure and can be the source of strong motivation.

EGO STATUS   With a comfortable degree of social acceptance, most individuals become concerned with status in their group. Group respect and the need to feel important depend heavily on the responses of other group members. Recognition from superiors and peers is a compelling drive for many people and may be responsible for the upward movement of a great many successful people.

Figure 19-7   Maslow's need hierarchy. [*Abraham H. Maslow, "Motivation and Personality," Harper & Row, New York, 1970.*]

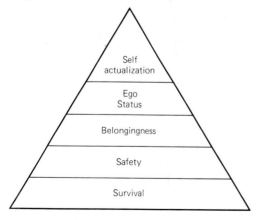

HUMAN RESOURCE MANAGEMENT IN AGRIBUSINESS

SELF-ACTUALIZATION   The highest level of need, and one that becomes important only when lower-level needs have been relatively well satisfied, is self-realization, the feeling of self-worth. This category of needs is highly abstract and takes a multitude of forms among different individuals. Self-actualization may be achieved through creative activities such as art, music, helping others in community activities, or building a business. The results of self-actualization are not that "Others need me," but rather that "I feel I've made an important and worthwhile contribution."

In our society, most people's survival and safety needs are relatively well taken care of, so these are seldom a strong motivation. Only when these needs are threatened do they become much of an issue. Although employees may feel good about a retirement plan, retirement benefits are seldom a factor in motivating them to higher levels of productivity. Even when job security becomes the focal point of labor negotiations, few would argue that such factors motivate employees to a very large degree, since they are becoming expected as normal and reasonable.

Belongingness or group acceptance can exert somewhat more pressure on people. Field hands paid an hourly rate may exert peer pressure on new workers not to work too hard, for fear that the newer workers will upset management expectation levels; in such cases, group rejection is usually the threat. Supervisors must recognize and encourage peer group acceptance and manager acceptance as important to employee performance.

Ego status or recognition is one of the most common and most productive needs through which agribusiness managers supervise and motivate employees. A great many people seem to be responsive to ego-need fulfillment. Nearly everyone feels "I want to be important and recognized." Managers who give employees recognition frequently, honestly, and positively are often rewarded with highly motivated personnel.

Recognition can take many forms. The easiest kind may be verbal; compliments are very effective when they are honest. It can be nonverbal: a pat on the back or simply a smile or nod of approval. Listening is also very powerful. Caring enough to listen to subordinates and to consider their opinions and feelings is one of the most powerful ways to recognize employees. Every successful manager has his or her own way of recognizing people effectively, but no matter what the technique, it is not accidental. It is purposeful management activity.

Self-actualization is not quite so easy to deal with in a management context because it comes from within the individual. Management can do best by simply (1) recognizing that some employees will be motivated by their own sense of self-accomplishment, (2) allowing this to happen, and (3) encouraging the proper environment for it, whenever possible.

Motivators and Hygienic Factors

A popular but somewhat controversial theory of employee motivation is one developed by Frederick Herzberg.[9] Herzberg argued that two separate kinds of factors explain workers' level of motivation. Each of these sets of factors is a separate continuum that affects workers' attitudes and performance. One class is called hygienic factors; the other is called motivators.

Hygienic Factors *Hygienic factors,* or *pain relievers,* are conditions necessary to maintain an employee's social, mental, and physical health. Research suggests that there are several such factors, including company benefits and policies, working conditions, job security, supervision, and pay. Herzberg argues that the presence of these factors does not make a worker happy, but if they are lacking, the employee is likely to become unhappy. Hence, hygienic factors are called pain relievers.

On a continuum, hygienic factors range from dissatisfaction to no dissatisfaction.

hygienic factors
Dissatisfaction←————————————→no dissatisfaction

These factors in and of themselves do not motivate people, but they are part of the environment, and when absent they can cause considerable employee discontent. For this reason, hygienic factors are sometimes referred to as *demotivators.* Low pay, constant fear of losing one's job, or dirty working conditions can, over a period of time, lead to disgruntled workers and poor performance, especially when these conditions are worse than those of another peer group.

Motivators *Motivators* are *reward producers,* or conditions that encourage employees to apply themselves, mentally and physically, more productively to their jobs. Motivators bring about commitment to the task. Most motivators are predominantly psychological, such as recognition, advancement, responsibility, challenging work, and the opportunity for further growth. The job itself becomes the major source of motivation. On a continuum, these factors range from no satisfaction to satisfaction.

motivators
No satisfaction←————————————→satisfaction

One of the controversies surrounding Herzberg's theory is whether money is a hygienic factor or a motivator. Many agribusinesses use money as an incentive to motivate employees to higher levels of performance. Proponents of such plans feel strongly that both salespeople on commission and field workers on wages tied to productivity are highly motivated to maximize their performance.

Yet Herzberg argues that these payment techniques are hygienic because they do not have the effect of increasing commitment to the job.

[9]Frederick Herzberg, *Work and the Nature of Man,* New York, World, 1966.

He says that pay incentives may work well temporarily, but once a particular pay and performance level has been reached, and the worker adapts to it, the pay itself is no longer a reason for productivity. In fact, if something happens to cut the pay level, the employee is likely to become frustrated and dissatisfied.

Salaried employees seem particularly susceptible to this phenomenon. Although they may work harder to achieve a pay raise, soon after it has been accomplished, their standard of living and expectations move up to form a new base point of normalcy; at the same time, their performance often regresses to a more comfortable level.

Although there is controversy surrounding Herzberg's idea that money is not truly a motivator, there is much to be gained from his theory. The message is that agribusiness managers should work to *enrich* the job. He suggests doing this through providing constant feedback, variety in tasks, and a means of making the job more important. This, he feels, will help the employee become more enthusiastic about the work.

TRANSACTIONAL ANALYSIS: A POSTSCRIPT

A popular and practical approach to understanding and supervising employees is the late Dr. Eric Berne's transactional analysis. Originally developed as a therapeutic tool, Dr. Berne's concepts have been applied widely to management and offer a useful, simple explanation of and language for discussing human behavior in business.[10]

P-A-C Model

Transactional analysis (TA) divides human behavior into three classes of ego states: parent, adult, and child. These ego states have nothing to do with age, but are simply descriptive of various types of feelings, thoughts, and behavioral patterns. In any situation, a person assumes one of these three ego states as either an automatic response based on past experiences, or a conscious response of controlled behavior.

Parent Ego State   The *parent ego*, sometimes referred to as the *learned concepts of life*, represents the values, attitudes, and behavioral patterns established early in life from authority figures, primarily parents (see Figure 19-8). The parent provides a role model from which the young child learns values and responses that usually serve as a basis of behavior throughout life. Three categories of the parent ego state are important to management: prejudiced parent, nuturing parent, and critical parent.
THE PREJUDICED PARENT   The *prejudiced parent* represents unfounded attitudes and opinions that are held without any logical basis or analysis. Prejudices may be either positive or negative, but in either case, they can drastically affect behavior. Sometimes referred to as *parent messages*, these prejudices often guide lives and have a strong influence on many decisions, such as the people with whom one associates,

[10]Dudley Bennett, *TA and the Manager*, New York, American Management Association, 1976.

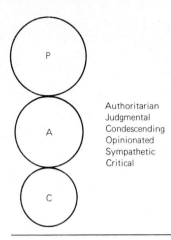

Authoritarian
Judgmental
Condescending
Opinionated
Sympathetic
Critical

Figure 19-8 Strong parent ego portrait.

one's lifestyle, where one lives, how one dresses, the job one takes, how one works, and an inexhaustible list of other factors. Although nonverbal examples transmit the strongest messages to young children, slogans and mottos also demonstrate the shoulds, oughts, musts, and should nots of life. Examples are:

Go to church on Sunday

Save for a rainy day

Red tractors are better than green tractors

We Smiths are community leaders

Salespeople are dishonest

Big business exploits the consumer

THE NURTURING PARENT   The *nurturing parent* represents attitudes and behavior that nurture and take care of others, just as parents offer sympathy, understanding, and warmth to their children. Nurturing behavior is common and appropriate to the supervisory role at times. In a very real way, managers must spend time consoling, encouraging, and listening to employees, just as a parent does with a child. Although nurturing is difficult for many men because of societal stereotypes, it can be a powerful and effective way for a supervisor to relate to subordinates.

THE CRITICAL PARENT   The *critical parent* refers to a stance involving critical attitudes and behavior. It is also thought to be learned from authority figures early in life. The manner by which one expresses critical feelings—tone of voice, gestures, posture, facial expressions, and words—is often similar to one's parents' behavior under similar conditions. Part of a supervisor's role includes reprimanding subordinates when necessary, which is purely the critical parent role.

Adult Ego State The *adult ego state* is often referred to as one's computer, because it presents logical thinking based on facts, like a computer (see Figure 19-9). In the adult state a person analyzes, estimates probabilities, computes dispassionately, and makes decisions. These decisions are not based on emotions or tradition, although both of these may be considered. Successful managers spend considerable professional time in their adult ego states.

Child Ego State The *child ego state* embodies people's feelings and emotions, or related childlike behavioral patterns. Nearly everything that happens in one's personal and professional lives is filtered through a screen of emotions that significantly affects the resulting behavior (see Figure 19-10).

THE NATURAL CHILD The natural child is the first and most significant subset of child ego state patterns. The *natural child* represents the full gamut of emotions and behavioral patterns that are natural even to very young children, such as happiness, sadness, anger, and fear. When a grown person is caught up in any of these basic emotions, the resulting behavioral patterns are likely to express these feelings in much the same manner as when that person was young. Of course, the emotion may be acted out in "big people" ways. An angry truck driver who has just been reprimanded by his supervisor may use language that is more profane, but his verbal outburst, clenched fists, horn honking, and gear stripping are probably reminiscent of a violent tricycle ride down a sidewalk following a scolding from his mother when he was 4 years old.

Children are also naturally impulsive and intuitive, and often "do what feels good"; so are many grown people in some parts of their life. Sometimes children are rebellious for no logical reason; they just feel like being contrary. So are employees on occasion.

Whenever a person is acting or feeling primarily childlike, the

---

Figure 19-9 Strong adult ego portrait.

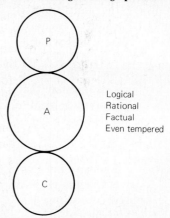

Logical
Rational
Factual
Even tempered

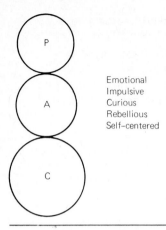

Emotional
Impulsive
Curious
Rebellious
Self–centered

Figure 19-10   Strong child ego portrait.

child ego state is present. Managers who recognize the role of the natural child can adjust their management styles to better cope with the circumstance.

THE LITTLE PROFESSOR   The *little professor* is a special set of childlike behavioral patterns that is especially important to managers. First, the little professor represents the natural creativity that seems to dwell in all humans. Unfortunately, parents and other authority figures often suppress this creativity in others by forcing them to fit into the same mold, and to think very much alike. But there does exist in all humans a tendency for creativity, if it can be released.

Of course, that creativity can cause problems, since it leads to unorthodox ideas and may create problems on the job. Creative people are often considered a bit "weird," and so seem hard to manage. They just do not fit in.

The little professor also represents one's natural intuitive ability to manipulate others to get what one wants. Many small children become quite skillful in coy and flirtatious behavior or temper tantrums that help them get what they want. For some, this style of behavior becomes a pattern that is carried to the job. Some secretaries know just how and when to ask their bosses for a special time off.

THE ADAPTED CHILD   The *adapted child* represents that time in one's early years when one did just what one was *supposed* to do, for no other reason than that one was supposed to do it. The adapted child suppresses natural tendencies and follows authority figures' wishes without question. Naturally, such people are easy to supervise, but they seldom originate new ideas or handle things on their own initiative.

Recognizing Ego States

Managers who can recognize ego states should be able to exercise appropriate supervisory action. Although the parent, adult, and child ego states cannot always be precisely defined or identified, many behavioral

HUMAN RESOURCE MANAGEMENT IN AGRIBUSINESS

clues will provide good indications of ego state. Managers can learn to watch for these clues and adjust their responses accordingly.

Clues include frequently used words and phrases, tone of voice, facial expressions, gestures, and posture (see Table 19-1). One clue does not generally give a strong indication of ego state, but a cluster of consistent clues is often meaningful, and a good basis for choosing management action.

When an employee is clearly acting from a child ego state, her or his behavior is somewhat predictable, especially if the manager has the advantage of past experience with the employee. A worker who is angry about a minor incident is not likely to be thinking rationally, but instead is emoting. The manager has several choices: to nurture the worker, listen to the worker's problem with a sympathetic ear, and calm the worker; or to be very firm, and order the employees to "shape up" or be fired. The manager could try to *kid* the employee out of a bad mood, or might try to *hook* the worker's adult ego state by asking questions that require logical reasoning to answer.

No one solution is best; it depends on the situation, the individuals, and the history of the problem. But the key is for the manager to recognize that there are alternatives and to choose the style of supervision that has the best chance of working.

Transactions Analyzed

A *transaction* is anything, verbal or nonverbal, that happens between two people. It involves both people's ego states. Analyzing transactions between people can be a powerful tool for managers who recognize that communications are an important part of successful supervision.

Whenever a person speaks, the communication originates from a specific ego state, and it is directed to a specific ego state in the other person. There are three types of transactions: complementary, crossed, and ulterior.

Complementary Transactions In *complementary transactions*, one person transmits a message and then receives an appropriate and acceptable response from the other person. In this kind of transaction, communication remains open and tends to continue.

There are many different types of complementary transactions; each encourages continued transactions, since the response is appropriate in the original communication. The most common complementary transactions are diagrammatically parallel: child–child ("Wow, is this fun!" "Yeah, let's do it tomorrow!"); adult–adult (see Figure 19-11); parent–parent ("You know, kids today just don't know how to work!" "Yeah, why just yesterday I saw this kid who . . ."); or parent–child (see Figure 19-12).

Crossed Transactions *Crossed transactions* are communications that do not mesh; an unexpected response is given from an inappropriate ego

TABLE 19-1 Ego State Clues

WORDS AND PHRASES	TONE OF VOICE	PHYSICAL EXPRESSION
Parent		
You should,	condescending	hands on hips
ought, must	consoling	drumming fingers
You can't . . .	critical	pointing finger
Don't . . .	sympathetic	looking down nose
Never, always,	judgmental	arms folded
maybe	worried	frowning
Because I		
said so		
If you ask me		
. . .		
Adult		
How many?	even	eye contact
When, where,	interested	level, alert
why?	intent	leaning forward
It's my opinion	natural	not tense
that . . .	moderated	
It seems to		
me . . .		
Child		
Wow! Gosh!	expressive	nervous
Do I hafto?	excited	frightened
Why me? I	happy	nail biting
won't!	sad	active
No!	angry	showing off
Please, can I?	whining	spontaneous
Swearing	defiant	
Look at me	curious	
Well, OK . . .	compliant	
I wish	impulsive	
I hope		

state, and the result is a gradual breakdown in communications (see Figures 19-13 and 19-14).

Crossed transactions often end in an argument, or at least ill feeling, and each ensuing set of transactions results in a more serious break. Quite frequently, the child gets hooked, that is, something is said that causes the person to move to the child ego state and automatically react on an emotional basis. The person may respond out of the hurt, angry, or rebellious ego state, or may revert to his or her own parent and attempt to heap ridicule on the other person. This one-upmanship generally causes an even worse cross in the next round.

Ulterior Transactions   *Ulterior transactions* contain two sets of transactions at the same time. The first is the surface message; the second is an ulterior message that is disguised but obvious to the other party.

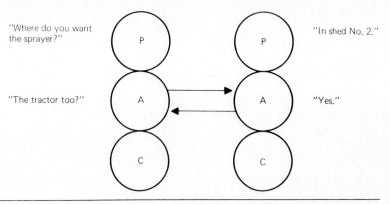

"Where do you want the sprayer?"

"In shed No. 2."

"The tractor too?"

"Yes."

Figure 19-11   Adult-adult complementary transaction.

Sarcastic messages of all kinds are considered ulterior messages (see Figure 19-15). They can come from any ego state, but are usually disruptive to communication.

Effective Communication   Effective communication is critical to good supervision. Managers who can analyze transactions have an effective tool for dealing with habitually difficult situations. It is, however, unreasonable to try to analyze all transactions. Too much analysis can result in a bad case of "analysis-paralysis" and can render a supervisor ineffective. Yet when a particular circumstance seems to repeatedly foster a breakdown in communications, careful analysis may provide much useful information about how to deal with the situation more productively.

It is the manager's responsibility to ensure good communication, not the subordinate's. Although one would hope that the subordinate would try to communicate objectively, the supervisor has no assurance of that, and so must assume that responsibility personally. Approaching

Figure 19-12   Parent-child complementary transaction.

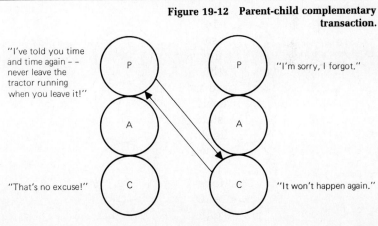

"I've told you time and time again – – never leave the tractor running when you leave it!"

"I'm sorry, I forgot."

"That's no excuse!"

"It won't happen again."

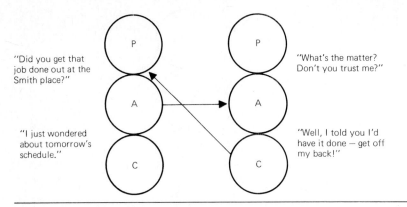

"Did you get that
job done out at the
Smith place?"

"I just wondered
about tomorrow's
schedule."

"What's the matter?
Don't you trust me?"

"Well, I told you I'd
have it done — get off
my back!"

Figure 19-13 Crossed transaction, adult/adult-child/child.

communication from the adult perspective can help the supervisor avoid getting hooked and losing control of the situation; professionals need to maintain control.

"Different Strokes for Different Folks"

Every person has the need to feel valued and recognized by others. In transactional analysis, any recognition of another person's presence is known as a *stroke*. It could be a word, simply "hi"; it could be a gesture—a smile or nod; it could be a touch—a handshake or a pat on the back. A stroke is anything that says, "I know you're there."

Strokes are necessary for growth and survival. Although it is not well understood, research shows that there is a connection between strokes and physical health. Infants who do not get sufficient physical stroking do not develop normally. Recent studies seem to indicate that persons who live alone have more health problems. Although the vast majority of people get enough attention to avoid being physically af-

Figure 19-14 Cross transaction, parent/child-parent/child.

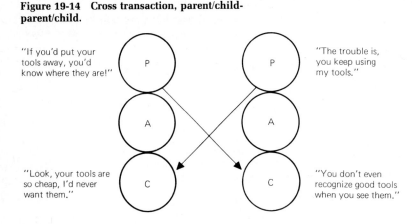

"If you'd put your
tools away, you'd
know where they are!"

"Look, your tools are
so cheap, I'd never
want them."

"The trouble is,
you keep using
my tools."

"You don't even
recognize good tools
when you see them."

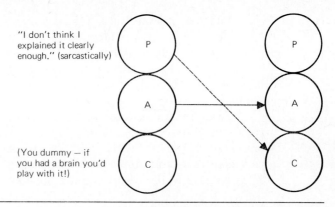

"I don't think I explained it clearly enough." (sarcastically)

P

A

(You dummy — if you had a brain you'd play with it!)

C

P

A

C

Figure 19-15   Ulterior transaction.

fected, strokes nonetheless play a very important role in emotional well-being.

Some people need many strokes in order to feel socially secure. They look for strokes wherever they can get them, and the job is one of their primary sources. In fact, hunger for strokes probably affects everyone's behavior on the job to some extent. But for some people, it is an utterly compelling drive.

Positive Strokes   *Positive strokes* are any form of recognition that leaves another person feeling good, alive, and significant. Friendships and close relationships are often built around positive strokes. People like those who stroke them, who care enough to listen. Positive strokes give real meaning to life for most people, and there are many kinds of positive strokes.

Positive Unconditional Strokes   *Positive unconditional strokes* convey the spoken or implied message, "I like you . . . you're OK with me." There are no conditions to the acceptance. This is thought to be the most meaningful kind of stroke; it is common among family members and close friends, but is frequently found in the business world as well. It is reflected in all kinds of behavior and conversation. Unconditional strokes may be affectionate or complimentary:

"Good morning!"

"That's a neat shirt!"

"I just don't know how we'd get along without you."

"You really know how to close a sale."

"Come join me for coffee."

"Your decision was well thought out."

Note that unconditional strokes enhance people's feelings about themselves. If the strokes are honest, genuine, and not overdone, they are of great benefit to a person's ego. When authentic unconditional strokes, sometimes called *warm fuzzies*, are given for something the other person is already proud of, they are easily believed and readily accepted.

Warm fuzzies cannot really be considered a management tool, since there cannot be any attempt to manipulate another's behavior with them. They are given freely, without strings. Yet managers who easily give recognition and show genuine approval fulfill important needs of subordinates, and the result is often positive motivation.

Positive Conditional Strokes   *Positive conditional strokes* are recognition given to intentionally modify another's behavior. Since it is management's job to motivate and guide the behavior of employees, positive conditional strokes are widely and appropriately used as a management tool.

Conditional strokes essentially say, "You're OK, if . . . " Acceptance of the other person is conditional on some expected behavior.

"If you keep that up, you'll get a bonus."

"I'm impressed when you work overtime."

"You look good today, for a change."

"If you make $1 million in sales, you'll get a trip to Acapulco."

Conditional strokes are sometimes called *plastic fuzzies*, because they resemble warm fuzzies but are a bit artificial. Though they qualify acceptance with an "if," they are not immoral or unethical; quite the contrary. They are a very popular and effective management and motivational tool. Plastic fuzzies help people feel good about themselves.

Negative Strokes   Negative forms of recognition also give attention and status to people. Negative strokes do not make people feel as good as positive strokes, but at least the person is getting some attention, and that is preferable to being ignored.

Negative strokes, sometimes called *cold pricklies*, most often come in the form of verbal criticism and reprimands. They usually originate from the critical parent ego state, and can easily hook the rebellious child, which tends to create real problems for the manager. They are meant to squelch and usually to hurt another person:

"What's the matter with you?"

"That's the trouble with these young kids."

"Can't you do anything right?"

"OK, I'll do it for you!"

Negative strokes are an effective way of getting attention. People who are ignored sometimes learn that inappropriate behavior can get them attention much faster and more predictably than any other type.

It is difficult to manipulate others into giving positive strokes, but it is easy to get negative strokes. As strange as it may sound, some workers may be so accustomed to negative strokes that negative strokes are the only thing they know how to get or how to handle. They may subconsciously create circumstances in which they get much-needed attention. It is possible that a person who is habitually late for work is looking for strokes.

Positive strokes are usually considered a more effective management technique than negative strokes. Clearly, however, recognition of employees is an extremely powerful form of motivating and supervising.

SUMMARY

Managing human resources is a fundamental responsibility of agribusiness managers. Managers must develop an organizational structure in which the responsibilities, authority, and accountability of individuals are clearly defined. Management must then direct and supervise daily activities, motivating and controlling employees to maximize productivity.

Many agribusinesses use a formal organizational chart to clarify the responsibilities, authority, and accountability of employees. Line organizations are structures in which everyone is in the chain of command and has direct responsibility for the primary functions of the business; in the line and staff organizational structure, specialists without authority are added to advise line managers; and in the functional organizational structure, specialists and advisors are given the authority to implement ideas in their area of special responsibilities.

Leadership is a challenging task for most agribusiness managers. There are many different styles of leadership, ranging from authoritarian to democratic to free rein. Management theorists have developed many models and theories to explain effective leadership. Blake and Mouton's managerial grid, Fiedler's contingency theory, McGregor's Theory X and Theory Y, and Drucker's management by objectives are all examples that have helped agribusiness managers become more effective leaders.

Motivating means stimulating employees to act in a specific way. Maslow explained people's basic needs as a hierarchy, and suggested that fulfillment of these basic needs is what motivates people. Herzberg pointed out that while some factors motivate people, other factors, such as money, become built into people's expectation level, thereby creating dissatisfaction when the factors are not satisfactory.

Transactional analysis is one of many models for understanding employees and what motivates them. It offers a simple language and framework for discussing various leadership problems.

Transactional analysis is a powerful tool that helps managers understand employees, but it should be considered only one additional tool. Managers need to examine many tools to find concepts that may be helpful to them.

There are no pat formulas or precise answers on the best way to manage people. Management is a complex process based on the individual characteristics of the leader, the led, and the situation. But there are many approaches and theories that can help the agribusiness manager a great deal.

DISCUSSION QUESTIONS

1. What gives a manager the right to issue orders to employees? Should the boss's orders always be followed? Why or why not?

2. The principles of single accountability and parity of responsibility and authority are often violated in business. What are the probable consequences of violating these principles? Have you personally experienced these situations? Explain.

3. Which type of formal organization would you prefer to work in, and why?

4. Identify power sources and status symbols in an organization in which you have worked or with which you have some familiarity. What impact, good or bad, did each have on the agribusiness?

5. Think of a manager or leader with whom you have worked or are familiar. How would you classify that person's leadership style?

6. What is your own feeling about Theory X, Theory Y? Where on this continuum would you be most likely to place yourself? Which type of leader do you believe is more effective, and why?

7. List at least five factors that you feel would motivate you on the job. List five factors that you consider hygienic. Do you think money is a motivator? Why or why not?

8. Draw an ego portrait of the typical manager and the typical employee. Explain why you have drawn it in this manner.

9. List at least five prejudiced-parent messages that can significantly affect people's job situations and supervision.

10. When is it appropriate for a manager to nurture an employee? To criticize? What response is each likely to elicit?

11. Give an example of a crossed transaction. Diagram the response.

12. How important are strokes in affecting people's behavior? Explain.

13. Sometimes people set others up to give them negative strokes. How can this make sense? What can a manager do about the situation?

AND NOW BACK TO GREENTHUMB

Review the case of Greenthumb, Inc., the business started by Marie and Bob Jordan, then answer the following questions.

QUESTIONS

1. How do you recommend Greenthumb be reorganized, and why?

2. Why have the current problems at Greenthumb surfaced? How could they have been avoided?

3. What are some of the possible sources of power in the informal organization at Greenthumb?

4. How does Greenthumb demonstrate the increasing problems of internal communication as a business grows?

APPENDIXES

OBJECTIVES

- Explore the job opportunities in agribusiness, now and in the future

- Suggest a practical entry into a professional agribusiness career

- Develop a systematic approach for finding and getting a job in agribusiness

- Review suggestions for getting off to a good start as a professional in agribusiness

Getting started in agribusiness requires special effort in finding the right opportunity.
A. In the store
B. In the office
C. In the field

THERE IS NO SUBSTITUTE FOR HARD WORK——Thomas A. Edison

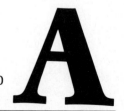

GETTING STARTED
IN AGRIBUSINESS MANAGEMENT

A

B

THE BUSINESS OF JOB HUNTING

So far, the authors have striven to develop basic management concepts as they apply to the running of an agribusiness. But if you stop to think, many of these concepts are applicable to a wider field of activity. Before you can act as an agribusiness manager yourself, you must find the kind of job that will give you practical, real-world experience to go along with the concepts you have already digested. That is where your new-found knowledge can help.

In a real sense, looking for a job constitutes a business proposition in and of itself. A great deal of time and money have been invested in what you must believe is a marketable product—yourself. Now that that product has been completed (though, of course, you will continue to develop through a lifetime), the task before you is to sell the product as effectively as possible. It may interest you to know that the field you are about to enter has much to offer and that your training has prepared you to meet its challenges.

The Challenge of Expanding Opportunities

Just a few years ago, those who made their living in agribusiness might have been dismissed as participating in a relatively backward industry. But the world crop shortages of the mid-1970s changed all that. Production agriculture and the myriad of agribusinesses supporting it became a focal point for growth, and many firms never before associated with agriculture struggled for a foothold in the market. Conglomerates that already owned agribusiness divisions began to allocate more of their resources to agribusiness ventures, and often gave their agribusiness divisions top priority. Publicly, agribusiness took on new prestige as a progressive industry with much growth potential. As many of the large firms that had previously viewed agriculture as a backward, low-return, high-risk industry began to tap the abundant production capabilities of North American agriculture, the number of opportunities for professional agriculturists began to increase. These opportunities have been increasing ever since.

Agriculture is the only major renewable resource in North America. Properly managed, it offers the potential for a constant export that regenerates itself and can even grow annually, whereas most other natural resources are gradually depleted. World demand for our agricultural production continues to grow, as world population increases and an increasing world standard of living puts foreign customers in a better position to buy our agricultural products. The Soviet Union, China, Western Europe, and many developing countries offer a growing market to help relieve our balance-of-payment problems. Because of the natural advantages of North America in food production, and because the economic system in the United States encourages productivity and efficiency, there is every reason to believe that American agriculture will continue to improve, offering outstanding opportunities for aggressive, well-trained young agriculturists.

It is true that the number of agricultural production units (farms, ranches, etc.) on this continent continues to fall. Rising labor costs and the availability of more efficient production methods have decreased and will continue to decrease the number of *people* directly involved in production agriculture. But this trend has been possible only because of the extensive and growing number of support services assisting and facilitating farm production. While the cost prohibits many people from getting into farming, the opportunity to work in the agribusinesses that supply and service farmers or market farm products is expanding rapidly.

Finding a Place in the Scheme
As the opportunities increase, it becomes more and more important for you to develop a strong sense of yourself and of your place in the scheme. A positive self-image begins with a strong sense of the qualities and background you have to offer.

What You Have to Offer For one thing, you can contribute a great deal of energy and enthusiasm. You have at least some technical agricultural competence that your employer can build on. Of course, there are endless things to learn, but your employer is expecting to help you learn the things you need to know, and your college training has been geared to teach you to learn quickly and fully. Your interest in and experience with agriculture is also valuable to your employer. At school you may have made many contacts on whom you can call if your company needs specialized advice. In short, your employer is interested in buying your loyalty, competence, enthusiasm, and willingness to learn and work.

Selecting a Company Deciding whether to work in a large corporate organization or a smaller local agribusiness is often difficult. Predictably, both prospects offer advantages and disadvantages; the final choice rests on the values and interests of the individual involved.

Larger firms tend to offer more prestige, particularly among students as they compare job offers. Even later, mention of employment with a well-known firm tends to generate a spark of recognition in conversation.

In addition, larger firms are usually more formally organized. Each job has a title and a job description. There is a formal, often extensive fringe benefit plan, and a training program may be detailed in advance.

Larger firms often require their employees to move from one location to another for promotions. Even at one location, there is usually ample opportunity to travel, sometimes extensively.

Smaller firms, on the other hand, offer much more of a "down home" flavor, since everyone in the company may know everyone else. There may be almost a family atmosphere, with all employees on a first-name basis. Since the local company usually has few locations, moving is not necessary. Power structures and benefit plans may not be so formal, travel is less frequent, and advancement paths are less clear. Responsibilities are often broader and delegated earlier. Training programs are usually on the job, but working closely with an experienced pro and having broader responsibilities earlier can be a very effective way to learn. Even very small, family-owned firms can offer good opportunities. Of course, advancement in the family-owned agribusiness may be limited unless provision is made for partial ownership after a few years. Plans to share ownership with employees of privately owned companies are growing in popularity. Usually, the stipulation is made that any ownership share will be sold back to the majority stockholder at termination of employment.

Selecting a Job Finding and deciding on your first job will be a very important and exciting step in your professional agribusiness career. In all likelihood, you have been preparing yourself for several months to several years for taking that first job, yet you may be somewhat confused about the kind of job you want or what firm you would like to work for.

Some new entries into the job market half expect agribusinesses to inundate them with job offers. When this does not occur, they should not interpret it as an indication that opportunities are lacking. It simply means that they must look for the opportunities rather than waiting for the opportunities to search them out.

Some people find it easier to get job offers than others because they have more contacts, more experience, a stronger record, or a more pleasant personality than others. Those who are not in this position must simply work harder to catch up.

Notice that we have not talked about finding the *right* job. There is no one right job. Most people could enjoy and prosper with many different alternatives. The difference between best and second best may be slight, so the important thing is to select an acceptable and appropriate opportunity. One of the most valuable experiences is to go to agribusiness managers in your home community and ask them what you can expect from different types of agribusiness jobs. They will almost always be delighted to spend time with you. Not only will you gain a great deal of useful general information, but you may get some excellent job leads from such people.

SETTING OBJECTIVES The first step in the job-selection process is to set both personal and professional objectives for yourself. Think through what you want out of life. What kinds of things do you enjoy? Do you want to travel, and how much? Do you want to work outdoors or in an office? How important are money, power, prestige? Do you have a strong geographical preference? If you are married, your spouse will play an extremely important role in answering these questions. It is a good idea to put your thoughts on paper. This may help to clarify some issues, such as values and priorities, that are partially hidden even from yourself.

DEVELOPING A STRATEGY Once you have decided what your goals and objectives are, you must develop a strategy for finding job opportunities that will satisfy your objectives. This means developing an action plan that specifies how to proceed. Will you mass-produce résumés, or will you depend largely on personal contacts? Will you devote most of your attention to campus interviews, or will you go to the field yourself? You may want to talk with your counselor or placement service as you develop your strategy.

BUDGET TIME AND MONEY   Be sure to budget adequate resources to do justice to your marketing effort. After all, you have invested much time (several years?) and money (thousands of dollars?) in this product. It does not make sense to wait until graduation or to consider only a few options in marketing yourself. Plan to spend money (borrowed if necessary) to make long-distance calls and to visit employers. Start early enough to do it properly several months before you are ready to go to work.

Where to Look for Jobs   Your choice of where to look for job opportunities will be influenced not only by your objectives but by the type of agribusiness that seems best. Many students make the error of looking only at agribusinesses that send professional recruiters to the school. While many of these firms offer excellent job opportunities, usually only the larger organizations can afford to recruit formally, and many of their opportunities are limited to sales jobs. A great many agribusiness opportunities are with smaller or local agribusiness firms that need to add new employees only occasionally, and so do not formally recruit. Searching out these alternatives requires a far different approach.

SCHOOL PLACEMENT SERVICE   Many schools do an excellent job of matching firms and students by organizing and facilitating job interviews. This is an excellent opportunity and should be used early and extensively by the student. Students should check this service for interesting possibilities at least weekly during their last year.

PROFESSORS AND TEACHERS   Instructors are often the best single source of information. Often they have a great number of personal con-

---

EXHIBIT

Job-search Checklist   **A-1**

Job Search Checklist

1. Evaluate your goals and objectives on paper.
2. Talk with counselors and teachers for ideas.
3. Develop a strategy — a time-phased plan.
   a. Determine what kinds of firms you would like to work with.
   b. Develop a list of specific companies that sound good.
   c. Find the name of an individual in each company.
   d. Initiate contact with each person.
   e. Send each person a resume and letter.
4. Interview with firms that may come to your school.
5. Interview trip.
6. Analyze alternatives.
7. Decide.
8. Don't look back.

tacts. Since they know both you and potential employers, they can be very helpful in locating possible jobs. Even if they do not have a list of firms that are currently hiring, they know the firms that have employed past graduates, and so are in a position to divulge some good leads. Do not hesitate to ask for help. Remember, the success of your school's agribusiness program depends on successful placement of its graduates. Your advisors want you to get a good job.

TRADE ASSOCIATIONS Nearly every agribusiness industry is represented in national (and often state) trade organizations. The offices of these organizations are in touch with members' needs. Some organizations go so far as to publish lists of available job openings. Libraries have special books listing state and national associations and their addresses.

GOVERNMENT AGENCIES With challenging and well-paying jobs in various agencies of the USDA, the government itself employs many agriculturists. The Farmers Home Administration, Soil Conservation Service, and Agricultural Stabilization Service are typical examples. Usually, it is best to contact a representative of the agency in which you are interested to get additional information. Sometimes students must take civil service exams to qualify for these jobs. Veterans and other special groups are given particular consideration by these agencies.

EMPLOYMENT AGENCIES The number of private firms that specialize in finding employees for agribusinesses are increasing. While most of these firms are quite reputable, some are less so. Reputable agencies usually work only with employers who are willing to pay the fees for the agency's services. If you are not sure about an agency, check it with the Better Business Bureau or with someone who knows the firm.

OTHER STUDENTS AND FRIENDS Some of the best information may come from others who are also in the job market. Some students worry about competing with each other, but this is seldom a problem. Each person is so different from every other person that the same jobs generally do not appeal to everyone. Work together and compare notes.

Often relatives and friends back home have some contacts. These contacts do not have to be for known job openings; simply making contact with someone in an established firm can be helpful. Managers in smaller firms may not decide to add a new person until someone contacts them and impresses them.

PERSONAL CONTACTS Your own personal contact network is likely to be your most productive source of information. Aggressive pursuit of many sources often uncovers unusual possibilities. One lead sometimes flows directly into another. Some of the books in your library or placement center, such as *The College Placement Annual* or *Moody's Industrials,* list hundreds of firms. If you are primarily interested in hometown firms, use the Yellow Pages to make a list of agribusinesses you might be interested in.

Résumés A résumé is a written summary of your personal, educational, and professional qualifications. Its purpose is to present prospective employers with enough information to determine whether they are interested in you. In some ways, it is a formal advertisement for yourself.

Résumés are developed individually, so no two are alike. However, most include identification of the candidate, career objectives, personal and professional experience that might be valuable to the job, employment history, and sometimes references with whom the employer can check (see Exhibit A-2).

Usually, résumés are limited to a single page. A recent photo may or may not be printed on the résumé or attached to it. It is important to include a personalized cover letter for each company that will receive the résumé. References should be drawn from non-family members who know you well. Among the references, be sure to include a previous

Sample Résumé	EXHIBIT A-2

DAVID K. COLEMAN

CURRENT ADDRESS
1028 State Street
West Lafayette, Indiana 47906
Phone: (317) 743-4681

PERMANENT ADDRESS
R. #2 Box 50-A
Summitville, Indiana 46070
Phone: (317) 536-2372

PERSONAL DATA
Birth Date: July 20, 1957
Marital Status: Single
Height: 6'1'', Weight: 175 lbs.
Health: Excellent
Available: May 7, 1979

JOB OBJECTIVITY
I am interested in a rewarding and challenging business career in sales or marketing. I would eventually be interested in a managerial position.

EDUCATION
Senior in Agricultural Economics.
Major grade point average: 5.07/6.0
Overall grade point average: 4.74/6.0
Graduation Date: December 1979
Have taken wide background of courses including:
Agronomy, Botany, Animal Science, Chemistry, English, and Communication.

ACTIVITIES AND HONORS
Purdue Pete, Purdue University Mascot
Interfraternity Council Junior Board under Development
Interfraternity Council Senior Board, Vice-President of Financial Affairs
GIMLET Leadership Honorary
GREEK photographer
Campaign worker, photographer for student body elections ticket
Elected Precinct Committeeman, Tippecanoe County
Old Masters Personal Host
Old Masters Central Committee
Nominee for the Bruce Kendall Award for Excellence in Communication

WORK EXPERIENCE
F.I.C.B. Summer Trainee (Albion Production Credit Association)
Free lance photographer
Mounds State Park Laborer
Farm Laborer
Purdue University, Ag Economics Dept.

REFERENCES AND ADDITIONAL INFORMATION FURNISHED UPON REQUEST employer who knows you well enough to evaluate you, but get the employer's permission first.

Some Tips for a Successful Career
There is no one clear path to a successful career in agribusiness. It seems trite to say that dedication, hard work, perseverance, and loyalty are necessary, yet the authors cannot resist the temptation to share a few tips that have proved useful to the many graduates they have worked with over the years.

Begin at the Grass-Roots Level Most people begin their professional careers in agribusiness physically handling products and servicing customers. This grass-roots experience is invaluable for understanding the fundamentals of agribusiness management. A strong argument can be made that these experiences are a prerequisite for any significant advancement into management. This phase of the professional career helps a person understand firsthand what it means to carry out management directions, to communicate with customers effectively, and to deal with the hectic activity of peak-season responsibility.

Sometimes these work experiences are at least partially gained in summer work or part-time jobs. Other times, working in several facets of the agribusiness may be part of a formal training program for new employees. Going through this process is extremely beneficial for gaining the respect of peers and, even more importantly, the respect of those who may ultimately become your subordinates.

Unfortunately, many young people become impatient with this phase of their professional development. After they have spent 2 or 4 years formally preparing themselves in post-high school training, they are anxious to get on with it. Many feel that a few weeks or months working very much as a laborer in an agribusiness are unnecessary and contribute little. Yet experienced people who have been through the same professional route continually say that a sound base of work experience makes for a far better manager.

Many agricultural graduates learn special skills in some phase of technical agriculture that are likely to be the focal point of their first job. Horticulture, agricultural mechanics, agronomy, animal science, and other specialized curricula all offer special opportunities for agribusiness jobs. Seldom will these entry-level jobs offer much opportunity to make extensive use of a broad range of management tools. But they do allow and usually require extensive use of technical know-how. These entry-level jobs offer the opportunity to really learn the practical technical skills and their application to real-world problems.

Employees who do quite well in performing their technical functions are usually promoted, often into jobs where their technical expertise is no longer as important as their communications, leadership, and general management skills. This phenomenon sometimes creates real frustration for many well-qualified, capable agriculturists who are well trained technically, but not well equipped for advancement into management. Seldom do people fail to reach their full professional potential because of lack of technical competence; rather, management and people skills are more frequently the limiting factors.

"Pay Your Dues"   Accept the initiation period during which all new employees must prove themselves to become accepted by their peers. This period is particularly troublesome for young college people who have difficulty relating to older workers who have no college training. It sometimes means being the butt of practical jokes and accepting less desirable jobs, but this period should not last forever, so grin and bear it.

Learn the Power Structure   In every agribusiness there are individuals who wield far more power than their formal position would suggest. Their power may result from seniority, proximity to real power, personality, or a number of other things. Although it may not be wise to play politics, it is equally unwise to ignore powerful people in organizations.

Make Your Boss Look Good   Nothing can get you more attention and favorable evaluations (including pay raises) than making your boss look good. If you can get your boss promoted, there will be an opening for you. Or, alternatively, the boss may take you along with him or her. When talking to others in the organization, speak of your boss with respect. Compliment your boss when appropriate, and express gratitude when you genuinely appreciate something.

Be a Team Member   A successful agribusiness operates as a team. Each member has specific assigned tasks, but the job is not complete when an individual finishes an individual task. The total team must work toward completion of the total task. This often means helping others, even at the expense of temporarily postponing completion of your own task, if that is in the best interest of the larger effort.

Be Visible   While teamwork is critical, it is also important to do something that is clearly your own. That is, make sure that at least some of the results of your efforts are noticeable to others. Sometimes this will involve some small extra project, which you may have initiated on your own, that you believe might be valuable to the company.

Make Suggestions   As a professional, you have a responsibility to watch for weak areas and suggest improvements. Do not be afraid to voice your ideas; suggestions make it clear that you care. Make your suggestions tactfully, and do not expect your idea to suddenly change the way the business is run. Have the patience to wait for an idea to take hold, and do not take lack of response as a personal rebuff. Remember to separate criticism of your ideas from criticism of you as a person. The old technique of "making the boss think she or he thought of it" can do wonders to get ideas accepted. Plant the seed and let it grow.

Recognize That Change Is Threatening People become accustomed to and comfortable with certain methods of operating a business. Whenever someone suggests changes, people may become threatened and resist changes. Recognize this principle and promote change cautiously.

Weigh the Cost of Being Right Whenever conflicts or differences of opinion arise, you must decide whether to push your ideas, and if so, how far. Even when you are absolutely certain you are correct, you may decide that your gain from pushing your idea is more than outweighed by the resulting ill feeling from the other person or persons. Weigh this carefully.

Allow People to Save Face In situations in which a conflict arises and it becomes obvious that you are in the right, avoid the temptation of forcing the other person to admit that he or she is wrong. Although there may be a lot of personal satisfaction in such an action, the embarrassment of the other person can create bitter feelings that you will have to live with for a long time. Always leave the other person with a way of saving face.

Manage Expectations All discontent is relative to expectation. If you tell someone that you can make a delivery by 3 P.M. and you arrive at 3:15, the customer is likely to be frustrated. If you promise delivery by 3:30 and arrive at 3:15, the customer will be impressed by your promptness. This is not to suggest that you should regularly underestimate your ability. It means that you should be realistic and not overstate what you can do.

Ask for Help It is amazing what people will do when you simply ask them, yet pride or ignorance often keeps people from asking for help directly. This technique is especially helpful for people who are new on the job. Experienced personnel are often eager to play a parental role and may even be protective.

Always Give a Little Extra For fast movement and a rewarding professional career, it pays to do a bit more than is expected of you in every aspect of your job. Do not leave at the stroke of 5 P.M.; stay a bit later. Get there a few minutes early each day. Make an extra phone call. Always doing a little bit more than what is expected can generate real benefits.

Professional Agribusiness Management

A *profession* is an occupation that requires specialized knowledge, which in turn requires long and intensive training. Professional agribusiness managers require the formal study of management methods as they apply to the agribusiness. Professionals must learn how to analyze, decide, plan, execute, and lead. Some of this learning is formal, in the classroom or in seminars and workshops. Some of this learning, perhaps the greater part of it, is *experiential,* or on the job; while some of the learning is personal, through reading books and self-examination. A professional manager is continually striving to become better and more effective.

A profession requires a certain code from its members. Although agribusiness managers do not have to take formal vows, there is clearly a code of conduct expected of professional managers. Legal regulations form one kind of base for acceptable management conduct, but ethical expectations go much deeper than simple legalities. Managers have a great moral and ethical responsibility to employees, stockholders, and the general public for effectively and efficiently managing the resources under their command. Professional agribusiness managers accept this responsibility.

A profession is also an occupation engaged in for financial rewards. Agribusiness managers have great opportunities for significant financial rewards. Owners and investors are fully aware of the importance of good management in protecting and increasing the value of their investment. Compensation in the form of salary and bonuses can make agribusiness management a very rewarding profession.

Agribusiness management *is* a profession. Becoming a professional manager of an agribusiness is an exciting challenge to meet.

SUMMARY
Agribusiness offers growing, almost unlimited opportunities for aggressive, well-trained young agriculturists. Yet job opportunities are not likely to seek out the applicant. A productive job search requires a systematic and logical approach, much as a marketing manager would plan to market a product. Objectives should be carefully thought through, a strategy mapped out, and the plan executed. An integral part of the job search involves seeking employment information from a variety of sources and then sending résumés and seeking personal interviews.

Finding an appropriate job requires a great deal of common sense and perseverance. There are a great many factors that contribute to an individual's success in agribusiness, and the true professional will meet the challenges presented by all of them.

DISCUSSION QUESTIONS
1.   Why are job opportunities in agribusiness looking particularly good now and in the future?

2.   Would you rather work in the agricultural division of a large national corporation or in a smaller, local agribusiness? Why?

3.   What business management concepts can easily be applied to marketing your services to prospective buyers? Show by illustration how each tool might be helpful.

4. Develop a résumé for yourself.

5. At the end of this Appendix, there are a number of tips for success on the job in agribusiness. Based on your own experience, suggest three more tips that you believe could be helpful to others.

MINICASE

Develop a three- to five-page paper spelling out the goals and objectives of your professional career.[1] Be sure to include:

1. A brief summary of your personal history

2. A brief description of yourself; what kind of person you are

3. Your major strengths and weaknesses

4. A specific statement of your career objectives (avoid general statements like "to be happy")

5. The kinds of work you think you might enjoy most

6. The importance to you of:
    a. money
    b. travel
    c. working outdoors
    d. working in agriculture
    e. working with farmers or ranchers
    f. being home every night

[1]If you have a spouse or "significant other," be sure to include his or her thinking in your responses.

GLOSSARY

B

GLOSSARY

Account A separate recording for a specific financial information category referring to the income or expenses of a business.

Accounts payable The amount of money owed to outside businesses for any items purchased on credit and for which payment is expected to be made in less than 1 year.

Accounts receivable The total amount customers owe to a business as payment for purchases. These accounts result from the granting of credit to customers.

Accounts receivable loan A loan for which the bank lists a business's accounts receivable as collateral.

Accountability Being answerable to another for performance.

Accounting period A predetermined regular interval for which accounts in the ledger are summarized.

Accrual basis of reporting The method of reporting revenue (income) in the statement of operations for the period during which it is earned (regardless of when it is collected), and reporting an expense in the period in which it is incurred (regardless of when the cash disbursement is made).

Accruals Those financial obligations that accumulate each day for which there has been no formal bill or invoice, such as taxes payable and wages payable.

Acid test A liquidity relationship that clearly delineates a firm's ability to meet immediate cash needs: (Cash + marketable securities + accounts receivable) ÷ total current liabilities = acid test.

Advantage The direct physical or operating result of a feature of a product.

Advertising Mass communication with potential customers, usually through public media.

Agribusiness Any business organization that supplies farm inputs or services, or that processes, distributes, or wholesales agricultural products, or retails them to consumers.

Agribusiness sector The diverse commercial enterprises that provide the inputs to the farm sector and the correct mix of "service" to products as they move through the food system to the final consumer. The total complex of agribusiness that collectively supplies agricultural products and markets, processes, and distributes agricultural products.

Balance sheet An accounting statement that shows the financial makeup and condition of a business at a specific time by listing what the business owns, what it owes, and what the owners have invested in the business. It shows a balance between assets and claims against them.

Benefit An interpretation of what an advantage of a product is likely to mean to a particular customer.

Bond A form of loan in which an organization issues a promise to pay back a certain sum of money to the bondholder at some specified future date.

Borrowing capacity The ability of a customer to meet loan-repayment obligations.

Break-even point (BE) The point at which income generated from sales just equals the total costs incurred from those sales. Break-even point is calculated by fixed cost ÷ contribution to overhead.

Budget A formal, written plan showing how a firm's resources—usually financial—are to be allocated during an operating period. It serves as a basis for monitoring performance and controlling operations.

Business An organization created to coordinate and manage private resources to generate a profit.

Capital The financial resources of a business comprising, in its broadest sense, all the assets of the business and representing both owned and borrowed funds.

Capital investment An investment in plant facilities or equipment that requires a long-term financial commitment.

Capitalism An economic system in which property is owned and controlled by private citizens.

Cash Funds that are immediately available for use without restriction, such as checking account deposits in banks, cash register money, and petty cash.

Cash budget A projection of a firm's income flow and cash needs on a periodic basis to enable management to plan, monitor, and control its cash (flow).

Centralized cooperative A large cooperative serving farmers in a wide geographical area through its own local facilities. Farmer-members own and control the centralized regional cooperative that, in turn, controls all local facilities. Control is from the top down.

Chain supermarket A group of eleven or more stores under one central management.

Closed shop laws Legislation that requires everyone working for a company that has a union contract to belong to that union.

Cold calls A method of prospecting that involves simply stopping by every farm or agribusiness in the market area without prior selection criteria.

Cold pricklies (Transactional analysis) A negative stroke; it most often comes in the form of verbal criticism and reprimands.

Collateral A pledge of a firm's assets to guarantee payment of a loan.

Collective bargaining A process in which employers and representatives of employees attempt to arrive at agreements governing the conditions under which the employees are willing to work for the employer.

Commercial finance companies Those finance companies that specialize in business and commercial loans.

Common-size statement A method of analyzing the profit and loss and balance sheet figures using percentages and comparing them with those of a group of similar-size businesses.

Common stock A specific share of ownership in a corporation that carries with it the privilege of exercising control through a vote in electing directors and the right to share in any profits or losses incurred by the business.

Compensatory balance A specified amount of money that must be retained in a bank account while a loan is outstanding.

Competitive pricing Pricing methods based on competitors' prices, simply setting prices at the "going rate."

Complementary transactions (Transactional analysis) One person transmits a message and then receives an appropriate and acceptable response from the other person. Communication remains open and tends to continue.

Compounding A method of calculating interest in which interest earned periodically is added to the principal and becomes part of the base on which future interest is earned.

Consensus A qualitative technique in which knowledgeable people associated with a business are each asked separately for their opinions about a particular situation.

Continuous production A total production network that involves the flow of inputs in an uninterrupted way through a standardized system to product outputs that are basically the same.

Contribution to overhead (CTO) That portion of income from each unit of sales that remains after variable costs are covered; it is applied toward the fixed or overhead costs: $CTO = SP - VC$ (selling price per unit minus variable cost per unit).

Control The process of monitoring performance, as compared with preestablished standards, for the purpose of making adjustments to ensure that goals will be accomplished.

Cool calls A method of prospecting that involves calling on those one believes to be likely prospects.

Cooperative A business corporation that is organized to serve the needs of its member-patrons rather than to make a profit on its own.

Cooperative advertising Local advertising that is cooperatively sponsored by the manufacturer and the local dealer or distributor through a cost-sharing program.

Coordinating An effort to ensure that all the gears of an organization mesh smoothly; that the actions of a group of people are unified and synchronized.

Corporation An artificial being endowed by law with the powers, rights, liabilities, and duties of a natural person. A corporation's assets are controlled by itself, not by the owners (stockholders) directly.

Cost-based pricing Pricing based on adding a constant margin onto the basic cost of the individual product or service.

Cost basis of valuation The practice by which valuable resources called assets are recorded at their acquisition price.

Cost of goods sold The total cost to the business of goods that were actually sold during the specified time period. This includes such items as raw materials, freight costs for shipping goods to the business, and any damaged or lost goods that must be absorbed.

CPM (critical path method) A method of scheduling that involves a diagrammatic representation of the network of activities in which a production operation is engaged. Similar to PERT.

Crossed transactions (Transactional analysis) Communications that do not mesh; an unexpected response is given from an inappropriate ego state; the result is a gradual breakdown in communications.

CTO pricing A method of encouraging extra sales by selling additional product above and beyond the sales projection at some price greater than the variable cost of handling the product so as to make a contribution to overhead.

Current assets An accounting term designating actual cash or assets that can be converted to cash during one normal operating cycle of the business, typically 1 year. It represents financial resources that might be quickly converted to cash to meet short-term financial obligations.

Current liabilities Those outsiders' claims on a business that will fall due within one normal operating cycle, usually 1 year.

Current ratio A liquidity relationship used to determine a firm's ability to meet its short-term obligations: Total current assets ÷ total current liabilities = current ratio.

Debenture note A promise issued in exchange for the loan of financial capital; it usually creates a security against the general assets of the firm or a specific part of the company's stock and property.

Decision making The process of choosing a course of action between alternatives for the purpose of achieving desired results. A logical procedure for identifying the problem, discovering alternative solutions, analyzing them, and choosing a course of action.

Delegation downward principle Authority should be delegated downward to the lowest level at which the decision can be made competently.

Demand A measure of the amount of a product or service that consumers are willing to buy at different prices. It shows the relationship between price and the quantity demanded.

Demand elasticity A measure showing the relative change in quantity demanded as price changes. It shows the responsiveness of quantity demanded to given changes in price.

Demand forecast Immediate, medium-range, and long-range forecasts of demand for a product that take into account not only trends of past performance in the agribusiness but also general economic and consumer-preference trends.

Democratic A style of leadership that favors a shared decision-making process.

Derived demand Demand that is based on the demand for another product with which the product is closely associated or used in the production process. The demand for most farm supplies is derived from the demand for farm products.

Direct selling A process that involves prospecting for new customers, precall planning, getting the customer's attention and interest, making presentations, handling objections, and closing the sale in a direct, one-on-one contact with customers.

Directing Guiding and supervising the activities of others to accomplish predetermined objectives.

Discount pricing A method of pricing that offers customers a reduction from the published or list price for specified reasons, such as volume purchases or preseason ordering.

Discounted loan A loan that has the amount of interest to be paid deducted from the cash sum at the time it is borrowed: Amount of loan − amount of interest paid = sum of available cash (discounted loan).

Diversification The technique of adding other lines of business that pose different risks and opportunities so that the likelihood of a loss in one area will be offset by the possibility of gain in another.

Early adopters Respected citizens (producers or consumers) who adopt new ideas quickly but with caution. They represent the next 13½ percent of the customers (after innovators) to try out a new idea, product, or service. They are opinion leaders in a community.

Early majority Deliberate people who see themselves as progressive, but not generally as leaders. This group represents the next 34 percent (after the early adopters) to try a new idea, product, or service.

Economic profit The residual income (left over) after the accounting cost (all actual measurable costs) and opportunity costs are subtracted from sales.

Economics The study of how the scarce resources of land, labor, capital, and management are combined to meet the needs of people, and how these needs are distributed.

Economies of scale A principle stating that larger plants, if efficient, can result in a lower cost per output unit because the larger size allows the plant to purchase more cheaply or operate more efficiently.

Efficiency A ratio measuring the output or production of a system or process per unit of input.

Elasticity A concept showing the relationship of two changing variables relative to each other. It reflects the responsiveness of one variable to changes in another.

Equal marginal return principle Using a variable input of limited quantity in several enterprises to the point where marginal returns among enterprises are equal.

Equity capital A source of funds that does not have to be repaid. It is secured either by reinvesting profits from the business or from investors who are willing to risk additional money in the business.

Evaluation The surveillance of progress to tell whether a plan is on course; it allows both the analysis of new information and the discovery of new opportunities.

Exchange functions of marketing The marketing functions that involve those activities that are concerned with the transfer of ownership in the marketing system.

Exit interview An in-depth interview with an employee at the time of termination that is designed to learn the employee's attitudes, reasons for leaving, and suggestions for improving the working relationship.

Expenditure That which is incurred whenever the business acquires an asset, whether it is used immediately or years later. It may or may not be a cash outflow at the time the asset is acquired.

Expenses The value of assets consumed by the business in acquiring, producing, and selling goods and services. Expenses include only those resources consumed by actual sales during the accounting period.

Extraction A production process that involves removing a product from its natural environment.

Fabrication A production process that involves changing the form of some basic material to make it more marketable.

Facilitating functions of marketing Those activities that help the market system to operate more smoothly; marketing activities that facilitate the physical flow and exchange function. These include financing, market information, risk-bearing, and standardization and grading the product.

Factor An organization that buys accounts receivable from a business at a discounted price and then collects directly from the individuals who owe money.

Farm sector The enterprises that produce grain, livestock, food, and fiber products.

Feature A descriptive, measurable fact about the product.

Federated cooperative A large cooperative serving a wide geographical area whose members are local cooperatives that are, in turn, owned and controlled by local farmers. Control is from the bottom up—from farmers to local cooperatives to the regional cooperatives.

Financial statement A summarized statement of the financial status of a business, usually prepared as a summary of accounts from the ledger. The most common financial statements are the balance sheet and income statement.

Fixed assets Those items that the business controls that have a relatively long life, such as land, buildings, and equipment.

Fixed costs Those costs that do not fluctuate with the volume of business; considered the costs of being in business.

Flexibility principle An organization should maintain its structural flexibility so that it can adjust to its changing internal and external environment.

Focus-group interview (FGI) A guided discussion among users of a product or service that is designed to discover consumer attitudes and opinions toward those products or services.

Forecast An estimate of future business activity on which operating plans are based.

Forward contracting Formalizing a binding agreement to buy or sell products at established terms for delivery at some specified future date.

Free marketing system A type of economic system in which consumer wants are expressed directly in the marketplace using a free price mechanism as the basis for allocation of scarce resources.

Free rein (laissez-faire) A no-leadership style because all decision making is relinquished to followers.

Functional organization A structure that grants staff specialists authority in the areas of their specialty.

Futures market A market in which promises to deliver or accept a standardized unit of product at some specified future date are traded. The futures market reflects anticipated future supply and demand situations.

General economic forecast A forecast of general economic conditions for a specific future period.

General partnership The association of two or more people as owners of a business in which each individual partner, regardless of the percentage of capital contributed, has equal rights and liabilities.

Gross margin The difference between total sales and the cost of goods sold. This is income remaining to cover operating expenses and leave a profit.

Gross margin ratio Gross margin expressed as a percent of sales: Sales − cost of goods sold ÷ sales = gross margin.

Hedging A process by which the risk of price changes is transferred from one party to another; establishing equal and opposite positions in the cash and futures markets for a specific commodity.

Hurwicz Decision making under uncertainty, called the alpha or coefficient of optimism strategy.

Indirect selling Providing service to customers and facilitating the marketing process.

Innovators Venturesome people who like to try new ideas. They represent the first 2½ percent of the customers to try a new idea, product, or service.

Input sector The commercial enterprises that provide supplies and services to farmers for production of agricultural products.

Interest The charges made by a lender for the use of money.

Intermediate-term loan A temporary grant of money to be paid back, usually in 1 to 5 years.

Intermittent production A total production network that involves variable outputs, variable procedures, and often variable inputs.

Inventory Those items that are held for sale in the ordinary course of business, or that have been purchased for use in producing goods and services to be sold.

Inventory turnover ratio An efficiency measure showing the relationship between inventory and sales volume. It shows the dollars of sales per dollar of inventory or the number of times that the value of inventory is sold during the period: Sales ÷ inventory = rate of turnover.

Job specification A written set of qualifications that are needed to perform a specific job satisfactorily.

Journal A chronological listing of all business transactions as they occur on a day-to-day basis.

Laggards Tradition-bound people who take so long to adopt new ideas that by the time the ideas are adopted, they no longer are new. This group is the last 16 percent to accept a new idea, product, or service.

LaPlace (Bayesian) Decision making under uncertainty, assuming equal probabilities of occurrence for all outcomes.

Late majority Skeptical people who adopt new ideas only after considerable evidence has been shown. This group represents the next 34 percent (after the early majority) to accept a new idea, product, or service.

Leadership The process of helping individuals or groups to accomplish organizational goals by unleashing each person's individual potential as a contribution to organizational success.

Leads Prospects that have been taken from knowledgeable sources.

Leasing A form of renting, usually involving a contractual agreement that specifies the terms of the arrangement and extends over a specified period of time.

Ledger Financial records in which transactions relating to a particular element of the business are recorded into individual accounts for eventual summarization into meaningful categories.

Lessee The person or organization who pays for the privilege of using the property of another for a specified period of time.

Lessor A person or organization who leases to another person or organization. The lessor maintains ownership through the lease period.

Leverage The concept of obtaining funds by using equity capital as a base for borrowing additional funds.

Liabilities Anything a business owes to others outside the business, such as bills and loans.

Limited partnership The association of two or more people as owners of a business in which some partners contribute money or ownership capital to the partnership without incurring the full legal liability of a general partner.

Line and staff organization A structure similar to line organization, but including a place for specialists, who have direct accountability to key line managers and are responsible for offering advice on problems and providing services in their area of specialty.

Line of credit A commitment by the lender to make available to the firm a certain sum of money, usually for a 1-year period, at a specified rate of interest at whatever time the firm needs the loan; also known as revolving loan.

Line organization A structure in which there is one simple, clear line of authority extending downward from top management to each person in the organization.

Linear projection A quantitative procedure for projecting past trends into a future time setting.

Local cooperative A cooperative that is organized and controlled by local member-patrons to serve their own needs.

Long-term liabilities Outsiders' claims against the business that do not come due within 1 year, such as bonded indebtedness, mortgages, and long-term loans.

Long-term loans A temporary grant of money for a duration usually of more than 5 years.

Loss-leader pricing A method of pricing that involves offering one or more products in a product mix at a specially reduced price for the purpose of attracting more customers who will hopefully purchase other regularly priced items.

Macroeconomics The study of how consumers, businesses, and government in the aggregate interact to allocate scarce resources.

Management by exception A management technique with the basic premise that management should not spend time on areas that are progressing according to plan, but should identify and concentrate on areas that are not meeting acceptable performance criteria.

Manager A person charged with the responsibility of planning, organizing, and controlling the activities of a business organization to accomplish objectives established by the owners.

Marginal cost The additional cost incurred in producing one more unit. It represents the change in total cost divided by the change in output.

Marginal rate of substitution The extra amount of input Y that will substitute for less of input X.

Marginal revenue The additional income generated by selling one more unit of product; it represents the change in total revenue divided by the change in output.

Market penetration Strength in a given market segment.

Market research The study of customers, competition, and trends in the marketplace, all of which should provide objective, analytical information on which to base marketing decisions.

Market segmentation The classification of customers into segments or categories according to applicable characteristics.

Marketable securities Investments in another company's stocks and bonds. These may be cashed in or sold during the accounting year.

Marketing The study of the flow of products from the producer through intermediaries to consumers.

Marketing audit An objective examination of a company's entire marketing program.

Marketing channel The path goods take from producer to consumers.

Marketing efficiency A measure of productivity of the marketing process in terms of the resources used and output generated during the marketing process.

Marketing management The management of the total process of identifying customer needs, developing products and services to meet these needs, establishing promotional programs and pricing policies, and implementing a system of distribution to customers.

Marketing margin The difference between product returns at two different levels in the marketing channel (i.e., the difference between the price paid by consumers and that received by producers).

Marketing mix The combination of price, product, promotion, and place strategies developed and implemented by a firm.

Minimal layer principle The number of levels of management should be kept as low as possible consistent with the goal of maintaining an effective span of control.

Mixed free enterprise system A free enterprise system on which some governmental restrictions are placed in order to lessen the hardships imposed on individuals as adjustments are made in the allocation of scarce resources.

Model An abstract presentation, usually in mathematical terms, that exhibits all the factors believed to be pertinent to a situation. It is used to understand and project the outcome of various possible circumstances.

Motivation A stimulus that produces action.

Net operating profit The amount left over after operating expenses are subtracted from the gross margin. It represents profit from operation of the primary business activity.

Net profit The amount that remains after taking into account any nonoperating income or expenses, such as interest or dividend earnings and interest expense.

Net worth (owners equity) The value of the owners' investment in the business. It is equal to the total assets of the business less all obligations to nonowners.

Nonprofit corporation A corporation that is exempt from certain forms of taxation, and that generally cannot directly enrich its owners financially.

Nonrecourse loan A program in which farmers could "seal" their grain in USDA-acceptable storage facilities and obtain a loan that was equal to the number of bushels in storage multiplied by the established support price for the commodity.

Notes payable Short-term loans or liabilities from individuals, banks, or other lending institutions that fall due within a year. Also included in this category is the specific portion of any long-term debt that will come due within a year.

Objectives Statements developed by top management, boards of directors, and chief executives to define what they believe to be the organization's mission.

Oligopoly A market dominated by a few large firms; for example, the farm-implement supply sector.

Operating expenses The expenses associated with actual operation of the business. Expenses not directly associated with operations, such as interest expense, penalties, and nonrelated legal expenses, are excluded.

Operational efficiency The dimension of marketing efficiency that measures the productivity of performing marketing services within the firm; it consists of the raw ratio of marketing output to marketing input.

Opportunity cost The income given up by not choosing the next best alternative for the use of resources.

Order point An agreed-upon level of depletion of warehouse stock of a specific product that warrants an order for more.

Organizing The grouping of activities and fitting together of people in the best possible relationships to get work done effectively and economically and to help achieve the objectives and goals of the enterprise.

Owner's equity (net worth) The value of the owners' investment in the business. It is equal to the total assets of the business less all obligations to nonowners.

Parity of responsibility and authority principle A person should have enough authority to carry out assigned responsibilities.

Parity price A calculated "fair price" that would give farmers the same degree of purchasing power in the current period as they had in an earlier "base" period.

Partnership A business owned by two or more people who jointly control the assets of the business.

Penetration pricing A pricing strategy that consists of offering a product at a low price, perhaps even at a loss, in order to obtain a great deal of exposure and to gain wide acceptance quickly.

Periodic inventory An actual physical count of stock on hand conducted at regular intervals.

Perpetual inventory A running account of stock on hand that is updated as sales occur.

PERT (program evaluation review technique) A method of scheduling that involves a diagrammatic representation of the network of activities in which a production operation is engaged. Similar to CPM.

Physical functions of marketing The marketing function that refers to the time, place, and form utility that are added to the product as it is transported, stored, and processed to meet customer wants.

Pipeline inventory The minimum amount of inventory needed to cover the period of time between the warehouse's reordering and its receipt of the additional stock.

Planning Forward thinking about courses of action based upon full understanding of all factors involved and directed at specific objectives.

Points Service charges, based on the face value of the loan, that are paid to the lending institution to secure the loan.

Policies General guidelines for handling various circumstances that are expected to arise frequently.

Posting The transferring of information from the journal to the ledger.

Preferred stock A specific share of ownership of a corporation that does not carry the privileges of voting for directors, but has a preferred position in receiving dividends and in redemption in the case of liquidation.

Prepaid expense Assets that represent prepayment of an item or service that will be used up in the near future and will become an expense. It represents something of value at the time the balance sheet is drawn up.

Present value The current value of an investment that will yield a specific amount on a given future date:

$$\text{Present value} = \frac{\text{expected income from investment}}{(1 + i)^n}$$

where i = interest rate and n = number of years.

Prestige pricing A method of pricing that appeals to an elite image and tends to equate price and quality: "You get what you pay for."

Price discovery The process by which the equilibrium of quantity and price is determined when producers and consumers meet in the marketplace.

Pricing efficiency The dimension of marketing efficiency that measures how adequately market prices reflect the production and marketing costs throughout the total marketing system.

Pro forma financial statements A projected profit and loss statement and balance sheet that are based on the best estimates of what the business will look like in the future. They serve as a tool by which to judge what the financial needs of the business will be during and at the end of the operating period.

Process layout An arrangement in which all like functions are grouped in the same place. It is related to intermittent production.

Product layout An arrangement that involves a step-by-step sequence of functions as the product is assembled. It is geared specifically to the continuous production process.

Product life cycles The predictable way in which sales and profits of a product respond as a product is introduced, grows rapidly, matures, and finally declines in the market place.

Product market sector The commercial enterprises that process and distribute the farm product to final users.

Product mix The combination of products sold.

Profession An occupation requiring specialized knowledge which, in turn, requires long and intensive training.

Profit and loss statement A summary of business operations during a specific period of time that demonstrates the profit or loss resulting from the combination of income and expenses.

Profit on sales ratio A ratio showing the relationship of profit to sales volume. It shows the profit generated on each dollar of sales: Net profit ÷ sales = POS.

Proprietorship A business owned and controlled by one person.

Prospecting The process of identifying and locating potential customers.

Psychological pricing A method of pricing that involves establishing prices that are emotionally more satisfying because they sound better. *Example:* Two for 99 cents instead of 50 cents each.

Receivables ratio A ratio showing the average number of days that sales are in accounts receivables: Receivables ÷ sales ÷ 360 days = days sales in receivables.

Regional cooperative A large cooperative serving farmers in a wide geographical area through its own outlets or through independent local affiliated cooperatives.

Responsibility The obligation to see a task through to completion.

Résumé A written summary of the personal, educational, and professional qualifications of a person in the job market.

Retained earnings That portion of the net gain on the owners' original investment that the owners have chosen to leave in the business as additional contributed capital.

Return on investment A management ratio combining (1) profits on sales and (2) return on investments that measures the performance of a business and the skill of the management team. A measure of profitability showing the profit generated for each dollar of investment, expressed as an annual rate: Profit ÷ investment = return on investment.

Revolving fund financing The unique feature of cooperatives that gives them the option of issuing patronage refunds in the form of stock.

The cooperative then revolves the stock periodically by allowing older stock to be cashed in.

Risk Decision making under the assumption that probabilities of occurrence can be assigned to each possible outcome.

ROI (return on investment) pricing Pricing based on the addition to the basic cost of the individual product or service an amount sufficient to earn a specified return on investment.

RONW (return on net worth) A ratio showing the profit per dollar of owners' investment or net worth, expressed at an annual rate: Net profit ÷ net worth = POEC (profit on equity capital).

Sales The dollar value of all the products and services that have been sold for cash or on credit during the period specified on the profit and loss statement.

Sales-call interview The act of establishing customer contact, developing or renewing a positive relationship, discovering the customer's needs, convincing the customer that one can meet those needs, and securing the customer's commitment.

Sales forecasting Estimating sales in dollars and physical units for a specific future period.

Sales promotions Programs and special offerings designed to motivate interested customers to make a positive buying decision.

Salesperson One who is responsible for assisting in the marketing-selling process through direct customer contact.

Savage Decision making under uncertainty, called the minimax regret strategy.

Selling The act of transferring ownership of goods and services.

Semivariable cost A cost that is partly fixed and partly variable.

Set-aside program A program in which farmers are paid to hold some of their acreage out of production each year.

Short-term loan A temporary grant of money to be paid back in 1 year or less. It may be a regular-term note, with a specific amount due at a specific time, or a revolving or line-of-credit loan.

Silent partner One of the partners of a business who has restricted management rights and responsibilities and so has limited liability for the organization's actions.

Simple rate of return The most commonly used capital investment analysis ratio, this term refers to the profit generated by an investment as a percent of the investment:

$$\frac{\text{Average net income} - \text{average depreciation}}{\text{Average investment}}$$

Simulation A systematic trial-and-error approach to problem solving that usually involves several possibilities derived from past operational experience and records. It is used to project probable results of varying circumstances.

Single-accountability principle No person should report to more than one boss.

Skimming the market A pricing strategy that introduces a product at a high price for some affluent customers, then gradually lowers the price, bringing it into range for less affluent customers.

Solvency Refers to a firm's ability to meet long-term financial obligations. It is usually measured by relating net worth or owner's equity to debt.

Solvency ratios Relationships that determine a firm's ability to meet long-run claims or debts. The three most common solvency ratios are: Total liabilities ÷ net worth = solvency; net worth ÷ total net assets = solvency; long-term debt ÷ net worth = solvency.

Span-of-control principle The number of people who can be supervised effectively by one individual is limited.

Stock A paper, in prescribed legal form, that represents each person's amount of ownership in a corporation.

Strategic marketing plan The logical integration of all business activities and resources to meet customers' needs and to generate a profit.

Strike An organized work stoppage by employees of an organization.

Stroke (Transactional analysis) Any recognition of another's presence by word, gesture, or touch.

Subchapter S corporation A closely held corporation for which subchapter S of the Internal Revenue Code makes it possible for the owners of the corporation to elect to be taxed as individuals rather than as a corporation.

Supply The quantities that producers are willing and able to put on the market at a series of different prices. It reflects the direct relationship between price and quantity supplied.

Supply elasticity A measure showing the change in quantity supplied as price changes. It shows the relative responsiveness of quantity supplied to price changes.

Synthesis The production process that involves culling a single product from a variety of raw materials.

Systems concept An approach that perceives the area under control as a total, interrelated, and interreacting system.

The close The salesperson's act of securing a commitment from the customer.

Total cost The sum of the total variable cost plus the total fixed cost.

Total fixed cost The total of all fixed costs incurred at any level of production. Fixed costs are those costs that are constant during the operating period, regardless of the level of production.

Total revenue The total income received during an operating period. The amount is equal to the number of units sold multiplied by the selling price.

Total variable cost The total of all variable costs incurred at any level of production. Variable costs are those costs that vary directly with the level of production during the operating period.

Trade credit Credit advanced by suppliers and vendors of the agribusiness firm.

Transactional analysis A popular and practical approach to understanding and supervising employees, developed by the late Dr. Eric Berne. It is based on the idea that human behavior can be classified into parent, adult, and child patterns.

Turnover ratio A ratio showing the relationship of sales to total assets. It is an efficiency measure that gives the dollars of sales annually for each dollar of assets in the firm or the number of times the firm generates sales equivalent to the value of its assets: Turnover = total sales ÷ total assets.

Ulterior transactions (Transactional analysis) One thing is said, but another is meant.

Uncertainty Decision making under the assumption that one or more of the possible outcomes has an unknown probability.

Underwriting An agreement made with a firm that specializes in buying a business's bonds and then reselling them to the general public.

Utility The value of a product or service to a consumer. As a product moves through the marketing system, it gains utility.

Variable cost Those costs that increase directly with the volume of sales. Considered the costs of doing business.

Vertical integration The process of adding on other marketing or production functions in addition to existing functions so as to become less dependent on other organizations.

Volume-cost analysis A tool for examining the relationship between costs and the volume of business.

Wage efficiency ratio An efficiency measure showing the relationship between labor cost and sales volume. It shows how many dollars of labor cost there were for each dollar of sales.

Wald Decision making under uncertainty, called the maximin strategy.

Warehouse receipts A means of using inventory as security for a loan.

Warm fuzzy (Transactional analysis) A positive unconditional stroke.

What the market will bear A method of pricing highly unique products and services by experimenting with various prices with the objective of finding and charging the maximum that consumers are willing to pay.

INDEX

INDEX

Strike, 397
Supply:
  curve, 95
  definition, 95
  elasticity, 101
  shift in, 95-96
Supply-demand analysis, 98-99
Synthesis, 354

Taylor, Frederick, 352
Theory X–Theory Y, 416
Total fixed cost, 91, 209-210
Total food system concept, 5-6
Total variable cost, 91, 210-211
Trade credit, 169
Transactional analysis, 423
Trial close, 336
Turnover ratio, 142

Ulterior transactions, 428
Uncertainty, 362
U.S.D.A., 4
Utility, 235-236
  form, 235
  place, 235
  possession, 235
  time, 235

Variable costs, 210
Vertical integration, 243
Volume-cost analysis, 208-221

Wage efficiency ratio, 144
Wagner–Connery Act, 396
Wald criterion, 363
Warehouse receipts, 168
Wealth of Nations, 83